Portfolio Theory and
Performance Analysis

Wiley Finance Series

Portfolio Theory and
Performance Analysis

Noël Amenc
and
Véronique Le Sourd

WILEY

Other Wiley Editorial Offices

John Wiley & Sons Inc., 111 River Street, Hoboken, NJ 07030, USA

Jossey-Bass, 989 Market Street, San Francisco, CA 94103-1741, USA

Wiley-VCH Verlag GmbH, Boschstr. 12, D-69469 Weinheim, Germany

John Wiley & Sons Australia Ltd, 33 Park Road, Milton, Queensland 4064, Australia

John Wiley & Sons (Asia) Pte Ltd, 2 Clementi Loop #02-01, Jin Xing Distripark, Singapore 129809

John Wiley & Sons Canada Ltd, 22 Worcester Road, Etobicoke, Ontario, Canada M9W 1L1

Wiley also publishes its books in a variety of electronic formats. Some content that appears
in print may not be available in electronic books.

British Library Cataloguing in Publication Data

A catalogue record for this book is available from the British Library

ISBN 0-470-85874-5

Typeset in 10/12pt Times by TechBooks, New Delhi, India
Printed and bound in Great Britain by Antony Rowe Ltd, Chippenham, Wiltshire
This book is printed on acid-free paper responsibly manufactured from sustainable forestry
in which at least two trees are planted for each one used for paper production.

Contents

Acknowledgements

This book owes much to the valuable advice of Mr Lionel Martellini, Professor at the Marshall School of Business at the University of Southern California in Los Angeles, whom we would particularly like to thank. We would also like to express our gratitude to Mr Peter O'Kelly for his considerable assistance in producing the definitive English version of our work. Finally, we address our thanks to Ms Laurence Kriloff for her patience and expertise in assisting us with the formatting of the electronic version of this manuscript. All errors and omissions remain, naturally, our own responsibility.

Biographies

Noël Amenc is professor of finance at the Edhec Business School, where he is in charge of the Risk and Asset Management research centre. Noël is also associate editor of the Journal of Alternative Investments. He is the author of numerous publications in the domain of portfolio management, notably in the areas of asset allocation and performance measurement. He also holds significant positions within the asset management industry, including head of research with Misys Asset Management Systems.

Véronique Le Sourd holds an advanced graduate diploma in applied mathematics from the Université Pierre et Marie Curie (Paris VI) and has worked as a research assistant within the finance and economics department of HEC Business School. She is currently a research engineer for Misys Asset Management Systems and associate researcher with the Edhec Risk and Asset Management Research Centre.

Introduction

Over the past 20 years, portfolio management has evolved enormously. Asset management was considered for many years to be a marginal activity, but it appears today to be central to the development of the financial industry, both in the United States and Europe.

The increasing number of cross-border merger and acquisition operations and the extremely high valuations that are put on those operations are evidence of the major financial establishments' desire to invest in a sector that they consider to be essential to their strategy of globalising and "financialising" their activities.

Asset management's transition from an "art and craft" to an industry has inevitably called integrated business models into question, favouring specialisation strategies based on cost optimisation and learning curve objectives.

In terms of production, the development of multi-management has given these new strategies a concrete identity. The considerable success of multi-management is linked not only to a re-examination of production conditions, which favours manager specialisation and asset class or management style economies of scale, but also satisfies a unanimous demand on the part of institutional and private investors, who wish to combine financial diversification (increasing number of classes or styles) with organisational diversification (increasing number of managers).

In the area of distribution, the concept of multi-distribution is benefiting from the breakdown of the integrated management doctrine, which led to multi-management.

The distribution of third-party funds, which was given the name "open architecture", began in the United States in the 1980s. It led to a significant reduction in the sales share of exclusively house funds (40% in 2000). This movement has also affected Europe, where the regional players are reacting to the arrival of major North American distribution centres, with the latter intending to profit from the financial consumerism encouraged by the development of the Internet. Forecasts of 50% of third-party funds distributed in Europe by 2010 seem realistic in view of recent strategic and commercial initiatives and the reduction that has been observed in the share of proprietary distribution networks compared with external networks. The costly acquisitions of independent American distribution specialists by the major traditional European commercial banks are evidence of the US/Europe convergence gamble in the area of fund distribution.

This evolution in the strategic paradigm has influenced financial thinking. A unique characteristic of the financial industry (and an advantage for researchers!) is that there is a strong degree of accessibility between the professional and academic worlds.

As a result, multi-distribution and multi-management are based on and affect a considerable amount of research in the area of fund performance analysis. Since multi-managers and multi-distributors are anxious to delegate their management in the best possible conditions, and sell the value-added constituted by manager selection to their clients, they undertake numerous initiatives and engage in extensive research to improve portfolio and fund performance analysis and measurement.

Moreover, specialisation is supported by the appearance of new concepts in the area of risk and performance analysis, grouped together under the term "style management". Since the beginning of the 1990s, this concept has revolutionised institutional management in North America. Its development in Europe is a key growth factor for the major international investment management firms.

Finally, as in any competitive environment, marketing practices are essential. With their characteristic artistry and audacity, major American managers have succeeded in basing their investment management process and performance marketing pitch on academic "evidence". They also justify their sales propositions with "scientific" proof of the soundness and universality of the underlying conceptual choices.

As such, faced with an abundance of tools and academic references, we felt that it was important to place all the practices, empirical studies and innovations in their context, given that they are always described as "major" by their promoters in the area of portfolio theory. That is the principal objective of this publication: to allow the professionals, whether managers or investors, to take a step back and clearly separate the true innovations from mere improvements to well-known, existing techniques; to situate the importance of innovations with regard to the fundamental portfolio management questions, which are the evolution of the investment management process, risk analysis and performance measurement; and to take the explicit or implicit assumptions contained in the promoted tools into account and, by so doing, evaluate the inherent interpretative or practical limits.

With that perspective in mind, the layout of this book connects each of the major categories of techniques and practices to the unifying and seminal conceptual developments of modern portfolio theory, whether these involve measuring the return on a portfolio, analysing portfolio risk or evaluating the quality of the portfolio management process.

1
Presentation of the Portfolio
Management Environment[1]

The first chapter will allow us to define portfolio management and describe how it is practised by professionals. Before coming to portfolio management itself, however, we will first define the basic elements that allow portfolios to be created, namely assets. These assets, which are traded on financial markets, are numerous and vary greatly in nature. It is commonplace to group them together into major categories.

1.1 THE DIFFERENT CATEGORIES OF ASSETS

The simplest way to group assets together is to consider asset classes. Each asset class corresponds to a level of risk. The assets in each group can then be split, at a more detailed level, into sub-groups. Equities are split into sectors of industrial activity or style, with the latter depending on whether the stocks are growth or value stocks or on the size of the company's market capitalisation. Bonds are grouped together according to criteria such as maturity or the quality of the issuer. The aim is to obtain groups of assets that behave in a similar way and are characterised by an exposure to risk factors (cf. Chapter 6).

The breakdown of assets into major asset categories also corresponds to management specialisation and the classification provides a reference for particular performance analysis methods. Placing portfolio assets in categories is part of a top-down approach to portfolio analysis, which establishes a discriminating link between the choice of an asset class and the return on the portfolio. Whether it involves a risk profile or a style, this top-down approach provides justification for managers concentrating their efforts on asset allocation as the principal source of performance.

1.1.1 Presentation of the different traditional asset classes

Assets are divided into three major classes: equities, bonds and money market instruments. Each class can then be subdivided into groups with common criteria. The class of derivative instruments can be added to these asset classes. The classification can also be carried out according to a geographical breakdown.

1.1.1.1 Equities

An ordinary share (equity) is a title of ownership that represents a share in a company. It gives the right to receive a dividend, with the amount of the dividend being calculated according to the company's earnings. The amount is therefore liable to vary from one year to the next. Equities constitute the most risky class of assets, but, as compensation, they provide a greater

---

[1] For more details on the subjects discussed in this chapter, we recommend Chapter 1 of Fabozzi (1995) and Boulier (1997).

return on investment over the long term than other types of assets. Equities can be broken down by industrial sector, or according to the size of the company's market capitalisation.

1.1.1.2   Bonds

Bonds are securities that represent a loan. They can be issued by a company or by a State. These securities give rise to regular payment of coupons, which constitute the interest on the loan, and redemption of the security at maturity. The cash flow is therefore known in advance. Bonds represent an investment that is less risky than equities, but also less lucrative over the long term. Their risk is analysed in two ways:

1. The risk of non-redemption or credit risk, evaluated according to the quality of the issuer, which is measured by a rating system. The rating, which is made public, contributes to an efficient market and allows the return on the bond to be linked to its risk.
2. The market risk, or interest rate risk, which is analysed as a function of the opportunity cost represented by the difference between the return ensured by the bond and that of the market for an equivalent maturity.

Bonds are grouped, consequently, into issuers or ratings and maturities.

1.1.1.3   Money market instruments

This final category of assets is not very risky, but the return on investment is lower. It involves short-term borrowing and lending for managing the cash in a portfolio.

These asset classes, which have different levels of risk, allow investors to spread their investments, according to the planned duration of the investment and the risk that the investor is willing to take. Investors can thus predict the average return on their investment. The diversification of the investment, both between different asset classes and within an individual class, is an important factor in portfolio management. Intuitively, it seems clear that this will allow the risk taken to be limited. This intuition on the reduction of risk through diversification was formalised by Markowitz in a mean–variance conceptual framework that we will present in Chapter 3.

1.1.1.4   Derivative instruments

This class of assets supplements the traditional assets, which are equities, bonds and money market instruments. It is made up of a large variety of assets, among which we can cite options, futures, forwards and swaps.

An option is a security that gives the right, but not the obligation, to buy, if it is a call, or to sell, if it is a put, the underlying instrument at a strike price fixed in advance. The purchase, or sale, is carried out at the date the contract expires, for a European option, or at that date at the latest, for an American option. The underlying instruments can be equities, indices, currencies, futures or interest rates.

A futures contract is a contract agreed between two parties through which the seller commits to transferring a financial asset to the buyer, at a date and a price that are fixed when the contract is made. A forward contract allows the same transaction to be carried out, but unlike futures, which are traded on an organised market, forward contracts are traded over the counter. Futures contracts allow portfolio risk to be hedged, and also allow the risk/return profile of the portfolio to be changed rapidly and at minimal cost.

A swap is a contract, agreed between two parties, which allows financial cash flows to be exchanged. More often than not it involves exchanging a fixed rate for a variable rate.

These assets are said to be derivative because their price depends on an underlying instrument. They play an important role in portfolio management. Their use allows portfolio managers to be more flexible and effective in developing and applying investment strategies than if they were limited to using the underlying instruments: equities, bonds and money market instruments. For example, derivative instruments allow the portfolio exposure to be modified in terms of assets and currencies, without modifying the real composition of the underlying portfolio. They also allow portfolio risk to be hedged and performance to be improved by using a leverage effect on the return.

1.1.2 Alternative instruments[2]

This class includes various investment vehicles: hedge funds, managed futures, commodities and funds called "alternative traditional" funds (private equity, venture capital, private debt and real estate). Among the different assets considered, hedge funds have experienced considerable growth. At the end of 2000, they accounted for more than 500 billion dollars in managed assets.

The success of alternative funds, notably hedge funds, is linked to two considerations:

1. On the one hand, the risk/return combination for these investments has, over the last 15 years, been better than that of the traditional asset classes.
2. On the other hand, and above all, their low correlation with the risks and returns of equities and bonds make them excellent diversification vehicles.

On this second point, numerous studies have highlighted the advantages of including an alternative class in the overall asset allocation. Beeman *et al.* (2000) demonstrated, using two optimisation models, one of which was based on a pure mean–variance approach, and the other on accumulated loss constraints (Probabilistic Efficient Frontier), that investing from 6% to 16% in hedge funds, depending on the objectives and risk constraints of the investor, significantly improved the efficient frontier of a diversified portfolio.

In spite of these undeniable advantages, we will not deal with the subject of performance analysis for alternative assets in the present publication. In view of the diversity of alternative investment vehicles and their characteristics, we feel that it would be necessary to adapt the risk and performance analysis models proposed by portfolio theory. Such an adaptation would assume a more thorough analysis of factorial approaches and would notably take into account the non-linearity of returns.[3]

The multi-style approach in alternative investment would also necessitate a review of the analysis concepts developed on the subject in traditional portfolio management. This series of adaptations seems to us to justify a specific publication (see Amenc *et al.*, 2003).

---

[2] For a detailed presentation of this asset class, the reader could refer to the work of Schneeweis and Pescatore (1999).

[3] For an initial approach to applying multi-factor models to alternative investment risk and performance analysis, see Schneeweis and Spurgin (1998).

1.1.3 Grouping by sector

Owing to its diversity, it is primarily the equity class that is concerned by this type of breakdown. The classification of assets by sector of activity leads, more often than not, to distinguishing the following major sectors: automobiles, banks, primary products, chemicals, construction, goods and services, energy, financial services, food processing, pharmaceuticals, distribution, technology, telecommunications and public services. The assets can also be grouped according to the size of their market capitalisation, or whether they present value or growth characteristics. We then refer to the style of the stocks.

Growth stocks can be defined as those that present a current or future growth rate that is above that of the economy, while value stocks are those that have a growth rate which is in line with that of the economy. To compensate, value stocks pay out dividends or have price/earnings (*P/E*) ratio that are higher than those of growth stocks.

This grouping of assets into homogeneous categories corresponds to a trend towards greater specialisation among managers. Many funds are invested in a single asset category. In order to offer managers a reference to evaluate their management, all the major market indices are now organised into ranges of sectors. Worldwide indices are now beginning to do the same. The Dow Jones group has just launched global sector indices for the major sectors of activity. The sector approach on the worldwide level tends to represent an increasingly significant share in managed portfolios. The fact that investors are anxious to have diversified portfolios has led firms in recent years to develop of funds of funds from specialised funds. We will return to this point in the third section of this chapter.

1.2 DEFINITION OF PORTFOLIO MANAGEMENT

A portfolio is defined as a grouping of assets. Portfolio management consists of constructing portfolios and then making them evolve in order to reach the return objectives defined by the investor, while respecting the investor's constraints in terms of risk and asset allocation. The investment methods used to reach the objectives range from quantitative investment, which originated in modern portfolio theory, to more traditional methods of financial analysis. Quantitative investment techniques are now among the most widely used fund management methods. They are generally grouped into two major categories: active investment management and passive investment management, with the term "passive investment" covering both index investment and portfolio insurance. A general idea of the major trends in investment management is given below.

1.2.1 Passive investment management

Passive investment management consists of tracking the market, without attempting to anticipate its evolution. It relies on the principle that financial markets are perfectly efficient, which means that financial markets immediately integrate all information liable to influence prices. It is therefore pointless to try to beat the market. The best technique in that case is to try to replicate a market index, i.e. invest in the same securities as those in the index in the same proportions. This type of investment is a direct result of equilibrium theory and the capital asset pricing model, which we will discuss in Chapter 4. It has led to the creation of index funds, i.e. funds that are indexed on the market. These funds have the lowest management fees. Index investment allows an investor to have a diversified portfolio, without having to carry out research security by security. In addition, since the composition of indices is relatively stable, the turnover rate in the portfolios is relatively low, which limits transaction costs.

Besides these classic index funds, funds called "tilted" index funds have been developed. These funds use a technique derived from that of classic index funds. The idea is to introduce an element of active investment, to try to obtain a performance that is better than that of the reference index, without exposing the portfolio to a market risk greater than that of the index. The goal is not to beat the index by a significant amount, but to beat it regularly. The difference in performance compared with the reference portfolio, measured by the tracking-error, is followed with precision and must remain within a relatively strict band. Management is based on analysis of the systematic portfolio risk, i.e. the share of risk that is not eliminated by diversification. The risk is broken down with the help of multi-factor models. These models allow the different sources of risk to be analysed and the portfolio oriented towards the most lucrative risk factors, which allows the tilt sought to be obtained. Multi-factor models are discussed in Chapter 6.

The index can also be tilted using more traditional methods, with a financial analysis-based stock picking strategy. The multi-factor analysis then guarantees that stock picking has not modified the overall exposure of the portfolio compared with that of the index. In certain cases a portfolio composition constraint is imposed by reducing the stock picking to a simple over- or underweighting of the stocks that make up the reference index.

To meet the expectations of investors who wish to protect themselves from a considerable loss of capital in the event of markets falling significantly, particular asset management methods have also been proposed. The methods are portfolio insurance and, more generally, methods that are called structured investment methods. These methods are still included in passive techniques, in the sense that the manager defines the rules on which the investment is based and does not modify those rules over the life span of the portfolio, whatever way the market evolves. The performance of the portfolio can thus be known in advance for each final market configuration.

In its simplest version, portfolio insurance consists of automatically readjusting the composition of the portfolio between money market instruments and risky instruments, depending on how the market evolves, in such a way that it never falls below a certain level of return (see Black and Jones, 1987, and Perold and Sharpe, 1988). In a more general way, allocation can be carried out between two asset classes, with one being riskier than the other, such as equities and bonds, for example. We come across this principle in the investment method called "tactical asset allocation", which consists of readjusting the proportions of each category of assets automatically, on the basis of a signal that indicates which asset class will perform best in the upcoming period. The forecasts that allow decisions to be taken are based on observation of economic or stock exchange cycles. The principle of portfolio insurance leads to buying the risky asset when it has progressed and selling it when it has depreciated. This is known as a "trend follower" strategy, i.e. one that tracks the market. It can be contrasted with "contrarian" type investment, which is used when carrying out the tactical asset allocation that was defined during the top-down investment process. This approach consists of periodical readjustment of the proportions, but is not performed automatically.

Portfolio insurance can also be carried out with the help of options. Options allow a floor value to be placed on a portfolio. This principle is used in funds with guaranteed capital and allows the investor to be sure to recover the amount invested, at the very least, when the investment period expires. This can be of interest when markets fluctuate to a considerable degree. On the downside, the investment will be less profitable than the market if the market has risen continually during the period. This is the cost of the insurance. For more details on this type of portfolio management and the methods used, see Chapter 5 of Amenc and Le Sourd (1998).

1.2.2   Active investment management

The objective of active investment management is to perform better than the market, or better than a benchmark that is chosen as a reference. Observation of financial markets shows that their theoretical efficiency is not perfect. They require a certain amount of time before they react to new information and asset prices are adjusted. As a result, there are short periods of time during which certain assets are not at their equilibrium value. Active investment management thus involves developing strategies to take advantage of temporary market inefficiencies. The choice of securities that will figure in the portfolio is an essential stage in this type of investment. The selection techniques are based on theoretical asset evaluation models, identifying the securities that should be purchased or sold, according to their upside or downside potential, which in turn is due to their under- or overvaluation by the market, with regard to the theoretical values proposed by the model(s) used. Portfolios that are actively managed contain fewer securities than those that are managed according to passive techniques, because detailed research into each security takes a considerable amount of time.

It is also possible to practise active investment management at the asset class, rather than security, level (active asset allocation or tactical allocation).

Funds that are managed through so-called "traditional" methods are also included in the area of active investment. These funds constitute a significant share of the funds that are available on the market. They are often relatively specialised. For the most part they use financial analysis, which consists of choosing each stock individually – the term used is "stock picking" – based on research into the balance sheets and financial characteristics of companies.

1.3   ORGANISATION OF PORTFOLIO MANAGEMENT AND DESCRIPTION OF THE INVESTMENT MANAGEMENT PROCESS[4]

Two opposing approaches are used to build portfolios: bottom-up and top-down. The bottom-up approach is the older and more traditional. It concentrates on individual stock picking. Evaluation of performance for those portfolios then consists of measuring the manager's capacity to select assets whose performance is better than the average performance of assets from the same class, or the same sector. The top-down approach gives more importance to the choice of different markets rather than individual stock picking. This approach is justified by research[5,6] that showed that the distribution of the different asset classes made the largest contribution to portfolio performance. More specifically, the top-down investment process is broken down into three phases, which are often handled by different people. Portfolio performance can then be analysed by attributing the contribution of each stage in the process to the overall portfolio performance in order to highlight the investment decisions that contributed the most to the overall performance result. The analysis of these results then contributes to improving portfolio management. For now, we will introduce the different phases in the investment management

---

[4] For more detailed information, cf. the introduction to Amenc and Le Sourd (1998).
[5] Cf. Brinson *et al.* (1986, 1991).
[6] A review of the interpretation of this research is presented in Chapter 7.

process and will reserve the description of the quantitative methods that allow them to be implemented for Chapter 7.

1.3.1 The different phases of the investment management process

1.3.1.1 Strategic asset allocation[7]

Strategic asset allocation is the first stage in the investment management process. It is an essential phase, since, following the top-down investment principle, a significant share of the portfolio's performance depends on this choice. Nevertheless, it is often the investment management phase to which the least amount of time is devoted. This type of allocation involves distributing the different asset classes within the portfolio, in accordance with the investor's objectives. This is the same as defining the benchmark, or reference portfolio. It is a long-term allocation strategy, which is defined by a management committee. The investment time scale is often around five years. This phase is described as *policy asset allocation* in the literature.

1.3.1.2 Tactical asset allocation

Tactical asset allocation consists of regularly adjusting the portfolio, in a systematic or discretionary way, to take advantage of short-term opportunities, while remaining close to the initial allocation. It therefore involves modifying the weightings of the asset classes compared with the reference portfolio while staying within the permitted level of tolerance. Among the methods used, the best known is *market timing*, which consists of increasing or decreasing the sensitivity of the portfolio to market variations, depending on whether an increase or decrease in the market is expected. We will return to the implementation of this technique in more detail in Chapter 7. The performance evaluation methods linked to the use of this technique will be discussed in Chapter 4.

1.3.1.3 Stock picking

This investment phase uses managers who are specialised in specific asset types and who ensure optimal selection of stocks within each asset group in the portfolio. All quantitative methods that allow these choices to be made can be used. Managers generally devote most time to this stage of the investment management process. This is where the different asset evaluation and portfolio optimisation models are applied.

1.3.2 The multi-style approach[8]

We have just described the classic portfolio management process. But as we saw in Section 1.1, assets can be classified according to their style. This leads to portfolio management that is linked to the style and specific manager characteristics. We can then allocate the portfolio between management styles instead of simple asset classes. This type of portfolio management was conceptualised by Sharpe (1988, 1992).

---

[7] For more detailed information, Chapter 9 of Farrell (1997) can be consulted.
[8] On this subject, one may consult Coggin *et al.* (1997), Duval (1999), Chapter 5 of Fabozzi and Grant (1999) and Fencke and Gascu (2001).

The multi-style approach is gaining in popularity because it provides a solution to the difficulty of a risk/return arbitrage approach through the beta alone (which we will discuss in Chapter 4) and is also a modern and structured approach to managers' standard stock picking practices: the value/growth distinction is often considered by practitioners to be a "refined" version of the P/E criterion.

More globally, the multi-style approach corresponds to a simplification/generalisation of the multi-factor approach (cf. Chapter 6) which, for its principles and application, is based on market consensus. The marketing departments of the major American asset management firms have proved very able at using the results of academic research to demonstrate the utility of a multi-style approach in the search for long-term performance persistence.

In practice, multi-style investment has enabled multi-management activity, which is based on the selection of style-specialised managers, to grow on the other side of the Atlantic (SEI and Russell are the best known exponents). Research shows that managers have a better chance of performing well in the long run if they specialise in a style of stocks.

This multi-management, which is called "manager of managers", has given a new lease of life to the concept of diversification and has brought true value-added to multi-management products. The latter were often perceived as diversified funds-of-funds which were themselves diversified, and for which no academic or empirical evidence could justify the management fees.

1.3.3 Performance analysis

The growth of mutual funds, and the resulting competition between different establishments, has led to a search for a clear and accurate presentation and analysis of results. This explains the increasing amount of academic and professional research devoted to performance measurement, which allows past results to be quantified, and performance analysis, which allows the results to be explained.

Performance analysis is the final stage in the portfolio management process. It provides an overall evaluation of the success of the investment management process in reaching its objective and also identifies the individual contribution of each phase to the overall result. Implementation of portfolio analysis requires perfect knowledge of the investment strategy followed. It was originally developed to meet the expectations of fund holders, who wished to have a clear view of how their portfolios were managed, possess an analysis of the risk taken and the level of return desired, and check that the objectives fixed were respected. It has allowed managers to evolve towards better control of the investment management process and has thus provided them with the means to bring about improvements. It allows the aspects of the process that have been productive to be strengthened and the aspects that have failed to reach the overall objective to be eliminated. It therefore has a twofold utility and is an essential phase in the investment management process.

The term "performance analysis" covers all the techniques that are implemented to study the results of portfolio management. These range from simple performance measurement to performance attribution. The first result that investors are interested in is the increase in their wealth. Performance measurement consists of measuring the difference in the value of the portfolio, or investment fund, between the beginning and the end of the evaluation period. Details will be given on this aspect in Chapter 2. Performance attribution breaks down the return to attribute the exact contribution of each phase in the process to the overall portfolio performance, thus allowing the manner in which the result was obtained to be understood. The intermediate step is performance evaluation, which explains how the measured return was obtained and whether the result is due to skill or luck. We can therefore determine whether the difference in performance compared with the benchmark comes from a different asset allocation, or from stock picking within each asset class, and see if the result was obtained through luck or skill. The analysis can be extended further for as long as we wish to obtain more detailed information. We can therefore quantify the favourable or unfavourable impact of each investment decision on the overall portfolio performance.

Performance attribution originated in the United States, where it has now been commonly used for a number of years. In France, its use is more recent. The fact that France is lagging behind the United States in this area can be partly explained by the investment differences between the two countries. In the United States, equity investment is predominant, notably through pension funds, which are very widespread. In France, on the other hand, bond investment has long dominated. As it happens, the first performance attribution methods developed were oriented more towards equity portfolio analysis. In addition, the introduction of quantitative techniques into the area of portfolio management was also more recent in France than in the United States.

However, the French context is evolving. Equity investment today represents a significant share of the market in France. The number of professionally managed funds in the financial markets is increasing. The mutual fund market is highly developed and the wide range of products proposed has served to strengthen the performance attribution requirements in order to be able to produce increasingly accurate reports and carry out manager selection over comparable bases. Investors wish to avail themselves of all the information necessary to make their choice. They are no longer satisfied with the overall performance value of their portfolio alone. They also want to see the performance broken down into asset classes.

The growth of performance attribution in France occurred at the same time as the evolution of investment towards a top-down process and the introduction of quantitative asset allocation techniques. Managers have become more and more specialised in different sectors and portfolio management is very often shared between several people. As a result, there is an increasing need for methods that allow the contribution of each manager to be individually attributed. The most frequently used technique in France involves breaking down performance into the different stages of the investment management process. Use of multi-factor models to analyse performance remains limited compared with the United States.

Nevertheless, certain difficulties can still limit the use of performance attribution. Breaking down performance into the different stages of the investment management process uses comparison with a benchmark, which must be adapted to the composition of the portfolio. It is therefore necessary to construct the benchmark with precision, because frequently the market indices are not representative of the investment strategy (this is the case notably for style indices). For this reason, asset management firms can turn to specialised firms or consultants, who develop and market specific indices. We will return to the problem of constructing benchmarks in more detail in Chapter 2. Performance attribution is more complex to implement for fixed income securities and derivatives, which are included in portfolios that use risk hedging techniques.

Finally, although portfolio attribution has grown in importance within asset management firms in France, it has not been widely disseminated to the general public. With few exceptions[9], the specialised press merely provides rankings based on predefined fund categories,

---

[9] Notably the ranking provided by the daily newspaper *Le Monde*, which is based on a multi-factor approach. We will return to this in Chapter 6.

without taking into account the real risk exposure or portfolio style. Therefore, nothing allows the highlighted performance to be qualified. In particular, it is impossible to distinguish between normal returns provided through exposure to different portfolio risks from abnormal performance (or outperformance) due to the manager's skill, whether through market timing or stock picking.

Without being a guarantee of future results, results obtained in the past help to establish the image of financial establishments. The area of performance analysis is therefore growing rapidly, since it meets the needs of both investors and portfolio managers.

1.4 PERFORMANCE ANALYSIS AND MARKET EFFICIENCY[10]

1.4.1 Market efficiency

Performance analysis is a means of judging the qualities of a manager and measuring the value-added of an active investment strategy compared with the simple replication of an index or a benchmark. For this aspect, it was developed within the framework of research into the efficiency of markets. The validation of the efficiency theory gave rise to empirical studies, which contributed to the development of performance measurement models. Analysis of the performance of active managers' funds, compared with the performance of the market, allows the form of market efficiency to be tested. The possibility for a manager to add value is linked to the gap between the valuation of the securities by the market and their equilibrium value. The existence of the gap depends on the time taken by the market to integrate new information, and therefore the level of efficiency of the financial markets.

The market is efficient if the prices of assets at any moment reflect all available information. Fama, who is responsible for the modern formalisation of market efficiency, defined the different forms:

- Efficiency is said to be strong if all information, public and private, is already contained in the asset prices. Following this hypothesis, it is not possible to achieve a better performance than the market.
- Efficiency is said to be semi-strong if the prices only reflect public information on the firms.
- Efficiency is said to be weak if today's prices reflect information contained in past prices. This form of efficiency allows for the existence of active investment possibilities for a person who has additional information, and thus allows for the possibility of achieving better performance than the market.

Efficiency translates the fact that there is no foreseeable trend in stock markets. We speak of the "random walk" of stock market prices. If we suppose that asset prices are determined in a rational manner, then only new information is liable to modify them. If the information is costly, then we can expect the search for information to increase the expectation of profit. This hypothesis was developed by Grossman and Stiglitz (1980). Their definition of market efficiency is broader than Fama's. They postulate that markets are efficient if the additional profit produced by actively managing a portfolio compensates exactly for the management fees. In so doing, they apply the definition given by Jensen (1978), which says that in an efficient market a forecast produces zero profits. We will return to the definition of efficiency

---

[10] Cf. Chapter 8 of Broquet and van den Berg (1992), Chapter 13 of Fabozzi (1995), Chapter 17 of Elton and Gruber (1995) and Fama (1970, 1991).

in Chapter 4 when we present the capital asset pricing model. A study by Ippolito (1989) validated Grossman and Stiglitz's hypothesis.

Therefore, investors may operate in two ways. They either simply observe the market prices, or they look for, and analyse, information. The former, who do not dispose of any particular information, would be well advised to practise passive investment, because they are not liable to obtain higher profits than the market. The latter can hope to obtain greater profits than the market but, on average, the excess profits that they obtain compensate exactly for the cost of searching for the information, all of which means that their net performance is on average equivalent to that of uninformed investors. Grossman and Stiglitz stress that if everybody adopted a passive strategy, then certain securities would be undervalued. It would then be possible to practise technical and fundamental analysis successfully. The search for information, which is undertaken in order to increase portfolio performance, thus plays a role in regulating markets and contributes to their efficiency. They deduce from this that the more markets are analysed, the more efficient they are.

Wermers (2000) shows that equity fund managers hold securities that beat the market by a quantity that is sufficient in practice to cover their expenses and transaction costs, which is consistent with Grossman and Stiglitz's equilibrium model. We also observe that funds with a high turnover, and therefore high transaction costs that affect the management fees, hold securities with a return that is on average higher than that of securities held in a fund with a low turnover. This reflects the stock picking skills of managers in very active funds.

1.4.2 Performance persistence[11]

The question of performance persistence in funds is often addressed in two ways. The first is linked to the notion of market efficiency. If we admit that markets are efficient, the stability of fund performance cannot be guaranteed over time. Nevertheless, according to MacKinlay and Lo (1998), the validity of the random market theory is now being called into question, with studies showing that weekly returns are, to a certain extent, predictable for stocks quoted in the United States[12]. This type of affirmation is, however, contested by other university research, which continues to promote the theory of market efficiency, according to which prices take all available information into account, and as a result of which active portfolio management cannot create added value.

The second part of the problem posed by the existence or non-existence of performance persistence is intended to be less theoretical or axiomatic and more pragmatic: "Are the winners always the same? Are certain managers more skilful than others?" Of course, if certain managers beat the market regularly, over a statistically significant period, they will prove *de facto* that active investment makes sense and cast doubt over the market efficiency paradigm. But that is not the purpose of the question. A manager who beats the market regularly by taking advantage of arbitrage opportunities from very temporary inefficiencies will not prove that the market is inefficient over a long period.

The professionals speak more willingly of checking whether an investment performance is the fruit of the real skill of the manager, and not just luck, rather than showing that the markets in which they invest are inefficient. In practice, one is often tempted to believe that a manager who has performed well one year is more likely to perform well the following year

---

[11] Cf. Grinold and Kahn (2000).
[12] This calling into question of efficient markets is responsible for the strong growth in tactical asset allocation (TAA) techniques.

than a manager who has performed poorly. The publication of fund rankings by the financial press is based on that idea. But the results of studies that tend to verify this assumption are contradictory and do not allow us to affirm that past performance is a good indicator of future performance. The results depend on the period studied, but generally it would seem that the poorest performances have more of a tendency to persist than the best performances. The results are also different depending on whether equity funds or bond funds are involved. The literature describes two phenomena that depend on the length of the period studied. In the long term (three to five years) and the short term (one month or less) we observe a reversal of trends: past losers become winners and vice versa. Over the medium term (six to 12 months), the opposite effect is observed: winners and losers conserve their characteristics over the following periods and in this case there is performance stability.

Empirical studies carried out to study the phenomenon of performance persistence have enabled performance measurement models to be developed and improved. The models that we present here will be explained in detail in the rest of the book.

A large amount of both academic and professional research is devoted to performance persistence in American mutual funds. The results seem to suggest that there is a certain amount of performance persistence, especially for the worst funds. But parts of these studies also suggest that managers who perform consistently better than the market do exist. In what follows we summarise the results of a certain number of studies. Kahn and Rudd (1995) present a fairly thorough study of the subject, in which they also refer to earlier basic research. The earliest observations generally lead to the conclusion that there is no performance persistence, while the most recent articles conclude that a certain amount of performance persistence exists. The authors, for their part, observed slight performance persistence for bond funds, but not for equity funds. Their study takes into account style effects, management fees and database errors. They conclude that it is more profitable to invest in index funds than in funds that have performed well in the past.

Among the studies that concluded that there was an absence of manager skill in stock picking, we can cite Jensen (1968) and Gruber (1996). Carhart (1997) shows that performance persistence in mutual funds is not a reflection of the manager's superior stock picking skills. Instead, the common asset return factors and the differences in fees and transaction costs explain the predictable character of fund returns. In addition, he observes that the ranking of funds from one year to another is random. The funds at the top of the rankings one year may perhaps have a slightly greater chance of remaining there than the others. In the same way, the worst ranked funds are very likely to be badly placed again or even disappear. However, the ranking can vary greatly from one year to the next and the winning funds of one year could be the losing funds of the following year and vice versa.

Other studies brought to light persistence in the performance of mutual funds. This is the case of Hendricks et al. (1993) who highlighted a phenomenon of performance persistence for both good managers and bad managers. Malkiel (1995) observed significant performance persistence for good managers in the 1970s, but no consistency in fund returns in the 1980s. His results also suggest that one should invest in funds that have performed best in the past. These funds perform better than the average funds over certain periods, and their performance is not worse than that of the average funds for other periods. However, he qualifies his results slightly with several remarks: the results obtained are not robust, the returns calculated must be reduced by the amount of the fees and the survivorship bias must be taken into account. In addition, the performance of the funds for the period studied is worse than that of the reference portfolios over the same period, both before and after deducting management fees. He also analyses fund fees to determine whether high fees result in better performance. The study finds no relationship between the amount of fees and the value of returns before those fees are deducted. He also concludes, like Kahn and Rudd (1995), that it can be much more profitable for investors to buy index funds with reduced fees, rather than trying to select an active fund manager who seems to be particularly skilful. Carhart (1997) observed performance persistence for managers whose performance was negative.

Brown *et al.* (1992) showed that short-term performance persisted, but that the survivorship bias attached to the database (i.e. the fact that funds that perform badly tend to disappear) could significantly affect the results of performance studies and could in particular give an appearance of significant persistence. Malkiel (1995) and Carhart (1997) also show that the persistence they identified could be attributed either to survivorship bias or to a poor choice of benchmark. Malkiel (1995) observes that around 3% of mutual funds disappear every year. As a result, performance statistics in the long run do not contain the results of the bad funds that have disappeared. So the survivorship bias is much more important than previous studies suggested. More recent studies have thus used databases that are corrected for survivorship bias. Malkiel therefore concludes that the investment strategy must not be based on a belief in return persistence over the long term. A study by Lenormand-Touchais (1998), carried out on French equity mutual funds for the period from 1 January 1990 to 31 December 1995, shows that there is no long-term performance persistence, unless a slight persistence in negative performance is counted. In the short term, on the other hand, a certain amount of performance persistence can be observed, which is more significant when the performance measurement technique used integrates a risk criterion.

Jegadeesh and Titman (1993) show, with NYSE and AMEX securities over the period 1965–1989, that a momentum strategy that consists of buying the winners from the previous six months, i.e. the assets at the top of the rankings, and selling the losers from the previous six months, i.e. the assets at the bottom of the rankings, earns around 1% per month over the following six months. This shows that asset returns exhibit momentum, which means that the winners of the past continue to perform well and the losers of the past continue to perform badly. Rouwenhorst (1998) obtains similar results with a sample of 12 European countries for the period 1980–1995.

Although the earliest studies were only based on performance measures drawn from the CAPM, such as Jensen's alpha, the more recent studies used models that took factors other than market factors into account. These factors are size, book-to-market ratio and momentum. Fama and French are responsible for the model that uses three factors (market factor, size and book-to-market ratio). In an article from 1996, Fama and French stress that their model does not explain the short-term persistence of returns highlighted by Jegadeesh and Titman (1993) and suggest that research could be directed towards a model integrating an additional risk factor. It was Carhart (1997) who introduced momentum, which allows short-term performance persistence to be measured as an additional factor. He suggests that the "hot hands" phenomenon (i.e. a manager's ability to pick the best performing stocks) is principally due to the momentum effect over one year described by Jegadeesh and Titman (1993). Using a four-factor model, Daniel *et al.* (1997) studied fund performance to see whether the manager's stock picking skill compensated for the management fees. The authors conclude that performance persistence in funds is due to the use of momentum strategies by the fund managers, rather than the managers being particularly skilful at picking winning stocks.

Brown and Goetzmann (1995) studied performance persistence for equity funds. Their re-sults indicate that relative (i.e. measured in relation to a benchmark) risk-adjusted performance persists. Poor performance also tends to increase the probability that the fund will disappear. Blake and Timmermann (1998) analysed the performance of mutual funds in the United Kingdom, underlining the fact that most performance studies concern American funds and that there are very few on European funds. As it happens, the "equity" mutual fund management industry in the United Kingdom is very advanced and is the one in Europe for which we have the most historical data. The study shows that equity funds perform slightly worse than the market on a risk-adjusted basis. Performance seems to persist to the extent that, on average, a portfolio made up of funds that have performed best in historical terms will perform better in the following period than a portfolio made up of funds that have performed worst in historical terms.

The different results observed for performance persistence according to the periods studied can be linked to the fact that more market trends, such as seasonal effects and day of the week effects, have been observed in recent years. However, if performance persistence exists in the short term, it is seldom seen over the long term and, as most studies stress, only performance persistence that is observed over a number of years would really allow us to conclude that it is statistically significant. In the absence of a period that is sufficiently long, it is not possible to distinguish luck from skill.

Finally, the studies that seek to check whether it is possible for the manager to add value within the framework of an efficient market were carried out on funds that were invested in a single asset class, generally equities or bonds. While the contribution of stock picking to performance in an efficient market is questionable, the same cannot be said for the contribution of asset allocation to performance. All the studies conclude that asset allocation is important in building performance and often the question of persistence cannot be separated from the asset allocation choices.

Moreover, we can observe that stock markets are subject to cycles. Therefore, certain investment styles produce better performances during certain periods and worse performances during others. The existence of these cycles can thus explain the performance of a specialised manager persisting over a certain period, if the cycle is favourable, and then suffering from a reversal in the trend when the cycle becomes unfavourable.

Table 1.1 summarises the results from the different studies presented in this section.

1.5   PERFORMANCE ANALYSIS AND THE AIMR STANDARDS[13]

Performance analysis must also allow the results of different managers to be compared, while ensuring that the comparisons involve funds of the same nature. In order to render the comparisons significant, and to ensure uniform calculation of performance and presentation of results, the Association for Investment Management and Research (AIMR) defined a set of standards in 1993. These standards were revised and a new edition published in 1997. The AIMR-PPS are constantly subject to AIMR-PPS Implementation Committee comments, interpretations and amendments These modifications are available on-line at the AIMR's web site (www.aimr.org) and in the AIMR's bimonthly letter (*AIMR Advocate*). The standards, which are called AIMR-PPS, for Performance Presentation Standards, were designed to be suitable for the American market and were not worldwide standards at the outset. The AIMR then put together the Global PPS Committee in 1995, including representatives from the major

---

[13] The AIMR standards are presented succinctly in Fabozzi (1995) and in detail in AIMR (1997). See also Chapter 18 of Fabozzi (1996), Jones and Peltzman (1997), Ernewein (1998) and MacKendrick (2000).

Table 1.1

Authors	Type of data/period/models	Results
Jensen (1968)	115 mutual funds 1945–1964	No evidence of performance persistence
Brown *et al.* (1992)	1976–1987 Investigation of the survivorship bias problem	Short-term performance persistence The survivorship bias attached to the database could significantly affect the result of performance studies and could in particular give an appearance of significant persistence
Hendricks *et al.* (1993)	1974–1988 165 of Wiesenberger's equity mutual funds	Performance persistence for both good and bad managers
Jegadeesh and Titman (1993)	1965–1989 Funds made up of NYSE and AMEX securities Three-factor model (the momentum factor is not included in the model)	Performance persistence for both good and bad managers Assets returns exhibit momentum: the winners of the past continue to perform well and the losers of the past continue to perform badly Performance persistence is due to the use of momentum strategies
Brown and Goetzmann (1995)	1976–1988 Wiesenberger's equity mutual funds Sample free of survivorship bias	Performance persistence for equity funds on a risk-adjusted basis Poor performance tends to increase the probability that the fund will disappear
Kahn and Rudd (1995)	1983–1993 for the equity funds 1988–1993 for the bond funds	Slight performance persistence for bond funds, but not for equity funds The analysis takes into account style effects, management fees and database errors
Malkiel (1995)	1971–1991 Analyse of fund fees Study of the survivorship bias	Significant performance persistence for good managers in the 1970s, but no consistency in fund returns in the 1980s. No long-term persistence The persistence identified could be due to survivorship bias
Fama and French (1996)	1963–1993 NYSE, AMEX and NASDAQ stocks Three-factor model (market factor, size and book-to-market ratio)	Their model does not explain the short-term persistence of returns highlighted by Jegadeesh and Titman (1993) Suggest that research could be directed towards a model integrating an additional risk factor
Gruber (1996)	1985–1994 270 of Wiesenberger's equity mutual funds Sample free from survivorship bias Single index and four index model	Evidence of persistence in performance

continues overleaf

Table 1.1 (*continued*)

Authors	Type of data/period/models	Results
Carhart (1997)	1962–1993 Equity funds made up of NYSE, AMEX and NASDAQ stocks Free from survivorship bias Four-factor model (Fama and French's three-factor model with momentum as additional factor)	Performance persistence for bad managers Short-term performance persistence is due to the use of momentum strategies Ranking of fund from one year to another is random
Carhart (1997)	1962–1993 Equity funds made up of NYSE, AMEX and NASDAQ stocks Free from survivorship bias Four-factor model (Fama and French's three-factor model with momentum as additional factor)	Performance persistence for bad managers Short-term performance persistence is due to the use of momentum strategies Ranking of fund from one year to another is random
Daniel *et al.* (1997)	1975–1994 2500 equity funds made up of stocks from NYSE, AMEX and NASDAQ Four-factor model Study of management fees	Performance persistence is due to the use of momentum strategies, rather than the managers being particularly skilful at picking winning stocks
Blake and Timmermann (1998)	1972–1995 Mutual funds in the United Kingdom Three-factor model	Performance persistence for equity funds: on average, a portfolio made up of funds that have performed best in historical terms will perform better in the following period than a portfolio made up of funds that have performed worst in historical terms
Lenormand-Touchais (1998)	1990–1995 French equity mutual funds	Short-term performance persistence, more significant when the performance measurement technique used integrates a risk criterion No long-term performance persistence, unless a slight persistence in negative performance is counted
Rouwenhorst (1998)	1980–1995 A sample of funds from 12 European countries	Performance persistence for both good and bad managers. Asset returns exhibit momentum

countries in the world, in order to define an international standard for performance presentation, the Global Investment Performance Standard (GIPS), which could be accepted in every country. In 1996, the European Federation of Financial Analysts' Societies (EFFAS) set up a parallel commission on performance measurement with the aim of developing performance presentation and measurement principles for Europeans and participating in the construction of a worldwide standard. The EFFAS commission soon became associated with the work of the Global PPS Committee. At the end of the project, the Global PPS Committee was renamed the GIPS Committee.

The definition of the GIPS[14] was rendered necessary by the existence of considerable differences in performance measurement and result presentation from one country to another. In addition, some countries have national regulations and others do not. The final version of the GIPS was published at the beginning of 1999 and investment firms were invited to comply with the standards from 1 January 2000. The GIPS resulted from the AIMR-PPS and therefore contain more or less the same fundamental requirements, namely accurate presentation and complete transparency of results. In fact, they complement the latter standards, for which they are an international version.

While the AIMR-PPS were implemented in the United States in a homogeneous environment and are suitable for the most developed markets, the GIPS was designed in such a way as to facilitate its acceptance in a large number of countries. The GIPS had to prove suitable for countries with different habits and cultures. Its scope is therefore wider than that of the AIMR-PPS. The standards are deliberately simple, in order to facilitate translation into different languages and integrate the different countries' varying levels of experience in the area of performance. They constitute a minimal worldwide standard for countries that do not have a performance measurement standard. The GIPS does not cover all aspects of performance measurement, evaluation and attribution, or all asset classes. It focuses for the moment on equities and fixed income securities, which cover most of the securities on the market. The standard will need to be developed to cover all categories of assets, such as derivatives, and to deal with additional aspects of performance. For example, it does not include any risk-adjusted performance measure, and nor do the AIMR-PPS. The development of such a measure was postponed in order to be able to implement a minimal standard quickly. Using the GIPS as a starting point, each country can define its national standard while including additional requirements that enable them, for example, to take national regulations or particular fiscal characteristics into account. In the case of a conflict between the GIPS and the country's local rules, the local rules must have precedence.

To accompany the GIPS, the Investment Performance Council (IPC) was set up in March 2000 by the AIMR. Its goal is to promote the use of the GIPS, not only as minimal rules to be used when the local rules are deficient, but also as a set of methods for calculating and presenting performance which is common to all countries. This globalisation of performance measurement has led the countries participating in the IPC or wishing to promote their financial management industry to implement a recognition and adaptation process with regard to the GIPS through a special procedure set up by the IPC: *Country Version of the GIPS (CVG) at the earliest opportunity.*

Following the development of the GIPS, the AIMR made some changes to the AIMR-PPS in order to render them entirely consistent with the GIPS. We will describe these changes in more detail in Chapter 2, along with the differences between the GIPS and the AIMR-PPS. The future objective of the GIPS committee is to converge the AIMR-PPS and GIPS to end up with a single worldwide standard for performance presentation. The requirements of the AIMR-PPS and GIPS are already being harmonised with that aim in mind.

Investment firms first sought to obtain AIMR-PPS certification, since these were the earlier standards. They can now request GIPS certification too. Whether it involves exercising the

---

[14] The complete text of the GIPS can be consulted on the AIMR web site at the following address: http://www.aimr.org/standards/pps/gips_standards.html.

AIMR-PPS or the GIPS, certain rules are requirements and others are simply recommendations. However, the recommendations are liable to become the requirements of the future. It
is therefore desirable for establishments to take them into account from the very start. Establishments that request certification must meet all the requirements and are then strongly
encouraged to implement regular internal checks to ensure that the certification is validated.
Since the GIPS and AIMR-PPS are fundamentally the same, a firm that meets the AIMR-
PPS conditions also meets the GIPS conditions. The requirements and recommendations are
described in Chapter 2.

1.6 INTERNATIONAL INVESTMENT:[15] ADDITIONAL ELEMENTS TO BE TAKEN INTO ACCOUNT

When we presented the major asset classes at the beginning of this chapter, we mentioned
the usefulness of having diversified portfolios to reduce the investment risks. Diversifying
a portfolio between several assets, or several asset classes, allows the risk to be reduced,
and therefore allows the performance to be improved for a given level of risk. This is because
correlations exist between returns on assets or asset classes. These correlations can be positive –
prices evolve in the same way – or negative – evolution occurs in the opposite direction. As we
will see in Chapter 3, the weaker the correlations between assets or asset classes, the greater
the reduction in portfolio risk. Therefore, for the same level of risk, the performance of a
diversified portfolio is better than that of a portfolio that is less diversified. As a result, it is in
the investor's interest to diversify her investments by seeking out those investments that have
a low level of correlation. Turning to international investment would then present significant
advantages, because it would allow the diversification possibilities to be increased, by offering
a wider choice of assets and markets.

However, the usefulness of international diversification is a very controversial subject. In
principle, the values of assets in each country are influenced by national economic factors, such
as interest rates, and by domestic politics. All of these constitute the specific risk of each country.
The economies of different countries are liable to evolve differently and the industrial structure
may also be different from one country to another. International diversification allows investors
to spread their risk between the specific levels of risk in each country and thereby eliminate part
of the risk. For the same level of return, the global risk of the portfolio is diminished. Portfolio
performance can therefore be improved, without increasing the risk. However, this is only true
to the extent that the financial markets in the different countries are not perfectly correlated.
Studies show that the correlation coefficients between the different countries, measured by
the correlations between their market indices, are strictly lower than one, if they are positive.
Moreover, the correlations between the different markets are globally weaker than correlations
between securities in the same market. Interesting risk reduction possibilities therefore exist.
We can observe, nevertheless, that the northern European countries (the United Kingdom,
Germany, France, The Netherlands and Switzerland) are closely correlated because those
countries have strong economic links. It is thus in the interest of European investors to diversify
their investments in the United States, Canada or Japan, rather than in other European countries.

On the other hand, if this economic reasoning of critical research has not exactly called
international diversification into question, it has lessened its attractiveness. We should cite

---

[15] It should be noted that the literature uses the term *international* to denote foreign investment only, excluding domestic investment, and the term *global* to denote worldwide investment, i.e. both foreign and domestic investment.

the study by Longin and Solnik (1995), which brought to light the fact that correlations between stock market returns in different countries were not constant and that they tended to be higher when the volatilities themselves were higher. Therefore, in a recessionary period, the benefits of diversification tend to diminish at the very moment when investors need them the most!

Moreover, Erb *et al.* (1996) showed that correlations between returns on the NYSE and those of most major stock markets were higher when the American economy was in recession than when it was growing. This work was also the subject of a more global study on the integration of financial markets, carried out by Dumas *et al.* (1997), using not only stock market return correlations from 12 countries in the OECD but also industrial production correlations. They note that stock market return correlations are always higher than production correlations. If we take into account the existence of national and worldwide business cycles, then the correlations between the stock markets are higher than those that would result from the market considering the countries' level of integration in the world market alone. This integration supplement can be interpreted as a sign of "sheep-like" behaviour from investors and managers. In spite of "rational" analysis of international asset allocation, taking into account the fundamentals of each of the geographical zones, they do not hesitate to sell an asset class, such as equities, globally, when they have doubts about the stock market returns on a leading exchange like New York. We may wonder whether this phenomenon is very different from the one observed when an index drops precipitously, where correlations between securities on the same market also tend to increase. At that stage, fundamental microeconomic analysis gives way to macroeconomic analysis (or panic!).

Finally, turning to international investment frequently leads, in practice, to new asset classes being defined. Investment can be carried out by buying securities directly or by investing in international funds. Even if it leads to an overall reduction in portfolio risk, this type of investment is a source of additional risk: exchange risk and political risk. These risks have differing levels of importance depending on whether developed countries with stable economies or emerging countries are involved. In emerging markets, the volatility of exchange rates is high. The political risk, which can be seen as the risk of expropriation or the risk of foreign exchange controls, is also higher. There are also difficulties linked to liquidity and efficiency problems in these markets. The exchange risk is in fact the only risk that is truly quantifiable. Traditionally, geographical analysis is distinct from exchange risk analysis. We thus identify the advantage of diversifying into international markets with low levels of correlation between them as a means of improving the efficient frontier of the portfolio and the exchange profits or losses linked to the fact that the assets selected for international allocation are expressed in different currencies. This approach actually considers the return on an international portfolio to be the result of a "principal" geographical factor that the manager controls and a "currency" effect that should be cancelled (hedging) or managed separately (currency overlay). We will consider that this residual view of the currency is neither consistent with modern approaches to portfolio risk, and notably the application of multi-factor models, nor with international diversification practices, notably with regard to bond portfolios, where investors bet more often on an appreciation of the currency than on a lowering of the interest rates in the country in question.[16]

In this publication, the particular requirements of international investment compared to national investment will be presented on an ongoing basis.

---

[16] On this question, it would be useful to refer to Levich and Thomas (1993).

1.7 CONCLUSION

The first chapter has allowed us to give an overview of portfolio management and the techniques that are involved. Performance analysis is considered today to be not only a set of portfolio return measurement techniques, but also a methodology for evaluating the whole investment management process. We therefore feel it is essential to reposition our arguments within the wider framework of portfolio management.

BIBLIOGRAPHY

Accoceberry, M., "Mesure de performances: Une clarification des procédés de gestion est indispensable", *MTF-L'Agefi*, no. 80, April 1996.

AIMR Performance Presentation Standards Handbook, 2nd edn, 1997.

AIMR, *Benchmarks and Performance Attribution, Subcommittee Report*, Final Draft, August 1998.

AIMR, *Global Investment Performance Standards*, April 1999.

Amenc, N. and Le Sourd, V., *Gestion quantitative des portefeuilles d'actions*, Economica, 1998.

Amenc, N., Bonnet, S., Henry, G., Martellini, L. and Weytens, A., *Alternative Investment*, 2003.

Beeman, D., Yip, K., Weinreich, J., Russell, C. and Barr, D., "Evolution of an Essential Asset Class – Absolute Return Strategies", *Journal of Investing*, vol. 9, no. 4, winter 2000, pp. 9–24.

Bergeruc, L., "La mesure de la performance des OPCVM actions françaises: le phénomène de persistance", *Banque et Marchés*, no. 50, January–February 2001.

Black, F. and Jones, R., "Simplifying Portfolio Insurance", *Journal of Portfolio Management*, fall 1987, pp. 48–51.

Blake, D. and Timmermann, A., "Mutual Fund Performance: Evidence from the UK", *European Finance Review*, vol. 2, 1998, pp. 57–77.

Boulier, J.-F., "Gestion quantitative", *Encyclopédie des marchés financiers*, Economica, 1997, pp. 572–582.

Brinson, G.P., Hood, L.R. and Beebower, G.L., "Determinants of Portfolio Performance", *Financial Analysts Journal*, July–August 1986.

Brinson, G.P., Singer, B.D. and Beebower, G.L., "Determinants of Portfolio Performance II: An Update", *Financial Analysts Journal*, May–June 1991.

Broquet, C. and van den Berg, A., *Gestion de portefeuille – Actions, Obligations, Options*, 2nd edn, De Boeck Université, 1992.

Brown, S.J. and Goetzmann, W.N., "Performance Persistence", *Journal of Finance*, vol. 50, no. 2, June 1995, pp. 679–698.

Brown, S.J., Goetzmann, W., Ibbotson, R.G. and Ross, S.A., "Survivorship Bias in Performance Studies", *Review of Financial Studies*, vol. 5, 1992, pp. 553–580.

Carhart, M.M., "On Persistence in Mutual Fund Performance", *Journal of Finance*, vol. 52, no. 1, March 1997, pp. 57–82.

Coggin, T.D., Fabozzi, F.J. and Arnott, R.D., *The Handbook of Equity Style Management*, 2nd edn, Frank J. Fabozzi Associates, 1997.

Daniel, K., Grinblatt, M., Titman, S. and Wermers, R., "Measuring Mutual Fund Performance with Characteristic-Based Benchmarks", *Journal of Finance*, vol. 52, no. 3, July 1997, pp. 1035–1058.

Dumas, B., Harvey, C.R. and Ruiz, P., "Are Common Swings in International Stock Returns Justified by Subsequent Changes in National Outputs?", *Cahier de Recherche*, no. 603/1997, HEC, 1997.

Duval, P., "La multigestion se développe", *Banque Magazine*, no. 599, January 1999.

Elton, E.J. and Gruber, M.J., *Modern Portfolio Theory and Investment Analysis*, 5th edn, Wiley, 1995.

Erb, C.B., Harvey, C.R. and Viskanta, T.E., "Political Risk, Economic Risk and Financial Risk", *Financial Analysts Journal*, no. 52, 1996, pp. 29–64.

Ernewein, A., "Les normes GIPS", *Revue Banque*, no. 591, April 1998.

Fabozzi, F.J., *Investment Management*, Prentice Hall International Editions, 1995.

Fabozzi, F.J., *Bond Portfolio Management*, Frank J. Fabozzi Associates, 1996.

Fabozzi, F.J. and Grant, J.L., *Equity Portfolio Management*, Frank J. Fabozzi Associates, 1999.

Fama, E.F., "Efficient Capital Markets: A Review of Theory and Empirical Work", *Journal of Finance*, vol. 25, no. 2, March 1970, pp. 383–417.

Fama, E.F., "Efficient Capital Markets II", *Journal of Finance*, vol. 26, no. 5, December 1991, pp. 1575–1617.

Fama, E.F. and French, K.R., "Multifactor Explanations of Asset Pricing Anomalies", *Journal of Finance*, vol. 51, no. 1, March 1996, pp. 55–81.

Farrell, Jr. J.L., *Portfolio Management, Theory and Application*, 2nd edn, McGraw-Hill, 1997.

Fencke, C. and Gascu, M., "La multigestion s'ouvre aux particuliers", *Banque Magazine*, no. 622, February 2001.

Grinold, R.C. and Kahn, R.N., *Active Portfolio Management: A Quantitative Approach for Producing Superior Returns and Controlling Risk*, 2nd edn, Irwin, 2000.

Grossman, S.J. and Stiglitz, J., "On the Impossibility of Informationally Efficient Markets", *American Economic Review*, 1980, pp. 393–408.

Gruber, M.J., "Another Puzzle: The Growth in Actively Managed Mutual Funds", *Journal of Finance*, vol. 51, 1996, pp. 783–810.

Hendricks, D., Patel, J. and Zeckhauser, R., "Hot Hands in Mutual Funds: Short-Run Persistence of Relative Performance, 1974–1988", *Journal of Finance*, vol. 48, March 1993, pp. 93–130.

Hong, H., Lim, T. and Stein, J.C., "Bad News Travels Slowly: Size, Analyst Coverage, and the Profitability of Momentum Strategies", *Journal of Finance*, vol. 55, no. 1, February 2000, pp. 265–295.

Ippolito, R., "Efficiency with Costly Information: a Study of Mutual Fund Performance, 1965–84", *Quarterly Journal of Economics*, vol. 104, 1989, pp. 1–23.

Jegadeesh, N. and Titman, S., "Returns to Buying Winners and Selling Losers: Implications for Stock Market Efficiency", *Journal of Finance*, vol. 48, 1993, pp. 65–91.

Jensen, M.C., "The Performance of Mutual Funds in the Period 1945–1964", *Journal of Finance*, vol. 23, 1968, pp. 389–416.

Jensen, M., "Some Anomalous Evidence Regarding Market Efficiency", *Journal of Financial Economics*, vol. 6, no. 2/3, 1978, pp. 95–101.

Jones, F.J. and Peltzman, L.J., "Fixed Income Attribution Analysis", *Managing Fixed Income Portfolios*, Frank J. Fabozzi, ed., Frank J. Fabozzi Associates, 1997.

Kahn, R.N. and Rudd, A., "Does Historical Performance Predict Future Performance?" *Barra Newsletter*, Spring 1995.

Kaplanis, E.C., "Coûts et avantages d'un portefeuille international", *Les Echos*, 21 and 22 March 1997.

Kothari, S.P. and Warner, J.B., "Evaluating Mutual Fund Performance", *Journal of Finance*, vol. 56, no. 5, October 2001, pp. 1623–1666.

Lenormand-Touchais, G., "Etude de la stabilité des performances: le cas des Sicav actions françaises", *Banque et Marchés*, no. 36, September-October 1998.

Levich, R. and Thomas, L., "The Merits of Active Currency Risk Management: Evidence from International Bond Portfolios", *Financial Analysts Journal*, September-October 1993.

Longin, F. and Solnik, B., "Is the Correlation in International Equity Returns Constant?", *Journal of International Money and Finance*, no. 14, 1995, pp. 2–26.

MacKendrick, D., "The GIPS Passport", *Performance and Risk Association Newsletter*, issue seven, July 2000.

MacKinlay, C. and Lo, A.W., "La théorie de la marche aléatoire en question", *L'Art de la Finance*, no. 7, *Les Echos*, April 1998.

Malkiel, B.G., "Returns from Investing in Equity Mutual Funds 1971 to 1991", *Journal of Finance*, vol. 50, no. 2, June 1995, pp. 549–572.

Perold, A. and Sharpe, W., "Dynamic Strategies for Asset Allocation", *Financial Analysts Journal*, January–February 1988, pp. 16–26.

Renard, E., "Attribution de performances: l'émergence d'un langage commun", *L'Agefi*, no. 86, December 1996.

Rouwenhorst, K.G., "International Momentum Strategies", *Journal of Finance*, vol. 53, no. 1, February 1998, pp. 267–284.

Schneeweis, T.R. and Pescatore, J.F., *The Handbook of Alternative Investment Strategies*, Institutional Investors, 1999.

Schneeweis, T.R. and Spurgin, R., "Multifactor Analysis of Hedge Funds, Managed Futures, and Mutual Fund Return and Risk Characteristics", *Journal of Alternative Investing*, no. 124, 1998.

Sharpe, W.F., "Determining a Fund's Effective Asset Mix", *Investment Management Review*, December 1988, pp. 59–69.

Sharpe, W.F., "Asset Allocation: Management Style and Performance Measurement", *Journal of Portfolio Management*, vol. 18, Winter 1992, pp. 7–19.

Simon, Y., *Encyclopédie des marchés financiers*, Economica, 1997.

Strul, R., "L'attribution de performance: outil du marketing", *Revue Banque*, no. 569, April 1996.

Wermers, R., "Mutual Fund Performance: An Empirical Decomposition into Stock-Picking Talent, Style, Transaction Costs, and Expenses", *Journal of Finance*, vol. 55, no. 1, February 2000, pp. 1655–1695.

Zheng, L. "Is Money Smart? A Study of Mutual Fund Investors' Fund Selection Ability", *Journal of Finance* vol. 54, no. 2, June 1999, pp. 901–933.

2
The Basic Performance Analysis
Concepts

In Chapter 1 we introduced the different aspects of portfolio management and underlined the importance of performance analysis. This chapter is essentially devoted to performance measurement, which is the first stage in performance analysis. We describe how to calculate the return on an asset, and then the return on a portfolio, for both national and international investment. We also specify the methods to be favoured to obtain results that comply with the AIMR standards. This chapter then addresses the initial elements that allow performance to be evaluated. It defines the references to be used to compare returns: benchmarks and peer groups. Finally, it introduces the notion of risk, which will be the subject of more detailed analysis in subsequent chapters.

2.1 RETURN CALCULATION

Ex post calculation of the return on a portfolio, or an investment fund, is the first element employed to determine its performance. In this section we first define the return on an asset, and then define the different calculation methods that apply to a portfolio.

2.1.1 Return on an asset[1]

2.1.1.1 Calculation over a period

A period is an interval of time during which an asset is held, without being modified. It is assumed that any eventual dividends are paid at the end of the period. The return on an asset can be calculated arithmetically or logarithmically.

Arithmetic return
The exact value of the return on an asset i for a period is obtained through an arithmetic calculation: we calculate the relative variation of the price of the asset over the period, increased, if applicable, by the dividend payment.
   The return on the asset R_{it} is given by

$$R_{it} = \frac{P_{it} - P_{i,t-1} + D_{it}}{P_{i,t-1}}$$

where

$P_{i,t-1}$ is the price of the asset at time $t-1$;
P_{it} is the price of the asset at time t; and
D_{it} is the dividend paid at time t.

---

[1] For additional information, see Charest (1997), who presents the different asset return calculation methods with their advantages, disadvantages and limits.

This formula allows the exact arithmetic return on a portfolio to be obtained easily, as a linear combination of the returns on the assets that make up the portfolio. In addition, the arithmetic expression allows the return to be separated into two terms:

- a term that comes from the increase in price: $(P_{it} - P_{i,t-1})/P_{i,t-1}$; and
- a term that comes from the dividend paid: $D_{it}/P_{i,t-1}$;

with the total return on the asset being equal to the sum of these two terms.

This calculation method does, however, present one disadvantage. The arithmetic returns for the sub-periods cannot be added together to obtain the return for a longer period. That is why we often use logarithmic returns, which can be aggregated over time.

Logarithmic return
With the same notation as before, the logarithmic return on an asset is obtained as follows:

$$R_{it} = \ln\left(\frac{P_{it} + D_{it}}{P_{i,t-1}}\right)$$

Since the logarithms can be aggregated, this formula allows us to obtain the return for a period of any length by simply adding the returns calculated for the elementary periods.

2.1.1.2   Calculation over several periods

The returns calculated for successive elementary time periods are then used to calculate the return for the whole period under consideration. To do that, we calculate their mean. There are two types of mean: the arithmetic mean and the geometric mean.

Arithmetic mean
The simplest calculation involves computing the arithmetic mean of the returns for the sub-periods, i.e. calculating

$$\bar{R}_a = \frac{1}{T}\sum_{t=1}^{T} R_{it}$$

where the R_{it} are obtained arithmetically and T denotes the number of sub-periods. We thus obtain the mean return realised for a sub-period.

Examples show that this mean overestimates the result, which can even be fairly far removed from the reality when the sub-period returns are very different from each other. The result also depends on the choice of sub-periods.

As an illustration, let us consider the example of an asset price that varies in the following manner:

$$P_0 = 100 \text{ at } t = 0; \qquad P_1 = 200 \text{ at } t = 1; \qquad P_2 = 100 \text{ at } t = 2$$

A direct calculation of the return for the period gives

$$R = \frac{P_2 - P_0}{P_0} = 0$$

But if we successively calculate the return for sub-period 1:

$$R_1 = \frac{P_1 - P_0}{P_0} = 1.0$$

and the return for sub-period 2:

$$R_2 = \frac{P_2 - P_1}{P_1} = -0.5$$

and we compute the mean, we obtain a mean return value for a sub-period that is equal to 0.25, which is not representative of the return that was actually realised for the period.

The arithmetic mean of the returns from past periods does, however, have one interesting interpretation. It provides an unbiased estimate of the return for the following period. It is therefore the expected return on the asset and can be used as a forecast of its future performance.

Let us now consider the case of returns obtained through a logarithmic calculation. Since these returns can be aggregated, the return for the entire period can be obtained directly by computing the sum of the returns for the sub-periods.

Geometric mean

The geometric mean (or compound geometric rate of return) allows us to link the arithmetic rates of return for the different periods, in order to obtain the real growth rate of the investment over the whole period. The calculation assumes that intermediate income is reinvested. The mean rate for the period is given by the following expression:

$$\bar{R}_g = \left[\prod_{t=1}^{T} (1 + R_{it}) \right]^{1/T} - 1$$

If we take the previous example again, then we now have

$$\bar{R}_g = [(1 + R_1)(1 + R_2)]^{1/2} - 1 = [(1 + 1)(1 - 0.5)]^{1/2} - 1 = 0$$

This calculation shows that the geometric mean gives the real rate of return that is observed over the whole period, which was not true for the arithmetic mean.

The example chosen is an extreme case to underline the difference in results between the arithmetic mean and the geometric mean. In general, the return values for successive periods are not that different, and the arithmetic mean and geometric mean give more similar results. However, the arithmetic mean always gives a value that is greater than the geometric mean, unless the R_t returns are all equal, in which case the two means are identical. The greater the variation in R_t, the greater the difference between the two means.

We indicated in the previous section that the arithmetic mean was interpreted as the expected return for the following period. However, if we are interested in the expected return over the long term, and not just in the forthcoming period, it is better to consider the geometric rate.

2.1.2 Portfolio return

Calculating the return, which is simple for an asset or an individual portfolio, becomes more complex when it involves mutual funds with variable capital, where investors can enter or leave throughout the investment period. There are several ways to proceed, depending on the area that we are seeking to evaluate. In this section we initially introduce the basic formula for calculating the return on a portfolio, and then describe the different methods that allow capital movements to be taken into account.

2.1.2.1 Basic formula

The simplest method for calculating the return on a portfolio involves applying the same formula as for an asset, or

$$R_{Pt} = \frac{V_t - V_{t-1} + D_t}{V_{t-1}}$$

where

V_{t-1} is the value of the portfolio at the beginning of the period;
V_t is the value of the portfolio at the end of the period; and
D_t is the cash flows generated by the portfolio during the evaluation period.

However, this formula is only valid for a portfolio that has a fixed composition throughout the evaluation period. In the area of mutual funds, portfolios are subject to contributions and withdrawals of capital on the part of investors. This leads to the purchase and sale of securities on the one hand, and to an evolution in the volume of capital managed, which is independent from variations in stock market prices, on the other. The formula must therefore be adapted to take this into account. The modifications to be made will be presented in the next section.

Furthermore, since a portfolio is defined as a linear combination of assets, its return is also expressed as a function of the returns on the assets that make up the portfolio, or

$$R_{Pt} = \sum_{i=1}^{n} x_{it} R_{it}$$

where R_{it} denotes the return on asset i during the period; and x_{it} denotes the weight of asset i in the portfolio at the beginning of the evaluation period.

The equivalence with the first formula is established in Appendix 2.1, which can be found at the end of the chapter. It should be noted that the use of the R_{it} returns obtained through arithmetic calculation give an exact formula, while logarithmic returns lead to an approximate result. Appendix 2.1 also specifies this point.

The use of one formula or the other depends on the data available. If we know the successive valuations of the portfolio, then it is quicker to use the first formula. If, on the other hand, the database is made up of asset returns, and we have historical data available on the evolution of their weights in the portfolio, then we use the second formula.

Therefore, the return on a market index, defined in theory as the weighted mean of all the securities that make up the index, with the weightings being obtained from the market capitalisation of each security, is calculated, in practice, by using the value of the indices quoted on the markets directly, or

$$R_{It} = \frac{I_t - I_{t-1}}{I_{t-1}}$$

where I_t denotes the value of the index at time t.

Finally, the second formula is used when we model the expected portfolio return. We will return to this subject in more detail in the next chapter.

2.1.2.2   Taking capital flows into account

Calculation methods have been developed to take into account the volume of capital and the time that capital is present in a portfolio. The earliest standards on this subject figure in a study published in 1968 by the *Bank Administration Institute (BAI)* (see Fisher, 1968). The methods that are currently listed and used are the internal rate of return, the capital-weighted rate of return (CWR) and the time-weighted rate of return. Each of these methods evaluates a different aspect of the return. This part of the chapter describes the different methods and presents the areas in which they are used.

Capital-weighted rate of return method
This rate is equal to the relationship between the variation in value of the portfolio during the period and the average of the capital invested during the period. Let us first consider the case where a single capital flow is produced during the period. The calculation formula is as follows:

$$R_{\text{CWR}} = \frac{V_T - V_0 - C_t}{V_0 + 1/2C_t}$$

where

V_0 denotes the value of the portfolio at the beginning of the period;
V_T denotes the value of the portfolio at the end of the period; and
C_t denotes the cash flow that occurred at date t, with C_t positive if it involves a contribution and C_t negative if it involves a withdrawal.

   This calculation is based on the assumption that the contributions and withdrawals of funds take place in the middle of the period. A more accurate method involves taking the real length of time that the capital was present in the portfolio. The calculation is then presented as follows:

$$R_{\text{CWR}} = \frac{V_T - V_0 - C_t}{V_0 + \dfrac{T-t}{T}C_t}$$

where T denotes the total length of the period.
   Let us now assume that there are n capital flows during the evaluation period. The formula is then generalised in the following manner:

$$R_{\text{CWR}} = \frac{V_T - V_0 - \sum\limits_{i=1}^{n} C_{t_i}}{V_0 + \sum\limits_{i=1}^{n} \dfrac{T-t_i}{T}C_{t_i}}$$

where t_i denotes the date on which the ith cash flow, C_{t_i}, occurs.
   This calculation method is simple to use, but it actually calculates an approximate value of the true internal rate of return of the portfolio, because it does not take the capitalisation of the contributions and withdrawals of capital during the period into account. If there are a large number of capital flows, then the internal rate of return, which we present below, will be more precise. The advantage of this method, however, is to provide an explicit formulation of the rate.

Internal rate of return method

This method is based on an actuarial calculation. The internal rate of return is the discount rate that renders the final value of the portfolio equal to the sum of its initial value and the capital flows that occurred during the period. The cash flow for each sub-period is calculated by taking the difference between the incoming cash flow, which comes from the reinvestment of dividends and client contributions, and the outgoing cash flow, which results from payments to clients. The internal rate of return R_I is the solution to the following equation:

$$V_0 + \sum_{i=1}^{n-1} \frac{C_{t_i}}{(1+R_I)^{t_i}} = \frac{V_T}{(1+R_I)^T}$$

where

T　denotes the length of the period in years; this period is divided into n sub-periods;
t_i　denotes the cash flow dates, expressed in years, over the period;
V_0　is the initial value of the portfolio;
V_T　is the final value of the portfolio; and
C_{t_i}　is the cash flow on date t_i, withdrawals of capital are counted negatively and contributions positively.

Since the formula is not explicit, the calculation is done iteratively. The internal rate of return only depends on the initial and final values of the portfolio. It is therefore independent from the intermediate portfolio values. However, it does depend on the size and dates of the cash flows, so the rate is, again, a capital-weighted rate of return.

Time-weighted rate of return (TWR) method

The principle of this method is to break down the period into elementary sub-periods, during which the composition of the portfolio remains fixed. The return for the complete period is then obtained by calculating the geometric mean of the returns calculated for the sub-periods. The result gives a mean return weighted by the length of the sub-periods. This calculation assumes that the distributed cash flows, such as dividends, are reinvested in the portfolio.

We take a period of length T during which capital movements occur on dates $(t_i)_{1 \leq i \leq n}$. We denote the value of the portfolio just before a capital movement by V_{t_i} and the value of the cash flow by C_{t_i}. C_{t_i} is positive if it involves a contribution and negative if it involves a withdrawal. The return for a sub-period is then written as follows:

$$R_{t_i} = \frac{V_{t_i} - (V_{t_{i-1}} + C_{t_{i-1}})}{V_{t_{i-1}} + C_{t_{i-1}}}$$

This formula ensures that we compare the value of the portfolio at the end of the period with its value at the beginning of the period, i.e. its value at the end of the previous period increased by the capital paid or decreased by the capital withdrawn.

The return for the whole period is then given by the following formula:

$$R_{\text{TWR}} = \left[\prod_{i=1}^{n} (1 + R_{t_i}) \right]^{1/T} - 1$$

This calculation method provides a rate of return per dollar invested, independently of the capital flows that occur during the period. The result depends solely on the evolution of the value of the portfolio over the period. To implement this calculation, we need to know the value and the date of the cash flows, together with the value of the portfolio at each of the dates.

There is one small reservation, however, when applying this method. To simplify matters, we often assume that all the cash flows occur at the end of the month, instead of considering the exact dates. In this case, the use of a continuous version of the rate smoothes the errors committed.

The BAI document provides an expression for this:

$$r_{\text{TWR}} = \frac{1}{T} \left[\ln\left(\frac{V_T}{V_0}\right) + \sum_{i=1}^{n-1} \ln\left(\frac{V_{t_i}}{V_{t_i} + C_{t_i}}\right) \right]$$

The link that exists between the discrete rate of return and the continuous rate is detailed in Appendix 2.2 of this chapter.

Comparison of the methods
The essential difference between the time-weighted rate of return and the capital-weighted rate of return is the following: the former measures the performance of the manager, whereas the latter measures the performance of the fund.

The time-weighted rate of return enables a manager to be evaluated separately from the movements of capital, which he does not control. This rate only measures the impact of the manager's decisions on the performance of the fund. It is thus the best method for judging the quality of the manager. It allows the results of different managers to be compared objectively. It is considered to be the fairest method and, for that reason, is recommended by the AIMR and is used by the international performance measurement bodies. The 1968 BAI document, which provided the earliest performance measurement standards, recommended the use of a time-weighted rate of return. This method requires the value of the portfolio to be known each time there is a contribution or withdrawal of funds. However, that information is not always available. In that case, there are methods that enable an approximate value of the rate to be obtained. We will return to this when we discuss the AIMR standards in Section 2.1.5.

The capital-weighted rate of return, for its part, allows the total performance of the fund to be measured and, by so doing, provides the true rate of return from the fund holder's perspective. The result in this case is strongly influenced by capital contributions and withdrawals.

The internal rate of return method allows us to obtain a more precise result than the capital-weighted rate of return when there are a significant number of capital flows of different sizes, but it takes more time to implement.

The capital-weighted rate of return and the internal rate of return are the only usable methods if the value of the portfolio is not known at the time the funds are contributed and withdrawn.

The existence of several methods for calculating returns, which give different results, shows that a return value should always be accompanied by more information. It is appropriate to indicate the calculation method used, together with the total length of time for the historical data and the frequency with which the returns were measured. With the increasing use of the AIMR standards, it has become usual to evaluate portfolios on a daily basis, while several years ago monthly or quarterly evaluations were considered sufficient. The increasingly frequent evaluations have enabled the impact of the capital flows on the result to be reduced, whatever the method used. Section 2.1.5 will give details on the standards developed by the AIMR for calculating returns.

Example

Table 2.1   Values of the portfolio and values of the cash flows

(years) Time t_i	Value of the portfolio V_{t_i}	Withdrawals($-$)/ payments($+$) C_{t_i}
0	0	10000	
1	0.5	10800	700
2	1.1	12000	-1500
3	1.5	12500	1000
4	1.9	11800	-1700
5	2.3	11500	500
6	2.6	12100	-1000
7	3.0	12300	

In order to illustrate the use of the different calculation methods, let us consider the following example. Table 2.1 contains the values of the cash flows that occurred during the period, together with the value of the portfolio before each cash flow. We therefore have all the information necessary to apply the different calculation formulas.

Calculation of the capital-weighted rate of return

This calculation only uses the initial and final values of the portfolio. It is not necessary to know the intermediate values. It does require, however, the values of the cash flows and the dates on which they occurred.

For the purposes of our example, the calculation formula is the following:

$$R_{CWR}^T = \frac{V_{t_7} - V_{t_0} - \sum_{i=1}^{7} C_{t_i}}{V_{t_0} + \sum_{i=1}^{7} \frac{T - t_i}{T} C_{t_i}}$$

Since the length of the period T is equal to three years, this expression gives a rate over three years. To obtain an annualised value for the rate, we use the relationship that allows returns that have been calculated for any period to be restated for a reference period, or

$$R_{Ref} = (1 + R_{Cal})^{T_{Ref}/T_{Cal}} - 1$$

where T_{Cal} denotes the length of the period that corresponds to the calculated return; and T_{Ref} denotes the length of the period for which we wish to obtain the result.

For our example, we therefore calculate:

$$R_{CWR} = \left(1 + R_{CWR}^T\right)^{1/3} - 1 = 13.26\%$$

Calculation of the internal rate of return

This rate is the solution to the following equation:

$$V_{t_0} + \sum_{i=1}^{6} \frac{C_{t_i}}{(1 + R_1)^{t_i}} = \frac{V_{t_7}}{(1 + R_1)^{t_7}}$$

By proceeding iteratively, we obtain $R_1 = 13.17\%$. Since the dates are expressed in years in the calculation formula, we obtain the annualised rate directly. This value is relatively close to the capital-weighted rate of return. The calculation formula shows that it could quickly become long and tedious if there were a large number of capital contributions and withdrawals.

Time-weighted rate of return calculation

This calculation uses both the successive portfolio valuations over the period and the cash flow amounts. The annualised value of the rate is calculated through the following formula:

$$R_{\text{TWR}} = \prod_{i=1}^{7} \left(\frac{V_{t_i}}{V_{t_{i-1}} + C_{t_{i-1}}} \right)^{1/T} - 1 = 14.26\%$$

The continuous value of the rate is obtained as follows:

$$r_{\text{TWR}} = \frac{1}{T} \left[\ln\left(\frac{V_T}{V_0} \right) + \sum_{i=1}^{6} \ln\left(\frac{V_{t_i}}{V_{t_i} + C_{t_i}} \right) \right] = 13.33\%$$

2.1.3   International investment

The calculations presented up to this point have been based on the assumption that the portfolios were invested in a single currency. However, portfolios generally contain assets from several countries, so it is necessary to convert the returns of the various securities to calculate the portfolio return in the reference country currency. In this section we first present exchange rates briefly and then explain the calculation formulas when returns are either hedged or not hedged against currency risk. In Section 2.3 we will return to the pros and cons of hedging against currency risk.

2.1.3.1   Exchange rates[2]

Definitions

Exchange rates allow the value of a security quoted in one currency to be converted into its equivalent value in another currency. We can therefore express the value of foreign assets in the currency of the country that has been chosen as a reference. It is appropriate to distinguish between the spot exchange rate and the forward exchange rate.

The spot rate is the rate used when the foreign currency must be converted into the local currency at the present time. The forward rate is used when agreement is reached today but the conversion will take place at a fixed date in the future. Forward rates are quoted on the markets for several future dates. Their values take the interest rate differential between the two countries into account.

The difference between the spot rate and the forward rate allows the forward premium to be defined by the following relationship:

$$\text{forward premium} = (\text{forward rate} - \text{spot rate})/\text{spot rate}$$

This quantity is called a "forward discount" if the spot rate is higher than the forward rate, which occurs when the interest rates in the reference country are lower than those in the foreign country. In what follows, the forward premium will be denoted by f.

The evolution of the spot exchange rate in percentage terms is called the "currency return". The variable TC will henceforth be used to refer to this quantity.

---

[2] For more detailed information, it would be useful to refer to Clarke and Kritzman (1996).

Exchange rate forecasting models[3]

The level of exchange rates for the different currencies and their prospective evolution determine the nature of the currency investment and the hedging choices. The forecasting of exchange rates is a complex area. Currency fluctuations are liable to be influenced by a multitude of factors. Economists use theoretical models, which allow them to anticipate the relative movements in exchange rates between different countries, according to economic characteristics. At equilibrium, there is a relationship between the relative levels of interest rates in different countries and exchange rates. If these relationships were always respected, then interest rates and asset prices would always reflect expected modifications in exchange rates, and the currency would not represent a separate risk in international investment. In fact, all that exists is a long-term tendency towards equilibrium, and factors such as taxes, exchange controls and transaction costs tend to distort the equilibrium. Exchange rates are therefore subject to unexpected fluctuations that investors must take into account in their investment strategy. The differentials compared with the models are used to forecast the long-term and short-term changes in rates. For more details on these models, see the Bibliography at the end of the chapter. In Rosenberg (1996) we also find a fairly complete inventory of the economic factors that influence exchange rates and the models that are used to forecast exchange rates. Among those models, we could mention the following:

1. Purchasing power parity, which is based on the principle that prices of identical goods must be the same in different countries after conversion. If purchasing power parity is respected, then an asset must have the same real return for the investor in the reference country and the foreign investor. This is translated by the relationship between the changes in the exchange rate and the inflation rates in the countries, considered over a period of time, which gives

$$\frac{d_{it}^{\text{Quot/Ref}}}{d_{i,t-1}^{\text{Quot/Ref}}} = \frac{I_t^{\text{Quot}}/I_{t-1}^{\text{Quot}}}{I_t^{\text{Ref}}/I_{t-1}^{\text{Ref}}}$$

where

$d_{it}^{\text{Quot/Ref}}$ denotes the price of the quotation currency for asset i at date t, expressed in the reference currency;

I_t^{Quot} denotes the price index in the country where the asset is quoted; and

I_t^{Ref} denotes the price index in the reference country.

The existence of currency risk comes from the observed differential compared to this theoretical principle.

2. The international Fisher effect, which links variations in the spot exchange rate with the difference in interest rates between the two countries.

3. The balance of payments equilibrium model, which links the balance of trade deficit to the levels of exchange rates. If the balance is negative, then there are more imports than exports. A return to equilibrium should therefore be observed if the reference currency depreciates compared with foreign currencies.

The performance decomposition of an international portfolio will be discussed in Chapter 7.

---

[3] Cf. Chapter 7 of Clarke and Kritzman (1996) and Rousseau (1997).

2.1.3.2   Calculating returns that are not hedged against currency risk

The expressions below calculate a return that is not hedged against currency risk: the result then depends on the variations in the currencies compared with each other.

Return on an asset
Arithmetic calculation.   The return on a foreign asset, expressed in the reference currency, depends on the return on the asset in the quotation currency and the return on the currency. To establish the relationship, we simply go back to the definitions. This gives: P_{it}^{Quot} is the price of asset i at time t expressed in the quotation currency; and $d_{it}^{\text{Quot/Ref}}$ is the price of the quotation currency for asset i at time t expressed in the reference currency; so the price P_{it}^{Ref} of asset i expressed in the reference currency is given by

$$P_{it}^{\text{Ref}} = P_{it}^{\text{Quot}} d_{it}^{\text{Quot/Ref}}$$

We can then calculate:

$$\left(1 + R_{it}^{\text{Ref}}\right) = \frac{P_{it}^{\text{Quot}} d_{it}^{\text{Quot/Ref}}}{P_{i,t-1}^{\text{Quot}} d_{i,t-1}^{\text{Quot/Ref}}} = \left(\frac{P_{it}^{\text{Quot}}}{P_{i,t-1}^{\text{Quot}}}\right)\left(\frac{d_{it}^{\text{Quot/Ref}}}{d_{i,t-1}^{\text{Quot/Ref}}}\right) = \left(1 + R_{it}^{\text{Quot}}\right)\left(1 + TC_{it}^{\text{Quot/Ref}}\right)$$

where

R_{it}^{Ref} denotes the return on security i in the reference currency;

R_{it}^{Quot} denotes the return on security i in the quotation currency; and

$TC_{it}^{\text{Quot/Ref}}$ denotes the return on the quotation currency for security i compared with the reference currency for the same period.

The return in the reference currency is therefore obtained by linking the return in the quotation currency to the exchange rate.

By developing the formula, we arrive at the following relationship:

$$R_{it}^{\text{Ref}} = R_{it}^{\text{Quot}} + TC_{it}^{\text{Quot/Ref}} + R_{it}^{\text{Quot}} TC_{it}^{\text{Quot/Ref}}$$

This expression involves a cross term, $R_{it}^{\text{Quot}} TC_{it}^{\text{Quot/Ref}}$, which is small compared with the other two. It is often set aside in order to simplify the calculations. We then write

$$R_{it}^{\text{Ref}} \approx R_{it}^{\text{Quot}} + TC_{it}^{\text{Quot/Ref}}$$

The use of logarithmic returns allows this formula to be obtained directly without having to use an approximation.

Logarithmic calculation.   To establish the relationship when the returns are logarithmic, we apply the same reasoning again. With the same notation, we now have

$$R_{it}^{\text{Ref}} = \ln\left(\frac{P_{it}^{\text{Quot}} d_{it}^{\text{Quot/Ref}}}{P_{i,t-1}^{\text{Quot}} d_{i,t-1}^{\text{Quot/Ref}}}\right) = \ln\left(\frac{P_{it}^{\text{Quot}}}{P_{i,t-1}^{\text{Quot}}}\right) + \ln\left(\frac{d_{it}^{\text{Quot/Ref}}}{d_{i,t-1}^{\text{Quot/Ref}}}\right) = R_{it}^{\text{Quot}} + TC_{it}^{\text{Quot/Ref}}$$

The fact that logarithms can be aggregated allows us to separate the return into two components: the appreciation of the security on the local market and the appreciation of the local currency compared with the reference currency.

Return on a portfolio

We saw previously that the return on a portfolio could be obtained either from successive portfolio valuations or as a linear combination of the asset returns. In the first case, the value of the portfolio in the reference currency is obtained from the asset prices expressed in the reference currency, or

$$V_{Pt}^{\text{Ref}} = \sum_{i=1}^{n} n_{it} P_{it}^{\text{Ref}}$$

where n_{it} denotes the number of securities of asset i held in the portfolio.

By replacing according to the values in the quotation currency, we obtain:

$$V_{Pt}^{\text{Ref}} = \sum_{i=1}^{n} n_{it} P_{it}^{\text{Quot}} d_{it}^{\text{Quot/Ref}}$$

where $d_{it}^{\text{Quot/Ref}} = 1$ if the asset is quoted in the reference currency.

All the calculation methods presented in Section 2.1.2 can then be applied to calculate the return on the portfolio. The cash flows that occur during the evaluation period follow the same transformation rules as the asset prices.

If we calculate the return on the portfolio from the returns on the assets that make up the portfolio, then we use the conversion relationships for the asset returns in the reference currency. We have

$$R_{Pt}^{\text{Ref}} = \sum_{i=1}^{n} x_{it} R_{it}^{\text{Ref}}$$

so

$$R_{Pt}^{\text{Ref}} = \sum_{i=1}^{n} x_{it} R_{it}^{\text{Quot}} + \sum_{i=1}^{n} x_{it} TC_{it}^{\text{Quot/Ref}} + \sum_{i=1}^{n} x_{it} R_{it}^{\text{Quot}} TC_{it}^{\text{Quot/Ref}}$$

if the returns are arithmetic, or

$$R_{Pt}^{\text{Ref}} = \sum_{i=1}^{n} x_{it} R_{it}^{\text{Quot}} + \sum_{i=1}^{n} x_{it} TC_{it}^{\text{Quot/Ref}}$$

if the returns are logarithmic.

2.1.3.3   Calculating returns that are hedged against currency risk

The return calculation formulas established above depend on variations in the exchange rate. The fluctuations in the different currencies compared with each other therefore constitute a risk for the investor: the currency risk. We will return to this in more detail in Section 2.3, which is given over to risk. In order to control the risk, it is possible to implement hedging.

Hedging instruments

Hedging against currency risk is carried out with the help of forward contracts on the exchange rate of the currency to be hedged. The purchase of a forward contract commits the holder to exchanging the reference currency for the foreign currency at the forward rate fixed by the contract. The return on a forward contract is equal to the difference between the currency return and the forward premium, or

$$R_{\text{ForwardContract}} = TC_{it}^{\text{Quot/Ref}} - f_{it}$$

This return is often referred to as the forward surprise.

Return on an asset

In order to establish the return on an asset that is hedged against currency risk, we consider a position made up of a foreign asset and forward contracts. The return on this position expressed in the reference currency is given by

$$\left(1 + R_{it}^{\text{Ref}}\right) = \left(1 + R_{it}^{\text{Quot}}\right)\left(1 + TC_{it}^{\text{Quot/Ref}}\right) + h\left(TC_{it}^{\text{Quot/Ref}} - f_{it}\right)$$

where h is the hedging ratio, i.e. the fraction of the total assets hedged. The value of h is between -1 and 0. The fact that this value is negative means that forward contracts must be sold to carry out the hedge. By developing the formula, we obtain

$$R_{it}^{\text{Ref}} = R_{it}^{\text{Quot}} + TC_{it}^{\text{Quot/Ref}} + R_{it}^{\text{Quot}} TC_{it}^{\text{Quot/Ref}} + h\left(TC_{it}^{\text{Quot/Ref}} - f_{it}\right)$$

If we set aside the cross term, then we have simply

$$R_{it}^{\text{Ref}} = R_{it}^{\text{Quot}} + TC_{it}^{\text{Quot/Ref}} + h\left(TC_{it}^{\text{Quot/Ref}} - f_{it}\right)$$

or the sum of the unhedged return on the asset and the gain or loss from the hedge against currency risk.

If $h = -1$, then the foreign asset position is completely hedged by the sale of a forward contract. The hedged return on the foreign asset is then equal to

$$R_{it}^{\text{Ref}} = R_{it}^{\text{Quot}} + f_{it}$$

or the sum of the return in the quotation currency and the forward premium.

If $h = 0$, then the return is not hedged. We then go back to the formula established in the section "Return on an asset" above. For values of h between -1 and 0, the hedge is partial.

Let us take $H = 1 + h$, the unhedged proportion of the asset, i.e. the exchange exposure ratio. We then have

$$R_{it}^{\text{Ref}} = \left(R_{it}^{\text{Quot}} + f_{it}\right) + H\left(TC_{it}^{\text{Quot/Ref}} - f_{it}\right)$$

This second formula means that the return is the sum of the completely hedged return and the return that comes from the forward contract position.

Return on a portfolio[4]

The formula established for an asset is generalised in the case of a portfolio made up of n assets. The choice of a partial or total hedge is made independently for each of the asset quotation currencies. The decomposition of the return on an international portfolio, as it is presented here, will be included in our discussion of performance attribution in Chapter 7.

---

[4] Cf. Grandin (1998), Fontaine (1997), and also Karnosky and Singer (1994).

By setting aside the cross term we have

$$R_{Pt}^{Ref} = \sum_{i=1}^{n} x_{it} R_{it}^{Quot} + \sum_{i=1}^{n} x_{it} TC_{it}^{Quot/Ref} + \sum_{j=1}^{m} h_j \left(TC_{jt}^{Quot/Ref} - f_{jt} \right)$$

where h_j denotes the hedge ratio for currency j; and m denotes the number of different currencies contained in the portfolio, $m \leq n$.

The cost of the hedge depends on the forward premium. This premium is positive when interest rates in the reference country are higher than those in the foreign country. It is negative if the opposite is true. Depending on the interest rate differential between the two countries, therefore, the hedge can have a cost or procure an additional gain.

2.1.4 Handling derivative instruments[5]

In Chapter 1 we mentioned the advantages of reserving a small share of the portfolio for investing in derivative instruments. The presence of this type of asset requires specific handling in order to determine its contribution to portfolio performance. The simplest method involves associating the derivative instruments with their underlying class. Equity options are thus associated with the equity class. We then measure the result when excluding the derivatives and can thereby measure their impact by calculating the difference between the two.

A more precise analysis allows us to break down the performance that is produced by derivative instruments. To simplify the argument, let us consider the case of a portfolio that contains options. We can then use similar reasoning with the other types of derivatives.

Let us remind ourselves that an option is a security that gives the right to purchase or sell the underlying asset at an exercise price that is fixed beforehand.

We will consider the case of a call, i.e. a buy option, which is held in a portfolio. C is the purchase price for the call. After time t its quoted value has become C_t. As a result, the performance is equal to $C_t - C$. By inserting the theoretical value of the option at the beginning of the period, denoted by V, it is possible to break down the performance into two terms. We can then write

$$C_t - C = (V - C) + (C_t - V)$$

The first term, $V - C$, measures the differential between the quoted price of the option and its theoretical price based on the quoted value of the underlying asset at the purchase date. The second term, $C_t - V$, measures the differential between the current quoted value of the option and its initial equilibrium price. This decomposition allows us to measure the derivatives' marginal contribution to portfolio performance. The first component evaluates the manager's skill in selecting undervalued options and the second component measures the manager's skill in selecting options that have an undervalued underlying asset. A positive value can be obtained for each of these components through either luck or skill. It is important to be able to distinguish between the two.

Both of the terms can be broken down again. The differential between the price of the option and its theoretical price at the purchase date can be broken down into volatility profit and formula profit. There are two ways of identifying an option that has been incorrectly valued compared with its underlying asset: estimating its volatility and using a formula to value the

---

[5] This approach refers to the work of Rubinstein (2000).

option theoretically. The volatility profit corresponds to an estimated value of the volatility that is above that which is implicitly used by the market. The formula profit corresponds to the value of the option, valued by the formula, which is above that quoted on the market. The component that comes from an incorrect valuation of the underlying asset can also be broken down into two terms: a first term that is exclusively linked to the asset and a second term that comes from the option only.

Analysing these different effects requires us to distinguish between several different option valuation formulas: first, the true formula, which is not known explicitly; second, the market formula, which can differ from the true formula if the market is not efficient; and finally, the formula chosen as a benchmark, which can, for example, be the standard binomial valuation model. In performance analysis the benchmark formula is used both to determine the true relative value of the option V and to break down the performance resulting from an incorrect valuation of the option into two parts. In the first case, the benchmark formula must be as close as possible to the true formula. In the second case, it must be as close as possible to the market formula. It may be necessary to choose a different benchmark formula for each case.

Let us take $C(s)$ as the initial theoretical value of the option, obtained by using the benchmark formula, and assume that the volatility s produced over the period was known at the beginning. The initial value of the option, C, is the value of the option measured with the help of the benchmark formula, but by using the implicit volatility σ. The profit that results from the volatility is obtained by calculating the difference, $C(s) - C$. This term translates into the option valuation error that results from incorrect anticipation of volatility by the market. The formula profit is then given by the difference, $V - C(s)$.

The asset profit is evaluated by measuring the performance of a benchmark strategy, assumed to be a forward contract on the underlying asset, $S_t - S(r/d)^t$, where S denotes the price of the asset at the date the option was purchased; S_t denotes the price of the asset at time t, the date on which the performance was evaluated; r denotes the annualised risk-free rate for the period; and d denotes the asset's dividend distribution rate, annualised over the period.

$S(r/d)^t$ gives the true value of the forward contract on the asset with delivery date t. If the market is efficient and risk-neutral, then the term measuring the profit that comes from the asset must be zero.

The last component comes from the option only. It evaluates the profit that results from the use of options rather than forward contracts. It is evaluated by calculating

$$C_t - V - \left(S_t - S(r/d)^t\right)$$

To sum up, the profit resulting from the option is broken down into:

(1) a term that comes from the volatility,
(2) a term that comes from the formula,
(3) a term that comes from the asset, and
(4) a term that comes from the option alone.

These four terms are added together to give the total profit on the option:

$$C_t - C = (C(s) - C) + (V - C(s)) + \left(S_t - S(r/d)^t\right) + \left(C_t - V - \left(S_t - S(r/d)^t\right)\right)$$

$$\quad\quad\quad\quad\quad (1) \quad\quad\quad\quad (2) \quad\quad\quad\quad (3) \quad\quad\quad\quad\quad\quad (4)$$

If the options are valued efficiently, then the sum of terms (1) and (2) is zero on average, whether or not the benchmark formula is close to the formula used by the market for valuing options. If the option is valued efficiently and, in addition, the benchmark valuation formula coincides with the market formula, then terms (1) and (2) are both equal to zero on average.

If the assets are valued efficiently, then term (3) must be zero. If it is not zero, the market is not risk-neutral and the value of this term measures the compensation that corresponds to the risk taken. If the assets are not valued efficiently, then term (3) is not zero and its value measures the manager's capacity to select options that have an incorrectly valued underlying asset.

In an efficient market context, term (4) is also zero.

2.1.5   The AIMR standards for calculating returns[6]

This section presents the rules defined by the Association for Investment Management and Research (AIMR) for calculating returns and presenting portfolio performance. The use of different calculation methods leads to different results. The rules were therefore developed with a view to harmonisation, in order to ensure the consistency of the calculations and data used between portfolios over time. Above all, the rules stress the importance of result presentation to allow comparisons between different investment firms. Some of the rules are mandatory, others are only recommendations. The use of the rules contributes to the competitiveness and credibility of the investment firms. Establishments that apply them can request AIMR certification. In what follows, the term "firm" will denote an investment firm in general.

2.1.5.1   Composite portfolios

A composite portfolio[7] is made up of a set of portfolios or asset classes that use the same investment strategies or have similar objectives. Before the AIMR standards were drawn up, managers used "representative" or "model" portfolios to market their performance. They were able to include the funds that had performed best and exclude those that had performed worst. To avoid that, the AIMR defined rules for grouping portfolios. The performance results presented must relate to those composite portfolios.

Requirements
The AIMR requests that all fee-paying discretionary portfolios be included in at least one composite. New portfolios must be included in a composite from the first sub-period following their creation. Portfolios must be excluded from composites from the first sub-period during which they are no longer managed, but they must be conserved for historical data purposes up to that sub-period. Portfolios must not be transferred from one composite to another without justification.

2.1.5.2   Performance calculation

Requirements
Performance calculation must be carried out on the basis of the total return, i.e. the gain in capital added to the income paid into the portfolio (dividends and coupons). The AIMR requests that the calculation method minimise the effects of capital contributions and withdrawals, in

---

[6] We restrict ourselves to the main ideas here. For a complete presentation of the standards, see AIMR (1997).
[7] The definition of a composite can be found in Chapter 1 of the AIMR document.

order to minimise the effects that are not under the manager's control. The calculation method used must therefore be a time-weighted rate of return. This rate can be calculated in three different ways: the first method is exact, the other two methods are approximate.

The first method involves valuing the portfolio on a daily basis and combining the results geometrically to obtain the return for the period. By choosing a day as a sub-period, we are sure that the impact of the capital contributions and withdrawals will be minimal. This method is considered to be the best because it calculates the true time-weighted rate of return. The calculation principle was presented in the section "Time-weighted rate of return method" above. The limitations of the method were also mentioned there: the value of the portfolio at the end of each day must be known. This does not pose a problem for the managers of mutual funds, but could pose a problem for other managers because daily valuation is time-consuming. In addition, the price of certain assets, such as certain categories of bonds or emerging market securities, can be difficult to determine on a daily basis. For those cases, we can turn to the approximate methods.

The two approximate methods proposed by the AIMR are the modified Dietz method and the unitary valuation method, which is called the modified BAI method.

The modified Dietz method calculates a capital-weighted rate of return, as defined in the section "Capital-weighted rate of return method" above, by taking the exact length of time that each cash flow is present in the portfolio. The major advantage of this method is that is does not require daily calculation of the portfolio value. The disadvantage is that it provides a less accurate estimate of the true time-weighted rate of return. This method is less favourable when comparing the performance of different managers, because it does not allow the capital contribution and withdrawal effects that cannot be controlled by the manager to be eliminated. These effects will however be minimal if the capital flows are small compared with the length of the sub-period.

The modified BAI method calculates an internal rate of return, as defined in the section "Internal rate of return method" above, by taking the exact dates of the cash flows into account. The advantages and disadvantages of this method are the same as those for the modified Dietz method.

The portfolios must be valued quarterly at the very least, but the AIMR recommends monthly valuation. Returns calculated for sub-periods must be linked geometrically to obtain the return for the total valuation period. An annualised rate is usually presented. However, for valuation periods of less than a year, the AIMR standards specify that returns must not be annualised.

Composite portfolio returns must be calculated by using the weights at the beginning of the period. Transaction costs must be deducted from the returns. Only performance obtained for portfolios that are really managed should be presented and not performance resulting from simulation of an investment strategy.

When cash is held in a portfolio, the return on the cash must be included in the portfolio return calculations, and the amount of the cash should be included in the value of the portfolio.

All documents that allow the performance calculation to be justified should be conserved.

Recommendations

The AIMR recommends that portfolios be valued on a daily basis, or at least each time a capital flow, or a market operation that is liable to distort the result, occurs. When a cash flow represents more than 10% of the value of the portfolio, the portfolio must be revalued at the date of the cash flow. It is recommended that the performance be calculated before the management fees are deducted, because these are not related to the strategy employed.

2.1.5.3   Presentation of results

Requirements

A 10-year performance record must be presented. If the firm has been in existence for less than 10 years, then all available historical data must be presented. Annual returns must be presented for all years.

2.1.5.4   Information to be published

Requirements

The firm must publish a complete list and description of all its composite portfolios. The description of a composite portfolio must include the number of portfolios that it contains and the amount of assets involved. It must also specify the percentage of the firm's total assets that the composite represents at the end of each period, for all periods after 1997. For periods before 1997, the firm has the choice of doing this at the beginning or at the end of the period. The firm must indicate whether performance results are calculated gross or net of management fees. If net results are presented, then the average weighted management fee must be disclosed. The performance presentation must also disclose the existence of a minimum asset size below which portfolios are excluded from a composite and mention the eventual inclusion of any non-fee-paying portfolios in the composites.

Recommendations

For exclusive presentation to the clients, it is recommended that performance be presented gross of investment management fees. The AIMR recommends that the weights of the portfolios included in the composite be indicated and that the cumulative composite returns for all periods be produced. There must be sufficient information for a client or a prospect to be able to evaluate the potential risk and the return characteristics of the portfolio or the investment strategy employed.

2.1.5.5   International portfolios

The AIMR gives special recommendations for calculating the performance of international portfolios. The recommendations essentially concern exchange rates. The performance must be presented in the currency chosen by the client. The firm chooses the exchange rate to be used to convert the performance, and the source of the exchange rates must then remain consistent for the whole period. To translate the end-of-month or end-of-quarter values from the quotation currency into the reference currency, the closing exchange rate at the end of the period must be used.

2.1.5.6   Portfolios that contain derivative instruments

For portfolios that contain a small proportion of derivative instruments, the AIMR recommends that the leverage effect resulting from this investment strategy be isolated in the portfolio performance calculation. The performance presented must indicate both the portfolio returns with the leverage effect and the restated returns with the leverage effect removed. The additional return provided by the share invested in derivative investments is then calculated as the difference between these two quantities.

2.1.5.7   The GIPS: what is different[8]

The most significant difference between the AIMR standards and the GIPS concerns the verification procedure for obtaining certification. There is only a single level of verification for the GIPS, whereas there is two-level verification for the AIMR standards. Verification is also easier to carry out because the firm only has to declare that it respects the GIPS. However, the GIPS strongly encourages the involvement of a third-party verifier. External verification by a third party is not mandatory for the moment, it is simply recommended.

The GIPS only require five years of historical data instead of 10 years for the AIMR standards. This is because most firms do not have sufficient historical records available. The following years should then be added progressively until 10 years of historical data are available, which means that the difference between the AIMR standards and GIPS will have disappeared by 2005.

Following the development of the GIPS, the AIMR made some changes to the AIMR standards in order to make them entirely consistent with the GIPS. The modifications are as follows. From 1, January 2000, portfolios must be valued monthly. Firms must present the percentage of composite assets that relates to non-fee-paying portfolios. All presentations must indicate the currency used to express the performance. The date that each composite was created must be presented. By 1, January 2005, firms will have to use trade-date accounting. Firms will have to use time-weighted rates of return adjusted for daily-weighted cash flows. Firms will have to account for dividends in a cumulative manner. By 1, January 2010, firms will have to value portfolios on the date of any external cash flow.

2.2   CALCULATING RELATIVE RETURN

The calculation of the return on a fund gives an absolute measurement of performance. However, it might be more relevant to measure performance in relation to a reference. We can thereby highlight the additional share of the return that comes from the investment strategy used and judge the manager's skill. The reference can be a benchmark or a group of portfolios with the same characteristics, which is called a peer group[9]. These are the two most common methods. We can also turn to a third method called *Portfolio Opportunity Distributions*.

2.2.1   Benchmarks[10]

A benchmark is simply a reference portfolio. It is used when the discretionary portfolio is put together and then when its performance is evaluated. It must therefore be chosen to reflect the diversity of the assets contained in the portfolio and the investment strategy employed. It must follow the same calculation rules as the portfolio that is being evaluated, particularly when taking dividends into account. The simplest benchmarks are constructed as a combination of market indices, with one index per group of assets. The benchmark can also be developed in a more elaborate manner in order to be as similar as possible to the managed portfolio. We describe the different types of benchmark that are used below, giving special attention to so-called "normal" benchmarks, which are custom-made benchmarks. This type of benchmark is being used more and more as portfolio management becomes increasingly specialised by

---

[8] Cf. Koenig (2001).
[9] Cf. on this subject, the AIMR articles (1995).
[10] Cf. Fabozzi (1995), Fogler (1989) and Rennie and Cowhey (1989).

sector, and since there is a desire to evaluate managers' performances in a more equitable and accurate manner.

2.2.1.1   Description of the different types of benchmark

Market indices

Market indices are quoted on stock exchanges and are therefore simple to use. However, they may not be sufficiently representative of the managed portfolio. For example, equity indices contain large capitalisation stocks and do not therefore allow the performance of a portfolio that contains small capitalisation stocks to be evaluated. We distinguish between several types of indices depending on their size. The broad indices include a very large number of stocks and are intended for institutions that do not often act directly in the markets. These indices include securities with a low level of liquidity. Investors who face the markets more frequently require more liquid indices. They use indices that are based on a more restricted number of stocks and made up of the main stocks in the listing only. However, these indices are less representative of the market and may appear too narrow for investors who wish to build an index portfolio. The more recent creation of a third category of indices, called mid-sized, provides a solution to the problems of the other two categories.

With the arrival of the euro and the progressive disappearance of the notion of domestic markets, it has been necessary to create new indices that focus on European securities, for both stocks (cf. Shakotko, 1998) and bonds (cf. Lee, 1999), in order to reflect the new economic and monetary context. Index management on a European scale requires available indices that reflect the evolution of the European markets, but also, more particularly, of the euro zone. Appendix 2.3 describes the main indices used in the different countries.

Generic investment style indices

These indices are developed by specialised firms (cf. Compton, 1997). They allow different investment styles to be measured: there are growth stock indices, value stock indices, large-cap and small-cap stock indices. These very specific indices are appropriate for a manager who has a well-defined investment style. For the other managers, we turn to benchmarks that describe the manager's style better: Sharpe benchmarks and normal portfolios.

However, numerous empirical studies, notably Brown and Mott (1997), have stressed the difficulty in selecting the securities that are included in the index composition, whether for style indices or benchmarks. In view of the instability of the attributes that characterise the style of the stocks contained in an index or a benchmark (for example, a stock with a low P/E ratio could be an undervalued growth stock or a value stock), it appears difficult to guarantee the style. In that context, it currently seems that there is no index that dominates the market.

In addition, the implementation of style indices is subject to intense competition, whether in the American market (notably Frank Russell, Wilshire Associates, S&P–Barra and Prudential Securities), or the international market (Boston International Advisors (BIA) have created style indices for 21 different countries and seven regional zones; Parametric Portfolio Associates, their competitor, offer the same set of indices). The result of the competition is that the references that make up the indices are very different from each other both in terms of composition and in terms of return. In 1997, technology, media and telecommunications (TMTs) represented 30.8% of the Prudential Securities International (PSI) large growth index, compared with 14.5% of the same type of index produced by S&P–Barra. In the same way, General Electric had the largest market capitalisation in the PSI large value index, while Exxon held that position in the Russell and S&P indices, and Wilshire reserved the status for IBM. It is clear that indices managed through and for the size effect introduce exposure to different sectors and geographic zones.

Furthermore, it should be noted that, for the same large-cap growth reference, the PSI index had a return, in 1982, that was less than 10%, compared with 22% for the S&P–Barra index. More generally, in recent years the largest differentials between the "best" and "worst" same-style indices were 13.8% in 1979 for growth stocks and 13.5% in 1984 for value stocks.

This diversity therefore poses the problem of the representativeness of style indices. Unlike market indices, style indices do not make any implicit or explicit reference to the qualities of the market portfolio, as described later in Chapter 4.

While numerous authors[11] have attempted to show that integrating absolute and simple criteria such as the volume of transactions or the market capitalisation of the securities selected in the index is a good "proxy" for the market representativeness criteria, no relative or calculated value such as the P/E or book-to-market ratio guarantees the representativeness of the style.

The Sharpe benchmarks

The Sharpe benchmarks allow us to solve the problem of the investment style indices being too specific (cf. Sharpe, 1992). It involves explaining the manager's style, no longer from a single index but from a series of indices. To do that, Sharpe proposes building a benchmark by performing multiple regressions on several specialised indices in order to obtain an index that is a linear combination of the different indices available and corresponds best to the management style to be evaluated. The list of indices that Sharpe proposes to use is specifically for the American market. In general, we choose indices that represent the different asset classes and describe the market in which the portfolio is invested in the most complete manner possible.

We will return to the practical use of this type of benchmark in Chapter 6, which discusses performance analysis with the help of multi-factor models, and Chapter 7, which addresses the subject of asset allocation.

Normal portfolios[12]

These are benchmarks that are tailor-made for each manager. They were developed from the principle that the portfolio manager's returns should be compared with the returns of a reference portfolio whose structure and composition are as similar as possible to those of the portfolio that is being evaluated. More often than not, portfolio managers are specialised in a single category of assets and therefore do not consider the complete universe of securities. Thus, broad indices are not suitable for evaluating their performance, because they contain securities that will not be included in the composition of the manager's portfolio. In addition, the proportions of each security in the indices are generally different from those chosen by the manager. The use of these indices as a benchmark could lead to an incorrect evaluation of the manager's performance. Managers could appear skilful if their style is favoured by the market, or their result could be qualified as poor if their style is not favoured by the market. We

---

[11] For more details on the question of index representativeness, one could consult Fabozzi and Molay (2000) and also Magill and Quinzi (1996), Athanasoulis and Shiller (2000), Black and Litterman (1990) and of course Roll (1977).

[12] Cf. Compton (1997), Luck (1995), who discusses the case of equity indices, and Christopherson (1998).

therefore prefer specialised benchmarks, the most frequently used being normal portfolios, to broad indices.

A normal portfolio is defined in the following way: it is a portfolio that is made up of a set of securities that contains all the securities from which the manager is liable to make his choice, weighted in the same way as they are weighted in the manager's portfolio.[13] A normal portfolio is therefore a specialised index. It allows the manager's performance to be determined by evaluating his capacity to select the best securities and/or the best sectors in his normal universe. If the manager's performance is worse than that of the normal benchmark, then we can conclude that the portfolio was managed poorly. This category of benchmark is therefore the one that allows for the most equitable evaluation of performance.

The objective in constructing a normal portfolio is to obtain an average characterisation of the portfolio to be evaluated. The definition of a normal portfolio for a particular manager is not unique. Several methods enable normal portfolios to be built. In the following paragraphs we will discuss the advantages and disadvantages of the different methods.

The simplest and most commonly used technique for building a portfolio involves drawing up a list of securities, based on the historical composition of the portfolios held by the manager. A second approach involves basing the list of securities on exposure to risk factors. The manager's average exposure to different risk indices is analysed to define the benchmark's exposures. A third method uses style indices to create a weighted combination of indices that corresponds to the manager's portfolio. The first two approaches rely on the same principle: establishing a reduced list of securities from a broad universe by setting criteria that could relate to the P/E ratio or exposure to certain factors. The portfolio is then constructed from the resulting list by attributing a weighting to each security. The two techniques differ in the security selection method and the choice of weightings. The three approaches allow us to carry out analyses that have different objectives.

The first approach allows us to determine whether managers select the best securities within their normal universe. The second approach allows us to study the macroeconomic sources of return and risk more precisely. The benchmark is based on the manager's portfolio risk factors. It is created by choosing securities similar to those selected by the manager and with an exposure to factors that is similar to the manager's average exposure. The benchmark therefore allows the manager's capacity to select securities from his universe to be evaluated, given his risk exposure profile. The third method is in fact the one developed by Sharpe, which was mentioned in the previous section and which will be considered in more detail in Chapter 6. The Sharpe benchmarks are therefore examples of normal benchmarks. This third approach allows us to say whether the manager's performance can be better than that of a combination of style indices. There are two techniques for determining the weightings assigned to each style index:

1. Analysis of the manager's portfolio returns (*returns-based analysis*).
2. Analysis of the style characteristics of the securities that make up the manager's portfolio (*portfolio-based analysis*).

These two techniques will be described in more detail in Chapter 6, in the section that discusses style analysis.

Among these different approaches, it is the first one, based on analysis of the historical composition of the manager's portfolio, that is the most commonly used. It is the simplest

---

[13] This definition is given in Christopherson (1989, p. 382).

to implement and the one that gives the most easily interpreted results. We will therefore concentrate on the successive stages required to create a benchmark using this method.

The stages that enable us to build a normal benchmark are as follows:

1. We first define the initial universe of securities.
2. We then choose the securities that will be included in the composition of the normal portfolio from this universe.
3. To finish, we choose the security weightings.

The initial universe of securities could, for example, be made up of a broad market index. On the American market we could, for instance, consider the Russell 3000 index, which contains the firms with the largest stock market capitalisation. We could also use the S&P500 index. From this initial list of securities, the following stage involves reducing the securities to those that the manager is really liable to select. To do that, the manager's selection criteria and decision rules must be known. The selection criteria could relate to a certain number of variables such as the market capitalisation, the return, the price-to-book ratio, the dividend rate, the historical beta and earnings variations. It should be noted that if the variables used to make the selection are independent, then the order in which one proceeds is of no importance. However, if the variables are correlated, then the result will depend on the order chosen.

Once the selection has been completed, we check the relevance of the sub-universe by comparing the overall trend of the manager's portfolio with that of the normal portfolio. Before that, however, the weight to be assigned to each security must be determined in order to make up the index. It is preferable for the adopted weighting method to be the same as the one chosen by the manager, because weighting differences lead to performance differences. Broad market indices such as the Russell and S&P500 are capital-weighted indices, but very often managers do not weight their portfolios in that way. Three types of capitalisation-based weightings can be used: equal weighting, which involves attributing the same weight to each stock irrespective of stock capitalisation; capitalisation weighting, which involves weighting each stock according to its percentage of the total value of the portfolio; and capitalisation weighting with break points, where the capitalisation-weighting rule is applied down to a certain capitalisation size and, beyond the threshold, each stock is given an equal weighting. It is also possible to have other types of weighting that are not based on capitalisation.

The advantage of capitalisation weighting is that it does not require the portfolio to be rebalanced when the portfolio asset prices fluctuate, which would be the case for an equally weighted portfolio. This therefore reduces liquidity problems and makes it easier to implement a passive investment strategy. Managers nevertheless tend to avoid using capitalisation weighting for their portfolios so as not to invest large sums in a single stock. They prefer to practise diversification between securities. As a result there are differences between managers' portfolios and capitalisation-weighted normal portfolios. Capitalisation weighting is nonetheless the most frequently chosen solution, because it facilitates passive investment compared with equal weighting, and because equal weighting does not constitute a satisfactory solution for all managers. In Chapter 6 we will present a more recent approach, which calculates the weightings to attribute to portfolio securities according to the style of the portfolio that is to be evaluated.

Normal portfolios are therefore more appropriate benchmarks than market indices because they take the investment style into account and thus provide a better evaluation of the manager. The use of these benchmarks does however pose a problem of objectivity when managers handle their own benchmarks. This type of benchmark also presents the disadvantage of having high management costs. However, they are the best references for evaluating a manager's performance and are being increasingly employed.

2.2.1.2 Benchmarks for international portfolios

In international investment management, the reference is the worldwide market portfolio, which, in theory, is made up of all the assets from the different countries, weighted by the market capitalisation of each market (cf. AIMR, 1998). In practice, we use an international index, for example the Morgan Stanley Capital Index Europe, Australasia and Far East (MSCI EAFE), as an approximation of this market portfolio. The choice of a specific benchmark for an investor involves determining the list of countries in which the investor wishes to invest and the investor's level of currency exposure, which leads, depending on the case, to the choice of a hedged or unhedged benchmark. The MSCI EAFE index is an example of an unhedged benchmark.

Unhedged benchmarks are used when there are no hedging strategies defined in the management mandate. They are used by investors who have a low level of allocation in foreign assets or investors who wish to actively manage their currency exposure. The currency activity is then used as a means of increasing the return or reducing the risk. The return for each country contained in the benchmark is obtained by combining the return on the asset in its local market with the return on the spot exchange rate. The benchmark therefore contains a currency component that includes both the surprise effect and the forward premium.

Hedged benchmarks are used when the currency risk, or at least part of the risk, is assumed to be hedged by the investment strategy. In the case of part of the risk being hedged, we use a partially hedged benchmark, which eliminates a fixed proportion of the currency risk. When the benchmark is completely hedged, the return for each of the countries that it contains is made up of the sum of the asset return in its quotation currency and the currency premium. In that case, the surprise effect of the spot exchange rate is eliminated.

2.2.1.3 Practical use of the benchmark

Once the benchmark has been defined and calculated, it can be used in a very simple way, initially, to determine the portfolio's performance. The manager's value-added is calculated as the difference between the return on the portfolio being evaluated and that of the benchmark. It should be noted that this value could be negative if the manager has not performed as well as the benchmark. In the following chapters we will present a more detailed approach to the interpretation of this quantity and the methods that enable a portfolio and its benchmark to be compared very precisely. With that aim in mind, we will successively discuss the Jensen measure in Chapter 4, multi-factor models in Chapter 6 and decomposition by asset group in Chapter 7.

We use the term "active return" to refer to the percentage of the return that is due to the manager's decisions. A manager's skill over a given period of time is therefore measured by the value of R_{At}, defined by

$$R_{At} = R_{Pt} - R_{Bt}$$

where R_{Pt} denotes the portfolio return for period t; and R_{Bt} denotes the benchmark return for period t.

This calculation can be carried out periodically, e.g. on a monthly basis. The series of active returns for the sub-periods is then used to obtain the active return on the portfolio for the whole period (cf. Baker, 1991).

If the sub-period returns have been calculated arithmetically, and then compounded geometrically, then calculating the cumulative asset return for the whole period is not equivalent to calculating the difference between the cumulative portfolio return and the cumulative benchmark return. On the other hand, if we have worked with logarithmic returns, the two calculations are equivalent. If we consider a period that is broken down into T sub-periods, then the logarithmic returns for the portfolio and the benchmark over the complete period are written as follows:

$$R_P^{\log} = \sum_{t=1}^{T} R_{Pt}^{\log}$$

$$R_B^{\log} = \sum_{t=1}^{T} R_{Bt}^{\log}$$

hence

$$R_P^{\log} - R_B^{\log} = \sum_{t=1}^{T} \left(R_{Pt}^{\log} - R_{Bt}^{\log} \right) = \sum_{t=1}^{T} R_{At}^{\log} = R_A^{\log}$$

Therefore, we again have an applied example of logarithmic returns allowing us to have simpler formulas.

Calculating the active return allows us to judge managers' results compared with their benchmark, but does not allow us to compare funds that use different benchmarks.

2.2.1.4   AIMR rules concerning the benchmark

The AIMR only provides recommendations concerning the benchmark. It is recommended to present the benchmark used for each composite. This benchmark must correspond to the portfolio's risk or the portfolio's investment style. It is also appropriate to indicate the composition differences between the portfolio and the benchmark.

For portfolios that have an international component, the same exchange rates must be used, where possible, to convert the portfolio and benchmark returns into the reference currency. When this is not possible, for example if the portfolio and the benchmark are valued at different times, the significant differentials must be provided.

2.2.2   Peer groups

The financial literature distinguishes between universes and peer groups (cf. Flynn, 1995). The universe is a broader entity, within which we can define peer groups. In more specific terms, a universe is a group of portfolios that is invested in the same market sector. A peer group, on the other hand, is a group of managers who invest in the same class of assets or who have the same investment style. Peer groups are therefore smaller and defined in a more precise manner than universes. In what follows we shall only consider peer groups.

Investment styles that characterise a peer group can be, for example, market capitalisation, growth stocks, value stocks or emerging markets. Peer groups are put together by selecting managers that correspond to the chosen criteria. We then calculate the funds' rates of return and establish a ranking within the group. The funds and managers are therefore evaluated in relation to funds that are managed in a similar fashion. The groups must be large enough for the comparisons to be statistically significant. The advantage of this method is that it permits comparisons with real portfolios, which are subject to taxes and transaction costs, while indices or combinations of indices used as benchmarks are theoretical portfolios that have no costs. Peer groups can be seen as benchmarks that are actively managed. There is, however, a problem with survivorship bias, because the worst-performing managers in the group disappear over time.

The use of peer groups is currently widespread, but to evaluate portfolio performance more accurately it is recommended to add other portfolio measurement tools such as risk-adjusted measures.

In order to avoid an arbitrary, before-the-fact ranking, fund performance analysis specialists have implemented a new statistical approach called clustering to make up peer groups. This involves maximising the distances between groups and minimising the distances within groups for each of the fund universes selected. The distance that is thereby "clustered" is determined by using Minkowski's concept of distance as a generalisation of the Euclidian distance after normalising the returns. Once they have been grouped together, the funds are qualified as belonging to a particular style according to their dominant common characteristics. The cluster approach is now considered to be a robust approach to fund classification because it does not assume any pre-specification of criteria. Like principal component analysis (PCA)-type factorial analysis, it involves an inductive approach and is therefore considered to be "objective" by practitioners. The optimal number of clusters that enables the funds to be grouped together is qualified *ex post* by applying tests that are considered today to be conceptually robust ("cubic clustering criteria", Sarle, 1983, and "pseudo-F statistic", Calinski and Harabasz, 1974).

2.2.3 A new approach: Portfolio Opportunity Distributions

A new manager evaluation concept, which is described by the term Portfolio Opportunity Distributions (POD), has been developed by Ronald Surz (cf. Surz, 1994, 1996, 1997). This method seeks to combine the advantages of using a benchmark with the advantages of using a peer group, while eliminating the disadvantages of both. The principle involves comparing the manager's results with those that would have been achieved by chance, after defining a comparison universe that is perfectly adapted to the manager being evaluated. The comparison universe is constructed in the following way. Starting from the set of securities that the manager is liable to include in his portfolio, we generate a large number of random portfolios. The portfolios are constructed in such a way as to respect the manager's investment criteria, namely the choice of management style, the allocation by industrial sector and the market capitalisation. We can thereby put together all the portfolios in which the manager could be planning to invest. The portfolios obtained therefore reflect the manager's decision-making process.

Once the universe has been defined, the performance of the manager's portfolio is compared with that of all the portfolios in the universe. This allows the manager to be evaluated in relation to his true performance possibilities. Here again this involves a comparison in relation to a reference group, but the definition of the peer group has been improved. One of the major problems in peer group comparisons is the difficulty involved in identifying a peer group that truly corresponds to the manager. When a fund has a very specific style, it may be difficult to find a sufficient number of funds of the same type to put together a significant group. The POD method thus enables a single reference peer group to be created for each manager. This method is particularly interesting for international portfolios because it enables broader universes to be obtained than when we use standard peer groups, since the sets of securities, management styles and accessible countries are broader than those available through peer groups.

Another disadvantage linked to the use of standard peer groups is survivorship bias, which comes from the disappearance over time of the worst-performing managers in the group. The POD method eliminates that problem, since the group portfolios are created by randomly selecting the securities. The group of portfolios then remains stable, since the portfolios are not really managed. There is no risk of disappearance.

In the section on peer groups (Section 2.2.2) we also mentioned that they should be sufficiently large for the comparisons to be statistically significant. Here again we could find ourselves limited by the number of funds available in the market. It was therefore necessary to study the results over several years so that they could be considered reliable. The POD method removes this disadvantage because it allows hundreds, or thousands, of portfolios to be constructed. All possible combinations of assets can be envisaged, as long as they satisfy the manager's investment criteria. Therefore, the manager's ranking compared with the reference universe could be analysed over a shorter period of time than that required by the use of standard peer groups. In addition, since the POD universes are created from a database of securities, the data that enable comparisons to be made are immediately available. The evaluation can therefore be carried out much earlier than when it is necessary to wait for the update of an independent database. Finally, POD universe comparisons are more appropriate than benchmark or peer group comparisons when identifying whether the manager's value-added was obtained through luck or skill.

As we have just seen, the POD method offers numerous advantages. The technique enables a peer group to be replicated while eliminating the problem of survivorship bias, since the portfolios used for comparison are not managed portfolios. It enables rankings to be established while being sure that the universe is both appropriate, since it is only based on securities that are liable to be chosen by the manager, and of sufficient size, since we can create as many portfolios as necessary. The manager's skill can be evaluated immediately, while with a benchmark it is necessary to wait several years to have a reliable statistical confidence interval. In practice, however, this method is not very widely used. Investment firms find it easier to turn to standard benchmarks or reference groups made up of funds that are actually managed. Nevertheless, it is probable that this strategy will be developed in the future because it enables the most appropriately adapted references to be obtained.

2.3   DEFINITION OF RISK[14]

The concept of return is not sufficient, on its own, to analyse the results of a portfolio. It is necessary to add a measurement of the risk taken. We have seen that the definition of a benchmark allows the portfolio risk to be characterised by the choice of asset categories in the portfolio composition. However, to analyse portfolio performance more precisely we need a quantitative measurement of risk. While return is an intuitive notion, the quantitative notion of risk comes from Markowitz's modern portfolio theory.

In this chapter we simply present the statistical definitions of risk indicators. The risk measures presented are measures of total risk. The notion of systematic risk, or beta, will be

---

[14] For more detailed information, see Chapter 2 of Broquet and van den Berg (1992), Elton and Gruber (1995), Grandin (1998), Sharpe (1985) and Zaouati (1995).

defined in Chapter 3 when the market model is presented. We will first present the individual risk indicators for each financial instrument, and then introduce a more general notion of risk, which will allow us to evaluate the risk of a portfolio that contains several asset classes.

In the following chapters we will return to the concept of portfolio risk in more detail. In Chapter 3, which is devoted to modern portfolio theory, we will give more specific details on the link between return and risk and will highlight the notion of reducing risk by diversifying the portfolio. In Chapter 4 we will present risk-adjusted performance measurement, which came from the capital asset pricing model (CAPM). Finally, in Chapter 6, which examines fundamental and macroeconomic factor models, and the applications of those models, we will present risk decomposition and analysis methods, which provide more information on portfolio risk analysis.

2.3.1   Asset risk

2.3.1.1   Variance

Intuitively, asset risk is characterised by the dispersion of the asset's returns around their average value. The statistical measurements are therefore the variance, σ_i^2, and the standard deviation, σ_i, with the former being the square of the latter. The variance is written as follows:

$$\sigma_i^2 = \frac{1}{T} \sum_{t=1}^{T} (R_{it} - \bar{R}_i)^2$$

where

R_{it} denotes the return on asset i for sub-period t;
$\bar{R}_i$ denotes the mean return on asset i over the whole period; and
T denotes the number of sub-periods.

A good estimation of the risk can be obtained by using the monthly returns over a period of three years.

The variance is the most widely used measure of risk. It is the definition of risk that Markowitz selected for his portfolio choice problem because it allows simple modelling to be obtained. We will return to this point in more detail in Chapter 3. The disadvantage of this measure is that it considers the risk of above-average returns and the risk of below-average returns in the same way, while investors are only worried about below-average returns. In the following section we present the semi-variance measure, which takes that difference into account.

2.3.1.2   Semi-variance: first definition[15]

Using the variance or standard deviation of returns to measure asset risk assumes that the returns are distributed normally. Although that hypothesis is respected over a short period, the same is not true for longer investment periods. Variance therefore represents a good measure of risk over a short investment period. Over a longer period, it is better to turn to a measure that takes the skewness of risk into account.

In 1959, Markowitz defined semi-variance as the most appropriate measure for characterising portfolio risk. The calculation principle is the same as that of the variance, apart from the fact

---

[15] Cf. Melnikoff (1998).

that only the returns that are lower than the mean are taken into account. It therefore provides a skewed measure of the risk, which corresponds to the needs of investors, who are only interested in the risk of their portfolio losing value. It is written as follows:

$$\frac{1}{T} \sum_{\substack{0 \leq t \leq T \\ R_{it} < \bar{R}_i}} (R_{it} - \bar{R}_i)^2$$

with the notation being the same as that used for variance.

As an analogy with the relationship between the standard deviation and the variance, we define a measurement called downside risk as the square root of the semi-variance.

If the distribution of returns is symmetrical, which is the case when returns are assumed to be distributed normally, then the semi-variance is equal to half of the variance and there is no difference between measuring the risk with one or other of the quantities. If, however, the distribution is skewed, then the two measures are not equivalent and it is not correct in that instance to use the variance instead of the semi-variance. The semi-variance is particularly well adapted to measuring the risk of derivative instruments, the distribution of which is generally not symmetrical.

In 1959, the use of this measurement was difficult for practical reasons, since computers were not yet very powerful. That is what led Markowitz to choose the variance, which is mathematically easier to implement. It is currently possible to use semi-variance, but the studies that include it are few and far between. However, in a conference that he gave in 1993, Markowitz indicated that he used semi-variance to measure risk when selecting portfolios for a securities house.

There is, however, a further obstacle to the use of semi-variance, other than the additional calculations required. The distributions of skewed returns are not stable over time. It is therefore difficult to estimate the semi-variance with the help of historical returns, as is commonly done for the variance.

The semi-variance theory was followed by a more general theoretical development: lower partial moments, of which semi-variance is a particular case.

2.3.1.3 Lower partial moments

The lower partial moment (cf. Nawrocki, 1996, 1999a, 1999b). measures the risk of falling below a target return set by the investor. The lower partial moment (LPM) of degree n for asset i is defined by

$$\text{LPM}_{in} = \frac{1}{T} \sum_{t=1}^{T} (\max(0, h - R_{it}))^n$$

where T denotes the number of observations; and h denotes the target return for the portfolio.

This measure can be calculated for several values of n. When $n = 2$, we find the semi-variance expression by taking the mean return for the period as the target return. The value of n allows the investor's aversion to risk to be represented. If $n < 1$, then the investor likes risk. If $n = 1$, then the investor is risk neutral. Finally, if $n > 1$, then the investor is risk averse. The higher the value of n, the higher the aversion to risk.

2.3.1.4   The shortfall risk

The notion of shortfall risk (cf. Leibowitz and Henriksson, 1989) allows the risk of obtaining lower returns to be characterised. In the approach developed by Leibowitz and Henriksson, portfolio risk is characterised using the probability of being above a target return. It is an intuitive definition of risk, which takes into account the skewed approach of investors in relation to risk, particularly over long investment periods. We will see in Chapter 7 how this notion can be associated with a mean–variance optimisation model to determine the optimal asset class allocation for a portfolio.

Following the same idea, Sortino and Price (1994) define portfolio risk in relation to an objective to be reached. It generalises the definition of semi-variance established by Markowitz by replacing the mean return with the notion of target return. They thus define the notion of a minimum acceptable return (MAR) as being the minimum return that must be obtained to reach an objective. Returns above the MAR constitute good occurrences and returns below the MAR constitute bad occurrences. Therefore, only the returns below the MAR are taken into account when calculating risk, since the risk is that of not reaching the objective fixed.

2.3.2   Link between the variations in returns on two assets

The complete characterisation of asset risk requires that the behaviour of the asset returns be compared with that of other assets. To do that, we use the covariance of the returns, defined by

$$\sigma_{ij} = \frac{1}{T} \sum_{t=1}^{T} (R_{it} - \bar{R}_i)(R_{jt} - \bar{R}_j)$$

The normalised version of this measure is the correlation coefficient, defined by

$$\rho_{ij} = \frac{\sigma_{ij}}{\sigma_i \sigma_j}$$

where σ_i and σ_j denote the standard deviations of assets i and j, respectively, and σ_{ij} denotes their covariance.

2.3.3   Other statistical measures of risk

Some additional statistics can help to characterise the risk of an asset. They are as follows:

1. The variation interval, which measures the amplitude between the highest return and the lowest return, or

$$\max_{1 \leq t \leq T} (R_{it}) - \min_{1 \leq t \leq T} (R_{it})$$

2. The absolute mean deviation, which measures the mean deviation between an asset's returns and its expected returns as an absolute value, or

$$\frac{1}{T} \sum_{t=1}^{T} |R_{it} - E(R_i)|$$

3. The probability of obtaining a negative return, which calculates the proportion of negative asset returns over a given period.

2.3.4   Risk indicators for fixed income investment

The measures of risk that have been presented so far have been specifically oriented towards equities. For bonds, we use specific indicators that measure the risk linked to distortion of the yield curve. Among the indicators, we find the following:

1. The duration, which measures a bond's sensitivity to a parallel shift in the yield curve. A portfolio's duration is calculated by adding together the durations of the securities that make up the portfolio, weighted by their relative value compared with the total value of the portfolio. The choice of a particular combination of securities allows us to obtain a portfolio with a fixed level of risk.
2. The convexity, which measures the duration's sensitivity to a distortion of the yield curve. It evaluates the curvature of the yield curve.

In Chapter 8, which is devoted to fixed income securities, we will cover these notions in more detail.

2.3.5   Foreign asset risk

The risk of a foreign asset comes, on the one hand, from variations in the returns on the asset in its quotation currency and, on the other, from variations in the quotation currency compared with the reference currency. The latter source of risk constitutes the currency risk. In this section we initially define currency risk and then formulate the risk decomposition of an unhedged asset. Finally, we present the calculation of hedged risk.

2.3.5.1   Currency risk

Currency risk is the additional risk taken on by the investor that results from the values of different currencies fluctuating against each other. The significance of the risk will vary, depending on whether the investment is in stocks or bonds. The risk can be considered to be low for an investment in stocks. If the portfolio is diversified between several countries, different variations in exchange rates will tend to compensate for one another. However, the risk is much more significant in the case of bonds because of the links that exist between interest rates and exchange rates. The decision on whether to hedge the currency risk, the choice of the degree of hedging and the hedging date can depend on several factors, including: the investor's anticipations in terms of exchange rate movements; the cost of the hedge; the level of risk exposure that the investor accepts; and the balance between the level of risk and the cost of the hedge.

2.3.5.2   Decomposition of the asset risk

The asset risk is broken down into the risk of the individual asset and the currency risk. In Section 2.1.3 we established an expression for the return on a foreign asset in the reference currency. Using that expression, we calculate the return variance expressed in the reference currency, or

$$\text{var}\big(R_{it}^{\text{Ref}}\big) = \text{var}\big(R_{it}^{\text{Quot}} + TC_{it}^{\text{Quot/Ref}}\big) = \text{var}\big(R_{it}^{\text{Quot}}\big) + \text{var}\big(TC_{it}^{\text{Quot/Ref}}\big)$$
$$+ 2\text{cov}\big(R_{it}^{\text{Quot}}, \; TC_{it}^{\text{Quot/Ref}}\big)$$

or in a more condensed manner:

$$\left(\sigma_i^{\text{Ref}}\right)^2 = \left(\sigma_i^{\text{Quot}}\right)^2 + \left(\sigma_{TC}^{\text{Quot/Ref}}\right)^2 + 2\rho_{i,TC}\sigma_i^{\text{Quot}}\sigma_{TC}^{\text{Quot/Ref}}$$

where

$(\sigma_i^{\text{Ref}})^2$ denotes the variance of asset i in the reference currency;

$(\sigma_i^{\text{Quot}})^2$ denotes the variance of asset i in the quotation currency;

$(\sigma_{TC}^{\text{Quot/Ref}})^2$ denotes the variance of the series of exchange rates; and

$\rho_{i,TC}$ denotes the correlation coefficient between the return on asset i in its quotation currency and the exchange rate.

2.3.5.3   Hedging against currency risk

The formula given above assumes that the currency risk is not hedged. With the same notation, the risk of an asset that is hedged against currency risk is as follows:

$$\left(\sigma_i^{\text{Ref}}\right)^2 = \left(\sigma_i^{\text{Quot}}\right)^2 + H^2\left(\sigma_{TC}^{\text{Quot/Ref}}\right)^2 + 2H\rho_{i,TC}\sigma_i^{\text{Quot}}\sigma_{TC}^{\text{Quot/Ref}}$$

where H denotes the currency exposure ratio. If $H = 0$, then the currency risk is completely hedged. If $H = 1$, then the risk is not hedged at all.

In order to show how to extend the calculation to the case of a portfolio, let us consider the simple case of a portfolio that is made up of a domestic asset and a foreign asset. The variance of the portfolio is given by the following:

$$\sigma_P^2 = x_d^2\sigma_d^2 + x_l^2\sigma_l^2 + H^2x_l^2\sigma_{TC}^2 + 2x_dx_l\sigma_{dl} + 2Hx_l(x_d\sigma_{d,TC} + x_l\sigma_{l,TC})$$

where

σ_d^2 denotes the variance of the domestic asset returns;

σ_l^2 denotes the variance of the foreign asset returns in the quotation currency;

σ_{TC}^2 denotes the variance of the exchange rates;

σ_{dl} denotes the covariance of the domestic asset returns with the foreign asset returns, expressed in the quotation currency;

$\sigma_{l,TC}$ denotes the covariance of the foreign asset returns expressed in the quotation currency with the exchange rates;

$\sigma_{d,TC}$ denotes the covariance of the domestic asset returns with the exchange rates;

x_d denotes the proportion of the portfolio invested in the domestic asset;

x_l denotes the proportion of the portfolio invested in the foreign asset, with $x_l = 1 - x_d$; and

H denotes the proportion of the portfolio exposed to currency risk.

As before, if $H = 0$, then the currency risk is completely hedged, and if $H = 1$, then the risk is not hedged at all.

The variance of the unhedged portfolio will be greater than that of the hedged portfolio if

$$x_l^2\sigma_{TC}^2 + 2x_l(x_d\sigma_{d,TC} + x_l\sigma_{l,TC}) > 0$$

2.3.6 The AIMR standards and risk

There are not yet many AIMR standards concerning risk (cf. AIMR, 1997). However, since there are many types of risk measures, the AIMR recommends presentation of both a measure of total risk and a measure of market risk in order to characterise the risk completely. The total risk is measured by the standard deviation and the market risk is measured by the beta. These measures must be provided for each composite portfolio and also taking into account the distribution of portfolio returns within the composite. In the latter case it is possible to weight the calculation with the values of the portfolios by using the value at the beginning of the period so as not to favour the best performing portfolios. Only portfolios managed over the whole period should be included in the calculation. Additionally, the presentation of the benchmark used provides a relative measure of the risk of the investment strategy.

The AIMR indicates that the Treynor, Sharpe and Jensen indices should be calculated for composite portfolios. These indicators, which measure risk-adjusted return, will be defined in Chapter 4.

2.3.7 Generalisation of the notion of risk: Value-at-Risk[16]

Until now we have presented specific risk indicators for each kind of financial instrument, such as the variance and beta for stocks, and the duration and convexity for bonds. However, operators in the financial markets manage portfolios that are diversified over several asset classes and need to be able to evaluate the global risk of an entire portfolio rapidly. The concept of Value-at-Risk (VaR) satisfies this need. It enables us to sum up the set of risks associated with a portfolio that is diversified over several asset classes in a single value. The principle differs from that of the measures that have been described thus far. While a measure such as variance characterises the average risk of the portfolio (the average uncertainty in the distribution of returns), VaR focuses on a value for possible losses; in that sense, it is a measure of extreme risk.

Historically, the risk measures presented at the beginning of this section were developed specifically for asset management, while VaR was developed for banking establishments. The significant losses experienced in recent years by certain financial institutions highlighted the need for a global measure of risk, which would allow the potential losses of a position to be evaluated rapidly. The calculation of the VaR provided these establishments with the means of evaluating the amount of capital to be held to guarantee their commitments. It then turned out that the VaR concept could be applied to all areas concerned with risk. Here we will limit the presentation of the VaR to its application to risk analysis and evaluation of a portfolio of securities.

In the area of portfolio analysis, the VaR allows us to use a single value to qualify all the risks borne by a portfolio which is made up of several financial instruments. The VaR measures the maximal loss that the portfolio can withstand over a given period and with a fixed probability in the event of the markets moving unfavourably. The regulatory authorities for financial establishments impose a confidence level of 99%, which means that there is only one chance in a hundred that the portfolio will experience a loss that is greater than the calculated VaR. The regulations also stipulate that a period of 10 days, which corresponds to the average market reversal period, be chosen. The VaR is therefore a short-term measure. The VaR is then given by the 1% quantile of the portfolio return probability distribution over 10 days. The VaR

---

[16] Cf. Esch *et al.* (1997), Boulier *et al.* (1997), Poncet (1998), Wiener (1997), Rizk and Mahjoub (1996), Marteau (1997), Gaussel *et al.* (2000) and Walter and Feghali (2000).

calculation allows us to evaluate whether the investment establishment can withstand the risk incurred, and more particularly to check whether the establishment possesses sufficient capital to cover the risk.

The principle of the VaR concept is therefore simple, but its practical implementation is more complex. The asset returns are assumed to be subject to common risk factors, which allow the portfolio return to be decomposed. By modelling the future evolution of the factors, it is possible to estimate the value of the portfolio at a future date and from there deduce its VaR. The first step therefore involves identifying the relevant risk factors for each portfolio. The problem of choosing risk factors will also be discussed for multi-factor models in Chapter 6.

2.3.7.1   VaR calculation methods

There are essentially three methods for calculating a portfolio's VaR: the analytical method, the historical method and the Monte Carlo method. The historical method and the Monte Carlo method calculate the exact values of the financial instruments contained in the portfolio before and after a market scenario is applied, while the parametric method assumes, to simplify matters, that the values of the financial instruments evolve in a linear fashion with those of the risk parameters. As far as the estimation of market scenarios is concerned, the parametric method and the Monte Carlo method specify the distribution law beforehand, while the historical method is based on observations of variations in risk factors over a given period. In the following paragraphs we describe the different calculation methods in more detail.

Analytical or parametric method
This is a probabilistic method. The risk factors are modelled by random variables that are distributed according to a theoretical law, which depends on a limited number of parameters. The properties of the law allow the distribution quantile, and therefore the VaR of the portfolio, to be estimated. To simplify the calculations we generally choose a normal distribution, which is completely characterised by its mean and its variance–covariance matrix. If the portfolio is made up of instruments with linear behaviour compared with the risk factors, then the portfolio volatility is obtained directly from the risk factors' variance–covariance matrix. The VaR is a linear function of the portfolio volatility. We will discuss the VaR calculation formulas in the case of a normal distribution below.

The normal distribution is assumed to be stationary, i.e. it will stay the same in the future. The portfolio return is decomposed in a linear fashion according to the risk factors and the portfolio's sensitivity to the factors over the period in question.

Formally, let F be the vector of n risk factors. F follows a standard normal distribution of dimension n and variance–covariance matrix Σ. Let λ_T be the vector of portfolio return sensitivities to the risk factors and T be the evaluation horizon. The portfolio return is written as follows:

$$R_{PT} = \lambda_T' F$$

The portfolio return, which is obtained as a linear combination of normal variables, again follows a normal law. By carrying out a transformation, we can then write

$$R_{PT} = \sqrt{\lambda_T' \Sigma \lambda_T}\, X$$

where X follows a standardised normal distribution.

We take Q as the probability that the loss on the portfolio shall not be above the calculated VaR amount. Q is generally chosen between 95% and 99%. Taking V_0 as the initial value of the portfolio, the VaR for the period T with probability Q is given by

$$\Pr(R_{PT}V_0 \geq VaR) = Q$$

or

$$VaR = -\sqrt{\lambda_T' \Sigma \lambda_T} N^{-1}(Q)V_0$$

where N^{-1} denotes the inverse of the standardised normal distribution.

This method is the one used by JP Morgan in RiskMetrics.[17] JP Morgan provides, free of charge, the returns, variances and covariances of the risk factors, estimated on the basis of historical data. The risk factors are in fact basic assets such as market indices for equities and zero-coupon rates for bonds.

The advantage of this method is that the data required to implement it are easily available. However, the method is strongly reliant on the assumption of normal returns. In reality, the historical return distributions of market variables are often quite far removed from a normal distribution. We observe in particular distributions with fat tails. In addition, this method does not take into account the non-linearity of certain financial instruments, such as derivative instruments, which can figure in portfolios.

Historical or non-parametric method
This method is the simplest and the most intuitive. It is based on historical series of risk factors to deduce an empirical distribution of portfolio returns. The form of the distribution is not therefore predefined. Here again we use the hypothesis that the distribution is stationary, i.e. that future behaviour will reproduce past behaviour. The VaR is then obtained by determining the portfolio return that corresponds to the confidence level chosen.

This method depends greatly on the choice of historical sample. For the estimation to be statistically significant, the sample period should not be too short. However, it should not be too long either because the characteristics of the factors evolve over time. In general, the last five years of historical data are taken. The advantage of this method is that it does not presuppose any particular form of distribution. Nevertheless, this makes it very sensitive to the quality of the data. All it needs is a small amount of incoherent data to distort the result. The method can be implemented quickly. It is also the method that requires the fewest calculations. It allows us to use as many risk factors as we wish, as long as we have historical data available on the factors. The method can be used for options whose behaviour is non-linear compared with the risk factors.

The Monte Carlo method
This method is not based on any particular assumptions about the form of the distribution. The first step is to identify the significant risk factors. We then construct the distribution of these factors from historical data, or from economic scenarios, in order to calibrate the model. Using the distribution, we then carry out a large number of pseudo-random selections, which allow us to evaluate the portfolio over the fixed time horizon. The set of values obtained for

---

[17] See the following websites: http://www.jpmorgan.com and http://www.riskmetrics.com.

each selection allows the distribution to be constructed. We extract the value of the portfolio that corresponds to the confidence level chosen. The VaR is then calculated as the difference between that value and the current value of the portfolio. The calculation principle is in fact the same as that of the historical VaR, except that the data used are now obtained through simulation.

The Monte Carlo simulation method is particularly appropriate for portfolios that contain non-linear instruments, such as derivatives. However, the method is cumbersome to implement because it requires a large number of simulations to be carried out to obtain a high level of accuracy in the result, which leads to numerous calculations.

The three VaR estimation methodologies can be considered to be complementary. However, the RiskMetrics method remains the most frequently used, because the data required to implement it are available to the general public.

The VaR is a measure that is used as a complement to the other portfolio risk characteristics. It characterises the risk over a fixed time horizon and allows the risks of the different portfolio components to be brought together: the volatility of equities, interest rate risk and option risk. The result is expressed in monetary units, enabling it to be compared directly with the value of the portfolio.

2.3.7.2 Choosing the analysis period

All the calculation methods described require historical data. This introduces the problem of choosing the optimal time period for the historical data. We often assume that the risk factors are stationary. If this assumption is valid, then the longer the historical period chosen, the more accurate the VaR calculation will be. However, studies tend to show that the stationary hypothesis is not always respected. It has been observed in reality that periods of high volatility in the market follow periods of lower volatility. In this case the result may not reflect current volatility if the historical period used to calculate the volatility is too long. Furthermore, there are regulatory constraints that impose minimal historical periods of one year. In order to obtain a satisfactory result it is thus possible to give higher weights to the most recent data.

The VaR is estimated on a daily basis, and its value over a 10-day horizon is deduced by applying a multiplication coefficient that is equal to the square root of 10. However, the use of the coefficient is only valid under the assumption of Gaussian (normal) returns. Whatever the return distribution, the volatility over 10 days is equal to the volatility for one day multiplied by the square root of 10.[18] But it is only under the hypothesis of Gaussian distribution that there is a linear relationship between the VaR and the portfolio volatility. It is therefore only in that case that we can deduce that the VaR over 10 days is obtained by multiplying the VaR over one day by the square root of 10. However, we often observe that the asset return distribution does not follow a Gaussian law. In particular, we notice the phenomenon of fat tails, i.e. that the probability density decreases very slowly to infinity. The historical VaR calculation method allows these cases to be handled, but it is then no longer possible to deduce the VaR over 10 days from the VaR for one day. The theory of extreme values, which we will return to later, allows this problem to be resolved. The case of the loss probability density decreasing slowly to infinity can be modelled by a function to the power of $-1/\alpha$. The VaR over 10 days is then

---

[18] As long as the null auto-correlation of returns hypothesis is respected.

obtained by multiplying the VaR over one day by $10^{1/\alpha}$. It should however be pointed out that this relationship is only valid for VaRs with high thresholds.

2.3.7.3   The VaR as a portfolio risk analysis tool

We have briefly presented the different methods for calculating the VaR of a portfolio. In fact, the VaR allows us to go further than a simple valuation of the loss amount when analysing portfolio risk. The traditional VaR calculation involves, as we have seen, aggregating the portfolio risks in order to obtain a single number that summarises all the portfolio risks. However, in doing that we lose information that could be used profitably to manage the portfolio and analyse portfolio risk. The VaR calculation process allows us to identify the different sources of portfolio risk and can thus provide more information than the value of the VaR itself. The VaR can in fact act as a portfolio risk management tool (cf. Aragonés *et al.*, 2001). To do so, it is necessary to define the composition of a portfolio's VaR and analyse the impact of a new transaction on the total VaR of the portfolio. This leads us to define the notion of VaR delta, which allows us to calculate the incremental VaR.

The goal of the incremental VaR is to define the contribution of each asset to the total VaR of the portfolio. The tool therefore allows the manager to evaluate whether the envisaged transaction will increase or decrease the total VaR of the portfolio. The total VaR of the portfolio is not equal to the sum of the VaRs of the assets that make up the portfolio, because there are correlations between the assets. The incremental VaR, for its part, is defined in such a way that the sum of the incremental VaRs is equal to the total VaR of the portfolio. It is obtained from the VaR's delta. The VaR's delta is the vector of the VaR's sensitivity to each asset. It is made up of partial derivatives of the portfolio's VaR with respect to each asset. The incremental VaR of asset i is then calculated by multiplying the ith component of the portfolio's VaR delta by the quantity of asset i held. If we denote the proportion of asset i held in the portfolio as x_i, then the incremental VaR for asset i in portfolio P, written $IVaR_i(P)$ is given by

$$IVaR_i(P) = x_i \frac{\partial VaR(P)}{\partial x_i}$$

When the VaR of a portfolio goes above a fixed limit, we look for transactions that would reduce the amount of the VaR. If the incremental VaR of an asset is positive, then it contributes to an increase in the total VaR of the portfolio. On the other hand, if the incremental VaR of the asset is negative, then introducing it into the portfolio will decrease the total VaR. To analyse a portfolio when we are seeking to reduce its VaR, we can proceed as follows. We break down the portfolio into a limited number of sub-portfolios and we calculate the contribution of each sub-portfolio to the total VaR of the portfolio. To do that we successively consider each sub-portfolio as an asset and the rest of the portfolio as another asset. Once we have identified the part of the portfolio that makes the most significant contribution to the VaR, we can carry out a more detailed asset-by-asset analysis of the sub-portfolio. We can therefore identify the foreseeable transactions that would reduce the VaR, and therefore the risk, of the portfolio.

The incremental VaR allows us to evaluate the benefits of a transaction under consideration, without completely recalculating the VaR of the portfolio, which saves time. It is also possible to choose one of two transactions as being more useful for reducing the portfolio's VaR. In Chapter 4 we shall see how the notion of incremental VaR is used to study the risk-adjusted return of a portfolio.

2.3.7.4   Additional techniques

The VaR measure gives an estimation of the potential loss of a portfolio in a market context that is qualified as being normal, i.e. not in a period of financial crisis. It does not therefore truly take into account the risk of loss that is linked to extreme variations in the factors. For example, the weaknesses of the VaR were exposed during the Asian and Russian crises. The losses observed were in reality greater than those that had been forecast by the models. This is partly explained by the fact that the calculations are more often than not based on the hypothesis of normal return distribution, which, as we have already mentioned, does not always correspond to the reality. The normal distribution underestimates the extreme events that are in fact essential for calculating the VaR. It is therefore necessary to complete the VaR result with what is known as stress testing, which allows the evolution of the portfolio in extreme conditions to be simulated through different scenarios. We can also use other distribution laws that generalise the normal law.

Extreme value theory
The methods used to calculate the VaR do not take into account extreme market conditions. The historical method, for example, is based on a period that is too short and too recent to integrate crisis situations in a more distant past. The analytical method and the Monte Carlo method use normal distributions, which do not allow extreme situations to be modelled. Extreme value theory (cf. Boulier *et al.*, 1998) can be used to develop stress scenarios that are consistent with past financial risks or to calculate a VaR that takes extreme values into account.

Extreme value theory is part of the historical analysis context for calculating the VaR. It allows the distribution of the largest value from a set of random observations to be observed, independently of the initial distribution. The goal is to study the effects of extreme market conditions, and/or the non-respect of the model's underlying assumptions, on the value of the portfolio, which allows the VaR measure to be completed.

Scenario analysis
An alternative to the historical simulations and the Monte Carlo simulations involves generating possible scenarios from experience, intuition and historical observations. We determine a certain number of scenarios that are liable to occur and the total value of the portfolio is estimated for each of these. The difference between the current value of the portfolio and its worst possible value is taken as a measure of risk. This method is quite time-consuming to implement.

Levy distributions
Levy distributions are characterised by two risk parameters, as opposed to a single risk parameter for normal distributions. The first parameter is volatility, as for the Gaussian distribution. The second parameter allows unforeseen movements in the market to be taken into account. It involves the characteristic exponent of the distribution, which is written as α and which has a value that varies between 0 and 2. A value that is equal to 2 gives the Gaussian distribution again. The lower the value of α, the greater the chance that large fluctuations will occur. If the α value is low, past data are only moderately useful for forecasting future evolution.

Technical progress has led to methods that require more calculations being used. This leads to the possibility of improving the results.

2.4 ESTIMATION OF PARAMETERS

The risk and return indicators presented in this chapter allow the result of the management of a portfolio for which the allocation is known to be evaluated *ex post*. Before moving on to portfolio selection models, we give more detailed information on the methods used to estimate the future values of asset risks and returns. The most commonly used method involves using a series of historical data. In this chapter we have described all the methods that allow these to be calculated. The standard practice is to take weekly asset returns for a period of three to five years. This method is the simplest, but it assumes that the future will reproduce the past, without modification. However, this is frequently untrue. To improve the results and to take the evolutions into account, we can make the recent period more important by assigning weightings to the returns. Returns can be forecast by using time series. We briefly describe the main models below.

There are also asset return forecasting methods based on the study of financial ratios that apply to companies. Financial analysis firms are specialised in this area. Here we present a probabilistic method, called a scenario method, which allows a mean asset return to be forecast, according to possible evolutions of the economy. To finish, we describe a method that allows the forecasts produced to be evaluated and a method that allows them to be combined, in line with their relative usefulness, in order to obtain a more reliable forecast.

2.4.1 Use of time series

A time series is made up of a series of observations on a variable over regular intervals. In the case that interests us, the variable considered is the return on an asset. The autoregressive moving average (ARMA) family of models, developed by Box and Jenkins (1970), then allows the future return to be expressed as the weighted mean of its past values and/or independent random variables (cf. Grinold and Kahn, 2000).

The simplest model is the AR(q) (autoregressive) model. The parameter in parentheses gives the order of the model. The return is expressed as the weighted sum of its past values and a random term, or

$$R(t) = a_0 + a_1 R(t-1) + \cdots + a_q R(t-q) + e(t)$$

The $(a_i)_{i=1,\ldots,q}$ are then evaluated with the help of a statistical procedure.

The MA(p) (moving average) model expresses the value of the variable at time t as a weighted sum of $p+1$ independent random values:

$$R(t) = e(t) + c_1 e(t-1) + \cdots + c_p R(t-p) + c_0$$

The ARMA(p,q) model is a combination of the two. In this family of models we can also find the ARIMA model, which is the ARMA model applied to the order one differences between the returns. This model is interested in the changes in returns, instead of being interested in the returns directly.

2.4.2   Scenario method[19]

This method is an alternative to the use of historical data in obtaining asset risk and return forecasts. It is also applied to the valuation of asset classes. In spite of its potential usefulness, it remains infrequently used. The principle involves defining economic scenarios and attributing a probability to each. For each of the scenarios, we forecast the asset return. From there, we define mean return and risk estimations for each asset, along with the covariance between the asset returns, through the following formulas:

$$E(R_i) = \sum_{s=1}^{S} p_s R_{is}$$

$$\text{var}(R_i) = \sum_{s=1}^{S} p_s (R_{is} - E(R_i))^2$$

$$\text{cov}(R_i, R_j) = \sum_{s=1}^{S} p_s (R_{is} - E(R_i))(R_{js} - E(R_j))$$

where

R_{is} denotes the forecast return on asset i over the estimation period if scenario s occurs;
p_s denotes the probability of scenario s occurring; and
S denotes the number of scenarios envisaged.

2.4.3   Forecast evaluation[20]

Whatever method is chosen to obtain a forecast of asset return, the quality of the estimations can be evaluated with the help of an information coefficient (IC). This coefficient measures, *ex post*, the correlation between the estimated return and the effective return produced. Its value is between 0 and 1. The higher the value, the more the method used can be qualified as being stable. It can be useful to combine several forecast sources by assigning a weighting that depends on the value of the IC to each. This allows the error committed to be reduced. As an illustration, let us look at what happens with two forecast sources.

We take F_1 and F_2 as the two forecasts. We denote the forecast error variance as $\text{var}(F_1)$ and $\text{var}(F_2)$ and the correlation between the errors as ρ_{12}. We take k as the weighting assigned to the first forecast method and $(1 - k)$ as the weighting assigned to the second method. We denote the combination of the two forecasts as C. We therefore have

$$C = k F_1 + (1 - k) F_2$$

The forecast error is then written as follows:

$$\text{var}(C) = k^2 \, \text{var}(F_1) + (1 - k)^2 \, \text{var}(F_2) + 2k(1 - k) \, \text{cov}(F_1, F_2)$$
$$= k^2 \, \text{var}(F_1) + (1 - k)^2 \, \text{var}(F_2) + 2k(1 - k)\rho_{12}\sqrt{\text{var}(F_1) \, \text{var}(F_2)}$$

The objective is to choose the best weightings to assign to each of the two methods in order to maximise the correlation between the forecast of the variable and its actual value, which

---

[19] Cf. Chapter 9 of Farrell (1997) and Broquet and van den Berg (1992).
[20] Cf. Chapter 8 of Farrell (1997) and Appendix 2.2 of this chapter.

is the equivalent of minimising the forecast error. To calculate the value of k that minimises the error, we calculate the differential coefficient of $\mathrm{var}(C)$ with respect to k and we equate the differential coefficient to zero:

$$\frac{\partial \mathrm{var}(C)}{\partial k} = k \left(2\,\mathrm{var}(F_1) + 2\,\mathrm{var}(F_2) - 4\rho_{12}\sqrt{\mathrm{var}(F_1)\,\mathrm{var}(F_2)} \right)$$
$$- 2\,\mathrm{var}(F_2) + 2\rho_{12}\sqrt{\mathrm{var}(F_1)\,\mathrm{var}(F_2)}$$

hence

$$k_{\mathrm{Optimal}} = \frac{\mathrm{var}(F_2) - \rho_{12}\sqrt{\mathrm{var}(F_1)\,\mathrm{var}(F_2)}}{\mathrm{var}(F_1) + \mathrm{var}(F_2) - 2\rho_{12}\sqrt{\mathrm{var}(F_1)\,\mathrm{var}(F_2)}}$$

It does involve a minimum for the $\mathrm{var}(C)$ function, because the differential coefficient is negative for $k < k_{\mathrm{Optimal}}$ and positive for $k > k_{\mathrm{Optimal}}$.

If the two forecast methods are completely independent, then

$$\rho_{12} = 0$$

and

$$k_{\mathrm{Optimal}} = \frac{\mathrm{var}(F_2)}{\mathrm{var}(F_1) + \mathrm{var}(F_2)}$$

If, in addition, the two methods have the same forecasting capability, or

$$\mathrm{var}(F_1) = \mathrm{var}(F_2)$$

then

$$k_{\mathrm{Optimal}} = 1/2$$

and

$$\mathrm{var}(C) = \frac{\mathrm{var}(F_1)}{2}$$

We have therefore split the error in half by using two independent forecasting sources.

If, on the other hand, the two methods are completely correlated, or

$$\rho_{12} = 1$$

and if we also assume that

$$\mathrm{var}(F_1) = \mathrm{var}(F_2)$$

then

$$k_{\mathrm{Optimal}} = 1/2$$

and

$$\mathrm{var}(C) = \mathrm{var}(F_1)$$

and in this case the error is identical to that which we would have obtained with a single forecasting method.

2.5   CONCLUSION

In this chapter we have presented the fundamentals of portfolio performance measurement. The first elements presented have limited informational content. The following chapters will allow us to extend the analysis through modern portfolio theory. We will first explain the principles of the theory and then develop its application to performance analysis.

APPENDIX 2.1   CALCULATING THE PORTFOLIO RETURN WITH THE HELP OF ARITHMETIC AND LOGARITHMIC ASSET RETURNS

We will establish the equivalence between the two expressions that allow the portfolio return to be calculated, namely

$$R_{Pt} = \frac{V_t - V_{t-1}}{V_{t-1}}$$

and

$$R_{Pt} = \sum_{i=1}^{n} x_i R_{it}$$

To simplify the calculations, we assume that there are no dividends paid during the evaluation period. The notation is as follows:

P_{it} is the price of asset i at time t;

n_{it} is the number of units of asset i in the portfolio at time t; this number is assumed to be constant between the beginning and end of the valuation period;

x_{it} is the weight of asset i held in the portfolio at time t, defined by

$$x_{it} = \frac{n_{it} P_{it}}{V_t}$$

R_{it} is the return on asset i at time t, defined by

$$R_{it} = \frac{P_{it} - P_{i,t-1}}{P_{i,t-1}}$$

if the calculation is arithmetic and

$$R_{it} = \ln\left(\frac{P_{it}}{P_{i,t-1}}\right)$$

if the calculation is logarithmic; and

V_t is the value of the portfolio at date t, defined by

$$V_t = \sum_{i=1}^{n} n_{it} P_{it}$$

Let us first consider the arithmetic calculation of portfolio return. We have

$$R_{Pt} = \frac{V_t - V_{t-1}}{V_{t-1}} = \frac{\sum_{i=1}^{n} n_{i,t-1} P_{it} - \sum_{i=1}^{n} n_{i,t-1} P_{i,t-1}}{V_{t-1}} = \sum_{i=1}^{n} \frac{n_{i,t-1}}{V_{t-1}} (P_{it} - P_{i,t-1})$$

$$= \sum_{i=1}^{n} \frac{n_{i,t-1} P_{i,t-1}}{V_{t-1}} \frac{P_{it} - P_{i,t-1}}{P_{i,t-1}} = \sum_{i=1}^{n} x_{it} R_{it}$$

which establishes the relationship we are looking for.

Let us now consider the case of the logarithmic calculation. We can establish a relationship between the arithmetic return and the logarithmic return on an asset:

$$R_{it}^{\text{arith}} = \frac{P_{it} - P_{i,t-1}}{P_{i,t-1}} = \frac{P_{it}}{P_{i,t-1}} - 1$$

hence

$$R_{it}^{\log} = \ln\left(\frac{P_{it}}{P_{i,t-1}}\right) = \ln\left(1 + R_{it}^{\text{arith}}\right)$$

We therefore have

$$\sum_{i=1}^{n} x_{it} R_{it}^{\log} = \sum_{i=1}^{n} x_{it} \ln\left(1 + R_{it}^{\text{arith}}\right) \approx \sum_{i=1}^{n} x_{it} R_{it}^{\text{arith}} = R_{Pt}$$

The approximation produced is based on a limited first-order development of the logarithmic function around 0. This approximation is possible because the R_{it} are assumed to be small over an elementary time period. If we extend the limited development of the logarithmic function to order 2, then we obtain:

$$\ln(1 + y) = y - \frac{y^2}{2} + \varepsilon(y^2)$$

Since the second term of the development is negative, the logarithmic returns slightly underestimate the asset returns. The portfolio return obtained from logarithmic asset returns is therefore slightly lower than that obtained with the help of arithmetic returns.

APPENDIX 2.2 CALCULATING THE CONTINUOUS GEOMETRIC RATE OF RETURN FOR THE PORTFOLIO

Taking the formula that gives the discrete geometric rate of return for a portfolio, we can establish its continuous equivalent. This result comes from the Bank Administration Institute's (1968) study.

We denote the discrete rates with an upper case R and the continuous rates with a lower case r. We established the following formula in the section "Time-weighted rate of return method" above

$$R_{\text{TWR}} = \left(\prod_{i=1}^{n} (1 + R_{t_i})\right)^{1/T} - 1$$

where

$$R_{t_i} = \frac{V_{t_i} - (V_{t_{i-1}} + C_{t_{i-1}})}{V_{t_{i-1}} + C_{t_{i-1}}}$$

We therefore have

$$1 + R_{\text{TWR}} = \left(\prod_{i=1}^{n} (1 + R_{t_i}) \right)^{1/T}$$

By taking the logarithm of each element, we obtain

$$\ln(1 + R_{\text{TWR}}) = \frac{1}{T} \sum_{i=1}^{n} \ln(1 + R_{t_i})$$

and by replacing R_{t_i} with its value, we can write

$$r_{\text{TWR}} = \frac{1}{T} \sum_{i=1}^{n} \ln\left(\frac{V_{t_i}}{V_{t_{i-1}} + C_{t_{i-1}}} \right)$$

Developing this formula:

$$r_{\text{TWR}} = \frac{1}{T}(\ln(V_{t_1}) - \ln(V_0) + \ln(V_{t_2}) - \ln(V_{t_1} + C_{t_1}) + \cdots + \ln(V_T) - \ln(V_{t_{n-1}} + C_{t_{n-1}}))$$

By grouping the terms together, we finally obtain:

$$r_{\text{TWR}} = \frac{1}{T} \left[\ln\left(\frac{V_T}{V_0} \right) + \sum_{i=1}^{n-1} \ln\left(\frac{V_{t_i}}{V_{t_i} + C_{t_i}} \right) \right]$$

APPENDIX 2.3   STOCK EXCHANGE INDICES[21]

On the one hand, stock exchange indices should allow rapid evaluation of the movements on a stock exchange in its entirety. This is the objective of indices that contain a small number of securities. Each stock exchange therefore has its representative index. These restricted indices are sufficient for evaluating the markets because they include the securities with the largest market capitalisation and therefore represent a high percentage of the total market capitalisation of the exchange.

On the other hand, the indices serve as references for investors. For that purpose, there are indices that contain a larger number of securities, along with indices that are specialised in a type of stock or sector. To these we can add the European indices, created recently, which represent the European market in its entirety, and the international indices.

The most commonly used calculation method for constructing indices is market capitalisation weighting, which corresponds to the construction of Markowitz's optimal portfolio. Nevertheless, among the best-known indices, the Dow Jones and the Nikkei are exceptions, because they are simple averages of the prices of the securities that make up the indices.

We describe the principal indices for the various stock exchanges below.

---

[21] For more details on the definitions and methods used for calculating indices, one can refer to Topsacalian (1996, 2000) and Chapter 4 of Spieser (2000).

French stock exchange indices

The Société des Bourses Françaises (SBF) publishes several indices that represent the French stock market. These indices are obtained from an arithmetic mean weighted by market capitalisation:

1. The CAC 40 index is the main reference index for the Paris Bourse. It is calculated from a sample of 40 French stocks on the primary market.[22] The stocks are taken from among the 100 leading companies on the exchange in terms of market capitalisation.
2. The SBF 120 index was created in 1991. It is made up of the 120 most active and most liquid stocks in the market, selected from the 200 leading firms in terms of market capitalisation. It contains the 40 stocks from the CAC 40. These stocks are quoted on the primary and secondary markets.
3. The SBF 80 index was created in 1997. It contains the 80 stocks from the SBF 120 that do not figure in the CAC 40.
4. The SBF 250 index replaced the CAC 240 index. It is made up of 250 French stocks that are quoted on the primary and secondary markets. It contains the 120 stocks from the SBF 120 index. The stocks are chosen for the degree to which they represent 12 economic sectors and the regularity of their prices.
5. The MIDCAC index is made up of 100 securities that are representative of the mid-capitalisation stocks quoted on the Paris Bourse. It contains securities that belong to the SBF 120 and SBF 250 indices, alongside securities that do not figure in any of the other indices. The goal of this index is to offer fund managers who are specialised in mid-cap stocks a reference database for qualifying their performance.

European stock exchange indices

In the United Kingdom, the Financial Times and the London Stock Exchange joined forces to produce the FTSE indices. There are a whole series of these, containing different numbers of securities:

- The FTSE 100 (or FOOTSIE) is the best known and most widely used index. It serves as a market indicator. It is made up of 100 stocks on the London Stock Exchange (LSE).
- The FTSE MID 250 is made up of 250 stocks on the LSE.
- The FTSE Actuaries MID 350 index combines the stocks from the FTSE 100 and the MID 250.
- The FTSE Small Cap index is made up of around 500 small company stocks.
- The FTSE Actuaries All-Share index contains around 600 stocks from the LSE. Its objective is to represent the whole market.

In Germany the indices quoted on the Frankfurt Stock Exchange are the DAX indices:

- The DAX 30 index is made up of 30 stocks selected from among the largest market capitalisations and the largest trading volumes.
- The DAX 100 index is made up of 100 continuously traded stocks.
- The MDAX index contains the 70 stocks that are in the DAX 100 and not in the DAX 30.
- The CDAX index is an index that is broadly composed.

---

[22] Until September 2000, the primary market was divided into a monthly settlement market and a spot market. The CAC 40 stocks were at that time taken from the monthly settlement market only.

We also find the FAZ index, developed by the Frankfurter Allgemeine Zeitung, and made up of the 100 largest listed stocks.

Finally, the following are the reference indices for some other European stock exchanges:

- In Amsterdam, the AEX index, made up of 25 stocks.
- In Brussels, the BEL 20 index, made up of 20 stocks.
- In Milan, the MIB 30 index, made up of 30 stocks.
- In Madrid, the IBEX 35 index, made up of 35 stocks.
- In Zurich, the SMI index, made up of 25 stocks.

American stock exchange indices

There are several stock exchanges in the United States and each one is evaluated by an index. The two dominant marketplaces are New York, with its two exchanges, the NYSE and AMEX, and Chicago. Another important exchange, the NASDAQ (National Association of Securities Dealers Automated Quotation), the exchange for high technology stocks, has no geographical location. All the transactions are carried out electronically. The best-known and most widely used indices are those produced by the newspapers (which is the case for the Dow Jones) and the ratings agencies (Standard & Poor's). The indices are constructed with firms that are quoted on several markets:

1. The Dow Jones Industrial Average (DJIA) index is the oldest index, created in 1884. It is published in the *Wall Street Journal*. It contains 30 industrial stocks and is used to measure the performance of the NYSE. It provides, however, biased information owing to its reduced size and its calculation method, since it is a simple average of the asset prices.
2. Another index that is limited in terms of size, the Major Market Index (MMI), was created by the Chicago Board of Trade (CBOT) to serve as a support for futures following Dow Jones & Company's refusal to allow its index to fill that role. It is made up of 20 securities with 17 belonging to the DJIA. This index is also dollar-weighted. Its objective is to reproduce the movements of the Dow Jones and its correlation with that index is around 97%.

The American agency Standard & Poor's has developed a whole range of indices. These indices are obtained from an arithmetic mean weighted by market capitalisation, which ensures better representation of market movements:

1. The S&P500 (Standard & Poor's Composite Index of 500 Stocks) is made up of 500 stocks that are traded on the NYSE with some stocks from the AMEX. This index is a reference index for the market. It is a medium-sized index.
2. The S&P100 contains 100 stocks from the S&P500 for which options are traded on the Chicago Board Options Exchange (CBOE) and the Chicago Mercantile Exchange (CME).
3. We could also mention the S&P400 and the S&P Small Caps.

The American market possesses several large-sized indices:

1. The NYSE Composite Index contains all the stocks on the NYSE, or more than 1700 securities grouped into 50 categories.
2. The Wilshire 5000 Equity Index is the largest of all the indices. Its objective is to represent virtually the entire capitalisation of the market and it contains all the stocks quoted on the NYSE and the AMEX along with a significant number of securities quoted on the

NASDAQ. In view of the number of stocks it contains, it is of limited use. Its size leads to large calculation requirements. For that reason it is only updated once a week.
3. The NASDAQ Composite is NASDAQ's best-known index. It contains more than 5500 firms, or all the American and foreign stocks quoted on the NASDAQ.
4. The Value Line index is calculated from a geometric mean. It is made up of more than 1700 stocks from the NYSE and the AMEX.

Finally, we will mention an index that was created recently, the Global Titan Index, which was launched in July 1999 and contains the 50 largest multinationals which are supposed to dominate the world economy in the twenty-first century.

Japanese stock exchange indices

The index that is used to measure the performance of the Tokyo Stock Exchange is the Nikkei Stock Average, or Nikkei 225. It contains 225 stocks selected from the Kabutocho. It is a price-weighted index. Two other indices are calculated from an arithmetic mean weighted by market capitalisation:

1. The Nikkei 300 index contains 300 securities from the first section of the Tokyo exchange. It was launched in October 1993.
2. The Topix index contains all the securities from the first section of the Tokyo exchange, or around 1250 securities.

International indices

There are several international indices issued by the major index-creating firms:

- the Morgan Stanley Capital International (MSCI) index;
- the FT/S&P Actuaries World Index issued by the Financial Times and Standard & Poor's; and
- the Dow Jones World Index.

These indices are calculated for every country that has a significant level of stock exchange activity. The weighting of each exchange in the index is proportional to the market capitalisation of the exchanges taken individually.

The European indices

The European indices were created recently. They enable the whole of the European market to be evaluated and complete the indices that evaluate each stock exchange individually. The indices are divided into two categories: the indices that contain the European Union countries and the indices that contain the euro zone countries only. There are several major families of European indices, with each of the major index-creating firms having its own indices.

Dow Jones Stoxx indices

These indices were created in February 1998. They are published by Dow Jones & Company in partnership with the German, French and Swiss Stock Exchanges. Luxembourg is not part of the composition of these indices, which do however contain Norwegian and Swiss stocks. This family of indices contains broad indices and narrow indices:

1. The Dow Jones Stoxx 50 index contains 50 stocks from 14 European Union countries (Luxembourg does not figure in the index) along with stocks from Switzerland and Norway.
2. The Dow Jones Euro Stoxx 50 contains 50 stocks from the 12 euro zone countries.
3. The Dow Jones Stoxx index contains 665 stocks that come from the same countries as the Dow Jones Stoxx 50.
4. The Dow Jones Euro Stoxx index contains 326 stocks from the 12 euro zone countries.

Securities to which foreigners do not have access are excluded from these indices.

FT/S&P Europe indices

These are the result of an association between the Financial Times group and Standard & Poor's and are divided into two FT/S&P indices and two S&P indices:

1. The FT/S&P Europe index is made up of the respective indices of the European Union countries plus Switzerland. It contains 702 stocks divided into seven economic sectors. The stocks are selected by decreasing order of market capitalisation in each sector. Only quoted stocks are retained.
2. The FT/S&P Eurobloc index brings together 353 stocks from the euro zone countries, excluding Luxembourg. Its composition follows the same principle as the FT/S&P Europe index.
3. The S&P Euroindex contains 158 companies from 10 euro zone countries (Luxembourg is not included). The securities are selected according to the same principle as for the S&P500.
4. The S&P Euro Plus index contains 200 companies from 14 countries (the euro countries, except Luxembourg, plus Denmark, Norway, Sweden and Switzerland).

FTSE indices

Two indices have been created by the FTSE Company in partnership with the Amsterdam Stock Exchange, the FTSE Eurotop 100 and the FTSE Eurotop 300, with the latter further divided into two categories, giving three indices:

1. The FTSE Eurotop 100 index is not exclusively devoted to the euro zone. It contains securities from 14 European Union countries (Luxembourg is not included). It is made up of the 100 most frequently exchanged European stocks on the basis of volumes handled over the previous three years.
2. The FTSE Eurotop 300 Eurobloc index contains the 130 largest market capitalisations in the euro zone, classified in decreasing order, without really taking into account their respective weightings within the European market.
3. The FTSE Eurotop 300 index for Europe contains 313 stocks from 14 countries. Its objective is to cover 65% of European capitalisation. Like its homologue for the euro zone, this index mainly takes into account the capitalisation of the stock.

Securities to which foreigners do not have access are excluded from these indices. British fund managers essentially use the two Eurotop 300 indices.

MSCI Europe indices

These indices were developed by Morgan Stanley Capital International and seek to account, as precisely as possible, for investment opportunities in all European Union and all euro zone countries respectively. The indices take all categories of stocks and therefore all capitalisation sizes into account:

1. The MSCI Europe index contains 561 stocks from the 15 European Union countries.
2. The MSCI EMU index contains 323 stocks from 11 euro zone countries.

The disadvantage of these indices is that the selection method could lead to the introduction of securities that are not very liquid, which constitutes an obstacle for index management.

European bond indices

Up until 1998, the main references in France for evaluating the performance of bond managers were the CNO (Comité de Normalisation Obligataire) indices, because French bond managers invested for the most part in the domestic market. From 1 January 1999 the domestic market is the euro market, which consisted of 11 countries in theory, but 10 in practice, because Luxembourg is not a recurring issuer. The CNO created two distinct indices for the market in government bonds in the euro zone. The broad index contains almost 270 securities and is intended to serve as a benchmark for fund managers. The restricted index is intended for front offices and is limited to the loans that are most representative of the yield curve in euros.

Apart from the CNO indices, all the other indices are produced by private investment firms: Salomon Smith Barney, JP Morgan, Lehman Brothers and Morgan Stanley.

Salomon Smith Barney indices

Salomon Smith Barney have been producing government indices on the American market for many years. They became interested in the European market when the euro was being implemented. Salomon Smith Barney calculate two euro indices:

1. The EGBI (Emu Government Bond Index) is a government index that is exclusively concerned with government loans from euro member countries.
2. The EBIGBI (Euro Broad Investment Grade Bond Index) is a non-government index that includes euro issues from non-sovereign issuers.

JP Morgan indices

JP Morgan only produces one category of bond index, for government securities, in most bond markets, including a certain number of emerging markets. JP Morgan now disseminates a bond index for the euro zone, the JPM EMU Bond Index, which, like the CNO and EGBI indices, is divided into segments according to the maturity of the security. It contains 228 loans and covers all government securities for nine European countries (Belgium, Finland, France, Germany, Ireland, Italy, The Netherlands, Portugal and Spain).

Lehman Brothers indices

Lehman Brothers produces government indices for developed and emerging countries, and also private sector indices. For Europe, the generic Lehman Brothers Euro-Aggregate Index is broken down into a multitude of sub-indices according to the nature of the issuer, the maturity and the sector of activity. This allows investors to break down the performance into the different market segments, notably government securities. There are approximately 7000 bonds, selected according to criteria relating to the liquidity and the total amount.

Morgan Stanley indices

Morgan Stanley has decided to produce European government and non-government bond indices through its subsidiary Morgan Stanley Capital International (MSCI), which already produces share indices. The bond indices are constructed according to the same logic as the SSB indices. The name used by MSCI for the indices will be MSCI ECI. Indices should soon be calculated for each of the countries in the euro zone, together with an aggregate index. All of the indices will be published in the press.

BIBLIOGRAPHY

Accoceberry, M., "Mesure de performances : Une clarification des procédés de gestion est indispensable", *MTF-L'Agefi*, no. 80, April 1996.

Aftalion, F., "Le point sur . . . Duration, convexité, immunisation", *Banque et Marchés*, no. 28, May–June 1997.

AIMR, *Performance Evaluation, Benchmarks, and Attribution Analysis*, AIMR, 1995.

AIMR Performance Presentation Standards Handbook, 2nd edn, 1997.

AIMR, *Benchmarks and Performance Attribution, Subcommittee Report*, Final Draft, August 1998.

Amenc, N. and Le Sourd, V., *Gestion quantitative des portefeuilles d'actions*, Economica, 1998.

Aragonés, J.R., Blanco, C. and Mascareñas, J., "Active Management of Equity Investment Portfolios", *Journal of Portfolio Management*, spring 2001, pp. 39–46.

Athanasoulis, S.G. and Shiller, R.J., "The Significance of the Market Portfolio", *Review of Financial Studies*, vol. 13, no. 2, 2000.

Baker, III E.D., "Performance Basics: Simple in Theory, Hard to Apply – Part I", *Performance Measurement: Setting the Standards, Interpreting the Numbers*, CFA, 1991.

Bishop, E., *Indexation*, Euromoney Books, 1990.

Black, F. and Litterman, R., "Asset Allocation: Combining Investor View with Market Equilibrium", Goldman Sachs, Quantitative Research Group, 1990.

Boulier, J.-F., Brabant, A., Dalaud, R. and Dieu, A.-L., "Risques de marché : vue de profil", *Quants*, CCF, December 1997.

Boulier, J.-F., Dalaud, R. and Longin, F., "Application de la théorie des valeurs extrêmes aux marchés financiers", *Banque et Marchés*, no. 32, January–February 1998.

Box, G. and Jenkins, G., *Time Series Analysis: Forecasting and Control*, Holden Day, 1970.

Brie, B. (de), "Performances des OPCVM : mode d'emploi", *Revue Banque*, no. 591, April 1998.

Broquet, C. and van den Berg, A., *Gestion de portefeuille – Actions, Obligations, Options*, 2nd edn, De Boeck Université, 1992.

Brown, M.R. and Mott, C.E., "Understanding the Differences and Similarities of Equity Style Indexes", in *The Handbook of Equity Style Management*, T.D. Coggin, F.J. Fabozzi and R.D. Arnott, eds, 2nd edn, Frank J. Fabozzi Associates, 1997.

Calinski, T. and Harabasz, J., "A Dendrite Method for Cluster Analysis", Communications in *Statistics*, no. 3, 1974, pp. 1–27.

Cambon, D., "Attribution de performance et création de valeur", *Journées EFE*, May 1997.

Charest, G., "Rendement, risque et portefeuille", in *Encyclopédie des marchés financiers*, Economica, 1997, pp. 1608–1660.

Christopherson, J., "Normal Portfolios and their Construction", in *Portfolio and Investment Management*, F.J. Fabozzi, ed., Probus Publishing, Chicago, 1989.

Christopherson, J.A., "Normal Portfolios: Construction of Customized Benchmarks", in *Active Equity Portfolio Management*, F.J. Fabozzi, ed., Frank J. Fabozzi Associates, 1998.

Clarke, R.G. and Kritzman, M.P., *Currency Management: Concepts and Practices*, The Research Foundation of the Institute of Chartered Financial Analysts, 1996.

Coggin, T.D., Fabozzi, F.J. and Arnott, R.D., *The Handbook of Equity Style Management*, 2nd edn, Frank J. Fabozzi Associates, 1997.

Compton, M.I., "Equity Style Benchmarks for Fund Analysis", in *The Handbook of Equity Style Management*, T.D. Coggin, F.J. Fabozzi and R.D. Arnott, eds, 2nd edn, Frank J. Fabozzi Associates, 1997.

Elton, E.J. and Gruber, M.J., *Modern Portfolio Theory and Investment Analysis*, 5th edn, Wiley, 1995.

Esch, L., Kieffer, R. and Lopez, T., *Value at Risk, Vers un risk management moderne*, De Boeck Université, 1997.

Fabozzi, F.J., *Investment Management*, Prentice Hall International Editions, 1995.

Fabozzi, F.J., *Bond Portfolio Management*, Frank J. Fabozzi Associates, 1996.

Fabozzi, F.J. and Molay, R.P., *Perspectives in Equity Indexing*, 2nd edn, Frank J. Fabozzi Associates, 2000.

Farrell, Jr. J.L., *Portfolio Management, Theory and Application*, 2nd edn, McGraw-Hill, 1997.

Fisher, L., "Measuring Rates of Return", *Measuring the Investment Performance of Pension Funds*, Bank Administration Institute, 1968.

Flynn, M.J., "Universes and Peer Groups: Construction and Use", *Performance Evaluation, Benchmarks, and Attribution Analysis*, AIMR, 1995.

Fogler, H.R., "Normal Style Indexes – An Alternative to Manager Universes?", *Performance Measurement: Setting the Standards, Interpreting the Numbers*, ICFA, 1989.

Fontaine, P., "Gestion des portefeuilles internationaux", in *Encyclopédie des marchés financiers*, Economica, 1997, pp. 548–571.

Gaussel, N., Legras, J., Longin, F. and Rabemananjara, R., "Au-delà de la VaR", *Quants*, CCF, Mars 2000.

Grandin, P., *Mesure de performance des fonds d'investissement, Méthodologie et résultats*, Economica, Gestion poche, 1998.

Grinold, R.C. and Kahn, R.N., *Active Portfolio Management: A Quantitative Approach for Producing Superior Returns and Controlling Risk*, 2nd edn, Irwin, 2000.

Jacquillat, B. and Solnik, B., *Marchés financiers, Gestion de portefeuille et des risques*, 3rd edn, Dunod, 1997.

Karnosky, D.S. and Singer, B.D., *Global Asset Management and Performance Attribution*, The Research Foundation of the Institute of Chartered Financial Analysts, Charlottesville, VA, 1994.

Koenig, P., "Normes AIMR /GIPS : vers un standard unique", *Banque Magazine* no. 622, February 2001.

Lee, P., "European Bond Indices: The Search for a True Index", *Euromoney*, March 1999.

Leibowitz, M.L. and Henriksson, R.D., "Portfolio Optimization with Shortfall Constraints: A Confidence-limit Approach to Maintaining Downside Risk", *Financial Analysts Journal*, March–April 1989.

Luck, C.G., "Style in Indexes and Benchmarks", *Performance Evaluation, Benchmarks, and Attribution Analysis*, AIMR, 1995.

Magill, M. and Quinzi, M., *Theory of Incomplete Markets*, MIT Press, 1996.

Malaise, P., "L'émergence de normes internationales en matière de mesure de performance", *MTF-L'Agefi*, no. 80, April 1996.

Marteau, D., "La *Value at Risk* est-elle un indicateur pertinent de mesure des risques ?", *Revue Banque*, no. 584, September 1997.

Melnikoff, M., "Investment Performance Analysis for Investors", *Journal of Portfolio Management*, vol. 25, no. 1, fall 1998, pp. 95–107.

Nawrocki, D., "Market Theory and the Use of Downside Risk Measures", *CHI Investment Software Research Paper Series*, 1996.

Nawrocki, D., "A Brief History of Downside Risk Measures", *Journal of Investing*, vol. 8, no. 3, fall 1999a, pp. 9–26.

Nawrocki, D., "The Case for the Relevancy of Downside Risk Measures", Working Paper, 1999b.

Peyrard, J., *Les marchés des changes : opérations et couvertures*, Vuibert, 1995.

Poncet, P., "Le point sur . . . Value at Risk", *Banque et Marchés*, no. 37, November–December 1998.

Rennie, E.P. and Cowhey, T.J., "The Successful Use of Benchmark Portfolios", *Improving Portfolio Performance with Quantitative Models*, AIMR, 1989.

Rizk, G. and Mahjoub, C., "Value at Risk : mode, garde-fou, ou indicateur efficient ?", *Revue Banque*, no. 572, July–August 1996.

Roll, R., "A Critique of the Asset Pricing Theory's Tests: On Past and on Potential Testability of the Theory", *Journal of Financial Economics*, no. 4, 1977, pp. 129–176.

Rosenberg, M., "Currency Forecasting: Theory and Practice", *Global Fixed Income Research*, Merrill Lynch, 1996.

Rousseau, P., "Prévision des taux de change", in *Encyclopédie des marchés financiers*, Economica, 1997, pp. 1502–1517.

Rubinstein, M., "Derivatives Performance Attribution", Working Paper, August 2000.

Sarle, W.S.,: "SAS Technical Report A-108, The Cubic Clustering Criterion", SAS Institute, 1983.

Shakotko, R., "A nouvel horizon nouveaux indices . . . ", *Revue Banque*, no. 594, July–August 1998.

Sharpe, W.F., *Investments*, 3rd ed., Prentice Hall, 1985.

Sharpe, W.F., "Asset Allocation: Management Style and Performance Measurement", *Journal of Portfolio Management*, vol. 18, winter 1992, pp. 7–19.

Simon, Y., *Encyclopédie des marchés financiers*, Economica, 1997.

Sortino, F.A. and Price, L.N., "Performance Measurement in a Downside Risk Framework", *Journal of Investing*, vol. 3, no. 3, fall 1994, pp. 59–64.

Spaulding, D., *Measuring Investment Performance – Calculating and Evaluating Investment Risk and Return*, McGraw-Hill, 1997.

Spieser, P., *Information Economique et Marchés Financiers*, Economica, 2000.

Surz, R.J., "Portfolio Opportunity Distributions: An Innovation in Performance Evaluation", *Journal of Investing*, vol. 3, no. 2, summer 1994, pp. 36–41.

Surz, R.J., "Portfolio Opportunity Distributions: A Solution to the Problems with Benchmarks and Peer Groups", *Journal of Performance Measurement*, vol. 1, no. 2, winter 1996.

Surz, R.J., "New and Improved Investment Performance Evaluation", *Journal of Performance Measurement*, vol. 2, no. 1, fall 1997.

Topsacalian, P., *Les indices boursiers sur actions*, Economica, 1996.

Topsacalian, P., "Le point sur . . . les indices boursiers", *Banque et Marchés*, no. 47, July–August 2000.

Walter, C. and Feghali, R., "Value-at-Risk : du modèle de risque au risque de modèle", *Banque Magazine*, no. 614, May 2000.

Wiener, Z., "Introduction to VaR (Value-at-Risk)", *Risk Management and Regulation in Banking Conference*, Jerusalem, 18 May 1997.

Zaouati, P., *La gestion quantitative*, Economica, 1995.

3

The Basic Elements of Modern Portfolio Theory[1]

In the previous chapter we presented the characteristic parameters of a portfolio, namely its return and risk, and described the measures that enable us to evaluate the results of portfolio management *ex post*. In the current chapter we discuss rational portfolio choice criteria and in particular arbitrage between risk and return. Markowitz was the first to quantify the link that exists between portfolio risk and portfolio return. By so doing, he founded modern portfolio theory.

The Markowitz model was the starting point for numerous developments in finance. It contains, in particular, the fundamental elements of the Capital Asset Pricing Model (CAPM), which was the basis for the first performance analysis models, and which will be the subject of Chapter 4.

3.1 PRINCIPLES[2]

An article by Markowitz, published in 1952, is the source of modern portfolio theory. Together with Sharpe and Miller he was awarded the Nobel Prize for his research in 1990. Markowitz developed a theory of portfolio choice in an uncertain future. He quantified the difference between the risk of portfolio assets taken individually and the overall risk of the portfolio. He demonstrated that the portfolio risk came from the covariances of the assets that made up the portfolio. The marginal contribution of a security to the portfolio return variance is therefore measured by the covariance between the security's return and the portfolio's return and not by the variance of the security itself. Markowitz thus established that the risk of a portfolio is lower than the average of the risks of each asset taken individually and gave quantitative evidence of the contribution of diversification.

The theory developed by Markowitz is based on maximising the utility of the investor's terminal wealth. This utility function is defined according to the expected return and the standard deviation of the wealth. The theory offers a solution to the problem of portfolio choice for a risk-averse investor: the optimal portfolios, from the rational investor's point of view, are defined as those that have the lowest risk for a given return. These portfolios are said to be mean–variance efficient.

To simplify matters, the model assumes that there is only one investment period. Before giving details on the Markowitz model itself, we will initially define the notions of utility functions and risk aversion.

---

[1] Cf. Briys and Viala (1995) and Charest (1997). For a brief historical overview of the theories developed in the wake of Markowitz, see the series of articles "The people who changed global investing" which appeared in *Global Custodian*, fall 1999, "Harry Markowitz" and "William Sharpe".

[2] Cf. Chapter 4 of Fabozzi (1995) and Chapter 4 of Broquet and van den Berg (1992).

3.1.1   Utility functions and indifference curves[3]

To develop utility theory it is first necessary to define the rules of rational behaviour. Von Neumann and Morgenstern (1947) characterised rational choices in uncertain situations in the form of axioms. A detailed formulation of these axioms is given in Fama and Miller (1972). Following these principles, investors know how to compare the different alternatives presented and establish an order of preference. They then remain consistent with regard to their choices. To those principles we can add the fact that investors always prefer having more to having less: the marginal utility of wealth, which is defined as the growth rate of the utility function, is therefore always positive.

The definition of a utility function involves reducing each situation to a value, so that investors can make their choice according to that value. The utility function must respect a certain number of properties, which must conserve the order, i.e. if x is preferred to y, then the utility of x must be greater than the utility of y. The utility function enables risky alternatives to be classified.

Generally speaking, the expected utility of an investor's wealth is written as follows:

$$\mathrm{E}\,[U(W)] = \sum_i p_i U(w_i)$$

where p_i denotes the probability of obtaining wealth equal to w_i at the end of the period; and i denotes the summation index for all the possible occurrences.

According to the axioms that characterise the rational behaviour of investors, and the fact that the latter prefer having more to having less, investors always seek to maximise the expected utility of their wealth. This expected utility is therefore the investor's natural objective function. The principle is thus to calculate the expected utility of the wealth in all possible situations, and then to choose the one for which the quantity is maximal.

Utility functions are specific for given individuals. They should not be compared with each other. They enable the investor's choices to be characterised and the investor's preferences to be defined by associating the portfolio's risk and return values. The set of risk/return combinations that gives the same level of utility forms an indifference curve. Markowitz's mean–variance approach assumes that investors have a quadratic utility function or that the distribution of portfolio returns is normal, i.e. that the moments with an order that is strictly greater than two are null. However, quadratic utility functions present the disadvantage of not respecting the condition of decreasing aversion to risk, as we will show in the following section.

3.1.2   Risk aversion[4]

Translating the preference axioms into a utility function enables us to define the risk premium and risk aversion with the help of the derivatives of the utility function. Markowitz defines the risk premium as being the maximum amount that an individual is prepared to give up to avoid uncertainty. It is calculated as the difference between the utility of the expected wealth and the expected utility of the wealth, or

$$U[\mathrm{E}(W)] - \mathrm{E}[U(W)]$$

The sign of the difference allows us to qualify the investor's behaviour with regard to risk:

---

[3] Cf. Chapter 4 of Copeland and Weston (1988), and Chapter 3 of Briys and Viala (1995).
[4] Cf. Chapter 4 of Briys and Viala (1995) and Chapter 10 of Elton and Gruber (1995).

- if $U[E(W)] > E[U(W)]$, then the utility function is concave and the individual is risk averse;
- if $U[E(W)] = E[U(W)]$, then the utility function is linear and the individual is risk neutral;
- if $U[E(W)] < E[U(W)]$, then the utility function is convex and the individual is risk seeking.

These definitions are given in Markowitz (1959). Within the framework of portfolio choice, investors are assumed to be risk averse.

The measure of absolute risk aversion (ARA) is given by[5]

$$ARA = -\frac{U''(W)}{U'(W)}$$

This measures the risk aversion for a given level of wealth.

The measure of relative risk aversion (RRA) is given by

$$RRA = -W\frac{U''(W)}{U'(W)}$$

Constant relative risk aversion means that the loss amount tolerated by an individual increases in proportion to the increase in the individual's wealth.

Let us now consider the example of a quadratic utility function, or

$$U(W) = aW - bW^2$$

and calculate its first two derivatives, or

$$U'(W) = a - 2bW$$

and

$$U''(W) = -2b$$

We deduce that

$$ARA = \frac{2b}{a - 2bW}$$

and

$$RRA = \frac{2bW}{a - 2bW} = \frac{2b}{\dfrac{a}{W} - 2b}$$

Calculation of the first derivative of ARA compared with the wealth W gives

$$\frac{d(ARA)}{dW} = \frac{4b^2}{(a - 2bW)^2} > 0$$

Absolute risk aversion is therefore an increasing function of W. In the same way

$$\frac{d(RRA)}{dW} = \frac{\dfrac{a}{W^2}2b}{\left(\dfrac{a}{W} - 2b\right)^2} > 0$$

Therefore, relative risk aversion is also an increasing function of W. This means that an individual becomes more risk averse as his wealth increases, which is counterintuitive. That

---

[5] This result and the following one are demonstrated in Elton and Gruber (1995).

is one of the disadvantages of the quadratic utility function. We would wish to have a utility function that leads to a decreasing absolute risk aversion and a constant relative risk aversion.

Let us now consider the example of a logarithmic utility function, or

$$U(W) = \ln(W)$$

Calculation of its first two derivatives leads to

$$U'(W) = \frac{1}{W}$$

and

$$U''(W) = -\frac{1}{W^2}$$

and hence

$$ARA = \frac{1}{W}$$

and

$$RRA = 1$$

The *ARA* function is then a decreasing function and the *RRA* function is constant. The logarithmic utility function is therefore consistent with the behaviour of a risk-averse investor.

Markowitz nevertheless chose the quadratic utility function for his model because it enables an expression that only uses the first two moments of the return distribution to be obtained. This greatly simplifies the problem posed and enables a mean–variance approach to be used to determine the optimal portfolio, as we shall explain below.

3.2   THE MARKOWITZ MODEL

Markowitz introduced a new concept that involved considering the portfolio as a whole, whereas previously investors had been interested in securities on an individual basis. It therefore considerably modified the practice of investment methods. Within the framework of this approach, the role of financial analysts nevertheless remains essential, since they provide the evaluation of the data used by the model. The Markowitz theory does not speak of efficient markets, but of efficient portfolios. An efficient portfolio is defined as a portfolio with minimal risk for a given return, or, equivalently, as the portfolio with the highest return for a given level of risk. The complete set of these portfolios forms the efficient frontier, which constitutes the convex envelope of all the portfolios that can be produced. Each investor uses his own forecasts and deduces his efficient frontier from these. Two investors who use different forecasts will not therefore have the same efficient frontier. We shall see in Chapter 4 that we only consider that all investors make the same forecasts within the framework of the CAPM.

The Markowitz model is based on the following assumptions. Individuals construct their portfolios in order to maximise the expected utility of their terminal wealth. Their utility function is an increasing function of their wealth and they are risk averse. They make their choice based only on the first two moments of the random distribution of their wealth: the expectation and the variance. Since the final wealth is determined by the return on the investment, it is therefore equivalent to basing it on the expected portfolio return and the variance of the portfolio return. The expected utility of an individual's terminal wealth is therefore a function of the mean and the variance of the portfolio return. Portfolios that result from maximising the investor's utility are, by definition, efficient portfolios.

The Markowitz approach is described as a mean–variance approach because it only takes those two parameters, mean return and return variance, into account, i.e. the first two moments of their distribution, to characterise the investor's portfolio. This is the same as assuming that higher order moments are null. This is only respected if the returns are normally distributed or if the investor's utility function is quadratic. The mean–variance approach is therefore based on a restrictive assumption.

The expected return of the portfolio is measured by the mean return. The risk, which corresponds to the uncertainty of obtaining the return, is measured by the variance. This measure of risk is not the one that best corresponds to the investors' viewpoint, because the risk of obtaining a result that is above average is considered in the same way as the risk of obtaining a result that is below average. Investors have a skewed approach to risk. They are only worried about the risk of below-average returns. Moreover, Markowitz proposed semi-variance as a good measure of risk in his article, but finally chose variance for practical implementation reasons. The variance facilitates simple modelling. It is also a good measure of risk under the assumption that returns are distributed normally, an assumption that is respected over a short time horizon. Over a longer time period, it can be useful to consider the risk of loss (shortfall risk). This notion was defined in Chapter 2.

3.2.1 Formulation of the model

Since a portfolio is a linear combination of assets, its expected return and variance are expressed as a function of its composition, or

$$E(R_P) = \sum_{i=1}^{n} x_i E(R_i)$$

$$\text{var}(R_P) = \sum_{i=1}^{n} \sum_{j=1}^{n} x_i x_j \text{cov}(R_i, R_j)$$

where

x_i denotes the proportion of asset i held in the portfolio;
$E(R_i)$ denotes the expected return of asset i; and
$\text{cov}(R_i, R_j)$ denotes the covariance between asset i and asset j.

The variance expression reveals the usefulness of diversification in reducing risk thanks to the correlation that exists between asset returns.

To achieve optimal diversification, Markowitz developed a mathematical portfolio selection model. This model enabled him to find the composition of all the portfolios that corresponded to the efficiency criterion he had defined, for a given set of securities, and thereby to construct the corresponding efficient frontier. Taking the definition of portfolio return and portfolio risk into account, the model involves minimising the variance for a given return or maximising the return for a given variance.

In its simplest version, the model is written as follows:

$$\text{minimise var}(R_P)$$

under the following conditions:

$$E(R_P) = E$$

$$\sum_{i=1}^{n} x_i = 1$$

The efficient frontier calculation involves finding the weightings of the assets that make up each portfolio. When there are no constraints, this problem is solved easily by using the Lagrange multiplier method. Appendix 3.1 presents the resolution method developed by Merton (1972).

We can define more elaborate models by adding linear constraints on the proportions of assets to hold, in particular non-negativity constraints. Elton and Gruber (1995) present the different cases in detail. In the presence of constraints, the exact methods for solving the problem use quadratic programming algorithms and the calculations can be time-consuming. We will come to that point in Section 3.3. We shall then see, in Section 3.4, that there are simplified resolution methods.

We should mention that all the points on the efficient frontier can be obtained with the help of two efficient portfolios only. Every portfolio on the efficient frontier can be written in the form of a linear combination of two distinct portfolios that are situated on the frontier. This result[6] is known as Black's theorem (1972). The theorem has interesting applications in the realm of mutual funds. Investors who wish to hold an efficient mean–variance portfolio can achieve this by spreading their investment over two efficient mutual funds. The risk/return combination is determined by the relative share attributed to each fund. Black's theorem is described as being a separation theorem because, following this principle, the selection of the investor's portfolio results from two successive stages. The individual securities are initially combined in order to form two funds that enable the whole of the efficient frontier to be generated, and the investor then chooses the allocation between the two funds.

3.2.2   Choosing a particular portfolio on the efficient frontier

The choice of a particular point on the efficient frontier is a function of the utility of each investor and the investor's aversion to risk. The investor chooses a portfolio that is at the point of tangent between the efficient frontier and the indifference curve. The portfolio is obtained by maximising the expectation of a function of his wealth's utility. We have seen that quadratic utility functions are often chosen because their expected utility is only expressed as a function of the portfolio's mean and variance.

The problem therefore involves maximising

$$U(R_P) = E(R_P) - 1/2\lambda \, \text{var}(R_P)$$

where λ denotes the investor's aversion to risk. The higher is λ, the more the investor is risk averse. As soon as λ is set, the investor's optimal portfolio is uniquely characterised.

The aversion to risk is difficult to define and can be characterised by the notion of shortfall constraints. This approach, which was presented in Farrell (1997), results from the work of Henriksson and Leibowitz (1989). The notion of "safety first" presented by Elton and Gruber (1995) is equivalent. It actually involves limiting the risk of bad occurrences. To do that, we

---

[6] For a demonstration of this result, see Chapter 7 of Briys and Viala (1995).

can define several criteria. The first criterion states that the best portfolio is the one that has the lowest probability of falling below a target return. The second criterion is to choose the portfolio that maximises the floor value of the return, with the constraint that the probability of falling below that floor should be lower than a target value. The third criterion is to choose the portfolio with the maximal expected return, with the constraint that the probability of falling below a floor value should be lower than a target value.

3.2.3 Impact of transaction costs when determining the optimal portfolio

The model developed by Markowitz does not take transaction costs into account. These costs nevertheless have a significant impact on portfolio performance. An active manager who plans to modify a portfolio periodically, to adhere to the new asset allocation proposed by the Markowitz model, should only reallocate the portfolio if the benefit procured by the modification outweighs the costs generated by the requisite transactions.

Transaction costs are difficult to estimate because they are not fixed. It is not in fact possible to know their exact value until the security trade has taken place. The costs can be broken down into three terms:

1. The commission, which is the tax per security paid to execute the transaction. This component is the lowest and the easiest to evaluate.
2. The differential between the requested price and the offered price (bid/ask spread), which is the cost inherent in trading the security. It cannot be known precisely until the transaction has taken place.
3. The liquidity or market impact cost, which is the additional cost of trading several securities compared with the cost of trading a single security. This last term is difficult to estimate because the two situations can never be observed at the same time.

For want of being able to value transaction costs precisely, we can give them a mean value based on historical observations. A result that is correct on average can be obtained by using the same value for all securities. A figure of 2% per security is considered to be a reasonable value.

To optimise the portfolio while taking transaction costs into account, one simply modifies the utility function in the following way:

$$U(R_P) = E(R_P) - 1/2\lambda \, \mathrm{var}(R_P) - TC$$

where TC denotes the amount of the transaction costs.

Introducing a penalty on the transaction costs into the utility function enables us to avoid selecting portfolios that would lead to a turnover that would be too high compared with the initial portfolio. The higher the chosen value of TC, the less the portfolio will evolve. If the TC value chosen is zero, then the optimal portfolio given by the model is independent of the transactions carried out to obtain it.

3.2.4 International diversification and currency risk[7]

International diversification can be useful in reducing risk through diversification because it enables the universe of securities to be enlarged. By investing in international assets that

---

[7] For a more detailed approach, see Fontaine (1997), Chapter 11 of Farrell (1997) and Chapter 26 of Elton and Gruber (1995).

have a low correlation with domestic assets, we can improve portfolio performance. However, the additional risks, such as currency risk or political risk, must be taken into account. As long as the portfolio is broadly diversified, the risk of an international portfolio is lower than that of a national portfolio. The efficient frontier of portfolios that invest in international assets dominates that of portfolios that only invest in domestic assets. In certain cases it is nevertheless useful to implement hedging against currency risk, the cost of which will be taken off the portfolio return.

3.3   EFFICIENT FRONTIER CALCULATION ALGORITHM

In Section 3.2, we discussed the Markowitz problem for the simple case where the proportions of assets held in the portfolios are not subject to any constraints. In practice, constraints frequently exist. For example, when short selling is not authorised, it is necessary to assume that all the assets have positive weights. We could also wish to limit the amount invested per security in order to ensure a certain amount of portfolio diversification. It is therefore essential to be able to integrate these types of constraint into the resolution methods.

Generally speaking, the constraints are written as follows:

$$a_i \leq x_i \leq b_i, \quad i = 1, \ldots, n$$

The impossibility of short selling corresponds to a specific case where

$$a_i = 0 \quad \text{and} \quad b_i = 1, \quad i = 1, \ldots, n$$

In his 1952 article, Markowitz proposed an algorithm, called the critical line algorithm, which allowed the composition of efficient frontier portfolios to be determined when the proportions of assets are subject to constraints. Sharpe gave a description of this algorithm in a publication in 1970. This is the earliest exact resolution method with constraints.

3.3.1   The Markowitz–Sharpe critical line algorithm[8]

We only present the principles of the resolution method here. The interested reader should consult the Reference list at the end of the chapter.

We first define the investor's objective function, as a function of the λ parameter, which measures the investor's aversion to risk. By varying λ, we obtain the characterisation of the complete efficient frontier. In the absence of constraints, the resolution is achieved by defining the Lagrangian associated with the problem and equating all its partial derivatives to zero. We thus obtain a linear system for which the resolution gives, for each value of λ, the proportions of the optimal portfolio being sought. If there are constraints on the proportions of assets, then for each value of λ, the solution will contain x_i values that will be equal to their lower limit, x_i values that will be located between their lower limit and their upper limit and x_i values that will have reached their upper limit. These variables will have down, in and up status, respectively.

Instead of equating all the partial derivatives of the Lagrangian to zero, we now assume that the derivatives are strictly positive compared with the variables with down status, and strictly negative compared with variables with up status. This is a specific case of the Kühn–Tucker conditions. Assuming that the status of each variable is known, it is easy to write the system of linear equations that allows the solution to the problem to be calculated. The problem actually

---

[8] A detailed presentation is given in Chapter 4 of Broquet and van den Berg (1992).

involves determining the status of each of the variables. The status depends on the value of λ. For each variable there is a critical value of λ for which the status of the variable changes. This value is calculated according to the parameters of the problem. We can then sequence the critical λ obtained for all the variables. The resolution algorithm involves giving an initial status to the variables in order to calculate a first solution that is valid up to the first critical λ. We then proceed sequentially by carrying out the necessary modifications each time a variable changes status. The portfolios that correspond to the critical λ are called "corner" portfolios. They are sufficient for calculating the whole efficient frontier.

3.3.2   Other algorithms

The main difficulty presented by the resolution of the Markowitz problem is the time required to calculate and invert the correlation matrix. At the time when Markowitz developed his model, this posed an even greater problem because the processing power of calculators was limited.

Among the different algorithms proposed for solving the Markowitz problem, we should mention the Wolfe method (1959). This is an exact resolution method that enables problems that use linear constraints on the weightings of assets to be handled. The principle involves reducing the initial quadratic problem to a linear problem, which can then be resolved by the simplex method, the advantage being to reduce the calculation time.

Research has also been directed at the use of gradient methods to resolve the problem. The advantage of these methods is that they allow large dimension problems to be resolved without storing the matrix completely. The reader wishing to obtain more detailed information on optimisation methods, can refer, for example, to Boots (1964) and Luenberger (1984).

The most interesting methods in terms of saving calculation time are those that are based on a simplification of the model. Sharpe worked on this subject and developed his empirical market model. This model allows the number of calculations to be reduced by proposing a simplified asset correlation structure. Furthermore, quadratic resolution methods are very sensitive to the quality of data (cf. Michaud, 1989) and do not always enable us to interpret the result obtained or understand why certain securities have been selected instead of others. A simpler optimisation method is described in Elton and Gruber (1995). This method is also based on Sharpe's market model. Before describing the simplified portfolio selection models, we first present the market model from which they were developed.

3.4   SIMPLIFIED PORTFOLIO MODELLING METHODS

3.4.1   Sharpe's single-index model[9]

The algorithms presented above are evidence of the extensive calculations required to construct the efficient frontier. Sharpe (1963) studied Markowitz's research and worked on the possibility of simplifying the calculations in order to develop the practical use of the model. The time needed to calculate the complete correlation matrix was an obstacle to the implementation of the model. Sharpe therefore postulated that the asset returns were made up of a factor that was common to all assets and a component that was unique for each security. Studies showed that the best explicative factor was the return of the market as a whole. This model is called the empirical market model or Sharpe's single-index model. It has no theoretical basis, unlike the

---

[9] Cf. Chapter 5 of Broquet and van den Berg (1992), Chapter 5 of Fabozzi (1995), Chapter 3 of Farrell (1997) and Chapter 7 of Elton and Gruber (1995).

CAPM which will be presented in the next chapter. This model does not contain the notion of equilibrium and does not make any particular assumption about the market or about investors. It only proposes a simplified view. This principle was used again in Arbitrage Pricing Theory (APT) which we will discuss in Chapter 6. The model is also used for testing the CAPM relationship empirically: it is used to estimate the beta empirically. It therefore allows the theory to be rendered operational.

3.4.1.1   Formulation of the model

Variations in asset returns have a linear dependency on factors that are common to the whole market and factors that are unique to each firm. The factors that are common to the whole market are represented by a market index. The empirical market model is therefore written as follows:

$$R_{it} = \alpha_i + \beta_i R_{Mt} + \varepsilon_{it}$$

where

R_{it} denotes the return on asset i;
R_{Mt} denotes the return on the market index;
ε_{it} denotes the specific return on asset i; and
α_i and β_i are the coefficients to be determined.

The coefficients of the line, α_i and β_i, are obtained by linear regression of the market returns on the asset returns for the same period. The method used is that of the ordinary least squares. The beta coefficient is given by

$$\beta_i = \frac{\text{cov}(R_{it}, R_{Mt})}{\text{var}(R_{Mt})}$$

Following on from the model definition, the residual terms ε_{it} are non-correlated with the market return. The total risk of an asset is therefore broken down into a term for systematic risk (or market risk) and a term for non-systematic risk (or diversifiable risk), or

$$\text{var}(R_{it}) = \beta_i^2 \, \text{var}(R_{Mt}) + \text{var}(\varepsilon_{it})$$

This relationship, when applied to a portfolio containing n securities in the same proportions, highlights the usefulness of diversification in reducing risk. The risk of this portfolio is written as follows:

$$\text{var}(R_{Pt}) = \beta_P^2 \, \text{var}(R_{Mt}) + \frac{1}{n^2} \sum_{i=1}^{n} \text{var}(\varepsilon_{it})$$

The second term of this relationship tends towards 0 for a sufficiently large n. Therefore, the risk of a broadly diversified portfolio is only made up of the market risk.

For all portfolios, the correlation coefficient between the index and the portfolio, raised to the square, gives the percentage of the total variance of the portfolio returns that is explained by the index movements.

3.4.1.2   Application to the resolution of the Markowitz problem

The use of this model allows the Markowitz problem correlation matrix calculation to be simplified considerably. We have:

$$\text{cov}(R_{it}, R_{jt}) = \sigma_{ij} = \beta_i \beta_j \sigma_M^2, \quad \text{if } i \neq j$$

since $\text{cov}(\varepsilon_i, \varepsilon_j) = 0$, the residual returns are non-correlated, and:

$$\text{var}(R_{it}) = \sigma_i^2 = \beta_i^2 \sigma_M^2 + \text{var}(\varepsilon_{it})$$

Instead of having to calculate the $n(n+1)/2$ terms from the complete matrix, only $(2n+1)$ terms remain to be determined, or

$$\beta_i, \quad i = 1, \ldots, n$$

$$\text{var}(\varepsilon_{it}) = \sigma_{\varepsilon_i}^2, \quad i = 1, \ldots, n$$

$$\text{var}(R_{Mt}) = \sigma_M^2$$

The α_i, β_i and $\sigma_{\varepsilon_i}^2$ terms are estimated through regression. The variance–covariance matrix is written as follows:

$$
\begin{pmatrix}
\beta_1^2 \sigma_m^2 + \sigma_{\varepsilon_1}^2 & \cdots & \beta_1 \beta_n \sigma_m^2 \\
\beta_2 \beta_1 \sigma_m^2 & \cdots & \cdot \\
\cdot & \cdots & \cdot \\
\cdot & \cdots & \cdot \\
\cdot & \cdots & \beta_{n-1} \beta_n \sigma_m^2 \\
\beta_n \beta_1 \sigma_m^2 & \cdots & \beta_n^2 \sigma_m^2 + \sigma_{\varepsilon_n}^2
\end{pmatrix}
= \sigma_m^2
\begin{pmatrix}
\beta_1^2 & \cdots & \beta_1 \beta_n \\
\beta_2 \beta_1 & \cdots & \cdot \\
\cdot & \cdots & \cdot \\
\cdot & \cdots & \cdot \\
\cdot & \cdots & \beta_{n-1} \beta_n \\
\beta_n \beta_1 & \cdots & \beta_n^2
\end{pmatrix}
+
\begin{pmatrix}
\sigma_{\varepsilon_1}^2 & 0 & \cdots & 0 \\
0 & \sigma_{\varepsilon_2}^2 & \cdots & 0 \\
\cdot & \cdot & \cdots & \cdot \\
\cdot & \cdot & \cdots & \cdot \\
0 & \cdot & \cdots & \sigma_{\varepsilon_n}^2
\end{pmatrix}
$$

If we consider the specific case of a broadly diversified portfolio, the value of its risk is simply

$$\sigma_P^2 = \beta_P^2 \sigma_M^2$$

or

$$\sigma_P = \beta_P \sigma_M = \sum_{i=1}^{n} x_i \beta_i \sigma_M$$

and its expected return is given by

$$E(R_P) = \alpha_P + \beta_P E(R_M) = \sum_{i=1}^{n} x_i \alpha_i + \sum_{i=1}^{n} x_i \beta_i E(R_M)$$

since the residual returns have a null mean. We therefore come back to a completely linear problem.

3.4.2   Multi-index models[10]

These models are a generalisation of the single-index model. They will be developed in more detail in Chapter 6 within the framework of factor models. In this chapter we shall only discuss

---

[10] Cf. Chapter 4 of Farrell (1997) and Chapter 8 of Elton and Gruber (1995).

their application to portfolio modelling. The principle is the same as in the case of a single-index model, namely to obtain a simplified representation of the assets' variance–covariance matrix. The covariances between assets are evaluated with the help of the covariances between indices. The multi-index models enable us to obtain a more accurate result than the single-index model, while still keeping the number of calculations to a reasonable level. This is also an empirical model.

If we assume that the returns are explained with the help of K indices, then the model is written as follows:

$$R_{it} = a_i + \sum_{k=1}^{K} b_{ik} I_{kt} + \varepsilon_{it}$$

By means of a rotation, it is always possible to come back to the case where indices are orthogonal, i.e. non-correlated between indices. The variance of an asset i is then written as follows:

$$\text{var}(R_{it}) = \sum_{k=1}^{K} b_{ik}^2 \, \text{var}(I_{kt}) + \text{var}(\varepsilon_{it})$$

and the covariance between two assets is written

$$\text{cov}(R_{it}, R_{jt}) = \sum_{k=1}^{K} b_{ik} b_{jk} \text{var}(I_{kt})$$

The number of terms to calculate to determine the variance–covariance matrix is now $kn + n + k$, or n betas for each of the k factors, n residual risks and k index variances. Since the value of k is always well below the value of n, these models enable the number of calculations to be reduced.

3.4.3　Simplified methods proposed by Elton and Gruber[11]

Elton and Gruber proposed techniques for determining optimal portfolios that give a better understanding of the choice of securities to be included in a portfolio. The calculations are easy to carry out and lead to similar results to those given by the Markowitz model with the complete matrix. These techniques also use the single-index model as their basis. The method is based on an optimal ranking of the assets, established with the help of the simplified correlation representation model. We determine a threshold in the list. All the securities located above the threshold will be part of the optimal portfolio. Those that are below the threshold will be excluded. The problem is to determine the value of the threshold. We subsequently determine the percentage to be assigned to each security, according to the characteristic parameters of each security and the value of the threshold.

The ratio used to rank the assets is given by

$$\frac{E(R_i) - R_F}{\beta_i}$$

---

[11] Cf. the appendix to Chapter 10 of Farrell (1997) and, for more details, Chapter 9 of Elton and Gruber (1995).

where

$E(R_i)$ denotes the expected return of asset i;
R_F denotes the risk-free rate; and
β_i denotes the beta of asset i defined by Sharpe's market model.

This is the return above the risk-free rate compared with the non-diversifiable risk. We will see in Chapter 4 that this quantity is called the Treynor ratio and is used to evaluate portfolio performance.

The ratio is calculated for all the assets from which the investor is liable to choose. The results are classified from the highest value to the lowest value. The higher the value of the ratio, the more desirable it is to hold the security in the portfolio. As a result, if a security is held in an optimal portfolio, then all the securities for which this ratio is higher are also held in the portfolio. In the same way, if a security is excluded from the portfolio, then all the securities with a lower ratio will also be excluded. There is therefore a threshold value above which we select securities, and below which we exclude them. This value is denoted by C^*. The procedure is therefore simple to implement, as long as we know the value of C^*. We can then select the securities to include in the portfolio and calculate the proportions to hold.

C^* is calculated through an iterative procedure, by successively introducing the securities from the list into the portfolio and by calculating the C_i value associated with a portfolio containing i securities. C_i is expressed as follows:

$$C_i = \frac{\sigma_M^2 \sum_{j=1}^{i} \frac{(E(R_j) - R_F)\beta_j}{\text{var}(\varepsilon_j)}}{1 + \sigma_M^2 \sum_{j=1}^{i} \frac{\beta_j^2}{\text{var}(\varepsilon_j)}}$$

with the notation being the same as that used to present the single-index model.

We stop adding securities when the ratio associated with the candidate security is lower than the value of C_i that was calculated for the portfolio. At the end of this procedure we know the list of assets that will figure in the optimal portfolio. What remains is to determine the proportion to attribute to each of them. Denoting by x_i the proportion of asset i to hold, we have:

$$x_i = \frac{Z_i}{\sum_{j \in P} Z_j}$$

where

$$Z_i = \frac{\beta_i}{\text{var}(\varepsilon_i)} \left(\frac{E(R_i) - R_F}{\beta_i} - C^* \right)$$

An optimal portfolio can be constructed using this method with the simple help of a spreadsheet.

3.5 CONCLUSION

The Markowitz model certainly represents a considerable conceptual advance in the area of portfolio theory, even though it is not easy to use it to select assets. The use of simplified models for asset returns enables the calculation time to be reduced. In addition, studies have shown that the results obtained with the index models were close to those obtained with the traditional Markowitz model. The Markowitz model is actually more commonly used to choose the allocation between the different asset classes in a portfolio, rather than for stock picking. The number of asset classes is limited and leads to a reasonable number of calculations. At this stage, we also wish to underline the extreme difficulty in estimating expected returns from historical data. The optimal nature of the estimators can be called into question and, as Merton (1980) and Jorion (1985) have shown, the statistical noise is significant within the framework of a final sample of data. Although the covariance estimation converges easily, that of the expected returns is very sensitive to the choice of historical data used. The Markowitz model also contains the foundations of the CAPM[12], the reference model for valuing assets, which will be presented in Chapter 4, and which contains all the basic elements of performance measurement theory.

APPENDIX 3.1   RESOLUTION OF THE MARKOWITZ PROBLEM

In this appendix we present a calculation method for determining the composition of portfolios on the efficient frontier, when there are no constraints on the proportions of assets. This method is developed in Merton (1972).

We take n risky securities. Let $E(R_i)$ be the expected return of security i, σ_i^2 be the variance of its returns and σ_{ij} be the covariance between the returns of security i and security j. Since the securities are risky, the variances are all non-null. We additionally assume that no security can be expressed as a linear combination of the other securities. This ensures that the variance–covariance matrix associated with the n securities, and written Ω, is non-singular, a necessary assumption to be able to invert it.

The efficient frontier associated with these n securities is defined as the location of the feasible portfolios with the smallest variance for a given expected return. We denote by x_i the proportion of the portfolio invested in asset i. Let $E(R_P)$ be the expected portfolio return and σ_P^2 its variance. The efficient frontier is the set of portfolios that are a solution to the following problem of minimisation under constraints:

$$\text{minimise } 1/2\sigma_P^2$$

under the following conditions:

$$\sigma_P^2 = \sum_{i=1}^{n}\sum_{j=1}^{n} x_i x_j \sigma_{ij}$$

$$E(R_P) = \sum_{i=1}^{n} x_i E(R_i)$$

$$\sum_{i=1}^{n} x_i = 1$$

It should be noted that there is no restriction on the x_i. The solutions could therefore contain proportions of negative assets, which corresponds to a situation where short selling is authorised.

---

[12] An interesting presentation showing how Sharpe's model leads on from the Markowitz model is given in Miller (1999).

We define the Lagrangian associated with the problem, or

$$L = \sum_{i=1}^{n}\sum_{j=1}^{n} x_i x_j \sigma_{ij} + \gamma_1 \left(E(R_P) - \sum_{i=1}^{n} x_i E(R_i) \right) + \gamma_2 \left(1 - \sum_{i=1}^{n} x_i \right)$$

where γ_1 and γ_2 are Lagrange multipliers.

A condition that is respected by the solution to the problem is to cancel the first derivatives of L compared with each variable. Let

$$\frac{\partial L}{\partial x_i} = \sum_{j=1}^{n} x_j \sigma_{ij} - \gamma_1 E(R_i) - \gamma_2 = 0, \quad i = 1, \ldots, n \tag{A.1}$$

$$\frac{\partial L}{\partial \gamma_1} = E(R_P) - \sum_{i=1}^{n} x_i E(R_i) = 0 \tag{A.2}$$

$$\frac{\partial L}{\partial \gamma_2} = 1 - \sum_{i=1}^{n} x_i = 0 \tag{A.3}$$

Since Ω was assumed to be non-singular, the x_i that respect these conditions minimise var(R_P) and are unique. Equation (A.1) defines a linear system of n equations, where the unknown n are x_i, $i = 1, \ldots, n$. If we denote the elements of Ω^{-1}, the inverse of matrix Ω, as v_{ij}, then the system solutions are given by

$$x_k = \gamma_1 \sum_{j=1}^{n} v_{kj} E(R_j) + \gamma_2 \sum_{j=1}^{n} v_{kj}, \quad k = 1, \ldots, n \tag{A.4}$$

To use (A.2) and (A.3) we multiply, on the one hand, (A.4) by $E(R_k)$ and we sum from $k = 1$ to n, or

$$\sum_{k=1}^{n} x_k E(R_k) = \gamma_1 \sum_{k=1}^{n}\sum_{j=1}^{n} v_{kj} E(R_j) E(R_k) + \gamma_2 \sum_{k=1}^{n}\sum_{j=1}^{n} v_{kj} E(R_k), \quad k = 1, \ldots, n \tag{A.5}$$

and, on the other hand, we sum (A.4) from $k = 1$ to n, or

$$\sum_{k=1}^{n} x_k = \gamma_1 \sum_{k=1}^{n}\sum_{j=1}^{n} v_{kj} E(R_j) + \gamma_2 \sum_{k=1}^{n}\sum_{j=1}^{n} v_{kj}, \quad k = 1, \ldots, n \tag{A.6}$$

In order to pare down the notation, we define the following constants:

$$A = \sum_{k=1}^{n}\sum_{j=1}^{n} v_{kj} E(R_j)$$

$$B = \sum_{k=1}^{n}\sum_{j=1}^{n} v_{kj} E(R_j) E(R_k)$$

$$C = \sum_{k=1}^{n}\sum_{j=1}^{n} v_{kj}$$

From (A.2), (A.3), (A.5) and (A.6), we obtain the following linear equation system:

$$E(R_P) = B\gamma_1 + A\gamma_2$$
$$1 = A\gamma_1 + C\gamma_2$$

which enables γ_1 and γ_2 to be calculated:

$$\gamma_1 = \frac{CE(R_P) - A}{BC - A^2}$$

$$\gamma_2 = \frac{B - AE(R_P)}{BC - A^2}$$

By replacing γ_1 and γ_2 with their value in (A.4), we finally obtain:

$$x_k = \frac{E(R_P) \sum_{j=1}^{n} v_{kj}(CE(R_j) - A) + \sum_{j=1}^{n} v_{kj}(B - AE(R_j))}{BC - A^2}, \quad k = 1, \ldots, n$$

which completely characterises the composition of the smallest variance portfolio for a given level of return.

We can then define the efficient frontier equation, i.e. the relationship between σ_P^2 and $E(R_P)$. To do that, we use (A.1), multiplied by x_i and summed from $i = 1$ to n, which gives

$$\sum_{i=1}^{n} \sum_{j=1}^{n} x_i x_j \sigma_{ij} = \gamma_1 \sum_{i=1}^{n} x_i E(R_i) + \gamma_2 \sum_{i=1}^{n} x_i$$

or, by replacing with the relationships that define the initial problem:

$$\sigma_P^2 = \gamma_1 E(R_P) + \gamma_2$$

By now replacing γ_1 and γ_2 with their value, we obtain:

$$\sigma_P^2 = \frac{CE^2(R_P) - 2AE(R_P) + B}{BC - A^2}$$

which is the equation of a parabola.

The extremum of the parabola defines the minimum variance portfolio. It is the point that cancels the first derivative of σ_P^2 compared with $E(R_P)$, or

$$\frac{d\sigma_P^2}{dE(R_P)} = \frac{2(CE(R_P) - A)}{BC - A^2} = 0$$

hence:

$$E(R_{P_{min}}) = \frac{A}{C}$$

By replacing in the expression for σ_P^2, we calculate:

$$\sigma_{P_{min}}^2 = \frac{1}{C}$$

We can express $E(R_P)$ as a function of σ_P in order to represent the efficient frontier on the $(\sigma_P, E(R_P))$ plane. We then obtain a hyperbola characterised by

$$E(R_P) = \frac{A}{C} \pm \frac{1}{C}\sqrt{(BC - A^2)C\left(\sigma_P^2 - \frac{1}{C}\right)}$$

Only the upper part of the hyperbola defines the efficient frontier, which we can also write with the help of the minimum variance portfolio characteristics, or

$$E(R_P) = E\left(R_{P_{\min}}\right) + \frac{1}{C}\sqrt{(BC - A^2)C\left(\sigma_P^2 - \sigma_{P_{\min}}^2\right)}$$

BIBLIOGRAPHY

Black, F., "Capital Market Equilibrium with Restricted Borrowing", *Journal of Business*, vol. 45, 1972, pp. 444–454.

Boots, J.C.G., *Quadratic Programming. Algorithms, Anomalies, Applications*, North-Holland, 1964.

Briys, E. and Viala, P., *Eléments de théorie financière*, Nathan, 1995.

Broquet, C. and van den Berg, A., *Gestion de portefeuille – Actions, Obligations, Options*, 2nd edn, De Boeck Université, 1992.

Charest, G., "Rendement, risque et portefeuille", in *Encyclopédie des marchés financiers*, Economica, 1997, pp. 1608–1660.

Copeland, T.E. and Weston, J.F., *Financial Theory and Corporate Policy*, 3rd edn, Addison-Wesley, 1988.

Elton, E.J. and Gruber, M.J., *Modern Portfolio Theory and Investment Analysis*, 5th edn, Wiley, 1995.

Fabozzi, F.J., *Investment Management*, Prentice Hall International Editions, 1995.

Fama, E.F. and Miller, M., *The Theory of Finance*, Holt, Rinehart & Winston, 1972.

Farrell, Jr J.L., *Portfolio Management, Theory and Application*, 2nd edn, McGraw-Hill, 1997.

Fontaine, P., "Modèles d'arbitrage et multifactoriels internationaux", in *Encyclopédie des marchés financiers*, Economica, 1997, pp. 1164–1185.

Henriksson, R.D. and Leibowitz, M.L., "Portfolio Optimization with Shortfall Constraints: A Confidence-limit Approach to Maintaining Downside Risk", *Financial Analysts Journal*, March–April 1989.

Jorion, P., "International Portfolio Diversification with Estimation Risk", *Journal of Business*, vol. 28, 1985, pp. 259–278.

Luenberger, D.G., *Linear and non Linear Programming*, 2nd edn, Addison-Wesley, 1984.

Markowitz, H., "Portfolio Selection", *Journal of Finance*, March 1952, pp. 77–91.

Markowitz, H., *Portfolio Selection: Efficient Diversification of Investments*, Wiley, 1959.

Merton, R.C., "An Analytic Derivation of the Efficient Portfolio Frontier", *Journal of Financial and Quantitative Analysis*, vol. 7, 1972, pp. 1851–1872.

Merton, R.C., "On Estimating the Expected Return on the Market: An Exploratory Investigation", *Journal of Financial Economics*, no. 8, 1980, pp. 323–362.

Michaud, R., "The Markowitz Optimization Enigma: Is Optimized Optimal?", *Financial Analysts Journal*, 1989, pp. 31–42.

Miller, M.H., "The History of Finance: An Eyewitness Account", *Journal of Portfolio Management*, vol. 25, no. 4, summer 1999, pp. 95–101.

Sharpe, W.F., "A Simplified Model for Portfolio Analysis", *Management Science*, January 1963, pp. 277–293.

Sharpe, W.F., *Portfolio Theory and Capital Markets*, McGraw-Hill, 1970.

Von Neuman, J. and Morgenstern, O., *Theory of Games and Economic Behavior*, Princeton University Press, 1947.

Wolfe, P., "The Simplex Method for Quadratic Programming", *Econometrica*, vol. 27, no. 3, July 1959.

4
The Capital Asset Pricing Model and its Application to Performance Measurement[1]

In Chapter 3 we described Markowitz's portfolio analysis model and presented the empirical market model. The latter was developed by Sharpe in order to simplify the calculations involved in the Markowitz model and thereby render it more operational. The next step in financial modelling was to study the influence of the behaviour of investors, taken as a whole, on asset prices. What resulted was a theory of asset valuation in an equilibrium situation, drawing together risk and return.

The model that was developed is called the Capital Asset Pricing Model (CAPM). Several authors have contributed to this model. Sharpe (1963, 1964) is considered to be the forerunner and received the Nobel Prize in 1990. Treynor (1961) independently developed a model that was quite similar to Sharpe's. Finally, Mossin (1966), Lintner (1965, 1969) and Black (1972) made contributions a few years later.

This model was the first to introduce the notion of risk into the valuation of assets. It evaluates the asset return in relation to the market return and the sensitivity of the security to the market. It is the source of the first risk-adjusted performance measures. Unlike the empirical market line model, the CAPM is based on a set of axioms and concepts that resulted from financial theory.

The first part of this chapter describes the successive stages that produced the model, together with the different versions of the model that were developed subsequently. The following sections discuss the use of the model in measuring portfolio performance.

4.1 THE CAPM

4.1.1 Context in which the model was developed

4.1.1.1 Investor behaviour when there is a risk-free asset

Markowitz studied the case of an investor who acted in isolation and only possessed risky assets. This investor constructs the risky assets' efficient frontier from forecasts on expected returns, variance and covariance, and then selects the optimal portfolio, which corresponds to his/her level of risk aversion on the frontier.

We always assume that the Markowitz assumptions are respected. Investors are therefore risk averse and seek to maximise the expected utility of their wealth at the end of the period. They choose their portfolios by considering the first two moments of the return distribution only, i.e. the expected return and the variance. They only consider one investment period and that period is the same for everyone.

---

[1] Numerous publications describe the CAPM and its application to performance measurement. Notable inclusions are Broquet and van den Berg (1992), Fabozzi (1995), Elton and Gruber (1995) and Farrell (1997).

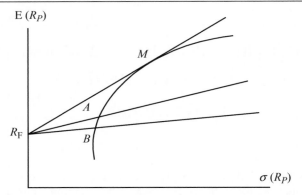

Figure 4.1   Construction of the efficient frontier in presence of a risk-free asset

Let us now consider a case where there is a risk-free asset. An asset is said to be risk-free when it allows a pre-determined level of income to be obtained with certainty. We shall write this asset's rate of return as R_F. Its risk is nil by definition. The investor can now spread his wealth between a portfolio of risky assets, from the efficient frontier, and this risk-free asset.

We take x to be the proportion of wealth invested in the risk-free asset. The remainder, or $(1 - x)$, is invested in the portfolio of risky assets, denoted as A. The expected return of the investor's portfolio P is obtained as a linear combination of the expected returns of its component parts, or

$$E(R_P) = x R_F + (1 - x)E(R_A)$$

and its risk is simply equal to

$$\sigma_P = (1 - x)\sigma_A$$

since the variance of the risk-free asset is nil and its covariance with the risky portfolio is also nil.

We can then eliminate x from the two equations and establish the following relationship:

$$E(R_P) = R_F + \left(\frac{E(R_A) - R_F}{\sigma_A}\right)\sigma_P \tag{4.1}$$

This is the equation of a straight line linking point R_F and point A. To be more explicit, let us see what happens graphically (see Figure 4.1). If we consider the representation of the Markowitz frontier on the plane $(\sigma_P, E(R_P))$, the point corresponding to the risk-free asset is located on the y-axis. We can therefore trace straight lines from R_F that link up with the different points on the efficient frontier.[2] The equation of all these lines is equation (4.1). Among this set of lines there is one that dominates all the others and also dominates the frontier of risky assets at every point. This is the only line that forms a tangent with the efficient frontier. The point of tangent is denoted as M.

The $R_F M$ line represents all the linear combinations of the efficient portfolio of risky assets M with a risk-free investment. It characterises the efficient frontier in the case where one of

---

[2] We assume that the return R_F is lower than the return on the minimal variance portfolio (located at the summit of the hyperbola). Otherwise, the principle that a risky investment must procure higher revenue than a risk-free investment would not be respected.

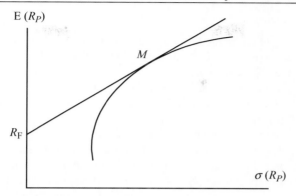

$E(R_P)$

M

R_F

$\sigma(R_P)$

Figure 4.2   Efficient frontier in presence of a risk-free asset

the assets is risk-free. The introduction of a risk-free asset therefore simplifies the result, since the efficient frontier is now a straight line. In addition, the risk of the portfolios is reduced for a given return, since the straight line dominates the efficient frontier of risky assets at every point. Investors therefore benefit from having such an asset in their portfolio.

The choice of a particular portfolio on the line depends on the investor's level of risk aversion. The more risk averse the investor, the greater the proportion of the portfolio that he/she will invest in the risk-free asset. If the opposite is true, then the investor puts most of the portfolio into risky assets. Two cases are possible. (1) The investor has a limitless capacity to borrow, i.e. to invest negatively in the risk-free asset, in order to invest a sum that is greater than his wealth in risky assets. In this case, the efficient frontier is the line to the right of point M. (2) The borrowing is limited, in which case the efficient frontier is a straight line up to the point of tangency with the risky asset frontier and is then the curved portion of the risky asset frontier, since the segment of the line located above no longer corresponds to feasible portfolios (Figure 4.2).

The previous study assumed that the borrowing interest rate was equal to the lending interest rate. This assumes that the markets are frictionless, i.e. that the assets are infinitely divisible and that there are no taxes or transaction costs. This assumption will also be used in developing equilibrium theory.

It has therefore been established that when there is a risk-free asset, the investor's optimal portfolio P is always made up of portfolio M with x proportion of risky assets and proportion $(1 - x)$ of the risk-free asset. This shows that the investment decision can be divided into two parts: first, the choice of the optimal risky asset portfolio and secondly the choice of the split between the risk-free asset and the risky portfolio, depending on the desired level of risk. This result, which comes from Tobin (1958), is known as the two-fund separation theorem.

This theorem, and Black's theorem, which was mentioned in Chapter 3, have important consequences for fund management. Showing that all efficient portfolios can be written in the form of a combination of a limited number of portfolios or investment funds made up of available securities greatly simplifies the problem of portfolio selection. The problem of allocating the investor's wealth then comes down to the choice of a linear combination of mutual funds.

The position of the optimal risky asset portfolio M has been defined graphically. We now establish its composition by reasoning in terms of equilibrium.

4.1.1.2   Equilibrium theory

Up until now we have only considered the case of an isolated investor. By now assuming that all investors have the same expectations concerning assets, they all then have the same return, variance and covariance values and construct the same efficient frontier of risky assets. In the presence of a risk-free asset, the reasoning employed for one investor is applied to all investors. The latter therefore all choose to divide their investment between the risk-free asset and the same risky asset portfolio M.

Now, for the market to be at equilibrium, all the available assets must be held in portfolios. The risky asset portfolio M, in which all investors choose to have a share, must therefore contain all the assets traded on the market in proportion to their stock market capitalisation. This portfolio is therefore the market portfolio. This result comes from Fama (1970).

In the presence of a risky asset, the efficient frontier that is common to all investors is the straight line of the following equation:

$$E(R_P) = R_F + \left(\frac{E(R_M) - R_F}{\sigma_M} \right) \sigma_P$$

This line links the risk and return of efficient portfolios linearly. It is known as the capital market line.

These results, associated with the notion of equilibrium, will now allow us to establish a relationship for individual securities.

4.1.2   Presentation of the CAPM

We now come to the CAPM itself (cf. Briys and Viala, 1995, and Sharpe, 1964). This model will help us to define an appropriate measure of risk for individual assets, and also to evaluate their prices while taking the risk into account. This notion of the "price" of risk is one of the essential contributions of the model.

The development of the model required a certain number of assumptions. These involve the Markowitz model assumptions on the one hand and assumptions that are necessary for market equilibrium on the other. Some of these assumptions may seem unrealistic, but later versions of the model, which we shall present below, allowed them to be scaled down. All of the assumptions are included below.

4.1.2.1   CAPM assumptions[3]

The CAPM assumptions are sometimes described in detail in the literature, and sometimes not, depending on how the model is presented. Jensen (1972a) formulated the assumptions with precision. The main assumptions are as follows:

1. Investors are risk averse and seek to maximise the expected utility of their wealth at the end of the period.
2. When choosing their portfolios, investors only consider the first two moments of return distribution: the expected return and the variance.
3. Investors only consider one investment period and that period is the same for all investors.

---

[3] These assumptions are described well in Chapter 5 of Fabozzi (1995), in Cobbaut (1997), in Elton and Gruber (1995) and in Farrell (1997), who clearly distinguishes between the Markowitz assumptions and the additional assumptions.

4. Investors have a limitless capacity to borrow and lend at the risk-free rate.
5. Information is accessible cost-free and is available simultaneously to all investors. All investors therefore have the same forecast return, variance and covariance expectations for all assets.
6. Markets are perfect: there are no taxes and no transaction costs. All assets are traded and are infinitely divisible.

4.1.2.2   Demonstration of the CAPM

The demonstration chosen is the one given by Sharpe (1964). See also Poncet *et al.* (1996). It is the simplest and the most intuitive, since it is based on graphical considerations.[4]

We take the risk-free asset and the market portfolio. These two points define the capital market line. When the market is at equilibrium, the prices of assets adjust so that all assets will be held by investors: supply is then equal to demand. In theory, therefore, the market portfolio is made up of all traded assets, in proportion to their market capitalisation, even though in practice we use the return on a stock exchange index as an approximation of the market return.

We now take any risky asset i. Asset i is located below the market line, which represents all efficient portfolios.

We define a portfolio P with a proportion x invested in asset i and a proportion $(1 - x)$ in the market portfolio. The expected return of portfolio P is given by

$$E(R_P) = xE(R_i) + (1 - x)E(R_M)$$

and its risk is given by

$$\sigma_P = \left[x^2 \sigma_i^2 + (1 - x)^2 \sigma_M^2 + 2x(1 - x)\sigma_{iM} \right]^{1/2}$$

where

σ_i^2 denotes the variance of the risky asset i;
σ_M^2 denotes the variance of the market portfolio; and
σ_{iM} denotes the covariance between asset i and the market portfolio.

By varying x, we construct the curve of all possible portfolios obtained by combining asset i and portfolio M. This curve goes through the two points i and M (see Figure 4.3).

The leading coefficient of the tangent to this curve at any point is given by

$$\frac{\partial E(R_P)}{\partial \sigma_P} = \frac{\partial E(R_P)/\partial x}{\partial \sigma_P/\partial x}$$

Now

$$\frac{\partial E(R_P)}{\partial x} = E(R_i) - E(R_M)$$

and

$$\frac{\partial \sigma_P}{\partial x} = \frac{2x\sigma_i^2 - 2\sigma_M^2(1 - x) + 2\sigma_{iM}(1 - 2x)}{2\sigma_P}$$

---

[4] The interested reader could refer to a more comprehensive demonstration in Chapter 9 of Briys and Viala (1995).

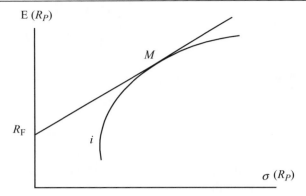

Figure 4.3 Curve of all portfolios made of the market portfolio and a risky asset

After simplifying, we obtain the following

$$\frac{\partial E(R_P)}{\partial \sigma_P} = \frac{(E(R_i) - E(R_M))\sigma_P}{x(\sigma_i^2 + \sigma_M^2 - 2\sigma_{iM}) + \sigma_{iM} - \sigma_M^2}$$

The equilibrium market portfolio already contains asset i since it contains all assets. Portfolio P is therefore made up of an excess of asset i, in proportion x, compared with the market portfolio. Since this excess must be nil at equilibrium, point M is characterised by $x = 0$ and $\sigma_P = \sigma_M$.

When the market is at equilibrium, the slope of the tangent to the efficient frontier at point M is thus given by

$$\frac{\partial E(R_P)}{\partial \sigma_P}(M) = \frac{(E(R_i) - E(R_M))\sigma_M}{\sigma_{iM} - \sigma_M^2}$$

Furthermore, the slope of the market line is given by

$$b = \frac{E(R_M) - R_F}{\sigma_M}$$

where σ_M denotes the standard deviation of the market portfolio.

At point M the tangent to the curve must be equal to the slope of the market line. Hence, we deduce the following relationship:

$$\frac{(E(R_i) - E(R_M))\sigma_M}{\sigma_{iM} - \sigma_M^2} = \frac{E(R_M) - R_F}{\sigma_M}$$

which can also be written as

$$E(R_i) = R_F + \frac{(E(R_M) - R_F)}{\sigma_M^2}\sigma_{iM}$$

The latter relationship characterises the CAPM. The line that is thereby defined is called the security market line. At equilibrium, all assets are located on this line.

This relationship means that at equilibrium the rate of return of every asset is equal to the rate of return of the risk-free asset plus a risk premium. The premium is equal to the price of the risk multiplied by the quantity of risk, using the CAPM terminology. The price of the risk is the difference between the expected rate of return for the market portfolio, and the return on the risk-free asset. The quantity of risk, which is called the beta, is defined by

$$\beta_i = \frac{\sigma_{iM}}{\sigma_M^2}$$

Beta is therefore equal to the covariance between the return on asset i and the return on the market portfolio, divided by the variance of the market portfolio. The risk-free asset therefore has a beta of zero, and the market portfolio has a beta of one. The beta thus defined is the one that already appeared in Sharpe's empirical market model.

By using the beta expression, the CAPM relationship is then written as follows:

$$E(R_i) = R_F + \beta_i(E(R_M) - R_F)$$

The CAPM has allowed us to establish that at equilibrium the returns on assets, less the risk-free rate, have a linear link to the return on the market portfolio, with the market portfolio being built according to Markowitz's principles.

This original version of the CAPM is based on assumptions that the financial markets do not completely respect. This first formula was followed by several other versions, which enabled the realities of the market to be taken into account to a greater degree. The different versions will be discussed in Section 4.1.3 below.

4.1.2.3 The contribution of the CAPM

The CAPM established a theory for valuing individual securities and contributed to a better understanding of market behaviour and how asset prices were fixed (cf. Chapter 3 of Farrell, 1997). The model highlighted the relationship between the risk and return of an asset and showed the importance of taking the risk into account. It allowed the correct measure of asset risk to be determined and provided an operational theory that allowed the return on an asset to be evaluated relative to the risk. The total risk of a security is broken down into two parts: the systematic risk, called the beta, which measures the variation of the asset in relation to market movements, and the unsystematic risk, which is unique for each asset. This breakdown could already be established with the help of the empirical market model, as we saw in Chapter 3. The unsystematic risk, which is also called the diversifiable risk, is not rewarded by the market. In fact, it can be eliminated by constructing diversified portfolios. The correct measure of risk for an individual asset is therefore the beta, and its reward is called the risk premium. The asset betas can be aggregated: the beta of a portfolio is obtained as a linear combination of the betas of the assets that make up the portfolio. According to the CAPM, the diversifiable risk component of each security is zero at equilibrium, while within the framework of the empirical market model only the average of the specific asset risks in the portfolio is nil.

The CAPM provides a reference for evaluating the relative attractiveness of securities by evaluating the price differentials compared with the equilibrium value. We should note that the individual assets are not on the efficient frontier, but they are all located on the same line at equilibrium. The CAPM theory also provided a context for developing manager performance evaluation, as we will show in Sections 4.2 and 4.3, by introducing the essential notion of risk-adjusted return.

By proposing an asset valuation model with the exclusive help of the market factor, Sharpe simplified the portfolio selection model considerably. He showed that optimal portfolios are obtained as a linear combination of the risk-free asset and the market portfolio, which, in practice, is approximated by a well-diversified portfolio. Equilibrium theory, which underlies the model, favoured the development of passive management and index funds, since it shows that the market portfolio is the optimal portfolio. The model also paved the way for the development of more elaborate models based on the use of several factors.

4.1.2.4   Market efficiency and market equilibrium

An equilibrium model can only exist in the context of market efficiency. Studying market efficiency enables the way in which prices of financial assets evolve towards their equilibrium value to be analysed. Let us first of all define market efficiency and its different forms.

The first definition of market efficiency was given by Fama (1970): markets are efficient if the prices of assets immediately reflect all available information. Jensen (1978) gave a more precise definition: in an efficient market, a forecast leads to zero profits, i.e. the expenses incurred in searching for information and putting the information to use offset the additional profit procured (cf. Hamon, 1997).

There are several degrees of market efficiency. Efficiency is said to be weak if the information only includes past prices; efficiency is semi-strong if the information also includes public information; efficiency is strong if all information, public and private, is included in the present prices of assets. Markets tend to respect the weak or semi-strong form of efficiency, but the CAPM's assumption of perfect markets refers in fact to the strong form.

The demonstration of the CAPM is based on the efficiency of the market portfolio at equilibrium. This efficiency is a consequence of the assumption that all investors make the same forecasts concerning the assets. They all construct the same efficient frontier of risky assets and choose to invest only in the efficient portfolios on this frontier. Since the market is the aggregation of the individual investors' portfolios, i.e. a set of efficient portfolios, the market portfolio is efficient.

In the absence of this assumption of homogeneous investor forecasts, we are no longer assured of the efficiency of the market portfolio, and consequently of the validity of the equilibrium model. The theory of market efficiency is therefore closely linked to that of the CAPM. It is not possible to test the validity of one without the other. This problem constitutes an important point in Roll's criticism of the model. We will come back to this in more detail at the end of the chapter.

The empirical tests of the CAPM involve verifying, from the empirical formulation of the market model, that the *ex-post* value of alpha is nil.

4.1.3   Modified versions of the CAPM[5]

Since the original assumptions of the CAPM are very restrictive, several authors have studied the consequences for the model of not respecting the assumptions. The studies address one assumption at a time. Chapter 14 of Elton and Gruber (1995) is very exhaustive on the subject. Among the versions of the model that were developed in this way, the most interesting from a practical application viewpoint are Black's zero-beta model and Brennan's model, which takes

---

[5] We can refer to Chapter 7 of Copeland and Weston (1988) for a detailed presentation with a demonstration of the Black and Merton models and to Chapter 8 for the Brennan model. Poncet *et al.* (1996) give a description without a demonstration of the Black and Merton models, Chapter 3 of Farrell (1997) presents the Black and Brennan models, and Chapter 14 of Elton and Gruber (1995) is devoted to the non-standard forms of the CAPM.

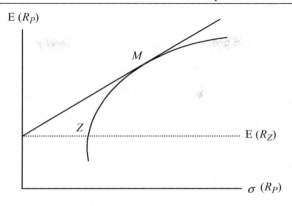

Figure 4.4   Minimum variance zero-beta portfolio (Z)

taxes into account. These two models will be shown in particular detail. This presentation is useful because it shows how the CAPM is adapted to the realities of the market. The different versions of the model are then applied in the area of portfolio performance measurement by allowing extensions to the Jensen measure. This will be developed in Section 4.2.

4.1.3.1   Black's zero-beta model[6]

Apart from the original version, this is the model that is most frequently used. This version was developed because two of the model's assumptions were called into question: (1) the existence of a risk-free asset, and therefore the possibility of borrowing or lending at that rate, and (2) the assumption of a single rate for borrowing and lending. Black (1972) showed that the CAPM theory was still valid without the existence of a risk-free asset, and developed a version of the model by replacing it with an asset or portfolio with a beta of zero. Instead of lending or borrowing at the risk-free rate, it is possible to take short positions on the risky assets.

The structure of the reasoning that enables this model to be produced is very close to that used to develop the basic model. We have the efficient frontier of risky assets, on which the market portfolio M is placed. We assume that we know how to determine the set of portfolios with zero beta, i.e. non-correlated with the market portfolio. These portfolios all have the same expected return $E(R_Z)$, since they all have the same systematic risk, namely a beta equal to zero. Among all these portfolios, only one is located on the efficient frontier: this is the portfolio with the minimum risk (see Figure 4.4).

We therefore have two portfolios on the efficient frontier: the market portfolio and the zero-beta portfolio, denoted by Z, with minimum variance. The complete efficient frontier can be obtained by combining these two portfolios. We invest x in portfolio Z and $(1 - x)$ in portfolio M. The expected return of this portfolio is written as follows:

$$E(R_P) = xE(R_Z) + (1 - x)E(R_M)$$

---

[6] For this model, we can also refer to Chapter 6 of Fabozzi (1995).

and its risk is

$$\sigma(R_P) = \left(x^2\sigma_Z^2 + (1-x)^2\sigma_M^2\right)^{1/2}$$

since the correlation between the market portfolio and portfolio Z is nil.

We then look for the slope of the tangent to point M that intersects the y-axis at point $E(R_Z)$. This slope is given by

$$\frac{\partial E(R_P)}{\partial \sigma(R_P)} = \frac{\partial E(R_P)/\partial x}{\partial \sigma(R_P)/\partial x}$$

We therefore calculate the partial derivatives of the expected return and risk of the portfolio, or:

$$\frac{\partial E(R_P)}{\partial x} = E(R_Z) - E(R_M)$$

and:

$$\frac{\partial \sigma(R_P)}{\partial x} = \frac{2x\sigma_Z^2 - 2\sigma_M^2(1-x)}{2\sigma(R_P)}$$

At point M, $x = 0$ and $\sigma(R_P) = \sigma_M$ so

$$\frac{\partial E(R_P)}{\partial \sigma(R_P)} = \frac{E(R_M) - E(R_Z)}{\sigma_M}$$

Furthermore, this line intersects the y-axis at the point $E(R_Z)$. Its equation is therefore finally written as follows:

$$E(R_P) = E(R_Z) + \left(\frac{E(R_M) - E(R_Z)}{\sigma_M}\right)\sigma(R_P)$$

The equation that is thereby established is identical in form to that of the capital market line of the basic model. The return on the risk-free asset is simply replaced by that of the zero-beta portfolio.

It is now possible to show that the return on any risky asset can be written using the return on the zero-beta portfolio and the return on the market portfolio. To do so, we proceed in the same way as when establishing the CAPM in the presence of a risk-free asset.

We consider the curve representing all the portfolios made up of a risky asset and the market portfolio. The slope of the tangent to this curve at point M is given by

$$\frac{(E(R_i) - E(R_M))\sigma_M}{\sigma_{iM} - \sigma_M^2}$$

This slope must be equal to the slope of our new market line, or

$$\frac{E(R_M) - E(R_Z)}{\sigma_M}$$

Hence

$$\frac{(E(R_i) - E(R_M))\sigma_M}{\sigma_{iM} - \sigma_M^2} = \frac{E(R_M) - E(R_Z)}{\sigma_M}$$

which finally gives the following:

$$E(R_i) = E(R_Z) + \frac{\sigma_{iM}}{\sigma_M^2}(E(R_M) - E(R_Z))$$

or

$$E(R_i) = E(R_Z) + \beta_i(E(R_M) - E(R_Z))$$

since

$$\beta_i = \frac{\sigma_{iM}}{\sigma_M^2}$$

The formula established is similar to that of the original CAPM, except that the return on the risk-free asset is replaced with the return on the zero-beta portfolio. The form of the CAPM is therefore conserved in the absence of a risk-free asset. This model is called the two-factor model.

Let us now return to the construction of zero-beta portfolios in more detail. A zero-beta portfolio is a portfolio with variations that are totally independent of market variations. We observe that most risky assets are positively correlated with each other. The best way to obtain a zero-beta portfolio is therefore to associate long and short positions on the assets, i.e. to carry out short selling on assets. The construction of zero-beta portfolios is not therefore possible unless short selling is authorised without any restrictions.

The CAPM cannot therefore be established without one or other of the following assumptions: the existence of a risk-free asset, which we can sell short without any limitations; or the absence of constraints on short selling of risky assets. It should be noted that generally there are restrictions on short selling. As a result, although this version of the model widens the framework for using the CAPM, it does not provide a solution in every case.

4.1.3.2 Model taking taxes into account: Brennan version

The basic CAPM model assumes that there are no taxes. The investor is therefore indifferent to receiving income as a dividend or a capital gain and all investors hold the same portfolio of risky assets. However, taxation of dividends and capital gains is generally different, and this is liable to influence the composition of the investors' portfolio of risky assets. Taking these taxes into account can therefore modify the equilibrium prices of the assets.

As a response to this problem, Brennan (1970) developed a version of the CAPM that allows the impact of taxes on the model to be taken into account. His model is formulated as follows:

$$E(R_i) = R_F + \beta_i(E(R_M) - R_F - T(D_M - R_F)) + T(D_i - R_F)$$

where

$$T = \frac{T_d - T_g}{1 - T_g}$$

and where

T_d denotes the average taxation rate for dividends;
T_g denotes the average taxation rate for capital gains;
D_M denotes the dividend yield of the market portfolio; and
D_i denotes the dividend yield of asset i.

By presenting this formula slightly differently, we have.

$$E(R_i) - R_F - T(D_i - R_F) = \beta_i(E(R_M) - R_F - T(D_M - R_F))$$

and we come back to a structure that is very similar to the basic CAPM. The returns on the asset and on the market are respectively decreased (or increased if T is negative) by a term proportional to the dividend yield and the taxes. When the tax rate on the dividends is equal to the tax rate on the capital gains, or $T = 0$, we do come back to the original model.

Investors can, for example, seek to avoid stocks that pay out large dividends. Such a strategy enables the return on the portfolio to be increased after deducting taxes, but, by distancing it from the market portfolio, it reintroduces a residual risk component.

4.1.3.3   Merton's continuous time version

Merton (1973) developed a continuous time version of the CAPM. His model is called the Intertemporal Capital Asset Pricing Model (ICAPM). In this model it is assumed that a state variable, for example the risk-free interest rate, evolves randomly over time. In this case, Merton shows that investors hold portfolios that result from three funds: the risk-free asset, the market portfolio and a third portfolio, chosen in such a way that its return is perfectly negatively correlated with the return on the risk-free asset. The two-fund separation model is replaced with a three-fund separation model. This third fund allows hedging against the risk of an unanticipated change in the future value of the risk-free rate (see also Elton and Gruber, 1995, and Copeland and Weston, 1998).

The expected return of an asset i at equilibrium is then written:

$$E(R_i) = R_F + \lambda_{i1}(E(R_M) - R_F) + \lambda_{i2}(E(R_{NF}) - R_F)$$

where

$$\lambda_{1i} = \frac{\beta_{iM} - \beta_{i,NF}\beta_{NF,M}}{1 - \rho_{NF,M}^2} \quad \text{and} \quad \lambda_{2i} = \frac{\beta_{i,NF} - \beta_{iM}\beta_{NF,M}}{1 - \rho_{NF,M}^2}$$

and where $\beta_{x,y}$ and $\rho_{NF,M}$ are defined as follows:

$$\beta_{x,y} = \frac{\sigma_{xy}}{\sigma_y^2} \quad \text{and} \quad \rho_{NF,M} = \frac{\sigma_{NF,M}}{\sigma_{NF}\sigma_M}$$

$E(R_{NF})$ denotes the expected rate of return of a portfolio that has perfect negative correlation with the risk-free asset R_F. All the rates of return are used in this model are continuous rates.

If the risk-free rate is not stochastic, or if it is not correlated with the market risk, then the third fund disappears, $\beta_{i,NF} = \beta_{NF,M} = 0$. We then come back to the standard formulation of the CAPM, except that the rates of return are instantaneous and the distribution of returns is lognormal instead of being normal.

The Merton model is a multi-period version of the CAPM. Assuming that the risk-free rate is stochastic leads to establishing a multi-factor (or multi-beta) version of the CAPM. Such a model can then be generalised to take other sources of extra-market risk into account, with the principle still being to make up a hedging portfolio for each source of risk and to determine the sensitivity of the assets to these portfolios. Nevertheless, this general theoretical approach does not specify the nature of the risk factors, or how to construct the portfolios to hedge the risks.

4.1.3.4   Model taking inflation into account

This model is a simple example of a generalisation of the CAPM for several factors. Here we assume that inflation is uncertain, which constitutes an additional risk factor on top of the basic model's market risk factor. The expected return at equilibrium of an asset i is now written as follows:

$$E(R_i) - R_F = \beta_{iM}(E(R_M) - R_F) + \beta_{iI}(E(R_I) - R_F)$$

where β_{iI} denotes the sensitivity of security i to the portfolio of securities held to hedge the inflation risk and $(E(R_I) - R_F)$ is the price of the inflation risk.

4.1.3.5   Model based on consumption: Breeden's (1979) CCAPM model

Here again we are dealing with a multi-period model, but one that is removed from the basic model since the returns on assets are no longer explained through the market return, but with the help of the consumption growth rate.

For each period t the return on asset i is written as follows:

$$R_{it} = \alpha_i + \beta_i C_t + e_{it}$$

where C_t denotes the consumption growth rate.

We also assume that the following conditions are respected:

$$E(e_{it}) = 0$$
$$E(e_{it}, C_t) = 0$$
$$\beta_i = \frac{\text{cov}(R_{it}, C_t)}{\text{var}(C_t)}$$

We can then establish the following equilibrium condition:

$$E(R_i) = E(R_Z) + \beta_i \gamma_1$$

where

γ_1 denotes the market remuneration for the consumption risk, with this risk being measured by the beta; and $E(R_Z)$ denotes the expected return on a zero-beta portfolio.

4.1.4   Conclusion

The presentation of some modified forms of the CAPM has allowed us to observe that the general structure of the basic model was quite well respected. We should however stress that these models were established by only modifying one assumption at a time. The advantage of these models is to be able to suggest improvements to the performance measurement indicators of the portfolios, while conserving a simple formula. We shall see the relevant applications in Section 4.2. The multi-factor forms of the model are already quite similar to the APT type models, to which Chapter 6 will be devoted.

4.2 APPLYING THE CAPM TO PERFORMANCE MEASUREMENT: SINGLE-INDEX PERFORMANCE MEASUREMENT INDICATORS[7]

When we presented the methods for calculating the return on a portfolio or investment fund in Chapter 2, we noted that the return value on its own was not a sufficient criterion for appreciating the performance and that it was necessary to associate a measure of the risk taken. Risk is an essential part of the investment. It can differ considerably from one portfolio to another. In addition, it is liable to evolve over time. Modern portfolio theory and the CAPM have established the link that exists between the risk and return of an investment quantitatively. More specifically, these theories highlighted the notion of rewarding risk. Therefore, we now possess the elements necessary for calculating indicators while taking both risk and return into account.

The first indicators developed came from portfolio theory and the CAPM. They are therefore more specifically related to equity portfolios. They enable a risk-adjusted performance value to be calculated. It is thus possible to compare the performance of funds with different levels of risk, while the return alone only enabled comparisons between funds with the same level of risk.

This section describes the different indicators and specifies, for each, their area of use. It again involves elementary measures because the risk is considered globally. We will see later on that the risk can be broken down into several areas, enabling a more thorough analysis.

4.2.1 The Treynor measure

The Treynor (1965) ratio is defined by

$$T_P = \frac{\mathrm{E}(R_P) - R_\mathrm{F}}{\beta_P}$$

where

$\mathrm{E}(R_P)$ denotes the expected return of the portfolio;
R_F denotes the return on the risk-free asset; and
β_P denotes the beta of the portfolio.

This indicator measures the relationship between the return on the portfolio, above the risk-free rate, and its systematic risk. This ratio is drawn directly from the CAPM. By rearranging the terms, the CAPM relationship for a portfolio is written as follows:

$$\frac{\mathrm{E}(R_P) - R_\mathrm{F}}{\beta_P} = \mathrm{E}(R_M) - R_\mathrm{F}$$

The term on the left is the Treynor ratio for the portfolio, and the term on the right can be seen as the Treynor ratio for the market portfolio, since the beta of the market portfolio is 1 by definition. Comparing the Treynor ratio for the portfolio with the Treynor ratio for the market portfolio enables us to check whether the portfolio risk is sufficiently rewarded.

The Treynor ratio is particularly appropriate for appreciating the performance of a well-diversified portfolio, since it only takes the systematic risk of the portfolio into account, i.e.

---

[7] On this subject, the interested reader could consult Broquet and van den Berg (1992), Elton and Gruber (1995), Fabozzi (1995), Grandin (1998), Jacquillat and Solnik (1997), and Gallais-Hamonno and Grandin (1999).

the share of the risk that is not eliminated by diversification. It is also for that reason that the Treynor ratio is the most appropriate indicator for evaluating the performance of a portfolio that only constitutes a part of the investor's assets. Since the investor has diversified his investments, the systematic risk of his portfolio is all that matters.

Calculating this indicator requires a reference index to be chosen to estimate the beta of the portfolio. The results can then depend heavily on that choice, a fact that has been criticised by Roll. We shall return to this point at the end of the chapter.

4.2.2   The Sharpe measure

Sharpe (1966) defined this ratio as the reward-to-variability ratio, but it was soon called the Sharpe ratio in articles that mentioned it. It is defined by

$$S_P = \frac{E(R_P) - R_F}{\sigma(R_P)}$$

where

$E(R_P)$ denotes the expected return of the portfolio;
R_F denotes the return on the risk-free asset; and
$\sigma(R_P)$ denotes the standard deviation of the portfolio returns.

This ratio measures the excess return, or risk premium, of a portfolio compared with the risk-free rate, compared, this time, with the total risk of the portfolio, measured by its standard deviation. It is drawn from the capital market line. The equation of this line, which was presented at the beginning of the chapter, can be written as follows:

$$\frac{E(R_P) - R_F}{\sigma(R_P)} = \frac{E(R_M) - R_F}{\sigma(R_M)}$$

This relationship indicates that, at equilibrium, the Sharpe ratio of the portfolio to be evaluated and the Sharpe ratio of the market portfolio are equal. The Sharpe ratio actually corresponds to the slope of the market line. If the portfolio is well diversified, then its Sharpe ratio will be close to that of the market. By comparing the Sharpe ratio of the managed portfolio and the Sharpe ratio of the market portfolio, the manager can check whether the expected return on the portfolio is sufficient to compensate for the additional share of total risk that he is taking.

Since this measure is based on the total risk, it enables the relative performance of portfolios that are not very diversified to be evaluated, because the unsystematic risk taken by the manager is included in this measure. This measure is also suitable for evaluating the performance of a portfolio that represents an individual's total investment.

The Sharpe ratio is widely used by investment firms for measuring portfolio performance. The index is drawn from portfolio theory, and not the CAPM like the Treynor and Jensen indices. It does not refer to a market index and is not therefore subject to Roll's criticism.

This ratio has also been subject to generalisations since it was initially defined. It thus offers significant possibilities for evaluating portfolio performance, while remaining simple to calculate. Sharpe (1994) sums up the variations on this measure. One of the most common involves replacing the risk-free asset with a benchmark portfolio. The measure is then called the information ratio. We will describe it in more detail later in the chapter.

4.2.3 The Jensen measure

Jensen's alpha (Jensen, 1968) is defined as the differential between the return on the portfolio in excess of the risk-free rate and the return explained by the market model, or

$$E(R_P) - R_F = \alpha_P + \beta_P(E(R_M) - R_F)$$

It is calculated by carrying out the following regression:

$$R_{Pt} - R_{Ft} = \alpha_P + \beta_P(R_{Mt} - R_{Ft}) + \varepsilon_{Pt}$$

The Jensen measure is based on the CAPM. The term $\beta_P(E(R_M) - R_F)$ measures the return on the portfolio forecast by the model. α_P measures the share of additional return that is due to the manager's choices.

In order to evaluate the statistical significance of alpha, we calculate the t-statistic of the regression, which is equal to the estimated value of the alpha divided by its standard deviation. This value is obtained from the results of the regression. If the alpha values are assumed to be normally distributed, then a t-statistic greater than 2 indicates that the probability of having obtained the result through luck, and not through skill, is strictly less than 5%. In this case, the average value of alpha is significantly different from zero.

Unlike the Sharpe and Treynor measures, the Jensen measure contains the benchmark. As for the Treynor measure, only the systematic risk is taken into account. This third method, unlike the first two, does not allow portfolios with different levels of risk to be compared. The value of alpha is actually proportional to the level of risk taken, measured by the beta. To compare portfolios with different levels of risk, we can calculate the Black–Treynor ratio[8] defined by

$$\frac{\alpha_P}{\beta_P}$$

The Jensen alpha can be used to rank portfolios within peer groups. Peer groups were presented in Chapter 2. They group together portfolios that are managed in a similar manner, and that therefore have comparable levels of risk.

The Jensen measure is subject to the same criticism as the Treynor measure: the result depends on the choice of reference index. In addition, when managers practise a market timing strategy, which involves varying the beta according to anticipated movements in the market, the Jensen alpha often becomes negative, and does not then reflect the real performance of the manager. In what follows we present methods that allow this problem to be corrected by taking variations in beta into account.

4.2.4 Relationships between the different indicators and use of the indicators

It is possible to formulate the relationships between the Treynor, Sharpe and Jensen indicators.

4.2.4.1 Treynor and Jensen

If we take the equation defining the Jensen alpha, or

$$E(R_P) - R_F = \alpha_P + \beta_P(E(R_M) - R_F) \tag{4.2}$$

---

[8] This ratio is defined in Salvati (1997). See also Treynor and Black (1973).

and we divide on each side by β_P, then we obtain the following:

$$\frac{E(R_P) - R_F}{\beta_P} = \frac{\alpha_P}{\beta_P} + (E(R_M) - R_F)$$

We then recognise the Treynor indicator on the left-hand side of the equation. The Jensen indicator and the Treynor indicator are therefore linked by the following exact linear relationship:

$$T_P = \frac{\alpha_P}{\beta_P} + (E(R_M) - R_F)$$

4.2.4.2 Sharpe and Jensen

It is also possible to establish a relationship between the Sharpe indicator and the Jensen indicator, but this time using an approximation. To do that we replace beta with its definition, or

$$\beta_P = \frac{\rho_{PM}\sigma_P\sigma_M}{\sigma_M^2}$$

where ρ_{PM} denotes the correlation coefficient between the return on the portfolio and the return on the market index.

If the portfolio is well diversified, then the correlation coefficient ρ_{PM} is very close to 1. By replacing β_P with its approximate expression in equation (4.2) and simplifying, we obtain:

$$E(R_P) - R_F \approx \alpha_P + \frac{\sigma_P}{\sigma_M}(E(R_M) - R_F)$$

By dividing each side by σ_P, we finally obtain:

$$\frac{E(R_P) - R_F}{\sigma_P} \approx \frac{\alpha_P}{\sigma_P} + \frac{(E(R_M) - R_F)}{\sigma_M}$$

The portfolio's Sharpe indicator appears on the left-hand side, so

$$S_P \approx \frac{\alpha_P}{\sigma_P} + \frac{(E(R_M) - R_F)}{\sigma_M}$$

4.2.4.3 Treynor and Sharpe

The formulas for these two indicators are very similar. If we consider the case of a well-diversified portfolio again, we can still use the following approximation for beta:

$$\beta_P \approx \frac{\sigma_P}{\sigma_M}$$

The Treynor indicator is then written as follows:

$$T_P \approx \frac{E(R_P) - R_F}{\sigma_P}\sigma_M$$

Hence

$$S_P \approx \frac{T_P}{\sigma_M}$$

Table 4.1   Characteristics of the Sharpe, Treynor and Jenson indicators

Name	Risk used	Source	Criticised by Roll	Usage
Sharpe	Total (sigma)	Portfolio theory	No	Ranking portfolios with different levels of risk Not very well-diversified portfolios Portfolios that constitute an individual's total personal wealth
Treynor	Systematic (beta)	CAPM	Yes	Ranking portfolios with different levels of risk Well-diversified portfolios Portfolios that constitute part of an individual's personal wealth
Jensen	Systematic (beta)	CAPM	Yes	Ranking portfolios with the same beta

It should be noted that only the relationship between the Treynor indicator and the Jensen indicator is exact. The other two are approximations that are only valid for a well-diversified portfolio.

4.2.4.4   Using the different measures

The three indicators allow us to rank portfolios for a given period. The higher the value of the indicator, the more interesting the investment. The Sharpe ratio and the Treynor ratio are based on the same principle, but use a different definition of risk. The Sharpe ratio can be used for all portfolios. The use of the Treynor ratio must be limited to well-diversified portfolios. The Jensen measure is limited to the relative study of portfolios with the same beta.

In this group of indicators the Sharpe ratio is the one that is most widely used and has the simplest interpretation: the additional return obtained is compared with a risk indicator taking into account the additional risk taken to obtain it.

These indicators are more particularly related to equity portfolios. They are calculated by using the return on the portfolio calculated for the desired period. The return on the market is approximated by the return on a representative index for the same period. The beta of the portfolio is calculated as a linear combination of the betas of the assets that make up the portfolio, with these being calculated in relation to a reference index over the study period. The value of the indicators depends on the calculation period and performance results obtained in the past are no guarantee of future performance. Sharpe wrote that the Sharpe ratio gave a better evaluation of the past and the Treynor ratio was more suitable for anticipating future performance. Table 4.1 summarises the characteristics of the three indicators.

4.2.5   Extensions to the Jensen measure

Elton and Gruber (1995) present an additional portfolio performance measurement indicator. The principle used is the same as that of the Jensen measure, namely measuring the differential between the managed portfolio and a theoretical reference portfolio. However, the risk considered is now the total risk and the reference portfolio is no longer a portfolio located on the security market line, but a portfolio on the capital market line, with the same total risk as the portfolio to be evaluated.

More specifically, this involves evaluating a manager who has to construct a portfolio with a total risk of σ_P. He can obtain this level of risk by splitting the investment between the market portfolio and the risk-free asset. Let A be the portfolio thereby obtained. This portfolio is situated on the capital market line. Its return and risk respect the following relationship:

$$E(R_A) = R_F + \left(\frac{E(R_M) - R_F}{\sigma_M} \right) \sigma_P$$

since $\sigma_A = \sigma_P$. This portfolio is the reference portfolio.

If the manager thinks that he possesses particular stock picking skills, he can attempt to construct a portfolio with a higher return for the fixed level of risk. Let P be his portfolio. The share of performance that results from the manager's choices is then given by

$$E(R_P) - E(R_A) = E(R_P) - R_F - \left(\frac{E(R_M) - R_F}{\sigma_M} \right) \sigma_P$$

The return differential between portfolio P and portfolio A measures the manager's stock picking skills. The result can be negative if the manager does not obtain the expected result.

The idea of measuring managers' selectivity can be found in the Fama decomposition, which will be presented in Chapter 7. But Fama compares the performance of the portfolio with portfolios situated on the security market line, i.e. portfolios that respect the CAPM relationship.

The Jensen measure has been the object of a certain number of generalisations, which enable the management strategy used to be included in the evaluation of the manager's value-added. Among these extensions are the models that enable a market timing strategy to be evaluated. These will be developed in Section 4.3, where we will also discuss multi-factor models. The latter involve using a more precise benchmark, and will be handled in Chapter 6.

Finally, the modified versions of the CAPM, presented at the end of Section 4.1, can be used instead of the traditional CAPM to calculate the Jensen alpha. The principle remains the same: the share of the return that is not explained by the model gives the value of the Jensen alpha.

With the Black model, the alpha is characterised by

$$E(R_P) - E(R_Z) = \alpha_P + \beta_P(E(R_M) - E(R_Z))$$

With the Brennan model, the alpha is characterised by

$$E(R_P) - R_F = \alpha_P + \beta_P(E(R_M) - R_F - T(D_M - R_F)) + T(D_P - R_F)$$

where D_P is equal to the weighted sum of the dividend yields of the assets in the portfolio, or

$$D_P = \sum_{i=1}^{n} x_i D_i$$

x_i denotes the weight of asset i in the portfolio. The other notations are those that were used earlier.

We can go through all the models cited in this way. For each case, the value of α_P is estimated through regression.

4.2.6 The tracking-error

The tracking-error is a risk indicator that is used in the analysis of benchmarked funds. Benchmarked management involves constructing portfolios with the same level of risk as an index, or a portfolio chosen as a benchmark, while giving the manager the chance to deviate from the benchmark composition, with the aim of obtaining a higher return. This assumes that the manager possesses particular stock picking skills. The tracking-error then allows the risk differentials between the managed portfolio and the benchmark portfolio to be measured. It is defined by the standard deviation of the difference in return between the portfolio and the benchmark it is replicating, or

$$TE = \sigma(R_P - R_B)$$

where R_B denotes the return on the benchmark portfolio.

The lower the value, the closer the risk of the portfolio to the risk of the benchmark. Benchmarked management requires the tracking-error to remain below a certain threshold, which is fixed in advance. To respect this constraint, the portfolio must be reallocated regularly as the market evolves. It is necessary however to find the right balance between the frequency of the reallocations and the transaction costs that they incur, which have a negative impact on portfolio performance. The additional return obtained, measured by alpha, must also be sufficient to make up for the additional risk taken on by the portfolio. To check this, we use another indicator: the information ratio.

4.2.7 The information ratio

The information ratio, which is sometimes called the appraisal ratio, is defined by the residual return of the portfolio compared with its residual risk. The residual return of a portfolio corresponds to the share of the return that is not explained by the benchmark. It results from the choices made by the manager to overweight securities that he hopes will have a return greater than that of the benchmark. The residual, or diversifiable, risk measures the residual return variations. Sharpe (1994) presents the information ratio as a generalisation of his ratio, in which the risk-free asset is replaced by a benchmark portfolio. The information ratio is defined through the following relationship:

$$IR = \frac{E(R_P) - E(R_B)}{\sigma(R_P - R_B)}$$

We recognise the tracking-error in the denominator. The ratio can also be written as follows:

$$IR = \frac{\alpha_P}{\sigma(e_P)}$$

where α_P denotes the residual portfolio return, as defined by Jensen, and $\sigma(e_P)$ denotes the standard deviation of this residual return.

As specified above, this ratio is used in the area of benchmarked management. It allows us to check that the risk taken by the manager, in deviating from the benchmark, is sufficiently rewarded. It constitutes a criterion for evaluating the manager. Managers seek to maximise its value, i.e. to reconcile a high residual return and a low tracking-error. It is important to look at the value of the information ratio and the value of the tracking-error together. For the same information ratio value, the lower the tracking-error the higher the chance that the manager's performance will persist over time.

The information ratio is therefore an indicator that allows us to evaluate the manager's level of information compared with the public information available, together with his skill in achieving a performance that is better than that of the average manager. Since this ratio does not take the systematic portfolio risk into account, it is not appropriate for comparing the performance of a well-diversified portfolio with that of a portfolio with a low degree of diversification.

The information ratio also allows us to estimate a suitable number of years for observing the performance, in order to obtain a certain confidence level for the result. To do so, we note that there is a link between the t-statistic of the regression, which provides the alpha value, and the information ratio. The t-statistic is equal to the quotient of alpha and its standard deviation, and the information ratio is equal to the same quotient, but this time using annualised values. We therefore have

$$IR \approx \frac{t_{\text{stat}}}{\sqrt{T}}$$

where T denotes the length of the period, expressed in years, during which we observed the returns. The number of years required for the result obtained to be significant, with a given level of probability, is therefore calculated by the following relationship:

$$T = \left[\frac{t_{\text{stat}}}{IR}\right]^2$$

For example, a manager who obtains an average alpha of 2.5% with a tracking-error of 4% has an information ratio equal to 0.625. If we wish the result to be significant to 95%, then the value of the t-statistic is 1.96, according to the normal distribution table, and the number of years it is necessary to observe the portfolio returns is

$$T = \left[\frac{1.96}{0.625}\right]^2 = 9.8 \text{ years}$$

This shows clearly that the results must persist over a long period to be truly significant. We should note, however, that the higher the manager's information ratio, the more the number of years decreases. The number of years also decreases if we consider a lower level of probability, by going down, for example, to 80%.

The calculation of the information ratio has been presented by assuming that the residual return came from the Jensen model. More generally, this return can come from a multi-index or multi-factor model. We will discuss these models in Chapter 6.

4.2.8 The Sortino ratio

An indicator such as the Sharpe ratio, based on the standard deviation, does not allow us to know whether the differentials compared with the mean were produced above or below the mean.

In Chapter 2 we introduced the notion of semi-variance and its more general versions. This notion can then be used to calculate the risk-adjusted return indicators that are more specifically appropriate for asymmetrical return distributions. This allows us to evaluate the portfolios obtained through an optimisation algorithm using the semi-variance instead of the variance. The best known indicator is the Sortino ratio (cf. Sortino and Price, 1994). It is defined on the same principle as the Sharpe ratio. However, the risk-free rate is replaced with the minimum acceptable return (MAR), i.e. the return below which the investor does not wish to drop, and the standard deviation of the returns is replaced with the standard deviation of the returns that are below the MAR, or

$$\text{Sortino ratio} = \frac{E(R_P) - MAR}{\sqrt{\frac{1}{T} \sum_{\substack{t=0 \\ R_{Pt} < MAR}}^{T} (R_{Pt} - MAR)^2}}$$

4.2.9 Recently developed risk-adjusted return measures

Specialised firms that study investment fund performance develop variations on the traditional measures, essentially on the Sharpe ratio. These measures are used to rank the funds and attribute management quality labels. We can cite, for example, Morningstar's rankings.

4.2.9.1 The Morningstar rating system[9]

The Morningstar measure, which is called a risk-adjusted rating (RAR), is very widely used in the United States. This ranking system was first developed in 1985 by the firm Morningstar. In July 2002, Morningstar introduced some modifications to improve its methodology. The measure differs significantly from more traditional measures such as the Sharpe ratio and its different forms. The evaluation of funds is based on a system of stars. Sharpe (1998) presents the method used by Morningstar and describes its properties. He compares it with other types of measure and describes the limitations of the ranking system.

The principle of the Morningstar measure is to rank different funds that belong to the same peer group. The RAR for a fund is calculated as the difference between its relative return and its relative risk, or

$$RAR_{P_i} = RR_{P_i} - RRisk_{P_i}$$

where RR_{P_i} denotes the relative return for fund P_i; and $RRisk_{P_i}$ denotes the relative risk for fund P_i.

The relative return and the relative risk for the fund are obtained by dividing, respectively, the return and the risk of the fund by a quantity, called the base, which is common to all the funds in the peer group, or

$$RR_{P_i} = \frac{R_{P_i}}{BR_g}$$

and

$$RRisk_{P_i} = \frac{Risk_{P_i}}{BRisk_g}$$

where g denotes the peer group containing the fund P_i;

---

[9] Cf. Melnikoff (1998) and see Sharpe's web site (http://www.stanford.edu/~wfsharpe/home.htm) for a series of articles describing the calculation methods.

R_{P_i} denotes the return on fund P_i, in excess of the risk-free rate;

$Risk_{P_i}$ denotes the risk of fund P_i;

BR_g denotes the base used to calculate the relative returns of all the funds in the group;

$BRisk_g$ denotes the base used to calculate the relative risks of all the funds in the group.

In the first version of the methodology, the risk of a fund was measured by calculating the average of the negative values of the fund's monthly returns in excess of the short-term risk-free rate and by taking the opposite sign to obtain a positive quantity:

$$Risk_{P_i} = -\frac{1}{T} \sum_{t=1}^{T} \min\left(R_{P_i t}, 0\right)$$

where T denotes the number of months in the period being studied; and $R_{P_i t}$ denotes the monthly return of fund P_i, in excess of the risk-free rate.

Risk calculation has been modified in the new version of the star rating. Risk is measured by monthly variations in fund returns and now takes not only downside risk but also upside volatility into account, but with more emphasis on downward volatility. Funds with highly volatile returns are penalised, whether the volatility is upside or downside. The advantages of this improvement can be understood by looking at Internet funds. These funds were not considered risky in 1999, as they only exhibited upside volatility. But their extreme gains indicated a serious potential for extreme losses, as has been demonstrated since. The new risk measure would have attributed a higher level of risk to those funds than the previous measure did. As a result, the possibility of strong short-term performance masking the inherent risk of a fund has now been reduced and it is more difficult for high-risk funds to earn high star ratings.

The base that is used to calculate the relative return of the funds is obtained by calculating the average return of the funds in the group. If the value obtained is greater than the risk-free rate for the period, then we use the result obtained, otherwise we use the value of the risk-free rate. We therefore have

$$BR_g = \max\left(\frac{1}{n} \sum_{i=1}^{n} R_{P_i}, R_F\right)$$

where n denotes the number of funds contained in the peer group; and R_F denotes the risk-free rate.

The base used to calculate the relative risk is obtained by calculating the average of the risks of the funds in the peer group, or

$$BRisk_g = \frac{1}{n} \sum_{i=1}^{n} Risk_{P_i}$$

In 1985, Morningstar defined four peer groups to establish its rankings: domestic stock funds, international stock funds, taxable bond funds and tax-exempt municipal bond funds. However, these four categories appear to be too few to make truly adequate comparisons. The improved star rating methodology[10] now uses 48 specific equity and debt peer groups. For example, equity funds are classified according to their capitalisation (large-cap, mid-cap and small-cap) and whether they are growth, value or blend. International stock funds are now subdivided into different parts of the world. By only comparing funds with funds from the

---

[10] For more details, see Morningstar's web site www.morningstar.com, from which it is possible to visit the specific web sites for each country.

same well-defined category, those that are providing superior risk-adjusted performance will be more accurately identified. For example, during periods favourable to large-cap stocks, large-cap funds received a high percentage of five-star rankings when evaluated in the broad domestic equity group. With the new system, only the best funds will receive five stars, as large-cap funds will only be compared with large-cap funds.

The ranking is then produced as follows. Each fund is attached to a single peer group. The funds in a peer group are ranked in descending order of their *RAR*. A number of stars is then attributed to each fund according to its position in the distribution of *RAR* values. The funds in the top 10% of the distribution obtain five stars; those in the following 22.5% obtain four stars; those in the following 35% obtain three stars; those in the next 22.5% obtain two stars; and, finally, those in the bottom 10% obtain one star.

The Morningstar measure is based on an investment period of one month, although funds are in fact held for longer periods, and a decrease in one month can be compensated for by an increase in the following month. This measure is not therefore very appropriate for measuring the risk of funds that are held over a long period.

4.2.9.2 Actuarial approach

In this approach (see Melnikoff, 1998) the investor's aversion to risk is characterised by a constant, W, which measures his gain–shortfall equilibrium, i.e. the relationship between the expected gain desired by the investor to make up for a fixed shortfall risk. The average annual risk-adjusted return is then given by

$$RAR = R - (W - 1)S$$

where

S denotes the average annual shortfall rate;
W denotes the weight of the gain–shortfall aversion; and
R denotes the average annual rate of return obtained by taking all the observed returns.

For an average individual, W is equal to two, which means that the individual will agree to invest if the expected amount of his gain is double the shortfall. In this case, we have simply

$$RAR = R - S$$

4.2.9.3 Analysis based on the VaR

The VaR was defined in Chapter 2 and the different methods for calculating it were briefly presented. As a reminder, the VaR measures the risk of a portfolio as the maximum amount of loss that the portfolio can sustain for a given level of confidence. We may then wish to use this definition of risk to calculate a risk-adjusted return indicator to evaluate the performance of a portfolio. In order to define a logical indicator, we divide the VaR by the initial value of the portfolio and thus obtain a percentage loss compared with the total value of the portfolio. We then calculate a Sharpe-like type of indicator in which the standard deviation is replaced with a risk indicator based on the VaR, or

$$\frac{R_P - R_F}{\dfrac{VaR_P}{V_P^0}}$$

where

R_P denotes the return on the portfolio;
R_F denotes the return on the risk-free asset;
VaR_P denotes the VaR of the portfolio;
V_P^0 denotes the initial value of the portfolio.

This type of ratio can only be compared for different portfolios if the portfolios' VaR has been evaluated for the same confidence threshold.

Furthermore, Dowd (1999) proposes an approach based on the VaR to evaluate an investment decision. We consider the case of an investor who holds a portfolio that he is thinking of modifying, by introducing, for example, a new asset. He will study the risk and return possibilities linked to a modification of the portfolio and choose the situation for which the risk-return balance seems to be sufficiently favourable. To do that, he could decide to define the risk in terms of the increase in the portfolio's VaR. He will change the portfolio if the resulting incremental VaR (IVaR) is sufficiently low compared with the return that he can expect. This can be formalised as a decision rule based on Sharpe's decision rule.

Sharpe's rule states that the most interesting asset in a set of assets is the one that has the highest Sharpe ratio. By calculating the existing Sharpe ratio and the Sharpe ratio for the modified portfolio and comparing the results, we can then judge whether the planned modification of the portfolio is desirable.

By using the definition of the Sharpe ratio, we find that it is useful to modify the portfolio if the returns and standard deviations of the portfolio before and after the modification are linked by the following relationship:

$$\frac{R_P^{\text{new}}}{\sigma_{R_P^{\text{new}}}} \geq \frac{R_P^{\text{old}}}{\sigma_{R_P^{\text{old}}}}$$

where R_P^{old} and R_P^{new} denote, respectively, the return on the portfolio before and after the modification; and $\sigma_{R_P^{\text{old}}}$ and $\sigma_{R_P^{\text{new}}}$ denote, respectively, the standard deviation of the portfolio before and after the modification.

We assume that part of the new portfolio is made up of the existing portfolio, in proportion $(1 - a)$, and the other part is made up of asset A in proportion a.

The return on this portfolio is written as follows:

$$R_P^{\text{new}} = aR_A + (1 - a)R_P^{\text{old}}$$

where R_A denotes the return on asset A.

By replacing R_P^{new} with its expression in the inequality between the Sharpe ratios, we obtain:

$$\frac{aR_A + (1 - a)R_P^{\text{old}}}{\sigma_{R_P^{\text{new}}}} \geq \frac{R_P^{\text{old}}}{\sigma_{R_P^{\text{old}}}}$$

which finally gives

$$R_A \geq R_P^{\text{old}} + \frac{R_P^{\text{old}}}{a}\left(\frac{\sigma_{R_P^{\text{new}}}}{\sigma_{R_P^{\text{old}}}} - 1\right)$$

This relationship indicates the inequality that the return on asset A must respect for it to be advantageous to introduce it into the portfolio. The relationship depends on proportion a. It shows that the return on asset A must be at least equal to the return on the portfolio before the modification, to which is added a factor that depends on the risk associated with the acquisition of asset A. The higher the risk, the higher the adjustment factor and the higher the return on asset A will have to be.

Under certain assumptions, this relationship can be expressed through the *VaR* instead of the standard deviation. If the portfolio returns are normally distributed, then the *VaR* of the portfolio is proportional to its standard deviation, or

$$VaR = -\alpha \sigma_{R_P} W$$

where

α denotes the confidence parameter for which the VaR is estimated;
W is a parameter that represents the size of the portfolio; and
σ_{R_P} is the standard deviation of the portfolio returns.

By using this expression of the VaR, we can calculate

$$\frac{VaR^{\text{new}}}{VaR^{\text{old}}} = \frac{W^{\text{new}} \sigma_{R_P^{\text{new}}}}{W^{\text{old}} \sigma_{R_P^{\text{old}}}}$$

which enables us to obtain the following relationship:

$$\frac{\sigma_{R_P^{\text{new}}}}{\sigma_{R_P^{\text{old}}}} = \frac{VaR^{\text{new}}}{VaR^{\text{old}}} \frac{W^{\text{old}}}{W^{\text{new}}}$$

We assume that the size of the portfolio is conserved. We therefore have $W^{\text{old}} = W^{\text{new}}$.

We therefore obtain simply, after substituting into the return on A relationship:

$$R_A \geq R_P^{\text{old}} + \frac{R_P^{\text{old}}}{a} \left(\frac{VaR^{\text{new}}}{VaR^{\text{old}}} - 1 \right)$$

The incremental VaR between the new portfolio and the old portfolio, denoted by IVaR, is equal to the difference between the old and new value, or $IVaR = VaR^{\text{new}} - VaR^{\text{old}}$.

By replacing in the inequality according to the IVaR, we obtain:

$$R_A \geq R_P^{\text{old}} + \frac{R_P^{\text{old}}}{a} \left(\frac{IVaR}{VaR^{\text{old}}} \right) = R_P^{\text{old}} \left(1 + \frac{1}{a} \frac{IVaR}{VaR^{\text{old}}} \right)$$

By defining the function η_A as

$$\eta_A(VaR) = \frac{1}{a} \frac{IVaR}{VaR^{\text{old}}}$$

we can write

$$R_A \geq (1 + \eta_A(VaR)) R_P^{\text{old}}$$

where $\eta_A(VaR)$ denotes the percentage increase in the VaR occasioned by the acquisition of asset A, divided by the proportion invested in asset A.

4.2.9.4 Measure taking the management style into account

The risk-adjusted performance measures enable a fund to be evaluated in comparison with the market portfolio, but do not take the manager's investment style into account. The style, however, may be imposed by the management mandate constraints rather than chosen by the manager. In this case it is more useful to compare management results with a benchmark that accurately represents the manager's style, rather than comparing them with a broad benchmark representing the market (cf. Lobosco, 1999). The idea of using tailored benchmarks that are adapted to the manager's investment style comes from the work of Sharpe (1992). We have already mentioned these benchmarks in the section devoted to benchmarks in Chapter 2, and we will come back to them in Chapter 6 with multi-factor models.

Lobosco (1999) proposes a measure called SRAP (Style/Risk-Adjusted Performance). This is a risk-adjusted performance measure that includes the management style as defined by Sharpe. It was inspired by the work of Modigliani and Modigliani (1997), who defined an equation that enabled the annualised risk-adjusted performance (RAP) of a fund to be measured in relation to the market benchmark, or

$$RAP_P = \frac{\sigma_M}{\sigma_P}(R_P - R_F) + R_F$$

where

σ_M denotes the annualised standard deviation of the market returns;
σ_P denotes the annualised standard deviation of the returns of fund P;
R_P denotes the annualised return of fund P; and
R_F denotes the risk-free rate.

This relationship is drawn directly from the capital market line. If we were at equilibrium, we would have $RAP_P = R_M$, where R_M denotes the annualised average market return.

The relationship therefore allows us to look at the performance of the fund in relation to that of the market. The most interesting funds are those with the highest RAP value. To obtain a relative measure, one just calculates the difference between the RAP for the fund and the RAP for the benchmark, with the benchmark's RAP measure being simply equal to its return.

The first step in measuring the performance of a fund, when taking the investment style into account, is to identify the combination of indices that best represents the manager's style. We then calculate the differential between the fund's RAP measure and the RAP measure of its Sharpe benchmark.

Lobosco gives the example of a fund with an annualised performance of −1.72% and a standard deviation of 17.48%. The market portfolio is represented by the Russell 3000 index, the performance of which for the same period is 16.54% with a standard deviation of 11.52%. The risk-free rate is 5.21%.

The risk-adjusted performance of this fund is therefore

$$RAP(Fund) = \frac{11.52}{17.48}(-1.72 - 5.21) + 5.21 = 0.64\%$$

Its performance in relation to the market portfolio is

$$RelativeRAP = RAP(Fund) - RAP(Market) = 0.64 - 16.54 = -15.90\%$$

If we now observe that the style of this fund corresponds to a benchmark, 61% of which is made up of the Russell 2000 index of growth stocks and 39% of the Russell 2000 index of growth stocks, the performance of this benchmark is now 2.73% with a standard deviation of 13.44%.

The risk-adjusted performance of this benchmark is given by

$$RAP(SharpeBenchmark) = \frac{11.52}{13.44}(2.73 - 5.21) + 5.21 = 3.08\%$$

and the relative performance of the portfolio compared to this benchmark is given by

$$RelativeRAP = RAP(Fund) - RAP(SharpeBenchmark) = 0.64 - 3.08 = -2.44\%$$

The relative performance of the fund is again negative, but the differential is much lower than compared with the whole market. The management style-adjusted performance measure is therefore a useful additional measure.

4.2.9.5   Risk-adjusted performance measure in the area of multimanagement

Muralidhar (2001) has developed a new risk-adjusted performance measure that allows us to compare the performance of different managers within a group of funds with the same objectives (a peer group). This measure can be grouped with the existing information ratio, the Sharpe ratio and the Modigliani and Modigliani measure, but it does contribute new elements. It includes not only the standard deviations of each portfolio, but also the correlation of each portfolio with the benchmark and the correlations between the portfolios themselves. The method proposed by Muralidhar allows us to construct portfolios that are split optimally between a risk-free asset, a benchmark and several managers, while taking the investors' objectives into account, both in terms of risk and, above all, the relative risk compared with the benchmark.

The principle involves reducing the portfolios to those with the same risk in order to be able to compare their performance. This is the same idea as in Modigliani and Modigliani (1997) who compared the performance of a portfolio and its benchmark by defining transformations in such a way that the transformed portfolio and benchmark had the same standard deviation.

To create a correlation-adjusted performance measure, Muralidhar considers an investor who splits his portfolio between a risk-free asset, a benchmark and an investment fund. We assume that this investor accepts a certain level of annualised tracking-error compared with his benchmark, which we call the objective tracking-error. The investor wishes to obtain the highest risk-adjusted value of alpha for a given portfolio tracking-error and variance. We define as a, b and $(1 - a - b)$ the proportions invested respectively in the investment fund, the benchmark B and the risk-free asset F. The portfolio thereby obtained is said to be correlation-adjusted. It is denoted by the initials CAP (for correlation-adjusted portfolio). The return on this portfolio is given by

$$R(CAP) = aR(manager) + bR(B) + (1 - a - b)R(F)$$

The proportions to be held must be chosen in an appropriate manner so that the portfolio obtained has a tracking-error equal to the objective tracking-error and its standard deviation is equal to the standard deviation of the benchmark.

The search for the best return, in view of the constraints, leads to the calculation of optimal proportions that depend on the standard deviations and correlations of the different elements in the portfolio. The problem is considered here with a single fund, but it can be generalised to the case of several funds, to handle the case of portfolios split between several managers, and to find the optimal allocation between the different managers. The formulas that give the optimal weightings in the case of several managers have the same structure as those obtained in the case of a single manager, but they use the weightings attributed to each manager together with the correlations between the managers.

Once the optimal proportions have been calculated, the return on the CAP has been determined entirely. By carrying out the calculation for each fund being studied, we can rank the different funds.

The Muralidhar measure is certainly useful compared with the risk-adjusted performance measure that had been developed previously. We observe that the Sharpe ratio, the information ratio and the Modigliani and Modigliani measure turn out to be insufficient to allow investors to rank different funds and to construct their optimal portfolio. These risk-adjusted measures only include the standard deviations of the portfolios and the benchmark, even though it is also necessary to include the correlations between the portfolios and between the portfolios and the benchmark. The Muralidhar model therefore provides a more appropriate risk-adjusted performance measure because it takes into account both the differences in standard deviation and the differences in correlations between the portfolios. We see that it produces a ranking of funds that is different from that obtained with the other measures. In addition, neither the information ratio nor the Sharpe ratio indicates how to construct portfolios in order to produce the objective tracking-error, while the Muralidhar measure provides the composition of the portfolios that satisfy the investors' objectives.

The composition of the portfolio obtained through the Muralidhar method enables us to solve the problem of an institutional investor's optimal allocation between active and passive management, with the possible use of a leverage effect to improve the risk-adjusted performance.

All the measures described in this section enable different investment funds to be ranked based on past performance. The calculations can be carried out over several successive periods on the basis that the more stable the ranking, the easier it will be to anticipate consistent results in the future.

4.3   EVALUATING THE MANAGEMENT STRATEGY WITH THE HELP OF MODELS DERIVED FROM THE CAPM: TIMING ANALYSIS

The first performance measurement indicators, which were drawn from portfolio theory and the CAPM (Sharpe, Treynor and Jensen), assume that portfolio risk is stationary. They measure the additional return obtained, compared with the level of risk taken, by considering the average value of the risk over the evaluation period. As a result, the measures only take the stock picking aspect into account. However, there is an investment management strategy, namely market timing, that involves modifying the level of the portfolio's exposure to market risk, measured by its beta, according to its anticipated evolution. To evaluate this type of strategy, one must turn to other models.

In this section we first present two performance analysis models, again based on the CAPM, which enable variations in the portfolio's beta over the investment period to be taken into account. They actually involve statistical tests, which allow for qualitative evaluation of a market timing strategy, when that strategy is followed for the portfolio. These models allow us to measure the portfolio's Jensen alpha, and to assess whether the result was obtained through the right investment decisions being taken at the right time or through luck. This section also presents a decomposition of the Jensen measure, which enables timing to be evaluated. The methods for implementing the market timing strategy itself will be presented in Chapter 7, which is devoted to the description and quantitative evaluation of the investment process.

4.3.1   The Treynor and Mazuy (1966) method[11]

This model is a quadratic version of the CAPM, which provides us with a better framework for taking into account the adjustments made to the portfolio's beta, and thus for evaluating a manager's market timing capacity. A manager who anticipates market evolutions correctly will lower his portfolio's beta when the market falls. His portfolio will thus depreciate less than if he had not made the adjustment. Similarly, when he anticipates a rise in the market, he increases his portfolio's beta, which enables him to make higher profits. The relationship between the portfolio return and the market return, in excess of the risk-free rate, should therefore be better approximated by a curve than by a straight line. The model is formulated as follows:

$$R_{Pt} - R_{Ft} = \alpha_P + \beta_P(R_{Mt} - R_{Ft}) + \delta_P(R_{Mt} - R_{Ft})^2 + \varepsilon_{Pt}$$

where

R_{Pt} denotes the portfolio return vector for the period studied;
R_{Mt} denotes the vector of the market returns for the same period, measured with the same frequency as the portfolio returns; and
R_{Ft} denotes the rate of the risk-free asset over the same period.

The α_P, β_P and δ_P coefficients in the equation are estimated through regression. If δ_P is positive and significantly different from zero, then we can conclude that the manager has successfully practised a market timing strategy.

This model was formulated empirically by Treynor and Mazuy (1966). It was then theoretically validated by Jensen (1972b) and Bhattacharya and Pfleiderer (1983).

4.3.2   The Henriksson and Merton (1981) and Henriksson (1984) models[12]

There are in fact two models: a non-parametric model and a parametric model. They are based on the same principle, but the parametric model seems to be more natural to implement. The non-parametric model is less frequently mentioned in the literature: we find it in Farrell (1997) and in Philips et al. (1996).

The non-parametric version of the model is older, and does not use the CAPM. It was developed by Merton (1981) and uses options theory. The principle is that of an investor who can split his portfolio between a risky asset and a risk-free asset, and who modifies the split over time according to his anticipations on the relative performance of the two assets. If the strategy is perfect, then the investor only holds stocks when their performance is better than that of the risk-free asset and only holds cash in the opposite case. The portfolio can be modelled by an investment in cash and a call on the better of the two assets. If the forecasts are not perfect, then the manager will only hold a fraction of options f, situated between -1 and 1. The value of f allows us to evaluate the manager. To do so, we define two conditional probabilities:

P_1 denotes the probability of making an accurate forecast, given that the stocks beat the risk-free asset;

---

[11] Cf. Broquet and van den Berg (1992), Elton and Gruber (1995), Farrell (1997), Grandin (1998), Jacquillat and Solnik (1997), Sharpe (1985), Taggart (1996), and Lhabitant (1994).
[12] Cf. Merton (1981), Henriksson and Merton (1981) and Henriksson (1984), and also Broquet and van den Berg (1992), Elton and Gruber (1995), Farrell (1997), Grandin (1998), Grinold and Kahn (1995), Jacquillat and Solnik (1997), Sharpe (1985), Taggart (1996), and Lhabitant (1994).

P_2 denotes the probability of making an accurate forecast, given that the risk-free asset beats the stocks.

We then have $f = P_1 + P_2 - 1$ and the manager has a market timing capacity if $f > 0$, i.e. if the sum of the two conditional probabilities is greater than one.

f can be estimated by using the following formula:

$$I_{t-1} = \alpha_0 + \alpha_1 y_t + \varepsilon_t$$

where $I_{t-1} = 1$ if the manager forecasts that the stocks will perform better than the risk-free asset during month t, otherwise 0; and $y_t = 1$ if the stocks actually did perform better than the risk-free asset, otherwise 0.

The coefficients in the equation are estimated through regression. α_0 gives the estimation of $1 - P_1$ and α_1 gives the estimation of $P_1 + P_2 - 1$. We then test the hypothesis $\alpha_1 > 0$.

Henriksson and Merton (1981) then developed a parametric model. The idea is still the same, but the formulation is different. It consists of a modified version of the CAPM which takes the manager's two risk objectives into account, depending on whether he forecasts that the market return will or will not be better than the risk-free asset return. The model is presented in the following form:

$$R_{Pt} - R_{Ft} = \alpha_P + \beta_{1P}(R_{Mt} - R_{Ft}) + \beta_{2P} D_t (R_{Mt} - R_{Ft}) + \varepsilon_{Pt}$$

where

$$D_t = 0, \quad \text{if } R_{Mt} - R_{Ft} > 0$$
$$D_t = -1, \quad \text{if } R_{Mt} - R_{Ft} < 0$$

The α_P, β_{1P} and β_{2P} coefficients in the equation are estimated through regression. The β_{2P} coefficient allows us to evaluate the manager's capacity to anticipate market evolution. If β_{2P} is positive and significantly different from zero, then the manager has a good timing capacity.

These models have been presented while assuming that the portfolio was invested in stocks and cash. More generally, they are valid for a portfolio that is split between two categories of assets, with one riskier than the other, for example stocks and bonds, and for which we adjust the composition according to anticipations on their relative performance.

4.3.3 Decomposition of the Jensen measure and evaluation of timing

The Jensen measure has been subject to numerous criticisms, the main one being that a negative performance can be attributed to a manager who practices market timing. As we mentioned above, this comes from the fact that the model uses an average value for beta, which tends to overestimate the portfolio risk, while the manager varies his beta between a high beta and a low beta according to his expectations for the market. Grinblatt and Titman (1989) present a decomposition of the Jensen measure in three terms: a term measuring the bias in the beta evaluation, a timing term and a selectivity term.

In order to establish this decomposition, we assume that there are n risky assets traded on a frictionless market, i.e. no transaction costs, no taxes and no restrictions on short selling. We assume that there is a risk-free asset. The assumptions are therefore those of the CAPM. We seek to evaluate the investor's performance over T time periods, by looking at the risk-adjusted returns of his portfolio. We denote r_{it} as the return on asset i in excess of the risk-free rate for period t; and x_{it} as the weight of asset i in the investor's portfolio for period t.

The return on the investor's portfolio for period t, in excess of the risk-free rate, is then given by

$$r_{Pt} = \sum_{i=1}^{n} x_{it} r_{it}$$

We denote by r_{Bt} the return in excess of the risk-free rate of a portfolio that is mean–variance efficient from an uninformed investor's viewpoint. We can then write

$$r_{it} = \beta_i r_{Bt} + \varepsilon_{it}$$

where

$$\beta_i = \frac{\text{cov}(r_{it}, r_{Bt})}{\text{var}(r_{Bt})}$$

and

$$E(\varepsilon_{it}) = 0$$

The portfolio return is then written as

$$r_{Pt} = \beta_{Pt} r_{Bt} + \varepsilon_{Pt}$$

where

$$\beta_{Pt} = \sum_{i=1}^{n} x_{it} \beta_i$$

and

$$\varepsilon_{Pt} = \sum_{i=1}^{n} x_{it} \varepsilon_{it}$$

In order to establish the decomposition, we consider the limit, in the probabilistic sense, of the Jensen measure, which is written as follows:

$$J_P = \hat{r}_P - b_P \hat{r}_B$$

where

b_p is the probability limit of the coefficient from the time-series regression of the portfolio returns against the reference portfolio series of returns;
$\hat{r}_P$ is the probability limit of the sample mean of the r_{Pt} series; and
$\hat{r}_B$ is the probability limit of the sample mean of the r_{Bt} series.

Formally, the probability limit of a variable is defined as

$$\hat{r}_P = p \lim \left[\frac{1}{T} \sum_{t=1}^{T} r_{Pt} \right]$$

It should be noted that b_P can be different from $\hat{\beta}_P$. This is the case when a manager practises market timing. $\hat{\beta}_P$ is then a weighted mean of the two betas used for the portfolio, while b_P is the regression coefficient obtained, without concerning oneself with the fact that the manager practises market timing.

We can write

$$\hat{r}_P = p \lim \left[\frac{1}{T} \sum_{t=1}^{T} r_{Pt} \right]$$

or, by replacing r_{Pt} with its expression:

$$\hat{r}_P = p \lim \left[\frac{1}{T} \sum_{t=1}^{T} (\beta_{Pt} r_{Bt} + \varepsilon_{Pt}) \right]$$

By arranging the terms in the expression we obtain:

$$\hat{r}_P = \hat{\beta}_P \hat{r}_B + p \lim \left[\frac{1}{T} \sum_{t=1}^{T} \beta_{Pt} (r_{Bt} - \hat{r}_B) \right] + \hat{\varepsilon}_P$$

By using this formula in the Jensen measure expression we obtain:

$$J_P = (\hat{\beta}_P - b_P)\hat{r}_B + p \lim \left[\frac{1}{T} \sum_{t=1}^{T} \beta_{Pt} (r_{Bt} - \hat{r}_B) \right] + \hat{\varepsilon}_P$$

This expression reveals three distinct terms:

1. a term that results from the bias in estimated beta: $(\hat{\beta}_P - b_P)\hat{r}_B$;
2. a term that measures timing:

$$p \lim \left[\frac{1}{T} \sum_{t=1}^{T} \beta_{Pt} (r_{Bt} - \hat{r}_B) \right];$$

3. a term that measures selectivity: $\hat{\varepsilon}_P$.

If the weightings of the portfolio to be evaluated are known, then the three terms can be evaluated separately. When the manager has no particular information in terms of timing, $\hat{\beta}_P = b_P$.

4.4 MEASURING THE PERFORMANCE OF INTERNATIONALLY DIVERSIFIED PORTFOLIOS: EXTENSIONS TO THE CAPM

Modern portfolio theory has demonstrated the usefulness of diversification in reducing port-folio risk. By enlarging the universe of available securities, international investment[13] offers additional diversification possibilities. Assets from different countries often have low levels of correlation. It is therefore possible to put together less risky portfolios than by limiting oneself to a single country. However, currency risk, which was defined in Chapter 2, has to be taken into consideration. The performance of international portfolios can then be evaluated with specific models, based on an international version of the CAPM.

---

[13] The advantages of international diversification are detailed in Chapter 11 of Jacquillat and Solnik (1997) and Chapter 11 of Farrell (1997).

4.4.1 International Asset Pricing Model[14]

Several authors have developed international versions of the CAPM. Among these, we could mention Solnik's model (1974a, 1974b), which is called the International Asset Pricing Model (IAPM). This model was established by following a similar framework to that used to obtain the continuous time version of the CAPM in the national case. The reference portfolio is now the worldwide market portfolio. The most widely used index in the United States, as an approximation of this portfolio, is the Morgan Stanley Capital Index (MSCI) Europe, Asia and Far East (EAFE). This is an index that is weighted according to the stock market capitalisations of each country. It covers more than 2000 companies from 21 countries. This model uses a risk-free rate from the country of asset i and an average worldwide risk-free rate, obtained by making up a portfolio of risk-free assets from different countries in the world. The weightings used are again the same as those used for the worldwide market portfolio. Solnik establishes the following relationship:

$$E(R_i) = R_{F_i} + \beta_i \left(E\left(R_{M_M}\right) - R_{F_M} \right)$$

where

β_i denotes the international systematic risk of security i, i.e. calculated in relation to the worldwide market portfolio;

R_{F_i} denotes the rate of the risk-free asset in the country of security i;

R_{F_M} denotes the rate of the average worldwide risk-free asset; and

R_{M_M} denotes the return on the worldwide market portfolio.

All the rates of return are expressed in the currency of the asset i country.

4.4.2 McDonald's model[15]

McDonald (1973) proposed a performance measure which is an extension to the Jensen measure. His model applies to a portfolio of stocks invested in the French and American markets. It is written as follows:

$$R_{Pt} - R_{Ft} = \Phi_P + \beta_{P1}^*(R_{M1,t} - R_{Ft}) + \beta_{P2}^*(R_{M2,t} - R_{Ft}) + e_{Pt}$$

where

$R_{M1,t}$ denotes the rate of return of the French market in period t;

$R_{M2,t}$ denotes the rate of return of the American market in period t;

R_{Ft} denotes the rate of return of the risk-free asset in the French market in period t;

$\beta_{P1}^* = x_1\beta_{P1}$ and $\beta_{P2}^* = x_2\beta_{P2}$, with x_1 and x_2 the proportions of the fund invested in each of the two markets and β_{P1} and β_{P2} the fund's coefficients of systematic risk compared to each of the two markets.

The overall excess performance of the fund Φ_P is broken down into

$$\Phi_P = x_1 d_{P1} + x_2 d_{P2}$$

where d_{P1} and d_{P2} denote the excess performance of each of the two markets.

---

[14] See Poncet *et al.* (1996) and Chapter 22 of Copeland and Weston (1988).
[15] Cf. Grandin (1998), Jacquillat and Solnik (1987) and Broquet and van den Berg (1992).

With this method we can attribute the contribution of each market to the total performance of the portfolio. This in turn allows us to evaluate the manager's capacity to select the best-performing international securities and to invest in the most profitable markets.

McDonald's model only considers investments in stocks and represents international investment in the American market alone. However, the model can be generalised for the case of investment in several international markets, and for portfolios containing several asset classes. This is what Pogue *et al.* (1974) propose.

4.4.3   Pogue, Solnik and Rousselin's model

Pogue *et al.* (1974) also proposed an extension to the Jensen measure for international portfolios (see also Grandin, 1998, and Jacquillat and Solnik, 1987). Their model measures the performance of funds invested in French and international stocks, without any limit on the number of countries, and in French bonds. The model is written as follows:

$$R_{Pt} = \alpha_P + x_{OF,P}\beta_{OF,P}(I_{OF,t} - R_{Ft}) + x_{AF,P}\beta_{AF,P}(I_{AF,t} - R_{Ft})$$
$$+ x_{WP}\beta_{WP}(I_{Wt} - R_{Wt}) + e_{Pt}$$

where

R_{Ft}	denotes the interest rate of the risk-free asset in the French market;
R_{Wt}	denotes the eurodollar rate;
$I_{OF,t}, I_{AF,t}, I_{W,t}$	denote the returns on the three representative indices: the French bond market index, the French stock market index and the worldwide stock market index for period t;
$x_{OF,P}, x_{AF,P}$ and x_{WP}	denote the proportion of the portfolio invested in each market;
$\beta_{OF,P}, \beta_{AF,P}$ and $\beta_{W,P}$	denote the systematic risk of each subset of the portfolio; and
α_P	denotes the portfolio's overall excess performance.

The result measures the manager's capacity to choose the most promising markets and his skill in selecting the best stocks in each market.

It is possible to go further into the analysis and breakdown of performance by using multi-factor models for international investment. These models will be presented in Chapter 6.

4.5   THE LIMITATIONS OF THE CAPM

4.5.1   Roll's criticism

Roll (1977) formulated a criticism of the CAPM. The core criticism relates to the fact that it is impossible to measure the true market portfolio.

Roll showed that the CAPM relationship implied that the market portfolio was efficient in the mean–variance sense. He deduced that to test the validity of the model, it was necessary to show that the market portfolio was efficient. However, the true market portfolio cannot be observed, because it must be comprised of all risky assets, including those that are not traded. Instead, we use a stock exchange index. The results of empirical tests are dependent on the index chosen as an approximation of the market portfolio. If this portfolio is efficient, then we conclude that the CAPM is valid. If not, we will conclude that the model is not valid. But these tests do not allow us to ascertain whether the true market portfolio is really efficient. Roll concludes from this that it is not possible to validate the CAPM empirically. This does not, nevertheless, mean that the model is not valid.

This criticism had consequences for the performance measurement models that were derived from the CAPM (Treynor and Jensen). If the index used as an approximation of the market portfolio is not efficient, then the portfolio performance result will depend on the index. By changing the index, the relative ranking of the portfolios is not necessarily maintained.

The fact that a portfolio which is not the true market portfolio is used leads to estimation errors in the betas. Some authors, such as Shanken (1987, 1992), present methods for correcting the measurement errors that are due to the fact that we are not observing the true market portfolio.

These criticisms have led to the development of other models. In the following chapter we shall successively present heteroskedastic models that enable better beta calculation and performance measurement models that do not depend on the market model. In Chapter 6 we shall present multi-factor models, which are mainly applied to portfolio risk analysis.

4.5.2 Conclusion

In spite of the criticism, the CAPM is widely appreciated as an asset valuation model. It has the advantage of being simple and is one of the best models for explaining returns. A consequence of the model was the development of passive management and index funds, the idea being that the best portfolio was the market portfolio. In the United States, Sharpe helped the firm Wells Fargo to set up its first index funds in the 1970s. The model gave rise to the first risk-adjusted performance measurement ratios. Among these, the Sharpe ratio is an indicator that is still widely used by the professionals.

However, without calling into question the contribution of the CAPM, the current consensus tends towards the idea that a single factor is not sufficient for explaining returns. Besides the market factor, two other factors have been identified: the size of the company and its book-to-market ratio. Fama and French[16] have carried out research on this subject. The firm Barra, for its part, has developed a more complete microeconomic model, which uses 13 fundamental factors. These factors are perfectly well known and defined, because they are directly linked to the securities (as such we speak of attributes), while in the case of the CAPM, the true theoretical market factor cannot be measured and must be approximated by a well-diversified market index. This approximation is one of the reasons for the criticism of the model formulated by Roll. On the basis of Roll's criticism, Ross proposed a multi-factor model that could be tested empirically. This model, while it presents the advantage over the Barra model of being based on an extension to the concepts of portfolio theory, proposes explaining the asset returns with the help of macroeconomic factors, without the theory specifying the number and nature of these factors, which makes it difficult to use. We will return to all of these models in detail in Chapter 6.

BIBLIOGRAPHY

Baker, III E.D., "Performance Basics: Simple in Theory, Hard to Apply – Part I", *Performance Measurement: Setting the Standards, Interpreting the Numbers*, CFA, 1991.

Bhattacharya, S. and Pfleiderer, P., "A Note on Performance Evaluation", *Technical Report* 714, Graduate School of Business, Stanford University, 1983.

---

[16] Fama and French have published several studies on the subject. See for example Fama and French (1995).

Black, F., "Capital Market Equilibrium with Restricted Borrowing", *Journal of Business*, no. 45, July 1972, pp. 444–455.

Breeden, D.T., "An Intertemporal Asset Pricing Model with Stochastic Consumption and Investment Opportunities", *Journal of Financial Economics*, vol. 7, 1979, pp. 265–296.

Brennan, M., "Taxes, Market Valuation and Corporate Financial Policy", *National Tax Journal*, no. 25, 1970, pp. 417–427.

Briys, E. and Viala, P., *Eléments de théorie financière*, Nathan, 1995.

Broquet, C. and van den Berg, A., *Gestion de portefeuille – Actions, Obligations, Options*, 2nd edn, De Boeck Université, 1992.

Cobbaut, R., "Théorie du marché financier", in *Encyclopédie des marchés financiers*, Economica, 1997, pp. 1954–1978.

Copeland, T.E. and Weston, J.F., *Financial Theory and Corporate Policy*, 3rd edn, Addison-Wesley, 1988.

Dowd, K., "A Value at Risk Approach to Risk–Return Analysis", *Journal of Portfolio Management*, vol. 25, no. 4, summer 1999, pp. 60–67.

Elton, E.J. and Gruber, M.J., *Modern Portfolio Theory and Investment Analysis*, 5th edn, Wiley, 1995.

Fabozzi, F.J., *Investment Management*, Prentice Hall International Editions, 1995.

Fama, E., "Efficient Capital Markets: A Review of Theory and Empirical Work", *Journal of Finance*, vol. 25, no. 2, March 1970, pp. 383–417.

Fama, E.F. and French, K.R., "Size and Book-to-Market Factors in Earnings and Returns", *Journal of Finance*, vol. 50, no. 1, March 1995, pp. 131–155.

Farrell, Jr J.L., *Portfolio Management, Theory and Application*, McGraw-Hill, 2nd edn, 1997.

Gallais-Hamonno, G. and Grandin, P., "Le point sur . . . Les mesures de performance", *Banque & Marchés*, no. 42, September–October 1999.

Grandin, P., *Mesure de performance des fonds d'investissement, Méthodologie et résultats*, Economica, Gestion poche, 1998.

Grinblatt, M. and Titman, S., "Portfolio Performance Evaluation: Old Issues and New Insights", *Review of Financial Studies*, vol. 2, 1989, pp. 393–421.

Grinold, R.C. and Kahn, R.N., *Active Portfolio Management*, Irwin, 1995.

Hamon, J., "Efficience faible. Efficience semi-forte", in *Encyclopédie des Marchés Financiers*, Economica, 1997, pp. 408–432.

Henriksson, R.D., "Market Timing and Mutual Fund Performance: An Empirical Investigation", *Journal of Business*, vol. 57, no. 1, 1984, pp. 73–96.

Henriksson, R.D. and Merton, R.C., "On Market Timing and Investment Performance II: Statistical Procedures for Evaluating Forecasting Skills", *Journal of Business*, vol. 54, no. 4, 1981, pp. 513–533.

Jacquillat, B. and Solnik, B., *Les marchés financiers et la gestion de portefeuille*, 2nd edn, Dunod, 1987.

Jacquillat, B. and Solnik, B., *Marchés financiers, Gestion de portefeuille et des risques*, 3rd edn, Dunod, 1997.

Jensen, M.C., "The Performance of Mutual Funds in the Period 1945–1964", *Journal of Finance*, vol. 23, May 1968, pp. 389–419.

Jensen, M.C., "Capital Markets: Theory and Evidence", *The Bell Journal of Economics and Management Science*, vol. 3, no. 2, autumn 1972a.

Jensen, M.C., "Optimal Utilization of Market Forecasts and the Evaluation of Investment Performance", in *Mathematical Methods in Investment and Finance*, G.P. Szego and K. Shell, eds., Elsevier, 1972b.

Jensen, M., "Some Anomalous Evidence Regarding Market Efficiency", *Journal of Financial Economics*, vol. 6, no. 2/3, 1978, pp 95–101.

Korajczyk, R.A., *Asset Pricing and Portfolio Performance – Models, Strategy and Performance Metrics*, Risk Books, 1999.

Lhabitant, F.-S., "Portfolio Performance: Theoretical and Empirical Investigations on the Swiss Mutual Fund Market", Mémoire de Diplôme, Master en Banque et Finance, Université de Lausanne, Ecole des Hautes Etudes Commerciales, October 1994.

Lintner, J., "The Valuation of Risk Assets and the Selection of Risky Investments in Stock Portfolios and Capital Budgets", *Review of Economics and Statistics*, February 1965, pp. 13–37.

Lintner, J., "The Aggregation of Investor's Diverse Judgements and Preferences in Purely Competitive Security Markets", *Journal of Financial and Quantitative Analysis*, vol. 4, no. 4, December 1969, pp. 347–400.

Lobosco, A., "Style/Risk-Adjusted Performance", *Journal of Portfolio Management*, vol. 25, no. 3, spring 1999, pp. 65–68.

McDonald, J., "French Mutual Fund Performance: Evaluation of Internationally Diversified Portfolios", *Journal of Finance*, vol. 28, no. 5, 1973, pp. 1161–1180.

Melnikoff, M., "Investment Performance Analysis for Investors", *Journal of Portfolio Management*, vol. 25, no. 1, fall 1998, pp. 95–107.

Merton, R.C., "An Intertemporal Capital Asset Pricing Model", *Econometrica*, vol. 41, September 1973, pp. 867–887.

Merton, R.C., "On Market Timing and Investment Performance I: An Equilibrium Theory of Value for Market Forecasts", *Journal of Business*, vol. 54, no. 3, 1981.

Miller, M.H., "The History of Finance: An Eyewitness Account", *Journal of Portfolio Management*, vol. 25, no. 4, summer 1999, pp. 95–101.

Modigliani, F. and Modigliani, L., "Risk-Adjusted Performance", *Journal of Portfolio Management*, winter 1997, pp. 45–54.

Mossin, J., "Equilibrium in a Capital Asset Market", *Econometrica*, October 1966, pp. 768–783.

Muralidhar, A.S., "Optimal Risk-Adjusted Portfolios with Multiple Managers", *Journal of Portfolio Management*, vol. 27, no. 3, spring 2001, pp. 97–104.

Philips, T.K., Rogers, G.T. and Capaldi, R.E., "Tactical Asset Allocation 1977–1994: The Long-Term Performance of TAA", *Journal of Portfolio Management*, fall 1996, pp. 57–64.

Pogue, G., Solnik, B. and Rousselin, A., "International Diversification: A Study of the French Mutual Funds", MIT, Working Paper, 1974.

Poncet, P., Portait, R. and Hayat, S., *Mathématiques financières: Evaluation des actifs et analyse du risque*, 2nd edn, Dalloz, 1996.

Roll, R., "A Critique of the Asset Pricing Theory's Tests", *Journal of Financial Economics*, March 1977, pp. 129–176.

Salvati, J., "Mesure de performance et gestion de portefeuille", in *Encyclopédie des marchés financiers*, Economica, 1997, pp. 1122–1139.

Shanken, J., "Multivariate Proxies and Asset Pricing Relations: Living with the Roll Critique", *Journal of Financial Economics*, vol. 18, 1987, pp. 91–110.

Shanken, J., "On the Estimation of Beta-Pricing Models", *Review of Financial Studies*, vol. 5, no. 1, 1992, pp. 1–33.

Sharpe, W.F., "A Simplified Model for Portfolio Analysis", *Management Science*, January 1963, pp. 277–293.

Sharpe, W.F., "Capital Asset Prices: A Theory of Market Equilibrium under Conditions of Risk", *Journal of Finance*, vol. 19, September 1964, pp. 425–442.

Sharpe, W.F., "Mutual Fund Performance", *Journal of Business*, January 1966, pp. 119–138.

Sharpe, W.F., *Investments*, 3rd edn, Prentice Hall, 1985.

Sharpe, W.F., "Asset Allocation: Management Style and Performance Measurement", *Journal of Portfolio Management*, vol. 18, winter 1992, pp. 7–19.

Sharpe, W.F., "The Sharpe Ratio", *Journal of Portfolio Management*, fall 1994.

Sharpe, W.F., "Morningstar's Risk-Adjusted Ratings", *Financial Analysts Journal*, July–August, 1998.

Simon, Y., *Encyclopédie des marchés financiers*, Economica, 1997.

Solnik, B., "The International Pricing of Risk: an Empirical Investigation of the World Capital Market Structure", *Journal of Finance*, May 1974b, pp. 365–378.

Solnik, B., "An International Market Model of Security Price Behavior", *Journal of Financial and Quantitative Analysis*, September 1974a, pp. 537–554.

Sortino, F.A. and Price, L.N., "Performance Measurement in a Downside Risk Framework", *Journal of Investing*, vol. 3, no. 3, fall 1994, pp. 59–64.

Taggart, Jr R.A., *Quantitative Analysis for Investment Management*, Prentice Hall, 1996.

Tobin, J., "Liquidity Preference as Behavior towards Risk", *Review of Economic Studies*, February 1958, pp. 65–85.

Treynor, J.L., "Toward a Theory of Market Value of Risky Assets", *Working Paper*, 1961, published in *Asset Pricing and Portfolio Performance – Models, Strategy and Performance Metrics*, Robert A. Korajczyk, ed., Risk Books, 1999.

Treynor, J.L., "How to Rate Management of Investment Funds", *Harvard Business Review*, vol. 43, January–February 1965, pp. 63–75.

Treynor, J.L. and Black, F., "How to Use Security Analysis to Improve Portfolio Selection", *Journal of Business*, vol. 46, no. 1, 1973, pp. 61–86.

Treynor, J. and Mazuy, K., "Can Mutual Funds Outguess the Market?", *Harvard Business Review*, vol. 44, July–August 1966, pp. 131–136.

5

Developments in the Field of Performance Measurement

In this chapter and the next we propose responses to criticisms of the CAPM. This chapter presents improvements to the model and alternative solutions. Chapter 6 addresses the difficulty of testing the CAPM by proposing a model that can be verified empirically.

In this chapter we first describe two models that allow the traditional CAPM to be improved and clarify certain elements of performance measurement. The first model is a heteroskedastic model, where the volatility depends on the past values of the process. The second is a conditional model, where the beta depends on economic variables, and which represents an evolution towards factor models. This second approach has been the subject of articles, written by Ferson and Schadt, which present its application to performance measurement. The application of the first approach to performance measurement has not been developed in the literature. Finally, this chapter ends with a presentation of performance measures that do not depend on the market model.

5.1 HETEROSKEDASTIC MODELS[1]

Numerous empirical studies on the performance of investment funds have been carried out with the help of traditional measures. The results of these studies often give negative Jensen alphas, and the Treynor and Mazuy and Henriksson and Merton methods tend to attribute a negative performance to informed investors. These studies also reveal that the results are not very stable over time. The results are therefore relatively unsatisfactory. However, the measurement methods used in these studies do not take into account the dynamic nature of the returns. More recent studies have shown that the use of conditional performance measurement models leads to more satisfactory results. Nevertheless, when we look at the modelling of returns with the help of models that integrate variations over time since the beginning of the 1980s, the application of these models to performance measurement has not been developed greatly in the literature. Notwithstanding this, models that use stochastic volatility are potentially useful.

5.1.1 Presentation of the ARCH models

The ARCH (autoregressive conditional heteroskedasticity) models were developed by Engle (1982) and generalised by Bollersev (1986), after the assumption of homoskedastic stock market returns was called into question. They allow us to model volatility stochastically, i.e. taking its variations over time into account, and therefore provide more detailed information.

There are several families of models. In what follows, $r_t, t = 1, \ldots, T$, denotes a series of returns. I_t denotes the available information, which is made up of the present and past values of the series.

---

[1] For more details, the interested reader could refer to Gouriéroux (1997) and Cuthbertson (1996).

5.1.1.1   The ARCH model

This model, which is the simplest, enables the conditional variance to be represented as a function of the squares of past forecast errors. It is formulated as follows:

$$r_t = \varepsilon_t$$

where

$$E(r_t/I_{t-1}) = E(\varepsilon_t/I_{t-1}) = 0$$

and

$$V(r_t/I_{t-1}) = h_t = c + \sum_{i=1}^{q} a_i \varepsilon_{t-i}^2$$

$E(r_t/I_{t-1})$ is a conditional expectation. It is the best forecast of r_t based on the information I_{t-1}. $V(r_t/I_{t-1})$ measures the conditional variance of the forecast errors.

If the model is applied to a return r_t defined in logarithmic form, or

$$r_t = \ln\left(\frac{P_t}{P_{t-1}}\right)$$

where P_t denotes the price of the asset at date t, then we have

$$E(r_t/I_{t-1}) = E(\ln(P_t/P_{t-1})/I_{t-1})$$

or

$$E(r_t/I_{t-1}) = E(\ln(P_t)/I_{t-1}) - E(\ln(P_{t-1})/I_{t-1})$$

so

$$E(\ln(P_{t-1})/I_{t-1}) = \ln(P_{t-1})$$

according to the properties of the conditional expectations.

Since $E(r_t/I_{t-1}) = 0$, according to the first condition of the model, we deduce that

$$E(\ln(P_t)/I_{t-1}) = \ln(P_{t-1})$$

The logarithm of the price is therefore optimally forecast by the logarithm of the price at the previous date. This corresponds to the market efficiency condition. The risk depends on evolutions in the past.

5.1.1.2   The GARCH model

This model is a generalisation of the previous model. The volatility now depends on both a linear combination of the forecast error squares (an autoregressive term) and past conditional variances (a moving average term). This model is written as follows:

$$r_t = \varepsilon_t$$

with

$$E(r_t/I_{t-1}) = 0$$

and

$$V(r_t/I_{t-1}) = h_t = c + \sum_{i=1}^{q} a_i \varepsilon_{t-i}^2 + \sum_{j=1}^{p} b_j h_{t-j}$$

5.1.1.3 The ARMA–GARCH model

This model, developed by Weiss (1986), allows us to be even more sophisticated by introducing dynamic modelling into the first-order moment. This moment is then represented by an autoregressive moving average (ARMA) model. The model is written as follows:

$$r_t = \mu + \varphi_1 r_{t-1} + \cdots + \varphi_p r_{t-p} + \varepsilon_t - \theta_1 \varepsilon_{t-1} - \cdots - \theta_q \varepsilon_{t-q}$$

with

$$E(\varepsilon_t/I_{t-1}) = 0$$

and

$$V(r_t/I_{t-1}) = V(\varepsilon_t/I_{t-1}) = h_t = c + \sum_{i=1}^{q} a_i \varepsilon_{t-i}^2 + \sum_{j=1}^{p} b_j h_{t-j}$$

5.1.1.4 The ARCH-M model

Engle *et al.* (1987) extended the previous model to relate it more closely to financial theory and reveal the existence of a risk premium. The model that they developed involves introducing the volatility into the conditional mean. The name ARCH-M means that the ARCH effect is situated in the mean. The model is written as follows:

$$r_t = \mu + \varphi_1 r_{t-1} + \delta_0 h_t + \delta_1 h_{t-1} + \varepsilon_t$$

with

$$E(\varepsilon_t/I_{t-1}) = 0$$

and

$$V(\varepsilon_t/I_{t-1}) = h_t = c + \sum_{i=1}^{q} a_i \varepsilon_{t-i}^2 + \sum_{j=1}^{p} b_j h_{t-j}$$

The δ_0 and δ_1 coefficients enable the short-term and long-term price of the risk to be calculated.

This brief presentation aims to give an overview of the possibilities for this family of models. But the formulas described above only involve assets that were studied independently. We now turn our attention to the simultaneous study of several assets in order to apply these models to portfolio management.

5.1.2 Formulation of the model for several assets

Although the formulation is relatively simple in the case of a single asset, as soon as we study several assets together the number of calculations to be carried out to estimate the covariances quickly becomes significant. The use of a factor model to explain the returns enables the number of calculations to be reduced, since the number of factors is considerably lower than the number of assets. Instead of introducing the ARCH formula into the returns directly, we introduce it into the factors, once the latter have been identified. The formula is therefore written in two stages. First, the asset returns are expressed with the help of factors, and then the ARCH modelling is applied to the factors. So as not to complicate the problem, we shall limit our presentation to cases where the returns are explained by a single factor: the market factor.

Let n be the number of assets under consideration. r_t denotes the vector of the returns associated with the assets. We seek to calculate the first- and second-order moments of r_t, or $E(r_t/I_{t-1})$ and $V(r_t/I_{t-1})$, which are respectively a vector of dimension n and a matrix of dimension (n,n). To do so we use the following model:

$$r_t = \beta f_t + u_t$$

where

$$r_t = \begin{pmatrix} r_{1t} \\ . \\ . \\ . \\ r_{nt} \end{pmatrix} ; \qquad u_t = \begin{pmatrix} u_{1t} \\ . \\ . \\ . \\ u_{nt} \end{pmatrix} ; \qquad \beta = \begin{pmatrix} \beta_1 \\ . \\ . \\ . \\ \beta_n \end{pmatrix}$$

$$E(u_t/I_{t-1}) = 0$$
$$V(u_t/I_{t-1}) = \sigma^2$$

σ^2 is a diagonal matrix of size (n,n) because, as in Sharpe's diagonal model, the error terms of each asset are independent of one another.

The factor f_t is modelled as follows:

$$f_t = \mu + \varepsilon_t$$

with

$$E(\varepsilon_t/I_{t-1}) = 0$$

and

$$V(\varepsilon_t/I_{t-1}) = h_t = c + \sum_{i=1}^{q} a_i \varepsilon_{t-i}^2 + \sum_{j=1}^{p} b_j h_{t-j}$$

(u_t) and (ε_t) are independent. With the help of this model, we can now calculate the conditional expectation vector of the n assets.

Each of the components of this vector is given by

$$E(r_{it}/I_{t-1}) = E((\beta_i f_t + u_{it})/I_{t-1})$$

or, by developing the term:

$$E(r_{it}/I_{t-1}) = \beta_i E(f_t/I_{t-1}) + E(u_{it}/I_{t-1})$$

from which, after calculation:

$$E(r_{it}/I_{t-1}) = \beta_i \mu + E(\varepsilon_t/I_{t-1}) + E(u_{it}/I_{t-1}) = \beta_i \mu$$

since

$$E(\varepsilon_t/I_{t-1}) = 0$$

and

$$E(u_{it}/I_{t-1}) = 0$$

We finally obtain:

$$E(r_t/I_{t-1}) = \begin{pmatrix} \beta_1 \\ \cdot \\ \cdot \\ \cdot \\ \beta_n \end{pmatrix} \mu$$

where μ is a scalar.

The elements of the variance–covariance matrix for the n assets are calculated as follows:

$$\mathrm{cov}(r_{it}, r_{jt}/I_{t-1}) = \mathrm{cov}(\beta_i f_t + u_{it}, \beta_j f_t + u_{jt}/I_{t-1})$$

By developing the above, we obtain:

$$\mathrm{cov}(r_{it}, r_{jt}/I_{t-1}) = \beta_i\beta_j\mathrm{var}(f_t/I_{t-1}) + \beta_i\mathrm{cov}(f_t, u_{jt}/I_{t-1})$$
$$+ \beta_j\mathrm{cov}(f_t, u_{it}/I_{t-1}) + \mathrm{cov}(u_{it}, u_{jt}/I_{t-1})$$

or, after calculation:

$$\mathrm{cov}(r_{it}, r_{jt}/I_{t-1}) = \beta_i\beta_j V(\varepsilon_t/I_{t-1})$$

for all $i \neq j$, because

$$\mathrm{cov}(f_t, u_{it}/I_{t-1}) = \mathrm{cov}(\varepsilon_t, u_{it}/I_{t-1}) = 0$$

since (u_t) and (ε_t) are independent, and

$$\mathrm{cov}(u_{it}, u_{jt}/I_{t-1}) = 0$$

since the assets' residual return terms are independent from each other.

For $i = j$, we have

$$\mathrm{var}(r_{it}/I_{t-1}) = \beta_i^2 V(\varepsilon_t/I_{t-1}) + V(u_{it}/I_{t-1})$$

which finally gives:

$$\mathrm{var}(r_{it}/I_{t-1}) = \beta_i^2 V(\varepsilon_t/I_{t-1}) + \sigma_i^2$$

The variance-covariance matrix for the n assets is therefore written:

$$V(r_t/I_{t-1}) = \begin{pmatrix} \beta_1^2 & \cdots & \beta_1\beta_n \\ \cdot & \cdots & \cdot \\ \cdot & \cdots & \cdot \\ \cdot & \cdots & \cdot \\ \beta_1\beta_n & \cdots & \beta_n^2 \end{pmatrix} V(\varepsilon_t/I_{t-1}) + \begin{pmatrix} \sigma_1^2 & 0 & \cdot\cdot & 0 \\ 0 & \cdots & & \cdot \\ \cdot & \cdots & 0 & \cdot \\ \cdot & & \cdots & 0 \\ 0 & \cdots & 0 & \sigma_n^2 \end{pmatrix}$$

5.1.3 Application to performance measurement

Let us consider a portfolio P made up of n assets, with each assigned a weighting x_{it}, $i = 1, \ldots, n$. The return on this portfolio is written as follows:

$$r_{Pt} = \sum_{i=1}^{n} x_{it} r_{it}$$

or, by replacing r_{it} with its expression:

$$r_{Pt} = \sum_{i=1}^{n} x_{it}(\beta_i f_t + u_{it})$$

which gives, by developing the above:

$$r_{Pt} = \left(\sum_{i=1}^{n} x_{it} \beta_i \right) f_t + \sum_{i=1}^{n} x_{it} u_{it}$$

hence, finally:

$$r_{Pt} = \beta_{Pt} f_t + u_{Pt}$$

by setting

$$\beta_{Pt} = \sum_{i=1}^{n} x_{it} \beta_i$$

and

$$u_{Pt} = \sum_{i=1}^{n} x_{it} u_{it}$$

To estimate the Jensen measure, we consider the following formula:

$$r_{Pt} = \alpha_P + \beta_{Pt} f_t + u_{Pt}$$

α_P and β_P are estimated through regression from time series on the portfolio and the market. Using a stochastic formula for the market factor provides a more accurate result.

5.2 PERFORMANCE MEASUREMENT METHOD USING A CONDITIONAL BETA

5.2.1 The model

The method is based on a conditional version of the CAPM (cf. Ferson and Schadt, 1996), which is consistent with the semi-strong form of market efficiency in the Fama (1970) sense.

The conditional formulation of the CAPM allows the return of each asset i to be written as follows:

$$r_{i,t+1} = \beta_{im}(I_t) r_{m,t+1} + u_{i,t+1} \tag{5.1a}$$

with

$$E(u_{i,t+1}/I_t) = 0 \tag{5.1b}$$

and

$$E(u_{i,t+1}r_{m,t+1}/I_t) = 0 \qquad\qquad (5.1c)$$

r_{it} denotes the return on asset i in excess of the risk-free rate, or

$$r_{it} = R_{it} - R_{Ft}$$

where R_{Ft} denotes the risk-free interest rate for period t.

In the same way, r_{mt} denotes the return on the market in excess of the risk-free rate, or

$$r_{mt} = R_{mt} - R_{Ft}$$

These relationships are valid for $i = 0, \ldots, n$, where n denotes the number of assets and for $t = 0, \ldots, T - 1$, where T denotes the number of periods.

I_t denotes the vector that represents the public information at time t. The beta of the regression, $\beta_{im}(I_t)$, is a conditional beta, i.e. it depends on the information vector I_t. Beta will therefore vary over time depending on a certain number of factors. When I_t is the only information used, no alpha term appears in the regression equation because the latter is null. The error term in the regression is independent from the information, which is translated by relationship (5.1b). This corresponds to the efficient market hypothesis.

Using asset return relationships, we can establish a portfolio return relationship. By hypothesising that the investor uses no information other than the public information, we deduce that the investor's portfolio beta, β_{Pm}, only depends on I_t. By using a development from Taylor, we can approximate this beta through a linear function, or

$$\beta_{Pm}(I_t) = b_{0P} + B'_p i_t$$

In this relationship, b_{0P} can be interpreted as an average beta. It corresponds to the unconditional mean of the conditional beta, or

$$b_{0P} = E(\beta_{Pm}(I_t))$$

The elements of the vector B_p are the response coefficients of the conditional beta with respect to the information variables I_t. i_t denotes the vector of the differentials of I_t compared with its mean, or

$$i_t = I_t - E(I)$$

From this we deduce a conditional formulation of the portfolio return:

$$r_{P,t+1} = b_{0P}r_{m,t+1} + B'_p i_t r_{m,t+1} + u_{P,t+1}$$

with

$$E(u_{P,t+1}/I_t) = 0$$

and

$$E(u_{P,t+1}r_{m,t+1}/I_t) = 0$$

The model's stochastic factor is a linear function of the market return, in excess of the risk-free rate, the coefficients of which depend linearly on I_t.

The model thereby developed enables the traditional performance measures, which came from the CAPM, to be adapted by integrating a time component. These applications are discussed in the following section.

5.2.2 Application to performance measurement[2]

5.2.2.1 The Jensen measure

The traditional Jensen measure does not provide satisfactory results when the risk and return are not constant over time. The model proposed enables this problem to be solved.

To evaluate the performance of portfolios, we employ an empirical formulation of the model which uses the term α_{CP}, or

$$r_{P,t+1} = \alpha_{CP} + b_{0P}r_{m,t+1} + B'_{p}i_{t}r_{m,t+1} + e_{P,t+1}$$

α_{CP} represents the average difference between the excess return of the managed portfolio and the excess return of a dynamic reference strategy. This model provides a better forecast of alpha. A manager with a positive conditional alpha is a manager who has a higher return than the average return of the dynamic reference strategy.

The first step involves determining the content of the information to be used. This is the same as using explanatory factors. Ferson and Schadt (1996) propose linking the portfolio risk to market indicators, such as the market index dividend yield (DY_{t}) and the return on short-term T-bills (TB_{t}), lagged by one period compared with the estimation period.

The dy_{t} and tb_{t} variables denote the differentials compared with the average of the variables DY_{t} and TB_{t}, or

$$\begin{cases} dy_{t} = DY_{t} - \mathrm{E}(DY) \\ tb_{t} = TB_{t} - \mathrm{E}(TB) \end{cases}$$

We therefore have

$$i_{t} = \begin{bmatrix} dy_{t} \\ tb_{t} \end{bmatrix}$$

or

$$B_{p} = \begin{pmatrix} b_{1P} \\ b_{2P} \end{pmatrix}$$

The conditional beta is then written as follows:

$$\beta_{P} = b_{0} + b_{1}dy_{t} + b_{2}tb_{t}$$

From which we have the conditional formulation of the Jensen model:

$$r_{P,t+1} = \alpha_{cp} + b_{0p}r_{m,t+1} + b_{1p}dy_{t}r_{m,t+1} + b_{2p}tb_{t}r_{m,t+1} + e_{p,t+1}$$

where α_{cp} represents the conditional performance measure, b_{0p} denotes the conditional beta, and b_{1p} and b_{2p} measure the variations in the conditional beta compared with the dividend yield and the return on the T-bills.

The coefficients are evaluated through regression from the time series of the variables.

---

[2] Cf. Ferson and Schadt (1996) and Christopherson *et al.* (1999).

5.2.2.2 The Treynor and Mazuy model

The non-conditional approach does not draw a distinction between the skill in using macroeconomic information that is available to everybody and a manager's specific stock picking skill. The conditional approach allows these to be separated.

The conditional formulation, applied to the Treynor and Mazuy model, involves adding a conditional term to the first-order term, or

$$r_{P,t+1} = \alpha_{CP} + b_{0P}r_{m,t+1} + B'_{P}i_t r_{m,t+1} + \gamma_P r_{m,t+1}^2 + e_{P,t+1}$$

where γ_P denotes the market timing coefficient. The conditional formulation is only used in the part that is shared with the Jensen measure and not in the model's additional term.

By using an information vector with two components, we obtain:

$$r_{P,t+1} = \alpha_{CP} + b_{0P}r_{m,t+1} + b_{1P}dy_t r_{m,t+1} + b_{2P}tb_t r_{m,t+1} + \gamma_P r_{m,t+1}^2 + e_{P,t+1}$$

The coefficients of the relationship are estimated through ordinary regressions.

5.2.2.3 The Henriksson and Merton model

The manager seeks to forecast the differential between the market return and the expectation of the return that is conditional on the available information, or

$$u_{m,t+1} = r_{m,t+1} - E(r_{m,t+1}/I_t)$$

Depending on whether the result of this forecast is positive or negative, the manager chooses a different value for the conditional beta of his portfolio.

If the forecast is positive, then

$$\beta_{up}(I_t) = b_{0up} + B'_{up}i_t$$

If the forecast is negative, then

$$\beta_d(I_t) = b_{0d} + B'_d i_t$$

Henriksson and Merton's conditional model is written as follows:

$$r_{P,t+1} = \alpha_{CP} + b_{0d}r_{m,t+1} + B'_d i_t r_{m,t+1} + \gamma_c r_{m,t+1}^* + \Delta' i_t r_{m,t+1}^* + u_{P,t+1}$$

with

$$\gamma_c = b_{0up} - b_{0d}$$
$$\Delta = B_{up} - B_d$$

and

$$r_{m,t+1}^* = r_{m,t+1} I\{r_{m,t+1} - E(r_{m,t+1}/I_t) > 0\}$$

where $I\{\cdot\}$ denotes the indicator function.

More explicitly, if $r_{m,t+1} - E(r_{m,t+1}/I_t) > 0$, then

$$r_{P,t+1} = \alpha_{CP} + b_{0up}r_{m,t+1} + B'_{up}i_t r_{m,t+1} + u_{P,t+1}$$

and if $r_{m,t+1} - E(r_{m,t+1}/I_t) \leq 0$, then

$$r_{P,t+1} = \alpha_{CP} + b_{0d}r_{m,t+1} + B'_d i_t r_{m,t+1} + u_{P,t+1}$$

By again taking our example of an information vector with two components, the model is written:

$$r_{P,t+1} = \alpha_{CP} + b_{0d}r_{m,t+1} + b_{1d}dy_t r_{m,t+1} + b_{2d}tb_t r_{m,t+1}$$
$$+ \gamma_c r^*_{m,t+1} + \delta_1 dy_t r^*_{m,t+1} + \delta_2 tb_t r^*_{m,t+1} + u_{P,t+1}$$

with

$$B_{up} = \begin{pmatrix} b_{1up} \\ b_{2up} \end{pmatrix}$$

$$B_d = \begin{pmatrix} b_{1d} \\ b_{2d} \end{pmatrix}$$

$$\Delta = \begin{pmatrix} \delta_1 \\ \delta_2 \end{pmatrix} = \begin{pmatrix} b_{1up} - b_{1d} \\ b_{2up} - b_{2d} \end{pmatrix}$$

The market timing strategy is evaluated by determining the coefficients of the equation through regression. In the absence of market timing, γ_c and the components of Δ are null. If the manager successfully practises market timing, we must have $\gamma_c + \Delta' i_t > 0$, which means that the conditional beta is higher when the market is above its conditional mean, given the public information, than when it is below its conditional mean.

5.2.3 Model with a conditional alpha

The evaluation of conditional performance enables the portfolio risk and return to be forecast with more accuracy. A better estimation of the beta leads to a better estimation of the alpha. But to be more specific in evaluating portfolio performance, we can assume that the alpha also follows a conditional process (cf. Christopherson et al., 1999). This allows us to evaluate excess performance that varies over time, instead of assuming that it is constant. The relationship given by the conditional alpha is written as follows:

$$\alpha_{CP} = a_P(i_t) = a_{0P} + A'_P i_t$$

The regression equation that enables the Jensen alpha to be evaluated is then written

$$r_{P,t+1} = a_{0P} + A'_P i_t + b_{0P}r_{m,t+1} + B'_P i_t r_{m,t+1} + u_{P,t+1}$$

By again taking the information model that is made up of two variables, the alpha component is written

$$\alpha_{CP} = a_{0P} + a_{1P}dy_t + a_{2P}tb_t$$

with

$$A_P = \begin{pmatrix} a_{1P} \\ a_{2P} \end{pmatrix}$$

The model is then written

$$r_{P,t+1} = a_{0P} + a_{1P}dy_t + a_{2P}tb_t + b_{0P}r_{m,t+1} + b_{1P}r_{m,t+1}dy_t + b_{2P}r_{m,t+1}tb_t + u_{P,t+1}$$

The coefficients of the equation are estimated through regression.

5.2.4 The contribution of conditional models

This section has examined the usefulness of introducing information variables into performance analysis. The study of mutual funds shows that their exposure to risk changes in line with available information on the economy. The use of a conditional measure eliminates the negative Jensen alphas. Their value is brought back to around zero. The viewpoint developed in Christopherson *et al.* (1999) is that a strategy that only uses public information should not generate superior performance. The methods for measuring the performance of market timing strategies, such as Treynor and Mazuy's and Henriksson and Merton's, are also improved by introducing a conditional component into the model.

5.2.5 Extensions to the model

The analysis can be extended to the case of an APT-type multifactor model, or

$$E(R_{i,t+1}/I_t) = \lambda_0(I_t) + \sum_{j=1}^{K} b_{ij}(I_t)\lambda_j(I_t)$$

for $i = 0, \ldots, N$ and $t = 0, \ldots, T - 1$.

The $b_{ij}(I_t)$ represent the conditional betas that measure the systematic risk of the asset compared with the K risk factors. $\lambda_j(I_t)$, $j = 1, \ldots, K$, are the risk premiums that correspond to the market's remuneration for each source of systematic risk. Each conditional beta is then modelled by a linear function of the information. The non-conditional version of the Arbritrage Pricing Theory (APT) model will be presented in detail in Chapter 6.

5.2.6 Comparison with the first model

The models presented in Sections 5.1 and 5.2 both involve a modified version of the CAPM. What they have in common is the use of expectations that are conditional on a piece of information. In the first approach, the beta of the model is constant, but the common factor, on which the return on the assets depends, varies over time. The evolution of this factor is modelled with the exclusive help of its past values. In the second case, the beta coefficient is no longer constant. Its evolution over time is modelled with the help of available information on the economic environment.

5.3 PERFORMANCE ANALYSIS METHODS THAT ARE NOT DEPENDENT ON THE MARKET MODEL

The Roll criticism, by underlining the impossibility of measuring the true market portfolio, cast doubt over the performance measurement models that refer to the market portfolio. Measures that were independent from the market model were therefore developed to respond to the criticisms of the model and propose an alternative. These measures are mainly used for evaluating a manager's market timing strategy.

5.3.1 The Cornell measure

The Cornell measure (cf. Cornell, 1979, and Grinblatt and Titman, 1989b) involves evaluating a manager's superiority as his capacity to pick stocks that have a higher return than their normal return. This measure does not use the market portfolio. The asset returns are the direct references used. The difficulty is to define the return that is considered to be "normal" for each asset.

In practice, the Cornell measure is calculated as the average difference between the return on the investor's portfolio, during the period the portfolio is held, and the return on a reference portfolio with the same weightings, but considered for a different period than the investor's holding period. The calculation can therefore only be carried out when the securities are no longer held in the investor's portfolio, i.e. at the end of the investment management period. The limitations of this measure relate to the number of calculations required to implement it and the possibility that certain securities will disappear during the period.

Formally, by using the notation from Section 4.3.3 in Chapter 4, presenting the decomposition of the Jensen measure, the asymptotic value of the Cornell measure can be written as follows:

$$C = \hat{r}_P - \hat{\beta}_P \hat{r}_B$$

By replacing $\hat{r}_P$ with its expression established in the previous chapter, or

$$\hat{r}_P = \hat{\beta}_P \hat{r}_B + p \lim \left[\frac{1}{T} \sum_{t=1}^{T} \beta_{Pt}(r_{Bt} - \hat{r}_B) \right] + \hat{\varepsilon}_P$$

we obtain:

$$C = p \lim \left[\frac{1}{T} \sum_{t=1}^{T} \beta_{Pt}(r_{Bt} - \hat{r}_B) \right] + \hat{\varepsilon}_P$$

i.e. the sum of the selectivity and timing components from the decomposition of the Jensen measure.

The Jensen and Cornell measures both attribute a null performance to an investor who has no particular skill in terms of timing or in terms of selectivity.

5.3.2   The Grinblatt and Titman measure and the positive period weighting measure

The Cornell measure does correct the problem of the Jensen measure, which wrongly attributes a negative performance to managers who practise market timing. But this measure requires the weightings of the assets that make up the managed portfolio to be known. Grinblatt and Titman (1989a, 1989b) proposed a measure that is an improvement on the Jensen measure, enabling the performance of market timers to be evaluated correctly, but which does not require information on portfolio weightings (see also Grandin, 1998, and Taggart, 1996).

This model is based on the following principle. When a manager truly possesses market timing skills, his performance should tend to repeat over several periods. The method therefore involves taking portfolio returns over several periods, and attributing a positive weighting to each of them. The weighted average of the reference portfolio returns in excess of the risk-free rate must be null. This condition reflects the fact that the measure attributes a null performance to uninformed investors.

The Grinblatt and Titman measure is thus defined by:

$$GB = \sum_{t=1}^{T} w_t(R_{Pt} - R_{Ft})$$

with

$$\sum_{t=1}^{T} w_t = 1$$

and

$$\sum_{t=1}^{T} w_t (R_{Bt} - R_{Ft}) = 0$$

where

R_{Pt} denotes the return on the portfolio for period t;
R_{Bt} denotes the return on the reference portfolio for period t;
R_{Ft} denotes the risk-free rate for period t; and
w_t denotes the weighting attributed to the return for period t.

A positive Grinblatt and Titman measure indicates that the manager accurately forecasts the evolution of the market.

This method presents the disadvantage of not being very intuitive. In addition, in order to implement it we need to determine the weightings to be assigned to the portfolio returns for each period.

5.3.3   Performance measure based on the composition of the portfolio: Grinblatt and Titman study

Grinblatt and Titman (1993) also proposed a method for evaluating market timing based on studying the evolution of the portfolio's composition (see also Grandin, 1998, and Taggart, 1996). The method is therefore fairly different from most other performance measurement methods. The methodology is similar to Cornell's (1979). The measure is based on the study of changes in the composition of the portfolio. It relies on the principle that an informed investor changes the weightings in his portfolio according to his forecast on the evolution of the returns. He overweights the stocks for which he expects a high return and lowers the weightings of the other stocks. A non-null covariance between the weightings of the assets in the portfolio and the returns on the same assets must ensue. The measure is put together by aggregating the covariances.

It is defined by

$$\sum_{i=1}^{n} \sum_{t=1}^{T} (r_{it} (x_{it} - x_{i,t-k})) / T$$

where r_{it} denotes the return on security i, in excess of the risk-free rate, for period t; and x_{it} and $x_{i,t-k}$ denote the weighting of security i at the beginning of each of the periods t and $t - k$.

The expectation of this measure will be null if an uninformed manager modifies the portfolio. It will be positive if the manager is informed.

This measure does not use reference portfolios. It requires the returns on the assets and their weightings within the portfolio to be known. Like the Cornell measure, this method is limited by the significant number of calculations and data required to implement it.

5.4   CONCLUSION

In this chapter we have described a certain number of performance measurement models that tend to provide solutions to the criticisms of the traditional measures drawn from the CAPM. We have presented heteroskedastic models that allow the non-stability of betas over time to be taken into account and performance analysis methods that do not depend on the market model. The heteroskedastic models are much more onerous to implement than the models presented in Chapter 4. As far as the models that do not depend on the market model are concerned, they require a large amount of data to be used and stored. For the moment, none of these methods is very widely used in evaluating managed funds. They are more frequently found in theoretical studies than used by professionals. The indicators based on the market model are still the most widely used. Improvements in performance measurement are more likely to be found in the area of multi-factor models, which are discussed in the next chapter.

BIBLIOGRAPHY

Bollersev, T., "Generalized Autoregressive Conditional Heteroskedasticity", *Journal of Econometrics*, vol. 31, 1986, pp. 307–327.

Christopherson, J.A., Ferson, W.E. and Turner, A.L., "Performance Evaluation Using Conditional Alphas and Betas", *Journal of Portfolio Management*, vol. 26, no. 1, fall 1999, pp. 59–72.

Cornell, B., "Asymmetric Information and Portfolio Performance Measurement", *Journal of Financial Economics*, vol. 7, no. 4, December 1979, pp. 381–390.

Cuthbertson, K., *Quantitative Financial Economics*, Wiley, 1996.

Engle, R., "Autoregressive Conditional Heteroskedasticity with Estimates of the Variance of UK Inflation", *Econometrica*, vol. 50, 1982, pp. 987–1008.

Engle, R., Lilien, P. and Robins, R., "Estimating Time Varying Risk in the Term Structure: the ARCH-M Model", *Econometrica*, vol. 55, 1987, pp. 391–407.

Fama, E.F., "Efficient Capital Markets: A Review of Theory and Empirical Work", *Journal of Finance*, vol. 25, no. 2, March 1970, pp. 383–417.

Ferson, W.E. and Schadt, R.W., "Measuring Fund Strategy and Performance in Changing Economic Conditions", *Journal of Finance*, vol. 51, no. 2, June 1996, pp. 425–461.

Gouriéroux, C., "Modèles hétéroscédastiques", in *Encyclopédie des marchés financiers*, Economica, 1997, pp. 1210–1220.

Grandin, P., *Mesure de performance des fonds d'investissement, Méthodologie et résultats*, Economica, Gestion poche, 1998.

Grinblatt, M. and Titman, S., "Mutual Fund Performance: an Analysis of Quarterly Portfolio Holdings", *Journal of Business*, vol. 62, no. 3, 1989a, pp. 393–416.

Grinblatt, M. and Titman, S., "Portfolio Performance Evaluation: Old Issues and New Insights", *Review of Financial Studies*, vol. 2, 1989b, pp. 393–421.

Grinblatt, M. and Titman, S., "Performance Measurement without Benchmarks: An Examination of Mutual Fund Returns", *Journal of Business*, vol. 66, no. 1, 1993, pp. 47–68.

Simon, Y., *Encyclopédie des marchés financiers*, Economica, 1997.

Taggart, Jr. R.A., *Quantitative Analysis for Investment Management*, Prentice Hall, 1996.

Weiss, A., "ARMA Models with ARCH Errors", *Journal of Time Series Analysis*, vol. 5, 1986, pp. 129–143.

6

Multi-Factor Models and their Application to Performance Measurement[1]

In Chapter 4 we described the Capital Asset Pricing Model (CAPM) and presented the associated criticisms. The model is based on very strong theoretical assumptions which are not entirely respected by the markets in practice. We have seen that the model assumes that the market portfolio is efficient in the mean–variance sense. However, the efficiency can only be ensured if the portfolio returns are normally distributed, or if the investors have a quadratic utility function. These assumptions are restrictive and difficult to justify. It has therefore not been possible to validate the model empirically in a rigorous fashion. The modified versions of the CAPM only provided partial solutions. The theorists thus sought to develop a more general model, while at the same time simplifying the assumptions. The result was a family of models that was referred to collectively as multi-factor models. These models constitute an alternative theory to the CAPM, but do not replace it. They are also linear models but, unlike the CAPM, there are no assumptions about the behaviour of investors. They also allow asset returns to be explained by factors other than the market index, and thus provide more specific information on risk analysis and the evaluation of manager performance.

In this chapter we begin by presenting multi-factor models from a theoretical point of view, and then describe the methods for choosing the factors and estimating the model parameters. Finally, we present the two main applications of these models, namely risk analysis and evaluation of portfolio performance.

6.1 PRESENTATION OF THE MULTI-FACTOR MODELS

The earliest model, which comes from Ross, is based on a key concept in financial theory: arbitrage valuation. A second category of models, based only on empirical considerations, was developed later. This section presents the structure of these two types of model.

6.1.1 Arbitrage models

In 1976, Ross proposed a model based on the principle of valuing assets through arbitrage theory (see also Roll and Ross, 1980). This model, called the Arbitrage Pricing Theory (APT) model, is based on less restrictive assumptions than the CAPM. While the CAPM assumes that asset returns are normally distributed, the APT does not hypothesise on the nature of the distribution. The APT model does not include any assumptions on individuals' utility functions either, but simply assumes that individuals are risk averse. This simplification of the assumptions allows the model to be validated empirically.

---

[1] For more details, the interested reader could consult Batteau and Lasgouttes (1997), Fedrigo *et al.* (1996), Marsh and Pfleiderer (1997), Chapters 8 and 16 of Elton and Gruber (1995), Chapter 4 of Farrell (1997) and Fontaine (1987).

The APT model still seeks to explain asset returns through common factors, but instead of the well-defined single factor in the CAPM, the model employs K factors and consequently constitutes a more general theory. The problem then consists of determining the value of K and the nature of the factors. That will be the subject of Section 6.2 of this chapter. The present section simply describes the theory underlying the model.

The APT model first postulates that a linear relationship exists between the realised returns of the assets and the K factors common to those assets, or

$$R_{it} = E(R_i) + \sum_{k=1}^{K} b_{ik} F_{kt} + \varepsilon_{it}$$

where

R_{it} denotes the rate of return for asset i;
$E(R_i)$ denotes the expected return for asset i;
b_{ik} denotes the sensitivity (or exposure) of asset i to factor k;
F_{kt} denotes the return of factor k with $E(F_k) = 0$; and
ε_{it} denotes the residual (or specific) return of asset i, i.e. the share of the return that is not explained by the factors, with $E(\varepsilon_i) = 0$.

The APT model assumes that markets are perfectly efficient and that the factor model for explaining the asset returns is the same for all individuals. The number of assets n is assumed to be very large compared with the number of factors K.

The residual returns of the different assets are independent from each other and independent from the factors. We therefore have

$$\text{cov}(\varepsilon_i, \varepsilon_j) = 0, \quad \text{for } i \neq j$$

$$\text{cov}(\varepsilon_i, F_k) = 0, \quad \text{for all } i \text{ and } k$$

Arbitrage reasoning then allows us to end up with the following equilibrium relationship:

$$E(R_i) - R_F = \sum_{k=1}^{K} \lambda_k b_{ik}$$

where R_F denotes the risk-free rate.

The details that allow us to obtain this relationship are presented in Appendix 6.1 at the end of this chapter. This relationship explains the average asset return as a function of the exposure to different risk factors and the market's remuneration for those factors.

λ_k is interpreted as the factor k risk premium at equilibrium. We define δ_k as the expected return of a portfolio with a sensitivity to factor k equal to 1, and null sensitivity to the other factors. We then have the following relationship:

$$\lambda_k = \delta_k - R_F$$

which allows us to write the arbitrage relationship in the following form:

$$E(R_i) - R_F = \sum_{k=1}^{K} (\delta_k - R_F) b_{ik}$$

This relationship can be interpreted as the equation of a linear regression, where the b_{ik} are defined as

$$b_{ik} = \frac{\text{cov}(R_{it}, \delta_k)}{\text{var}(\delta_k)}$$

The b_{ik} are the sensitivities to the factors (factor loadings).

This formula shows the CAPM as a specific case of the APT model, as long as we assume that the returns are normally distributed. We then simply take the market portfolio as the only factor.

The APT model allows us to use several factors to explain the returns, which gives it an advantage, in theory, over the CAPM. The market portfolio no longer has any particular role. It is simply one factor among many. The APT model does not require it to be efficient, as was the case for the CAPM. Finally, the APT model can be extended to the case of investment over several periods, while the CAPM only considers a single period.

Since the theory does not give the number and the nature of the factors, this model has been the object of numerous empirical validation tests to identify the most significant factors. The results of these tests will be presented in Section 6.2, which discusses the choice of factors and model estimation.

The models in this category are called longitudinal, or chronological, models, a reference to the fact that the returns are explained for each period.

6.1.2 Empirical models

The models drawn from arbitrage theory associate a risk premium λ_k with each factor. This risk premium is a characteristic of the factor and is completely independent from the securities. Another approach, which is empirical, proposes making the expected returns dependent on security-specific factors. In the first case the risk premiums constitute responses to outside influences. They reflect the link that exists between economic forces and the securities markets. The sensitivity of assets is evaluated in relation to factors that are qualified as macroeconomic, such as the return on the bond market, unanticipated changes in inflation, changes in exchange rates and changes in industrial production. In the second case the factors are security-specific attributes and are not linked to the economy. This type of factor will be described more precisely later in the chapter, when the Barra model is presented.

The empirical models make less restrictive assumptions than the APT-type models and no longer use arbitrage theory. They do not presume that there is an explanatory factorial relationship for the returns realised in each period t. They directly postulate that the average returns on the assets, or more precisely the average risk premiums, can be decomposed with the help of factors. Therefore, only one calculation stage remains, while the APT model required two. For each asset i, the relationship is written as follows:

$$E(R_i) - R_F = \sum_{k=1}^{K} b_{ik}\alpha_k + \varepsilon_i$$

where

b_{ik} denotes the value of factor k that is specific to firm i;

α_k denotes the coefficient associated with factor k, corresponding to the market's remuneration for that factor; and

ε_i denotes the specific return on asset i.

The factors that are used in this model are derived from financial analysis. They consist of financial ratios such as the P/E ratio, the dividend growth rate, the dividend yield, the earnings yield, and also the return for a past period and the market capitalisation. They are given the general term of fundamental factors. These models are called cross-sectional or fundamental, in reference to the factors. In Section 6.2 we will present the model developed by the firm Barra, which is the best known in this category of model.

The CAPM can also be seen as a specific case of this type of model. In this case the only factor that explains the security's risk premium is its beta, which does indeed constitute a security-specific factor.

6.1.3　Link between the two types of model

From a formal point of view, the relationship that gives the factorial expression of an asset's average return is similar to the second APT equation, apart from the fact that it contains an additional residual return term. As we saw previously, the empirical model is written as follows:

$$E(R_i) - R_F = \sum_{k=1}^{K} b_{ik} \alpha_k + \varepsilon_i$$

and the second APT equation is written as

$$E(R_i) - R_F = \sum_{k=1}^{K} \lambda_k b_{ik}$$

These two equations are cross-sectional. All that would be needed for the two equations to be strictly identical, apart from the names of the variables, would be to add a residual term to the APT equation. The empirical model is therefore drawn directly from the arbitrage model formula. The difference between the two models is in the interpretation of the variables.

In the case of the APT model, b_{ik} denotes the sensitivity of asset i to factor k. These b_{ik} have been estimated through regression with the help of the first APT equation. In the case of the empirical models, b_{ik} denotes the value of factor k specific to firm i. These b_{ik} factors are actually interpreted as the assets' exposures to the attributes. The b_{ik} are known beforehand. The α_k in the empirical model and the λ_k in the APT model are then estimated through similar procedures. These variables, called risk premiums, represent the market's remuneration for the factors.

We should stress that the variables that dominate in each of the two models are not the same. The second APT equation focuses on the risk premiums (the lambdas) associated with the economic factors that describe the market. The empirical models, for their part, favour the betas, i.e. the exposures, that are characteristic of the firms. The two approaches thus correspond to different philosophies.

6.2　CHOOSING THE FACTORS AND ESTIMATING THE MODEL PARAMETERS

As we mentioned in Section 6.1, multi-factor model theory does not specify the number or nature of the factors. That is where the main difficulty resides. The use of these models therefore requires a prior phase for seeking and identifying the most significant factors, as well as estimating the associated risk premiums. A certain number of empirical studies have been carried out on this subject. They give guidance on the choices, but the combinations of factors that allow the returns on a group of assets to be explained are not necessarily unique.

In addition, two major techniques are opposed in identifying the common factors for the assets. A first method, which is called an exogenous or explicit factor method, consists of determining the factors in advance. The choice of factors at that stage is arbitrary and tests are then carried out to conserve the most significant factors only. A second method, which is called an endogenous or implicit factor method, involves extracting the factors directly from the historical returns, with the help of methods drawn from factor analysis. Although the second method enables the evolution of returns to be monitored, the problem of interpreting the factors is posed.

In view of the nature of the factors considered and the identification method chosen, the multi-factor models used in practice can be grouped into three categories:

1. The first category brings together models where the factors are macroeconomic variables. The choice of these variables comes from empirical studies carried out to test the APT model. The factor loadings are calculated through regression.
2. The second category comprises models where the factor loadings are functions of the firms' attributes and the factors are estimated through regression. This is the approach used by the American firm Barra. The factors are said to be fundamental factors.
3. The third category consists of models where the factors are extracted from the return database through factor analysis or principal component analysis. This is the approach that was used for the first tests on the APT model to determine the number of explanatory factors. The principal application of this approach is in portfolio risk analysis and control. It is used by the American firms Quantal and Advanced Portfolio Technology (APT). The latter has a French subsidiary called Aptimum.

In the first two categories the factors are explicit. In the third, they are implicit. The empirical formulation common to these models can be written as follows:

$$R_{it} = b_{i1} F_{1t} + \cdots + b_{iK} F_{Kt} + u_{it}$$

where $i = 1, \ldots, n$, with n the number of assets, and $t = 1, \ldots, T$, with T the number of sub-periods. For the first category of models, we know F and we estimate b; for the second, we know b and we estimate F; and for the third, we estimate b and F simultaneously. Note that for the first and third category models an additional stage is necessary to estimate the risk premiums associated with the factors, once the b coefficients are known.

In this section we describe the characteristics of each model in detail and present the methods for evaluating the parameters.

6.2.1 Explicit factor models

6.2.1.1 Explicit factor models based on macroeconomic variables

These models are derived directly from APT theory. The risk factors that affect asset returns are approximated by observable macroeconomic variables that can be forecast by economists. The choice of the number of factors, namely five macroeconomic factors and the market factor, comes from the first empirical tests carried out by Roll and Ross with the help of a factor analysis method. The classic factors in the APT models are industrial production, interest rates, oil prices, differences in bond ratings and the market factor. In order to be able to use them as factors, the series of economic variables must be restated. They must first be centred, so that their mean is null, and then we must calculate the innovations of each series, i.e. the unanticipated changes in the series, which will enable the asset returns to be explained. The innovations are obtained by taking the residuals of the autoregressive processes adapted to each series. The principle behind this method is described clearly in Chen *et al.* (1986).

The procedure for estimating the model for a given market and period can then lead to the retention of certain factors only. This procedure, inspired by that used by Fama and MacBeth (1973) to test the CAPM, is carried out in two stages.

The first stage uses the first APT equation, or

$$R_{it} = \alpha_i + \sum_{k=1}^{K} b_{ik} F_{kt} + \varepsilon_{it}$$

The R_{it} returns for a set of assets are observed for a fixed period and with a certain frequency. For example, we could consider the weekly returns on French stocks over the past five years. The number of time periods must be greater than the number of assets. Roll and Ross worked on the American market using daily returns. In view of the large number of assets, they grouped them together into portfolios to perform the study. They constructed around 40 portfolios with 30 securities in each. The criterion chosen for making up the portfolios was a ranking of the securities in descending order of market capitalisation. There was another advantage to grouping the securities together in portfolios, which justified the fact that it was used by Fama and MacBeth: it enabled the error introduced by using the results of the first regression to carry out the second regression to be reduced. The F_{kt} are the series of innovations of the factors obtained from the economic variables observed for the same period and with the same frequency as the asset returns. The factor loadings b_{ik} for each asset are estimated through regression. By developing the contents of the matrices, this regression is written as follows:

$$\begin{pmatrix} R_{11} & \cdots & R_{n1} \\ \cdot & \cdots & \cdot \\ \cdot & \cdots & \cdot \\ \cdot & \cdots & \cdot \\ R_{1T} & \cdots & R_{nT} \end{pmatrix} = (\alpha_1 \ldots \alpha_n) + \begin{pmatrix} F_{11} & \cdots & F_{K1} \\ \cdot & \cdots & \cdot \\ \cdot & \cdots & \cdot \\ \cdot & \cdots & \cdot \\ F_{1T} & \cdots & F_{KT} \end{pmatrix} \begin{pmatrix} b_{11} & \cdots & b_{n1} \\ \cdot & \cdots & \cdot \\ \cdot & \cdots & \cdot \\ \cdot & \cdots & \cdot \\ b_{1K} & \cdots & b_{nK} \end{pmatrix} + \begin{pmatrix} \varepsilon_{11} & \cdots & \varepsilon_{n1} \\ \cdot & \cdots & \cdot \\ \cdot & \cdots & \cdot \\ \cdot & \cdots & \cdot \\ \varepsilon_{1T} & \cdots & \varepsilon_{nT} \end{pmatrix}$$

Roll and Ross (1980) describe the econometric aspects of this regression.

The second stage then involves estimating, through regression, the risk premiums λ_k associated with each factor. A cross-sectional regression of the expected asset returns against the factor loadings obtained during the first regression is then performed. The equation for this regression comes from the second APT equation, or

$$E(R_{it}) = \lambda_0 + \sum_{k=1}^{K} b_{ik} \lambda_k$$

where $\lambda_0 = R_F$ is the rate of return of the risk-free asset. Explicitly, the second regression is written

$$\begin{pmatrix} R_{11} & \cdots & R_{n1} \\ \cdot & \cdots & \cdot \\ \cdot & \cdots & \cdot \\ \cdot & \cdots & \cdot \\ R_{1T} & \cdots & R_{nT} \end{pmatrix} = \begin{pmatrix} \lambda_{01} \\ \cdot \\ \cdot \\ \cdot \\ \lambda_{0T} \end{pmatrix} + \begin{pmatrix} \lambda_{11} & \cdots & \lambda_{K1} \\ \cdot & \cdots & \cdot \\ \cdot & \cdots & \cdot \\ \cdot & \cdots & \cdot \\ \lambda_{1T} & \cdots & \lambda_{KT} \end{pmatrix} \begin{pmatrix} b_{11} & \cdots & b_{n1} \\ \cdot & \cdots & \cdot \\ \cdot & \cdots & \cdot \\ \cdot & \cdots & \cdot \\ b_{1K} & \cdots & b_{nK} \end{pmatrix} + (u_1 \ldots u_n)$$

The result of this regression is a time series of λ_{kt}. The average premium for the period is obtained by calculating

$$\bar{\lambda}_k = \frac{1}{T} \sum_{t=1}^{T} \lambda_{kt}$$

We then carry out a statistical test to check whether this average premium is significantly positive. At the end of this second stage we only retain, for the model, factors that have a significant risk premium. To be rigorous, it is then necessary to carry out the whole procedure again with the number of factors really identified and recalculate the factor loadings and risk premiums for the factors retained only.

Empirical validation studies of the APT[2] model highlight the fact that only a small number of factors have a significantly positive risk premium. In addition, the results vary depending on the period studied and the country. The research and identification phase for the model is therefore essential, so that only the "right" factors are retained. It is also necessary to re-evaluate the model periodically to ensure that it corresponds to the returns to be analysed.

At the end of the model's research and identification stage, we have, for a given period, the following relationship:

$$E(R_i) = \lambda_0 + \sum_{k=1}^{K} b_{ik} \lambda_k$$

in which all the parameters are known: the number of factors K, the factor loadings b_{ik} and the risk premiums λ_k. The risk premiums do not depend on the assets, only on the factors.

By replacing $E(R_i)$ with its expression in the first APT equation, we obtain the following:

$$R_{it} = \lambda_0 + \sum_{k=1}^{K} b_{ik} \lambda_k + \sum_{k=1}^{K} b_{ik} F_{kt} + \varepsilon_{it}$$

Assuming that the loadings and risk premiums of the factors are stable, we can forecast, in theory, the return on the asset for the upcoming period with the help of forecasts on the factors, since the factors are well-defined variables. ε_{it} then measures the differential between the forecast and realised variable. This should however be used with care, because empirical studies tend to prove that factor loadings and risk premiums are not stable over time.

The use of the APT model for analysing portfolio risk and performance is discussed in Section 6.4.

6.2.1.2   Explicit factor models based on fundamental factors

This approach is much more pragmatic. The aim now is to explain the returns on the assets with the help of variables that depend on the characteristics of the firms themselves, and no longer on identical economic factors, for all assets. The modelling no longer uses any theoretical assumptions but considers a factorial breakdown of the average asset returns directly. The model assumes that the factor loadings of the assets are functions of the firms' attributes. The realisations of the factors are then estimated by regression. Here again the choice of explanatory variables is not unique. Studies suggest that only two factors should be added to the market factor: this is the case for the studies carried out by Fama and French. Carhart,

---

[2] See, for example, the Chen *et al.* (1986) study on American stocks and the Hamao (1988) study on Japanese stocks.

for his part, proposed a four-factor model. Other studies led to a long list of very specific factors: this is the case for those carried out by the authors of the Barra model. For example, an article by Connor (1995) studies the explanatory power of 13 fundamental factors. We have chosen to limit ourselves here to a few examples of models. However, the subject of characterising explanatory factors for returns is vast and research articles on the subject are published regularly. The *Journal of Finance*, for example, constitutes an interesting source of information on the subject.

Fama and French's three-factor model[3]

Fama and French have carried out several empirical studies to identify the fundamental factors that explain average asset returns, as a complement to the market beta. They highlighted two important factors that characterise a company's risk: the book-to-market ratio and the company's size measured by its market capitalisation. Fama and French (1993) therefore propose a three-factor model, which is formulated as follows:

$$E(R_i) - R_F = b_{i1}(E(R_M) - R_F) + b_{i2}E(SMB) + b_{i3}E(HML)$$

where

$E(R_i)$	denotes the expected return of asset i;
R_F	denotes the rate of return of the risk-free asset;
$E(R_M)$	denotes the expected return of the market portfolio;
SMB (small minus big)	denotes the difference between returns on two portfolios: a small-capitalisation portfolio and a large-capitalisation portfolio;
HML (high minus low)	denotes the difference between returns on two portfolios: a portfolio with a high book-to-market ratio and a portfolio with a low book-to-market ratio;
b_{ik}	denotes the factor loadings.

The b_{ik} are calculated by regression from the following equation:

$$R_{it} - R_{Ft} = \alpha_i + b_{i1}(R_{Mt} - R_{Ft}) + b_{i2}SMB_t + b_{i3}HML_t + \varepsilon_i$$

Fama and French consider that the financial markets are indeed efficient, but that the market factor does not explain all the risks on its own. They conclude that a three-factor model does describe the asset returns, but specify that the choice of factors is not unique. Factors other than those retained in their 1993 model also have demonstrable and demonstrated explanatory power.

Carhart's (1997) four-factor model

This model is an extension of Fama and French's three-factor model. The additional factor is momentum, which enables the persistence of the returns to be measured. This factor was added to take into account the anomaly revealed by Jegadeesh and Titman (1993). With the same notation as above, this model is written

$$E(R_i) - R_F = b_{i1}(E(R_M) - R_F) + b_{i2}E(SMB) + b_{i3}E(HML) + b_{i4}(PR1YR)$$

where *PR1YR* denotes the difference between the average of the highest returns and the average of the lowest returns from the previous year.

---

[3] Cf. Fama and French (1992, 1995, 1996) and Molay (2000).

The Barra model[4]

The Barra multi-factor model is the best known example of the commercial application of a fundamental factor model. Barra disseminates research articles written by members of the firm on its web site. These articles situate the Barra model within the context of multi-factor models and compare it with other approaches. We could, for example, cite Engerman (1993), Grinold (1991), Rosenberg (1987) and Rudd (1992).

The Barra model assumes that asset returns are determined by the fundamental character-istics of the firm such as the industrial sector, the size and earnings. The systematic risk of an asset can then be explained by its sensitivity with regard to these characteristics. The charac-teristics constitute the exposures or betas of the assets. The approach therefore assumes that the exposures are known and then calculates the factors. The returns are characterised by the following factorial structure:

$$R_{it} = \sum_{k=1}^{K} b_{ikt}\alpha_{kt} + u_{it}$$

where

R_{it} denotes the return on security i in excess of the risk-free rate;
b_{ik} denotes the factor loading or exposure of asset i to factor k;
α_k denotes the return on factor k; and
u_i denotes the specific return on asset i.

The specific returns on the assets are assumed to be non-correlated with each other and non-correlated with the factor returns.

The factors used in this model belong to two categories: factors linked to the industrial sector and the risk indices. The former measure the differences in behaviour among securities that belong to different industries. The latter measure the differences in behaviour among securities for the non-industrial side.

Barra's model for American stocks defines 52 industrial categories. The list of industries is given in Barra (1998). We then determine the exposure of the securities in the universe to those industries: each security is attributed a weighting in the different industries. If the security is only attached to a single industrial sector, then the exposure to the "industry" factor takes a value of one or zero, depending on whether the security belongs to that group of industries or not. The assets of firms whose activity is spread over several industries are split between the different groups concerned with a percentage corresponding to the share of activity in that industry. The "industry" factors are orthogonal in their construction.

For the second category of factors, the model uses a precise list of 13 risk indices. Each of these indices is constructed from a certain number of fundamental pieces of information called descriptors, the combination of which best characterises the risk concept to be described. Barra (1998) presents these indices and their descriptors in detail. The list of risk indices, ranked in descending order of importance, is as follows:

1. *volatility*, a risk index based on both the long-term and short-term measurement of volatility;
2. *momentum*, an index that measures the variation in returns related to recent behaviour of the stock prices: the stocks that had a positive return in excess of the risk-free rate over the period are separated from those that had a negative return;

---

[4] For more details, one can consult Sheikh (1996).

3. *size*, an index that measures the difference in asset returns due to differences in market capitalisation;
4. *size non-linearity*, an index that measures the deviations from linearity in the relationship between the returns and the logarithm of their market capitalisation;
5. *trading activity*, an index that measures the volume of trades for each asset (the assets with the most significant trading activity are the most interesting for institutional investors: the returns on those stocks may behave differently than the returns of stocks that are not widely held by the institutions);
6. *growth*, an index that uses historical growth and profitability measures to forecast future earnings growth;
7. *earnings yield*, an index that is obtained by combining the historical earnings-to-price ratios with the values that were predicted by analysts: assets with the same earnings yield have returns that behave similarly;
8. *value*, an index that separates value stocks from growth stocks by using their book-to-price ratio;
9. *earnings variability*, an index that measure the variability in earnings by using both historical measures and analysts' forecasts;
10. *leverage*, an index that measures the financial leverage of the company;
11. *currency sensitivity*, an index that measures the sensitivity of the stock return to the return on a basket of foreign currencies;
12. *dividend yield*, an index that gives a forecast of the dividend yield from historical dividend data and the behaviour of the market price of the stock;
13. *non-estimation universe indicator*, an index for companies that are outside the estimation universe. It allows the factor model to be extended to stocks that are not part of the estimation universe.

The exposures to the risk indices are put together by weighting the exposures to their descriptors. The weightings are chosen in such a way as to maximise the explanatory and forecasting power of the model. Since the units and orders of magnitude are different depending on the variables, the exposures to the descriptors and risk indices are normalised according to the following formula:

$$b_{\text{normalised}} = \frac{b_{\text{raw}} - \langle b_{\text{raw}} \rangle}{std[b_{\text{raw}}]}$$

where $\langle b_{\text{raw}} \rangle$ denotes the mean value of exposure to a risk index for the whole universe of assets; and $std[b_{\text{raw}}]$ denotes the standard deviation of the exposure values for the whole universe of assets.

The result is that the exposure to each risk index has a null mean and a standard deviation equal to 1.

The Barra model therefore contains a total of 65 factors. Using this model in practice implies that we know the risk indices and that they are regularly updated. We therefore start by observing the characteristics of the companies at the beginning of each period. These characteristics are used to calculate the companies' factor loadings. These loadings or exposures constitute the b_{ikt} measured at the beginning of period t. They represent the risk indices and industry groups. The returns on the factors, α_{kt}, and the specific returns, u_{it}, are then estimated through a multiple regression, using the Fama–MacBeth procedure (Fama and MacBeth, 1973). To do this, the asset returns, R_{it}, in excess of the risk-free rate, are regressed on the factor exposures.

We obtain time series of factor realisations, for which we calculate the mean. We then test whether the mean is significantly different from zero. The model therefore proceeds in a single step. The model must be updated regularly to integrate the new information that comes from the companies. Barra estimates the returns of the 65 factors monthly.

The Barra model can also be used as an APT model in which the macroeconomic factors are replaced with microeconomic factors or fundamental attributes. We then calculate the assets' factor loadings. The model formulated by Barra is therefore consistent with the APT model.

The results are then used to estimate the variance–covariance matrix of asset returns. This aspect will be detailed in Section 6.4 when the Barra portfolio risk analysis model is presented.

6.2.2 Implicit or endogenous factor models[5]

The idea behind this approach is to use the asset returns to characterise the unobservable factors. It is natural to assume that the factors that influence the returns leave an identifiable trace. These factors are therefore extracted from the asset returns database through a factor analysis method and the factor loadings are jointly calculated. This approach was originally used by Roll and Ross to test the APT model. In this section we discuss the principle of factor analysis and its use in evaluating multi-factor models. Finally, we present a valuation method, called semi-autoregressive, which was developed more recently. The disadvantage of an implicit search for factors, however, is that it does not allow the nature of the factors to be identified.

6.2.2.1 The principle of factor analysis[6]

Factor analysis is a set of statistical methods that allows the information contained in a group of variables to be summarised, with the help of a reduced number of variables, while minimising the loss of information due to the simplification. In the case of factor models, this technique allows us to identify the number of factors required for the model and to express the asset returns with the help of several underlying factors. The method enables the explanatory factors and the factor loadings to be obtained simultaneously, but it does not give any information on the nature of the factors, which we must then be able to interpret.

From a mathematical point of view the returns of n assets considered over T periods are equated with a data cloud in the space R^n. The principle involves projecting this cloud into a sub-space of lower dimension, defined by factor axes, while explaining as much of the cloud's variability as possible. The strong correlations that exist between the returns on the assets enable this result to be reached. The search for factor axes is carried out from the calculation of the eigenvalues and eigenvectors of the asset returns' variance–covariance matrix. The weight of the factor axes is measured by the factor loadings. There are two factor analysis methods: (1) factor analysis based on the principle of maximum likelihood, which involves an optimal reproduction of the correlations observed, and (2) principal component analysis, which involves extracting the maximum variance.

If the number of assets is significant, then we group the assets into portfolios to carry out the study, so that the number of correlations to be calculated remains reasonable. Studies have shown that the results obtained depend on the criterion used to form the portfolios. Moreover,

---

[5] Cf. Fedrigo *et al.* (1996).
[6] Cf. Chapter 2 of Fontaine (1987), and Batteau and Lasgouttes (1997).

the greater the number of securities, the more the number of factors increases. These factors also vary depending on the period considered.

Maximum likelihood method

This method, which is called classic factor analysis, aims to reproduce the correlation between the variables as well as possible. Each of the variables observed is described linearly with the help of K common factors, which take into account the correlation between the variables, and a specific factor (or residual term), which expresses the share of variance that is specific to each security. The factors are modelled by random variables of normal density. Since the factors are assumed to be independent, the variables have a multivarious normal distribution. In the case that interests us, the variables are asset returns.

The method involves expressing the asset returns variance–covariance matrix as the sum of a positive eigenvalue matrix of rank K and a diagonal matrix, or

$$V = BB' + D$$

where B, with a dimension of $n \times K$, denotes the factor loading matrix b_{ik}, and D denotes the variance–covariance matrix of the residuals. This matrix is diagonal because the residuals are not correlated.

The advantage of the procedure is to obtain a value of K that is as small as possible, or at least much smaller than the number of initial variables.

Roll and Ross used this method, or more specifically Lawley and Maxwell's (1963) maximum likelihood method, to identify the number of factors in the APT model and to estimate the b_{ik} factor loadings of the assets.

Principal component analysis

The principle consists of searching for linear combinations of the n initial vectors, such that the new vectors obtained are eigenvalues of the initial variance–covariance matrix. The most widely used algorithm is Hotelling's (1933).

The procedure is as follows. We begin by extracting the index which best explains the variance of the original data. This constitutes the first principal component. We then extract the index which best explains the variance of the original data that was not explained by the first component. The second index is therefore, through its construction, non-correlated with the first. We then proceed sequentially. The iterative procedure can be repeated, in theory, until the number of indices extracted is equal to the number of variables studied: we thereby reproduce the original variance–covariance matrix exactly. In practice, since the components have decreasing explanatory power, we evaluate the quantity of information returned at each stage with the help of the associated eigenvalue, and we stop the procedure when the component obtained is no longer significant. The dimension of the new space for explaining the returns is therefore chosen in such a way as to limit the loss of information. The K explanatory factors retained are the eigenvectors associated with the K largest eigenvalues from the matrix. When the returns are widely dispersed, the number of high eigenvalues is significant, which leads to a space of large dimension. If, on the other hand, there is strong correlation between the returns, then a limited number of components is sufficient to explain most of the variance–covariance matrix.

Comparing the two approaches

The maximum likelihood method is better adapted to the Ross model. The principal component analysis method, for its part, corresponds more to a description of the returns. This method does, however, have an advantage over the first in that it does not make any particular assumptions about the distribution of the returns. Researchers nevertheless prefer the method based on maximum likelihood, which uses Gaussian laws, the properties of which are well known. The real distributions of the returns are not in fact very far removed from a multi-normal law and the method provides a more accurate test of the number of factors in the model.

6.2.2.2   Estimating the risk premiums

Factor analysis allows us to obtain the number of factors that explain the returns, and simultaneously the value of those factors and an estimation of the matrix of factor loadings. That is the advantage of the method compared with explicit factor models, where it was necessary to have one of the two variables, factors or factor loadings, to estimate the other. For what follows, i.e. estimating risk premiums, the principle remains the same as for explicit factor models: the factor loadings are regressed as a cross-section on the expected asset (or portfolio) returns to obtain the value of the risk premiums and their statistical significance. We thereby obtain the $\lambda_k, k = 0, \ldots, K$, such that

$$E(R_i) = \lambda_0 + b_{i1}\lambda_1 + \cdots + b_{iK}\lambda_K, \quad i = 1, \ldots, n$$

where n denotes the number of assets.

6.2.2.3   Interpreting the factors

The implicit factor estimation method has the disadvantage of not allowing a direct economic interpretation of the factors obtained. We can simply say that each factor, obtained as a linear combination of the asset returns, is a portfolio with a sensitivity to itself equal to one, and null sensitivity to the other factors. This is due to the orthogonal nature of the factors.

Since we are unable to name the implicit factors, we can explain the factors with the help of known indicators and thus come back to an explicit factor decomposition from the implicit decomposition. We proceed in the following manner. Taking R_{it} as the return on asset i explained by k implicit factors:

$$R_{it} = \mu_i + \beta_{i1}F_{1t} + \cdots + \beta_{ik}F_{kt} + \varepsilon_{it}$$

where the F_{jt} denote the non-correlated implicit factors. We have $\text{cov}(F_i, F_j) = 0$ and $\text{var}(F_i) = 1$.

We regress an explicit factor on the implicit factors:

$$R_{mt} = \mu_m + \beta_{m1}F_{1t} + \cdots + \beta_{mk}F_{kt} + \varepsilon_{mt}$$

By calculating

$$\text{cov}(R_i, R_m) = \beta_{i1}\beta_{m1} + \beta_{i2}\beta_{m2} + \cdots + \beta_{ik}\beta_{mk}$$

and

$$\text{var}(R_m) = \beta_{m1}^2 + \beta_{m2}^2 + \cdots + \beta_{mk}^2$$

and calculating the quotient of these two quantities, we obtain a beta that we can equate with the CAPM beta and which gives us the coefficient of the explicit factor R_{mt} in the decomposition of the return R_{it}. By doing this for all the explicit factors, we reach an explicit decomposition of the return R_{it}, having started with its implicit decomposition.

6.2.2.4 Semi-autoregressive approach[7]

The underlying idea is to postulate that there is an approximate linear relationship between the returns and the factor loadings. If we have more returns than loadings, then the latter can be approximated with the help of a sub-sample of returns. These approximations are then regressed as a cross-section on the returns for a different period to estimate the associated factors. This method differs from the conventional factor extraction techniques, such as factor analysis based on maximum likelihood and principal component analysis, even if the idea used is also the replication of the factors with the help of linear combinations of asset returns.

This method does not make any assumptions about the return distributions. It provides a simple asymptotic variance–covariance matrix of the estimated factors, which can be used to control the measurement errors. This is useful both for testing the model and for using it to evaluate the performance of a portfolio compared with a benchmark, while taking the measurement errors into account.

The asset returns are assumed to be generated by the following model approximated to K factors:

$$R_{it} = \mathrm{E}(R_{it}) + b_{i1} F_{1t} + \cdots + b_{iK} F_{Kt} + \varepsilon_{it}$$

for $i = 1, \ldots, n$ and $t = 1, \ldots, T$. The notation and conditions on the variables are those of the APT model, or

F_{kt}, is the unobservable risk factors with $\mathrm{E}(F_k) = 0$;
b_{ik}, is the factor loadings, which are assumed to be constant over the period studied; and
ε_{it}, is the specific risk of each asset with $\mathrm{cov}(\varepsilon_i, F_k) = 0$ for all i and k and $\mathrm{cov}(\varepsilon_i, \varepsilon_j) = 0$ for $i \neq j$.

The APT equilibrium relationship allows us to write

$$\mathrm{E}_t(R_{it}) = \lambda_{0t} + \lambda_{1t} b_{i1} + \cdots + \lambda_{Kt} b_{iK}$$

where $(\lambda_{1t} \ldots \lambda_{Kt})$ denotes the vector of the risk premiums associated with the factors; and λ_{0t} denotes the return on a zero-beta portfolio.

By combining the two APT equations and expressing:

$$s_{kt} = F_{kt} + \lambda_{kt}$$

we can then write

$$R_{it} = \lambda_{0t} + s_{1t} b_{i1} + \cdots + s_{Kt} b_{iK} + \varepsilon_{it}$$

for $i = 1, \ldots, N$ and for $t = 1, \ldots, T$.

The factor loadings b_{ik} are not observable, so they must be constructed through approximations, obtained with the help of the returns. To do so, we write the equation for an asset i for

---

[7] Cf. Mei (1993) and Batteau and Lasgouttes (1997).

$t = 1$ to K. We then obtain the following system:

$$\begin{pmatrix} s_{11} & \cdots & s_{K1} \\ \cdot & \cdots & \cdot \\ \cdot & \cdots & \cdot \\ \cdot & \cdots & \cdot \\ s_{1K} & \cdots & s_{KK} \end{pmatrix} \begin{pmatrix} b_{i1} \\ \cdot \\ \cdot \\ \cdot \\ b_{iK} \end{pmatrix} = \begin{pmatrix} R_{i1} - \lambda_{01} - \varepsilon_{i1} \\ \cdot \\ \cdot \\ \cdot \\ R_{iK} - \lambda_{0K} - \varepsilon_{iK} \end{pmatrix}$$

or, in a more condensed manner:

$$\Psi b_i = \gamma_i$$

The matrix Ψ is assumed to be non-singular, i.e. with no redundant factors. The system can be transformed by expressing

$$\tilde{s}_t = (\Psi^{-1})' s_t$$
$$\tilde{b}_i = \Psi b_i$$

in order to normalise the factors and the factor loadings. With this notation we can write

$$R_{it} = \lambda_{0t} + \tilde{s}_{1t} \tilde{b}_{i1} + \cdots + \tilde{s}_{Kt} \tilde{b}_{iK} + \varepsilon_{it}$$

where i varies from 1 to n and t varies from $K + 1$ to T. Since

$$\tilde{b}_i = \Psi b_i = \gamma_i = \begin{pmatrix} R_{i1} - \lambda_{01} - \varepsilon_{i1} \\ \cdot \\ \cdot \\ \cdot \\ R_{iK} - \lambda_{0K} - \varepsilon_{iK} \end{pmatrix}$$

by replacing $\tilde{b}_i$ with its expression for $t > K$, we have

$$R_{it} = \lambda_{0t} + \tilde{s}_{1t}(R_{i1} - \lambda_{01} - \varepsilon_{i1}) + \cdots + \tilde{s}_{Kt}(R_{iK} - \lambda_{0K} - \varepsilon_{iK}) + \varepsilon_{it}$$

By grouping the terms, we finally obtain:

$$R_{it} = \tilde{s}_{0t} + \tilde{s}_{1t} R_{i1} + \cdots + \tilde{s}_{Kt} R_{iK} + \eta_{it}$$

with

$$\tilde{s}_{0t} = \lambda_{0t} - \sum_{j=1}^{K} \tilde{s}_{jt} \lambda_{0j}$$

and

$$\eta_{it} = \varepsilon_{it} - \sum_{j=1}^{K} \tilde{s}_{jt} \varepsilon_{ij}$$

for $t = K + 1, \ldots, T$.

We have therefore transformed a model with K factors into a semi-autoregressive model with K lags. We can then carry out a cross-sectional regression of R_{it} on $(1, R_{i1}, \ldots, R_{iK})$ to obtain an estimation of the normalised factors $\tilde{s}_{kt}$. The regression is written as follows:

$$
\begin{pmatrix} R_{1t} \\ . \\ . \\ . \\ . \\ R_{nt} \end{pmatrix} = \begin{pmatrix} 1 & R_{11} & \cdots & R_{1K} \\ . & . & \cdots & . \\ . & . & \cdots & . \\ . & . & \cdots & . \\ . & . & \cdots & . \\ 1 & R_{n1} & \cdots & R_{nk} \end{pmatrix} \begin{pmatrix} \tilde{s}_{0t} \\ \tilde{s}_{1t} \\ . \\ . \\ . \\ \tilde{s}_{Kt} \end{pmatrix} + \begin{pmatrix} \eta_{1t} \\ . \\ . \\ . \\ \eta_{nt} \end{pmatrix}
$$

for $t = K + 1, \ldots, T$

The model is called semi-autoregressive because the autoregressive terms only vary in i and not in i and t.

6.2.2.5   A specific example: the model used by the firm Advanced Portfolio Technology (APT)[8]

This firm, which has been operating for around 15 years, has developed a model that renders the APT theory operational, with the difficulty being to determine the right factors to explain the returns. The model was drawn from several observations. First, it is not realistic to wish to fix the model's factors once and for all. Next, the factors that influence asset returns are not directly observable. The factors that make asset prices move are not the economic variables themselves, but the share of unanticipated change in the variables, i.e. the difference between the forecast and the realised value. The best solution for determining the factors is therefore to observe the asset prices. To do that, the asset returns are measured at regular intervals, e.g. every three days, or every week, or every month, over the whole study period. If the universe under consideration contains many assets, then this will lead to a large amount of data. It is then necessary to group the assets together to extract the factors.

The founders of the firm APT do not carry out traditional factor analysis, such as, for example, that used by Roll and Ross to test their model. They developed a specific statistical estimation technique which enables the factors to be estimated from a large sample of variables. They carried out tests on their model with the help of Monte Carlo simulations and showed that their procedure enabled the true factorial structure of the model to be obtained, while factor analysis applied to large data samples could pose problems. It again involves an implicit estimation of the factors, since the procedure does not make any initial assumptions about the nature of the factors.

The procedure is as follows. From the data observed we calculate the covariances between the assets. We observe at that stage that certain assets behave similarly, while others evolve independently or in the opposite way. The assets can then be grouped into homogeneous classes, i.e. into groups with similar covariances. The common characteristics of each group obtained in this way can be seen as a manifestation of the effect of the factor that we are seeking to measure. By then combining the individual returns of the securities in the group, we calculate the return for each group, which enables us to obtain an index for each group. These indices constitute the factors. They are constructed in such a way as to be non-correlated between themselves, which is an advantage compared with the economic variables, which are often correlated. These indices then allow the factor loading coefficients for each asset to be calculated, together with the specific asset return component that is not taken into account by the factors. These calculations are carried out through regression. For each asset we obtain one

---

[8] See the Internet site http://www.apt.co.uk.

coefficient per factor and a coefficient that is specific to the asset. The return on the asset is then simply expressed as the weighted sum of the product of each coefficient times the return on the factor, plus the specific component of the asset.

In solving this problem the choice of the optimal number of factors is important. The more precise the information we wish to obtain, the more we will tend to increase the number of factors. However, the model is useful insofar as it allows us to retain a limited number of factors. To reach the optimal number of factors, the factor model is then tested for a period that is different from the estimation period to check that no important factors have been omitted. The model obtained uses 20 factors.

After identifying the risk factors implicitly, the firm APT also proposes explaining the asset returns with the help of known explicit factors. To do this, the explicit factors are decomposed with the help of implicit factors, in accordance with the principle described in Section 6.2.2.3 concerning the interpretation of implicit factors. We thus calculate the weighting of each explicit factor in the decomposition of the asset returns. For example, the coefficient of the explicit factor, R_{mt}, is given by

$$
\gamma_{im} = \frac{\sum_{j=1}^{k} \beta_{ij} \beta_{mj}}{\sum_{j=1}^{k} \beta_{mj}^2}
$$

where β_{ij} denotes the coefficients of the decomposition of the return on asset i according to the implicit factors; and β_{mj} denotes the coefficients of the decomposition of the explicit factor m according to the implicit factors.

The model can handle all kinds of assets, stocks, bonds, indices, currencies and raw materials and covers all countries, including emerging countries. The calculations are carried out using three and a half years of historical data and weekly returns.

6.2.3   Comparing the different models

Comparisons between the different models relate to both the explanatory power of the different types of factors and the methods for estimating the parameters. The first problem that arises is the choice between an explicit factor model and an implicit factor model.

The explicit factor models appear, at least in theory, to be simpler to use, but they assume that we know with certainty the number and nature of the factors that allow asset returns to be explained and that the latter can be observed and measured without error. However, we have seen that factor model theory does not indicate the number and nature of the factors to be used. The choice is therefore made by relying on empirical studies, but there is no uniqueness to the factors, nor are the factors necessarily stable over time. Fedrigo *et al.* (1996) describe the influence of errors on the models fairly thoroughly. They detail the consequences of a measurement error, the omission of a correct factor or the addition of an irrelevant factor. The models are useful, however, to the extent that they allow economic interpretation of the factors, since the factors are known beforehand.

As far as the choice of factors is concerned, two trends are opposed, namely economic factors or fundamental factors. From the point of view of the model itself, models that use macroeconomic factors, such as the APT model, focus essentially on the values of the risk premiums associated with the factors, in order to identify the most highly remunerated sources of risk. The fundamental factor models focus on the factors themselves, to identify those that have the greatest influence on asset returns. Moreover, certain authors, such as Grinold (1991) and Engerman (1993), affirm that macroeconomic factors are the most appropriate for explaining expected asset returns, but that fundamental factors are preferable for modelling and portfolio risk management. They therefore justify the choices made by Barra. This can be explained by the fact that the fundamental factors depend on the assets and are therefore more liable to take into account the inherent risks of each company.

Using an implicit factor model solves the problem of the choice of factors, since the model does not make any prior assumptions about the number and nature of the factors and should therefore enable the true model to be determined. The limitation in using this type of model then comes from the difficulty in interpreting the factors obtained. This is doubtless why those models are far less developed in the literature and seem to have been the subject of fewer applications to date. It is nevertheless possible, as we saw in Section 6.2.2.3, to come back to an explicit decomposition from the implicit decomposition. The implicit models are also very useful for analysing and monitoring portfolio risk, because they are better at taking into account market evolutions. We will return to this subject in Section 6.4. To finish, we note a final advantage of implicit factor models. As we have seen throughout this chapter, it is common to model the dependency of returns compared with the factors through a linear relationship. This is because it is the easiest way to proceed. But the true model may be non-linear. In that case an implicit factor model enables a better approximation of any eventual non-linearities by adding supplementary factors.

6.3   EXTENDING THE MODELS TO THE INTERNATIONAL ARENA[9]

Extensions to Ross's arbitrage model, and multi-factor models in general, have been developed for international portfolios in order to respond to criticism of the international CAPM. The factors used in these models come from a longer list of factors: as well as the national factors, international factors are added, along with specific factors for exchange rates. Certain factors can explain both returns and exchange rates. Most models assume that the factorial structure of exchange rates includes both factors that are common to financial assets and exchange rates and factors that are specific to exchange rates. A large number of models assume that the realisation of the factors does not depend on the currency under consideration. Only Fontaine (1987) proposes a model where the factors depend on the currency. It could be justifiable to consider that the factors do not depend on the currency for economic factors such as oil production, which is expressed in barrels, but it is not true for factors that are expressed in monetary units.

The international multi-factor models have been the subject of many studies. It is not possible to cite them all here. One could refer to Fontaine (1987) and Fontaine (1997) which constitute a thorough study of the subject. Here we simply present the general form of the models and give some indications about the factors used.

6.3.1   The international arbitrage models

The assumptions are those of arbitrage models in the national framework, to which some additional assumptions linked to the international context have been added. Investors make

---

[9] Cf. Fontaine (1997) and Chapter 5 of Fontaine (1987).

the same forecasts on the exchange rate variations. They assume the same factor model for the asset returns expressed in their domestic currency. In each country, there is a risk-free asset. The return on that asset expressed in the currency of another country is assumed to be generated by the factor model of that country. It is then appropriate to check whether the factor model for explaining the returns depends on the currency in which the returns are expressed or not. We can then establish the capital asset pricing relationship in the international context.

The model described is that of Fontaine (1987). This model assumes that there are $N + 1$ assets and $L + 1$ countries. The first $L + 1$ assets are the risk-free assets. The reference country is identified by the index 0. The return on each asset i from the reference country expressed in the currency of that country is written as follows:

$$R_{i0}^0 = E(R_{i0}^0) + \sum_{k=1}^{K} b_{ik}^0 F_k^0 + \varepsilon_{i0}^0$$

where

R_{i0}^0 denotes the return on asset i from the reference country in the reference currency;

$E(R_{i0}^0)$ denotes the expected return on asset i from the reference country in the reference currency;

b_{ik}^0 denotes the sensitivity (or exposure) of asset i to factor k in the reference currency;

F_k^0 denotes the return on factor k in the reference currency with $E(F_k^0) = 0$; and

ε_{i0}^0 denotes the residual (or specific) return on asset i from the reference country in the reference currency with $E(\varepsilon_{i0}^0) = 0$.

The return on an asset i from country j in currency j is written as follows:

$$R_{ij}^j = E(R_{ij}^j) + \sum_{k=1}^{K} b_{ik}^j F_k^j + \varepsilon_{ij}^j$$

This model assumes therefore that the F_k factors depend on the currency under consideration, or $F_k^0 \neq F_k^j$.

To then be able to express the returns on the assets from the different countries in a common currency, we need the exchange rates. The exchange rates are also governed by a factor model:

$$TC_j^0 = E(TC_j^0) + \sum_{k=1}^{K} b_{jk}^0 F_k^0 + \varepsilon_{jj}^0$$

where TC_j^0 denotes the exchange rate that enables us to switch from currency j to the reference currency.

These elements now permit us to study the impact of the exchange rate on the factorial structure of the returns. To do so, let us consider the return on an asset i from country j. The return in the reference currency is written as follows:

$$R_{ij}^0 = R_{ij}^j + TC_j^0 + C_{ij}^j$$

where C_{ij}^j denotes the covariance between the exchange rate TC_j^0 and the return R_{ij}^j. By replacing TC_j^0 and R_{ij}^j with their expressions, we obtain the following:

$$R_{ij}^0 = E(R_{ij}^j) + \sum_{k=1}^{K} b_{ik}^j F_k^j + \varepsilon_{ij}^j + E(TC_j^0) + \sum_{k=1}^{K} b_{ik}^0 F_k^0 + \varepsilon_{jj}^0 + C_{ij}^j$$

It is then necessary to express all the factors in the same currency. We have

$$F_k^0 = F_k^j + TC_j^0 + C_{kj}^0 - (\sigma_j^0)^2$$

where C_{kj}^0 denotes the covariance between the exchange rate TC_j^0 and the factor F_k^0; and $(\sigma_j^0)^2$ denotes the variance of the exchange rate TC_j^0. This expression comes from Ito's lemma.

By replacing F_k^j with its expression as a function of F_k^0, we obtain:

$$R_{ij}^0 = E(R_{ij}^j) + \sum_{k=1}^K b_{ik}^j \left(F_k^0 - TC_j^0 - C_{kj}^0 + (\sigma_j^0)^2 \right) + \varepsilon_{ij}^j + E(TC_j^0)$$

$$+ \sum_{k=1}^K b_{ik}^0 F_k^0 + \varepsilon_{jj}^0 + C_{ij}^j$$

We can also replace TC_j^0 with its factorial expression, which gives

$$R_{ij}^0 = E(R_{ij}^j) + \sum_{k=1}^K b_{ik}^j \left(F_k^0 - \left(E(TC_j^0) + \sum_{k=1}^K b_{jk}^0 F_k^0 + \varepsilon_{jj}^0 \right) - C_{kj}^0 + (\sigma_j^0)^2 \right) + \varepsilon_{ij}^j$$

$$+ E(TC_j^0) + \sum_{k=1}^K b_{ik}^0 F_k^0 + \varepsilon_{jj}^0 + C_{ij}^j$$

By grouping the terms together, we obtain:

$$R_{ij}^0 = E(R_{ij}^j) + E(TC_j^0) + C_{ij}^j + \sum_{k=1}^K b_{ik}^j \left(-E(TC_j^0) - C_{kj}^0 F_k^0 + (\sigma_j^0)^2 \right)$$

$$+ \sum_{k=1}^K \left(b_{ik}^j + b_{jk}^0 \left(1 - \sum_{k=1}^K b_{ik}^j \right) \right) F_k^0 + \left(1 - \sum_{k=1}^K b_{ik}^j \right) \varepsilon_{jj}^0 + \varepsilon_{ij}^j$$

If we define

$$E_{ij}^0 = E(R_{ij}^j) + E(TC_j^0) + C_{ij}^j + \sum_{k=1}^K b_{ik}^j \left(-E(TC_j^0) - C_{kj}^0 F_k^0 + (\sigma_j^0)^2 \right)$$

$$b_{ik}^0 = \sum_{k=1}^K \left(b_{ik}^j + b_{jk}^0 \left(1 - \sum_{k=1}^K b_{ik}^j \right) \right)$$

$$d_{ij}^0 = 1 - \sum_{k=1}^K b_{ik}^j$$

then the expression can be written in a more condensed manner:

$$R_{ij}^0 = E_{ij}^0 + \sum_{k=1}^K b_{ik}^0 F_k^0 + d_{ij}^0 \varepsilon_{jj}^0 + \varepsilon_{ij}^j$$

The factorial structure of the model therefore finds itself modified compared with the national case, since an additional factor appears which is common to all assets from country j. This is the term ε_{jj}^0 which is specific to the exchange rate in country j. d_{ij}^0 represents the sensitivity of asset i to this factor. This sensitivity is null if asset i does not belong to country j.

The following conditions are respected:

$$\text{cov}(F_k^0, \varepsilon_{ij}^j) = 0$$

$$\text{cov}(\varepsilon_{jj}^0, \varepsilon_{ij}^j) = 0$$

$$\text{cov}(\varepsilon_{ij}^j, \varepsilon_{i'j}^j) = 0 \quad \text{for all } i \neq i'$$

$$\text{E}(F_k^j) = 0$$

$$\text{E}(\varepsilon_{ij}^j) = 0$$

$$\text{E}(\varepsilon_{jj}^0) = 0$$

The arbitrage relationship is obtained by constructing the risk-free portfolio. It is written as follows:

$$\text{E}_{ij}^0 = \lambda_0^0 + \sum_{k=1}^{K} \lambda_0^k b_{ik}^0 + M_j^0 d_{ij}^0$$

where

M_j^0 denotes the risk premium of the exchange factor;

λ_0^k denotes the risk premium of factor k; and

λ_0^0 denotes the return on the risk-free asset of the reference country expressed in the reference currency.

If we assume that the returns are hedged against exchange rate risk, then the additional term due to the currency exchange is eliminated and we obtain a relationship of the same form as the arbitrage relationship in the national case.

Fontaine's model assumes that the realisations of the factors depend on the currency. That is therefore the most general case. Other authors assume that the factors do not depend on the currency, or $F_k = F_k^j$.

6.3.2 Factors that explain international returns

Marsh and Pfleiderer (1997) studied the importance of two essential factors in international investment: the country and the industrial sector. If the industries are worldwide, i.e. if the markets are integrated, then the country factor should not be significant, because its effect is already contained in the industry factor. If the industries are not worldwide, i.e. if the markets are segmented, then companies that belong to the same industrial sector but different countries have different characteristics and the country factor therefore becomes significant.

A model that is classically proposed to study the effects of factors is the following. If we take an asset i belonging to industrial sector j and country k, the return is expressed by

$$\tilde{R}_{ijkt} = \text{E}(\tilde{R}_{ijkt}) + \tilde{G}_t + \tilde{I}_{jt} + \tilde{C}_{kt} + \tilde{e}_{ijkt}$$

where

$\tilde{G}_t$ denotes the global market factor represented by an international index;

$\tilde{I}_{jt}$ denotes the industrial factor;

$\tilde{C}_{kt}$ denotes the country factor; and

$\tilde{e}_{ijkt}$ denotes the residual return.

This model assumes that all assets in the same country have the same sensitivity to the country factor and that all assets in the same industrial sector have the same sensitivity to the industry factor. This assumption is not very realistic. Marsh and Pfleiderer therefore propose the following model:

$$\tilde{R}_{ijkt} = A_i + a_i \tilde{G}_t + b_{ij} \tilde{I}_{jt} + c_{ik} \tilde{C}_{kt} + \tilde{e}_{ijkt}$$

where each factor is now assigned an asset-specific sensitivity.

The model was tested with and without the global market factor. In both cases the country factor outweighs the industry factor. When present, the market factor explains around a third of the returns. Marsh and Pfleiderer's article cites other studies that reached the same conclusion.

This result casts doubt over Barra's factor model, which gives considerable importance to the industry-based factors. The result is consistent with the risk models used by Quantal, which stipulate that the industrial classification is not generally a good basis for measuring risk.

As in the national case, there are several methods for identifying "international" factors:

1. Exogenous methods based on time series. These models use international index-type variables above all, grouping together the effect of several variables.
2. Methods based on factor analysis of asset returns, which enable the factors to be extracted and the factor loadings to be calculated, but which do not allow us to identify the variables represented by the factors.
3. Methods based on company attributes (fundamental factors). Grinold *et al.* (1989) describe a multi-factor model in the international framework based on the experience of the firm Barra. This model consists of isolating the currency effect and then decomposing the local portfolio return into a market term, an industrial sector term and a common factor term. These factors are company attributes such as, for example, size, volatility or earnings. Grinold *et al.* find that the country factor is on average more important than the industry factor but that, at a more detailed level, the most important industry factors are more important than the least important country factors.

6.4   APPLYING MULTI-FACTOR MODELS

The use of multi-factor models is beginning to be more widespread among professionals, after remaining in the research domain for many years. Roll and Ross's (1984) article describes, for example, the possible applications of the APT model to portfolio management. The main disadvantage of these models, compared with the CAPM, is that the theory does not define the nature of the factors. In addition, the fact that they are difficult to implement was long considered to be an obstacle to their use. However, their use has now been facilitated by the improved calculation speed. Unlike the models drawn from the CAPM, the multi-factor models do not really allow us to measure the advantage of a particular portfolio for an investor in terms of optimality, as Salvati (1997) explains, because they do not make any particular assumptions about investors' behaviour. These models are not aimed at comparing the overall levels of portfolio risk. They are, however, explanatory models that study several different areas of risk. They allow us to identify all the sources of risk to which a portfolio is subjected, and to measure the associated remuneration. This results in better control over portfolio management: orienting the portfolio towards the right sources of risk leads to an improvement in its performance.

Risk analysis and performance evaluation through multi-factor models are therefore connected. The procedure is as follows. A manager seeks to reach a certain level of performance by orienting his portfolio toward the most highly remunerated risk factors. He carries out risk analysis at the beginning of the period to construct his portfolio, then analyses the performance at the end of the period and attributes the contribution of each risk factor to the overall performance. He can thus check whether the result obtained corresponds to his original expectations and then evaluate the decisions that were rewarding and those that were not.

It is possible to construct a wide variety of multi-factor models. The choice of a model for studying a particular portfolio depends on the nature of the portfolio. In this section we give details on how the different factor models that were presented at the beginning of the chapter are used to analyse portfolio risk and performance.

6.4.1   Portfolio risk analysis[10]

Using the factorial structure of asset returns it is easy to calculate the variance and covariance of the securities with the help of the variance and covariance of the factors. This produces a factorial structure for asset risk that measures the standard portfolio risk. This structure separates the risk into a component drawn from the model and a specific component.

Risk analysis is important for both passive investment and active investment. Passive investment index funds generally do not contain all the securities in their reference index when there are a large number of securities. The manager must then analyse the portfolio risk regularly to check that it is sufficiently close to the risk of the index. The factorial decomposition of the risk ensures better monitoring of his portfolio's tracking-error. In active investment, risk analysis allows us to determine the factors that have the greatest influence on asset prices according to the remuneration they produce in a well-diversified portfolio. Highlighting the risk factors also allows us to construct portfolios that are not sensitive to a particular factor. The factorial decomposition of risk therefore allows risk to be managed better.

We present examples of risk models below: the Barra model, the model used by the firm Quantal, and application of the firm Aptimum's model to risk analysis.

6.4.1.1   Barra's risk model[11]

The risk analysis model developed by Barra is drawn from their multi-factor model. We saw previously that the asset returns in that model are characterised by the following factorial structure:

$$R_{it} = \sum_{k=1}^{K} b_{ikt}\alpha_{kt} + u_{it}$$

where

R_{it} denotes the return on security i in excess of the risk-free rate;
b_{ik} denotes the exposure or factor loading of asset i with regard to factor k;
α_k denotes the return on factor k; and
u_i denotes the specific return of asset i.

---

[10] Cf. Burmeister et al. (1997) and Chapter 4 of Farrell (1997).
[11] Cf. Kahn (1995) and Chapter 3 of Grinold and Kahn (1995) with the technical appendix to the chapter, Sheikh (1996), Barra (1998) and Grinold and Kahn (2000).

The specific returns are assumed to be non-correlated between themselves and non-correlated with the factor returns, or

$$\text{cov}(u_i, u_j) = 0 \quad \text{for all } i \neq j$$

and

$$\text{cov}(u_i, \alpha_k) = 0$$

The next step is to calculate the asset return variance–covariance matrix with the help of the variance–covariance matrix of the risk factor returns that are common to this set of assets, which allows the number of calculations required to be reduced.

The variance–covariance matrix for the returns on the securities is therefore given by

$$V = B\Omega B^{\text{T}} + \Delta$$

where

Ω denotes the variance–covariance matrix for the factor returns;
B denotes the matrix of the assets' factor loadings; and
Δ denotes the variance matrix for the asset-specific returns. This matrix is diagonal because the terms that are specific to each asset are not correlated between themselves.

Explicitly, the elements of the assets' variance–covariance matrix therefore have the following structure:

$$V_{ij} = \sum_{k_1, k_2 = 1}^{K} b_{ik_1} \omega_{k_1 k_2} b_{jk_2} + \Delta_{ij}$$

where

V_{ij} denotes the covariance between asset i and asset j;
$\omega_{k_1 k_2}$ denotes the covariance of factor k_1 with factor k_2; and
Δ_{ij} denotes the specific covariance of asset i with asset j. This term is therefore null if $i \neq j$.

The matrix V is estimated with the help of the matrix B, the securities' loadings for the common factors, the matrix Ω, the variance–covariance of the factors, and the matrix Δ, the variances of the security-specific returns.

Barra's choice of fundamental factors should integrate evolutions in the composition of the portfolio and its risk characteristics better than macroeconomic factors, because these factors take the evolution of companies' risk characteristics into account. However, unlike the macroeconomic factor models, where the factors' variance–covariance matrix is calculated with the help of observed data, the matrix for the fundamental factor models is calculated with estimated data.

The portfolio risk is then calculated from the portfolio composition and V_{ij}. Let h_p be the vector of size n defining the asset weightings in portfolio P. The exposures to the factors of portfolio P are given by

$$x_P = B^{\text{T}} h_P$$

The variance of portfolio P is then written

$$\sigma_P^2 = h_P^{\text{T}} V h_P = x_P^{\text{T}} \Omega x_P + h_P^{\text{T}} \Delta h_P$$

Barra use the real composition of the portfolio over time by conserving the historical monthly data. We can carry out an identical analysis to calculate the active risk or tracking-error of the portfolio. As a reminder, this is the component of risk due to the differential between the portfolio and its benchmark. It will be denoted in what follows by the variable Ψ_P^2. Taking h_B as the vector of benchmark weightings, we define the differential between the portfolio composition and the benchmark composition as

$$h_{PA} = h_P - h_B$$

We then have

$$x_{PA} = B^T h_{PA}$$

and hence

$$\Psi_P^2 = h_{PA}^T V h_{PA} = x_{PA}^T \Omega x_{PA} + h_{PA}^T \Delta h_{PA}$$

The multi-factor risk model allows us to analyse the risk of a portfolio that has already been constituted. The risk is broken down according to the different sources of risk. The residual share of the risk that is not explained by the factors can thus be identified. In the case of active portfolio management, this risk decomposition can be compared with that of a passively managed reference portfolio. The differentials observed indicate that the manager expects higher remuneration for certain factors.

With the help of the portfolio risk expressions established from the factors, we can accurately calculate the marginal contribution of each factor to the portfolio risk, for both the total risk of the portfolio and its active risk. This allows us to see the assets and factors that have the greatest impact on the portfolio risk.

The marginal contribution of a security to the total risk of the portfolio, written as *MCTR*, for the marginal contribution to total risk, is defined by the partial derivative of the risk compared with the weighting of the security:

$$MCTR = \frac{\partial \sigma_P}{\partial h_P^T} = \frac{V h_P}{\sigma_P}$$

The *n*th component of the *MCTR* vector is the partial derivative of σ_P compared with the *n*th component of the vector h_P. We can see it as the approximate change in portfolio risk given an increase of 1% in the weighting of asset *n* financed by a 1% decrease in cash. The same type of reasoning can be applied to calculate the marginal contribution of a factor, written *FMCTR*, to the total risk of the portfolio. The marginal contribution of a factor enables us to measure the change in risk brought about by a modification in the exposure to that factor. We have

$$FMCTR = \frac{\partial \sigma_P}{\partial x_P^T} = \frac{\Omega x_P}{\sigma_P}$$

By noting that

$$x_P^T FMCTR = \frac{x_P^T \Omega x_P}{\sigma_P} = \frac{h_P^T V h_P - h_P^T \Delta h_P}{\sigma_P}$$

then $x_P^T(j) FMCTR(j)$ gives the contribution of factor *j* to the total risk of the portfolio and $h_P^T \Delta h_P / \sigma_P$ gives the contribution of the asset-specific risks to the total risk of the portfolio.

We can use the same reasoning with the active risk of the portfolio and successively calculate the marginal contributions of the assets to that risk, or

$$MCAR = \frac{\partial \Psi_P}{\partial h_{PA}^{\mathrm{T}}} = \frac{V h_{PA}}{\Psi_P}$$

and the marginal contributions of the factors, or

$$FMCAR = \frac{\partial \Psi_P}{\partial x_{PA}^{\mathrm{T}}} = \frac{\Omega x_{PA}}{\Psi_P}$$

Following this phase, performance analysis will allow us to check whether the portfolio risk choices were judicious. This will be developed later in the chapter.

6.4.1.2   The Quantal risk model[12]

Quantal developed and use a risk model based on implicit factors extracted from asset returns. These factors are generated by using the most recent four to six months of daily returns and giving more importance to the most recent trends to avoid including irrelevant data from the past. The analysis is carried out at the level of the securities and is not limited by the definition of a country or an industrial sector. The statistical model used is consistent with the APT model. The choice of a short period makes the model very sensitive to recent movements in the market and gives a good view of the portfolio risk and a better forecast of its tracking-error.

The choice of an implicit model to explain the risk allows us to determine, in order of importance, the factors that have the greatest influence on the evolution of returns, while the use of predefined factors could lead to improper factors being included or certain factors being omitted. This allows us to carry out a better analysis of portfolio risk.

For example, in the case of benchmarked investment, a portfolio can be constructed in such a way as to be exposed to the same risk factors as the reference portfolio, without having to be invested in exactly the same securities, and can thus conserve a minimal tracking-error.

6.4.1.3   The model developed by the firm APT (Advanced Portfolio Technology)

We have already discussed this company and its model, which is based on the search for implicit factors, in Section 6.2.2.5. The principle used is the same as Quantal's. In practice, the calculations are carried out by using historical data on 180 weekly returns with a database of 30 000 securities from different countries. The model extracts 20 factors through the statistical method presented in Section 6.2.2.5. The factors are orthogonal, i.e. independent, and they have strong explanatory power. The estimations are performed again every quarter by integrating the new data for the most recent quarter and eliminating the data from the earliest quarter.

This model is used to establish a ranking of mutual funds by risk category in order to be able to compare their performance within a single category. The ranking has appeared in *Le Monde* and other European newspapers[13] since the beginning of 1999. This ranking includes the risks taken by the manager, with the different areas of those risks being studied. The factor model established allows the fund and asset returns to be broken down into a certain number of

---

[12] Cf. Quantal's web site: http://www.quantal.com.
[13] *El Pais* in Spain, *The Guardian / Money Observer* in the United Kingdom, *Le Soir* in Belgium, *La Stampa* in Italy, *Süddeutsche Zeitung* in Germany, *Tageblatt* in Luxembourg, *Le Temps* in Switzerland and *Der Standard* in Austria.

coefficients of sensitivity to the risks that are common to all the assets. The values of these coefficients allow the risks of the funds to be evaluated. Precise knowledge of the risks then allows the mutual funds to be grouped into peer groups with very similar risk profiles. The ranking can then be established within each group.

APT compare their method with that of arbitrarily chosen explicit factor models. The explicit factors can be interpreted, but they are liable to be correlated. APT prefer to favour the explanatory power of the returns rather than interpretation of the factors. In addition, as we indicated in Section 6.2.2.3, a transition from implicit factors to explicit factors is then possible.

In this section we have presented three types of risk analysis model: one based on explicit factors and the other two based on implicit factors. Implicit factor models are particularly interesting for monitoring the risk, and, by extension, the performance, of an index portfolio, because they allow the exposure to different risk factors to be controlled accurately. To do that, we analyse the index to be replicated. We can then construct the index portfolio so that it is as close as possible to the index by exposing it to the same risks, with the same factor loadings as the index. This allows us to conserve the minimal portfolio tracking-error and to achieve the desired performance. Since the implicit factor models integrate evolutions in the market better than the explicit factor models, they allow more reliable results to be obtained.

6.4.2 Choice of portfolio

The simplified structure of the asset returns' variance–covariance matrix allows the portfolio optimisation methods to be implemented with fewer calculations. This point was addressed in Section 3.4 of Chapter 3.

6.4.3 Decomposing the performance of a portfolio[14]

The multi-factor models have a direct application in investment fund performance measurement. The models contribute more information to performance analysis than the Sharpe, Treynor and Jensen indices. We have seen that the asset returns could be decomposed linearly according to several risk factors common to all the assets, but with specific sensitivity to each. Once the model has been determined, we can attribute the contribution of each factor to the overall portfolio performance. This is easily done when the factors are known, which is the case for models that use macroeconomic factors or fundamental factors, but becomes more difficult when the nature of the factors has not been identified. Performance analysis then consists of evaluating whether the manager was able to orient the portfolio towards the most rewarding risk factors. *Ex post* observation of the level of returns compared with the consensus returns allows us to evaluate whether the manager was right or not to deviate from the benchmark by orienting the portfolio towards certain factors.

Analysis of portfolio performance with the help of a multi-factor model is applied to relatively homogeneous asset classes, for example French stocks, or international stocks, or a category of bonds. The factors identified depend on the type of asset under consideration.

All the models presented below generalise the Jensen measure. The share of return that is not explained by the factors constitutes the residual return and allows us to calculate the information ratio, as it was defined in Chapter 4.

---

[14] Cf. Roll and Ross (1984).

6.4.3.1   The multi-index model: Elton, Gruber, Das and Hlavka's model[15]

This model constitutes the first improvement compared with the single-index model. The indices quoted on the markets are indices that are specialised by asset type. The use of several indices therefore gives a better description of the different types of assets contained in a fund, such as stocks or bonds, but also, at a more detailed level, the large or small market capitalisation securities and the assets from different countries. The multi-index model is simple to use because the factors are known and easily available. The empirical validation studies are however more recent than those carried out on the APT model.

The Elton *et al.* model is a three-index model that was developed in response to a study by Ippolito (1989) which shows that performance evaluated in comparison with an index that badly represents the diversity of the assets in the fund can give a biased result. Their model is presented in the following form:

$$R_{Pt} - R_{Ft} = \alpha_P + \beta_{PL}(R_{Lt} - R_{Ft}) + \beta_{PS}(R_{St} - R_{Ft}) + \beta_{PB}(R_{Bt} - R_{Ft}) + \varepsilon_{Pt}$$

where

R_{Lt} denotes the return on the index that represents large-cap securities;
R_{St} denotes the return on the index that represents small-cap securities;
R_{Bt} denotes the return on a bond index; and
ε_{Pt} denotes the residual portfolio return that is not explained by the model.

Elton *et al.* position themselves within the framework of the efficient market hypothesis defined by Grossman and Stiglitz (1980), which assumes that the markets are efficient if the additional return produced by the active management of a portfolio simply compensates for the management fees. The manager's performance corresponds to the excess return that is not explained by the three indices. The model allows for better integration of the nature of the fund and identification of the manager's style as a function of the significance of each index in the performance result.

This model can be used to evaluate the manager's market timing capacity with regard to each of the market sectors by adding a quadratic term for each index. We then obtain a generalisation of the Treynor and Mazuy model.

6.4.3.2   The APT model[16]

The use of the APT model to analyse performance was developed for the first time by Connor and Korajczyk (1986). The principle is the same as for the Jensen measure or the multi-index model, namely to separate the predictable part of performance, explained by the model, from the manager's contribution. If the factors have been chosen well, then this model should enable the strategy followed by the manager to be described more accurately than by the three-index model presented above.

As we mentioned during the theoretical presentation of this model, the essential difficulty is in choosing the right factors. Connor and Korajczyk use macroeconomic factors. They selected the following five factors: the forward structure of rates, the bond premium, the unanticipated unemployment rate, unanticipated inflation and the residual market factor.

---

[15] Cf. Elton *et al.* (1993), and also Elton and Gruber (1995), Fabozzi (1995) and Grandin (1998).
[16] Cf. Elton and Gruber (1995), Grandin (1998), and Roll (1997) who cites the method used by Connor and Korajczyk.

Once the average return decomposition model has been established for each asset over a given period, we can study the performance of a portfolio made up of n assets, chosen from among the assets that were used to construct the model. We have

$$E(R_{it}) - R_F = \sum_{k=1}^{K} \beta_{ik} \lambda_k$$

where β_{ik} and λ_k are known.

The return on the portfolio is written as follows:

$$R_{Pt} = \sum_{i=1}^{n} x_i R_{it}$$

with x_i being the weightings of the assets in the portfolio.

The composition of the portfolio is assumed to be fixed over the period under consideration. The study period actually has to be broken down into as many sub-periods as there are modifications to the portfolio and the results then have to be aggregated over a complete period. By aggregating the results obtained for each asset at the portfolio level, we can then decompose its total return according to the risk factors.

The return forecast by the model is therefore:

$$E(R_P) = R_F + \sum_{k=1}^{K} \lambda_k \beta_{Pk}$$

where

$$\beta_{Pk} = \sum_{i=1}^{n} x_i \beta_{ik}$$

The differential between the observed portfolio return and its expected return, or $R_{Pt} - E(R_P)$, gives the share of return that is not explained by the model, and therefore attributable to the manager. The share of return explained by factor k is given by $\lambda_k \beta_{Pk}$.

This decomposition allows the performance differential between two portfolios to be explained by the different exposure to the factors.

Since the performance analysis is carried out *ex post*, the study period can be included in the period that was used to establish the model. It is then necessary to update the model regularly by continually taking, for example, five-year rolling periods of historical data.

6.4.3.3 Barra's model for analysing the performance of equity portfolios[17]

Barra promote a performance analysis and attribution model called Equity Portfolio Performance Analysis, based on their risk model. It involves evaluating performance in relation to the risks taken, with the help of the multi-factor risk analysis model, and identifying the sources of portfolio performance. The model uses the historical monthly composition of the portfolio. Performance attribution allows us to identify the management decisions and asset allocation

---

[17] Cf. Barra's internet site: http://www.barra.com, and Meier (1991, 1994). The models for bond portfolios will be presented in Chapter 8.

strategies that made the greatest contribution to the portfolio return and to determine whether the return is sufficient with regard to the risk taken to achieve it. We can therefore evaluate the manager's skill in achieving returns for the different categories of risk.

In Barra's performance attribution model the multi-factor models are integrated in a very thorough analysis that also handles evaluation of the investment management process, an aspect that will be detailed in Chapter 7. The performance of the portfolio is compared with that of a benchmark which can be chosen from among a list of specific benchmarks or can be custom built. The asset allocation component is separated from the stock picking component for each market sector, with the latter then being analysed with the help of a factor model. For the moment, we only describe the application of multi-factor models to analysis for each market sector. Using the model's risk indices and calculated risk premiums, the portfolio return is decomposed according to the same principle as that used for the APT model. We thereby determine the share of return that comes from each of the risk factors.

With the notation being the same as that used in Section 6.4.1.1, in which we described Barra's risk model, we recall that the return on a portfolio made up of n assets is written as follows:

$$R_{Pt} = \sum_{k=1}^{K} x_{Pkt} \alpha_{kt} + u_{Pt}$$

where

$$x_P = B^\mathrm{T} h_P$$

and

$$u_{Pt} = \sum_{i=1}^{n} h_{Pit} u_{it}$$

and where

α_k denotes the return on factor k;
u_i denotes the specific return on asset i;
B denotes the factor loading matrix; and
h_P denotes the vector that defines the weightings of the assets in the portfolio.

The coefficients x_{Pkt} denote the portfolio's exposures to the factors at the beginning of the period studied. R_{Pt} and α_{kt}. denote the returns realised by the portfolio and the factors, respectively. The return attributed to factor k is therefore written as follows:

$$R_{Pkt} = x_{Pkt} \alpha_{kt}$$

and the portfolio-specific return is given by u_{Pt}. This specific return measures the manager's skill in selecting individual securities.

The performance decomposition can also be performed on the portfolio's active return.

Studying the performance and interpreting the results then leads to a review of the investment plan. Performance attribution thus allows for a better understanding of the results and improved portfolio management.

Barra initially developed multi-factor models for each country and then developed a model that was adapted to international multi-currency portfolios. The latter model analyses portfolio performance as a function of the allocation by country, and then uses a specific model for each country. In the case of international portfolios, the major source of performance identified is the choice of allocation by country and by currency.

6.4.3.4 Implicit factor model for performance analysis

Once the model has been identified, we obtain a decomposition of the expected return on each asset according to the different factors. We can then explain the share of the portfolio return that is due to each factor and isolate its residual return. The principle is then the same as for an APT-type explicit factor model, apart from the fact that we cannot necessarily name the factors and the factors thus remain difficult to interpret. For that reason the models actually are more often used to manage portfolio risk than to explain portfolio performance.

However, as we already indicated in Section 6.4.1.3, the firm APT's implicit factor model is used to rank the performances of mutual funds and investment funds. Once the funds have been split into groups with similar risk profiles, they are ranked by level of performance within each group. The ranking obtained presents a restated performance on which a judgement is expressed. The level of risk taken in comparison with funds in the same category is also qualified with a system of stars. We can therefore evaluate the quality of management for each fund and analyse the source of the performance according to the risks taken to achieve it.

6.4.4 Timing analysis

The timing analysis methods, which were presented in Chapter 4 and which allow us to analyse the evolution of the portfolio's exposure to market risk, are generalised in the case of a multi-factor model. To do so, one simply adds a quadratic term to the equation for each of the factors. We thus obtain a Treynor and Mazuy-type formula. This allows us to study the variation in the portfolio's exposure to the different risk factors in correlation with the factor trends.

6.4.5 Style analysis

The concept of management style has become more and more prominent in recent years in equity management services. We observe that securities produce different performances according to the category to which they belong and the time periods considered. In Chapter 1 we presented the different investment styles and described the usefulness of the multi-style approach. Managers can construct portfolios based on a pure investment style or else spread the portfolio over several investment styles. Multi-style portfolios can also be obtained by combining funds where the managers follow well-defined styles. It is then necessary to have an appropriate model to analyse the performance of those portfolios and a benchmark that corresponds to the structure of the portfolio. The choice of benchmark is very important. It would not be fair to compare the performance of a manager who follows a very precise style with that of a benchmark representing the whole of the market, or that corresponds to a style that is different from his. A manager may, for example, produce a performance that is worse than the performance of the market as measured by a broad index if the style that he employs is not the most favourable over the period under consideration. He could nevertheless display particular skill within his style by producing a performance that is better than the benchmark that corresponds to his specific style; we should not consider in that case that the manager has performed badly. The opposite situation may also arise. A manager may produce a perfor-mance that is better than the broad index, but worse than the index corresponding to his style; he should not in that case be considered to be a good manager in the style that he employs. Studying performance in comparison with a specific benchmark allows us to avoid those kinds of errors.

Two types of method allow the style of a portfolio to be analysed. The first, called return-based style analysis, is based solely on the study of past portfolio returns. It does not require the composition of the portfolio to be known. It is drawn from the style analysis model developed by Sharpe (1992). The second method, called portfolio- or factor-based style analysis, analyses the style of the portfolio by studying each of the securities that make up the portfolio. We shall present these two types of analysis while specifying their respective advantages and disadvantages. Before that, however, we introduce and examine the issue of style indices on which the whole analysis is based.

6.4.5.1 Style indices[18]

The need to measure the performance of different investment styles led to the development of style indices. The style indices for the American market are principally developed by four companies: Frank Russell, Wilshire Associates, Barra, in association with Standard & Poor's, and Prudential Securities International.

The Frank Russell Company produces three types of style index: a large-cap index based on the Russell 1000 index, the Russell 3000 index and the Russell Top 200 index, a mid-cap index, and a small-cap index using both the Russell 2000 and Russell 2500 indices. Standard & Poor's publish large-cap indices for growth and value stocks in partnership with Barra. These indices are based on the S&P Composite, MidCap 400 and SmallCap 600 indices. Wilshire Associates and Prudential Securities publish style indices for the following three categories: large-cap, mid-cap and small-cap. There are also international style indices. Boston International Advisors (BIA) created style indices for 21 countries and seven regions for the following four major style categories: large value, large growth, small value and small growth. Parametric Portfolio Associates (PPA) have also developed a similar set of international indices. We will describe the main indices in more detail below.

The Russell Growth and Value indices are available for the three Russell large-cap indices: the Top 200 index, the Russell 1000 index and the Russell 3000 index. The mid-cap style indices are based on the Russell MidCap index and the small-cap style indices are based on the Russell 2000 index and the Russell 2500 index. These three indices use the same calculation method. The securities are ranked on the basis of their *P/E* ratio and their long-term growth rate. This ranking determines whether a stock tends to be a growth stock or a value stock. Around 30% of the securities in the large-cap index appear in both the growth and value indices, but in different proportions. The rest of the stocks appear in only one index.

The Russell 3000 index contains the 3000 largest companies in the United States, which together represent 98% of American stock market capitalisation. The Russell 2000 index corresponds to the bottom two-thirds of the list of the 3000 largest American corporations. The Russell 1000 index contains the 1000 largest companies. The Russell 2500 corresponds to the Russell 3000 index with the 500 largest capitalisations taken away. The Top 200 index contains the 200 largest firms. The MidCap index contains the 800 firms that come after the 200 largest firms in descending order of market capitalisation. The combination of the Top 200 index and the MidCap index constitutes the Russell 1000 index.

---

[18] Cf. Brown and Mott (1997) and Mott and Coker (1995).

The S&P/Barra Growth and Value indices are constructed from the S&P500 index on the basis of the *P/E* ratios of the securities. The securities with the lowest *P/E* ratios are integrated into the value index and the securities with the highest *P/E* ratios go into the growth index. The two indices are constructed in such a way as to have approximately the same capitalisation. Since the companies in the growth index have a larger market capitalisation, this index only contains 40% of the securities. The rest of the securities make up the value index. The same methodology is used to construct the S&P MidCap and SmallCap indices.

The S&P500 index, which is also called the S&P Composite, is constructed so as to be representative of the New York Stock Exchange in terms of industrial sectors. The stocks in the S&P MidCap 400 index are chosen according to their size and their industrial characteristics. The S&P SmallCap 600 index was introduced in October 1994. It contains companies chosen according to their size, their industrial characteristics and their liquidity. The SmallCap, MidCap and S&P Composite indices do not overlap. Certain companies in the MidCap index have a larger market capitalisation than those in the S&P500 and certain companies in the SmallCap index have a larger market capitalisation than those in the MidCap index.

The Wilshire Growth and Value indices are constructed from the Top 750 large-cap index, the MidCap 750 index and the Next 1750 small-cap index, eliminating securities that do not have growth characteristics for the former, or value for the latter. The Wilshire Top 750 index contains the securities with the largest market capitalisation in the Wilshire 5000 index, an index that had over 7000 securities halfway through the year 1996. The Wilshire MidCap index is a little smaller than the Russell MidCap and S&P MidCap indices. It contains the 250 smallest market capitalisation securities in the Top 750 index and the 500 largest market capitalisation securities in the Next 1750 index.

For the same style we therefore have several indices. However, we observe that the performance of these indices is different, even though they represent the same investment style. The differences observed are anything but negligible, as they can reach several basis points. The reason for this is that the indices are based on different universes of securities and are calculated using different methods. For example, Russell and Standard & Poor's create their indices on the basis of the *P/E* ratio, while Wilshire and PSI use a scanning technique based on several criteria. The choice of a particular index from among the different indices available for the same style is therefore difficult, and all the more so because the resulting performance analysis depends on the reference index chosen. To solve this problem we can seek to identify pure style indices. To do this, we carry out factorial analysis on the returns of the style indices that belong to the same style category. The first component then constitutes a pure style component, which can be seen as the intersection of the indices under consideration. By proceeding in that way for each style category, we obtain a set of pure style indices[19]. These indices can then be used as a basis for constructing normal portfolios made up of several style indices.

6.4.5.2   Sharpe's style analysis model[20]

The theory developed by Sharpe stipulates that a manager's investment style can be determined by comparing the returns on his portfolio with those of a certain number of selected indices. Intuitively, the simplest technique for identifying the style of a portfolio involves successively

---

[19] On the subject of implementing the technique for constructing "pure" indices, see Amenc and Martellini (2001).
[20] Cf. Sharpe (1992), Fabozzi (1995) and Hardy (1997).

comparing his returns with those of the different style indices. The goodness of fit between the portfolio returns and the returns on the index is measured with the help of a quantity called R^2, which measures the proportion of variance explained by the model. If the value of R^2 is high, then the proportion of unexplained variance is minimal. The index for which the R^2 is highest is therefore the one that best characterises the style of the portfolio. But managers rarely have a pure style, hence Sharpe's idea to propose a method that would enable us to find the combination of style indices which gives the highest R^2 with the returns on the portfolio being studied.

The Sharpe model is a generalisation of the multi-factor models, which is applied to classes of assets. Sharpe presents his model with 12 asset classes. These asset classes include several categories of domestic stocks, i.e. American in the case of the model: value stocks, growth stocks, large-cap stocks, mid-cap stocks and small-cap stocks. They also include one category for European stocks and one category for Japanese stocks, along with several major bond categories. Each of these classes corresponds, in the broad sense, to a management style and is represented by a specialised index.

The model is written as follows:

$$R_{Pt} = b_{P1} F_{1t} + b_{P2} F_{2t} + \cdots + b_{PK} F_{Kt} + e_{Pt}$$

where

F_{kt} denotes the return on index k;

b_{Pk} denotes the sensitivity of the portfolio to index k and is interpreted as the weighting of class k in the portfolio; and

e_{Pt} represents the portfolio's residual return term for period t.

In this model the factors are the asset classes, but unlike ordinary multi-factor models, where the values of the coefficients can be arbitrary, here they represent the distribution of the different asset groups in the portfolio, without the possibility of short selling, and must therefore respect the following constraints:

$$0 \le b_{Pk} \le 1$$

and

$$\sum_{k=1}^{K} b_{Pk} = 1$$

These weightings are determined by a quadratic program, which consists of minimising the variance of the portfolio's residual return.

The style analysis thus carried out allows us to construct a customised benchmark for the portfolio. To do so, we simply take the weightings obtained for each style index. This type of benchmark is called a Sharpe benchmark. We referred to it previously in Chapter 2. It corresponds to a passive portfolio of the same style as the portfolio to be evaluated. The difficulty lies in choosing a period of suitable length to be representative of the manager's style. A period that is too short is insufficient for evaluating a manager's style, but a benchmark constructed from a period that is too long may not fully reflect recent changes in the manager's style. Using a period of three years for constructing a benchmark is recommended. The benchmark established in that way is created *ex post*, although it would be useful for it to exist at the beginning of the period for which we are evaluating the manager. In order to have an appropriate benchmark for the manager's portfolio available permanently, we can proceed in rolling periods by always using the last three years of historical data to construct the reference for the upcoming period. We then update the benchmark by continually advancing it by one period (a quarter or a month) over time.

Once the coefficients of the model have been determined for a representative period and the benchmark has been constructed, the manager's performance is calculated as being the difference between the return on his portfolio and the return on the benchmark. We thereby isolate the share of performance that comes from asset allocation and is explained by the benchmark. The residual share of performance not explained by the benchmark constitutes the management's value-added and comes from the stock picking, within each category, that is different from that of the benchmark. It is the manager's active return. The proportion of the variance not explained by the model, i.e. the quantity $1 - R^2$, measures the importance of stock picking quantitatively.

When a fund is assigned to several managers, the style for the whole fund is obtained by aggregating the styles obtained for each manager with their respective weightings. In the case of international portfolios, the style analysis can be carried out by country, by considering the different style indices within each country, or else globally, by using international style indices.

The Sharpe model uses an analysis that is called return-based, i.e. based solely on the returns. The advantage of this method is that it is simple to implement. It does not require any particular knowledge about the composition of the portfolio. The information on the style is obtained simply by analysing the monthly or quarterly returns of the portfolio through multiple regression. The sources of the historical portfolio returns are explained by the combination of style indices that best represents the returns on the portfolio as a whole. The necessary data are the historical portfolio returns and the returns on a set of specified indices. But the major disadvantage of this method lies in the fact that it is based on the past composition of the portfolio and does not therefore allow us to correctly evaluate the modifications in style to which it may have been subjected during the evaluation period. This method therefore assumes that the managers have a consistent style during the period, or that only minimal and progressive style modifications occurred. As long as these conditions are respected, the method described works well.

When the study period is fairly long, there can be no certainty about style consistency over time. Past data may not be representative of the current portfolio. In this case the result obtained is actually the average style of the portfolio over the period. If style modifications occur, then the method tends to detect them late or sometimes not detect them at all. When several groups of indices are available for analysing the style, the results can differ according to the group of indices used. To get a view of the evolution of the portfolio style over time, we can carry out the analysis again for rolling sub-periods, after carrying out the analysis for the complete period. With quarterly returns we take, for example, three-year periods by rolling over one quarter. The successive results show the evolution in the manager's style. This is a quick way to analyse the evolution of the style without having to know the portfolio composition in detail.

Certain managers seek to add value by switching from one style and/or sector to another and by predicting the style or sector that will be favourable in the upcoming period. These managers are called sector rotators or style rotators. The style analysis and benchmark creation described in this section are not suitable for analysing this type of manager. It is better in that case to use a broad benchmark. However, the analysis presented allows us to identify this type of manager rapidly. The rolling period analysis gives results that are spread over all styles instead of tending towards a specific style. The style is therefore inconsistent. The

R^2 calculated to validate the benchmark is low and it is virtually impossible to predict the future on the basis of the past. The benchmark evaluated by rolling period evolves greatly from one period to another. While the average style benchmark turnover in one year is between 20% and 30%, that of a style rotator can reach 100%.

We have seen that the main disadvantage of the return-based method was that it was essentially based on past data. Furthermore, linear statistic modelling poses the problem of the meaning of the term "residual". We must consider that the classic assumptions of the linear model are always true and, consequently, that the optimality properties of the linear regression estimators will always remain valid. In particular, it is classic to rely on the "central limit" theorem to justify the fact that the random residual of the model (an effect that results from the addition of multiple unspecified random factors) has a distribution that is similar to the Laplace–Gauss law. This allows the parameters of the estimated model to be "Studentised" and thus allows their "significance" to be qualified statistically.

Apart from that statistical assumption, style analysis presents other statistical difficulties:

1. The linear regression uses past data and the past cannot be representative of the future (the problem with the non-stationarity of the processes).
2. The constraint imposed by the Sharpe model on the weight of the factors (positive and with a sum equal to 1) tends to distort the regression results obtained (DeRoon *et al.*, 2000). The correlation between the error term and the benchmark or benchmarks chosen may not be equal to 0.

6.4.5.3   Portfolio-based analysis

The principle of portfolio-based analysis is to analyse each of the securities that make up the portfolio (cf. Borger, 1997). The securities are studied and ranked according to the different characteristics that allow their style to be described. The results are then aggregated at the portfolio level to obtain the style of the portfolio as a whole. This method therefore requires the present and historical composition of the portfolio, together with the weightings of the different securities that it contains, to be known precisely. The analysis is carried out regularly in order to take account of the evolution of the portfolio composition and the evolution of the characteristics of the securities that make up the portfolio. The results obtained therefore correspond to the characteristics of the portfolio currently held by the manager and thus liable to influence his future performance, while the method described previously was based on the past characteristics of the portfolio. This method therefore enables better monitoring of the evolution of the portfolio. The method is partly drawn from the work of Fama and French, which we presented earlier in the chapter, who showed that asset returns could be explained by a small number of fundamental factors. In particular, Fama and French identified the size, measured by the market capitalisation, and the book-to-market ratio.

As we saw in Chapter 1, the style is essentially analysed according to two facets. Assets are classified, on the one hand, according to their market capitalisation, and, on the other, according to whether they are growth stocks or value stocks. For the size criterion, they are generally separated into two groups: large-cap securities and small-cap securities. To do this, all securities are ranked in decreasing order of market capitalisation. We can then define the two groups so that the total market capitalisation of each group is the same. In this case the small-cap stock group will contain more securities than the large-cap stock group. We can also choose to separate the two groups by observing the level at which the performance differences between the securities become significant. In addition, we can define a third intermediate category containing mid-cap securities.

We observe that the investment styles and the fundamental factors are linked: a style can be described by a set of fundamental factors. The stocks can be split into value stocks and growth stocks by observing the values of the securities' fundamental characteristics. Value stocks are characterised by high returns. Several variables allow them to be identified. The first is the book/price (B/P) ratio, which measures the book value compared with the market value. Value stocks are characterised by a high B/P ratio, but it is more difficult to justify stocks with a low B/P ratio being growthstocks. Value stocks are also characterised by a high earnings/price (E/P) ratio. This ratio measures the amount of earnings compared to the market value. We can also identify value stocks on the basis of the yield/priceratio, which measures the value of the dividend compared to the market value, i.e. the return on the security. Certain securities cannot be included in either the growth or the value category. This is the case, for instance, for companies that have made a loss. The different securities are therefore classified in line with the value of the fundamental characteristics that are chosen to describe the styles. We can then check whether the different groups obtained do have different performance characteristics.

Once the study has been carried out security by security, the results are used to evaluate the style of the portfolio as a whole. The portfolio's market capitalisation is obtained, for example, by calculating the weighted mean of the market capitalisation of the securities that make up the portfolio. We proceed in the same way for all the fundamental characteristics of the portfolio. The study must be carried out regularly, because the characteristics of the securities are liable to evolve over time.

It is also possible to turn to factor analysis for implicit identification of the factors that characterise the style of the portfolios, rather than presupposing the nature of the fundamental factors associated with each style (cf. Radcliffe, 2000). This approach, which is not very widely used today in practice, is an attempt to respond to a criticism, which is difficult to refute, of the security characteristic-based style analysis techniques. Numerous studies (notably Lucas and Riepe, 1996) have highlighted the difficulty of a priori classification of securities according to their characteristics. On the one hand, commonly used attributes such as the book/price or earnings/price ratios are unstable and depend as much on market conditions as on company-specific qualities. On the other hand, the characteristics of a large number of securities do not allow satisfactory discriminatory analysis to be carried out. In a Bienstock and Sorensen (1992) study, it appears that only 20% of the stocks, from a sample of 3000, can, to a significant degree, be classified as value or growth. Such a limitation would lead to the construction of style benchmarks that would be too narrow and would either not correspond to the actual investment management carried out or, if the manager wished to guarantee his style by respecting this constraint, significantly restrict the investment opportunities. Finally, when the investor chooses stocks that present the desired characteristics, he selects other undesired attributes, which should be analysed, with the stocks (exposure to a country, to a sector, etc.). This complicates the a priori construction of the benchmark or portfolio that is representative of the allocation desired.

6.4.5.4   Comparing the two methods

The return-based method is the most widely used because it is the simplest to implement. There is no need to know the securities that make up the portfolio, nor their proportions. It is therefore the only method that can be used when there are no data available on the composition of the portfolio[21]. This *ex post* analysis does not however allow the managers' a priori respect of investment constraints to be managed. In addition, this technique has the disadvantages of the methods that use regression, namely a risk of the model being wrongly specified when the style indices are chosen. The return-based approach nevertheless has allowed the use of customised benchmarks to be developed and generalised, where previously one merely tended to compare portfolios with broad indices.

The portfolio-based method requires more information on the portfolio, but in exchange it provides more precise information. It is based on the style characteristics used by the manager to construct and maintain his portfolio and allows the investment strategies followed to be studied. The manager therefore has the possibility of evaluating the results of his forecasts and gaining a better understanding of the reasons for the over- or underperformance highlighted by performance attribution. The portfolio-based approach integrates the evolution of the portfolio style over time to a greater degree. While the return-based method could simply reveal a style differential sustained by the portfolio, the decomposition of the portfolio makes it possible to understand the security in the portfolio or the investment strategy that created the differential. This technique allows us to notice rapidly that a manager is holding securities that do not correspond to his style. But the main weakness of this approach is the frequently subjective character of the classifications. Since the style analyses performed within this approach are specific to each manager, it is difficult for them to be reproduced by an external third party. This can turn out to be a major disadvantage when an external consultant is used to certify or evaluate the quality of the management performance analysis provided to the institutional investor. As a result, we often see objectives shared between the methods[22]. The techniques that rely on the portfolio-based analysis approach are used for the *internal* implementation of the monitoring process for risks, compliance with investment constraints and performance attribution. Since an analysis that is exclusively based on the returns is considered to be more objective, it is more often used for an *external* view of performance measurement and its adjustment in relation to the risk taken and the style used by the manager over the analysis period.

Within the area of multimanagement, we find this breakdown again. Only multimanagers who have access, through their information system, to all the daily operations of their delegated managers favour portfolio-based analysis. Managers of funds-of-funds use techniques that are only based on returns.

6.4.5.5   Style benchmarks

In Chapter 2 we defined normal benchmarks. This type of benchmark allows more accurate performance evaluation of a portfolio that is managed according to a particular style. The two methods for analysing the portfolio style that we have just described are used to construct appropriate normal portfolios for the managers' styles. The manager's portfolio can then be represented as a weighted combination of style indices.

In order to determine the weightings to assign to each style index, we analyse the style of the manager over a given period using one of the two methods described above. We thus obtain a set of weights that represent the manager's style at the end of the time period. The reference

---

[21] In 1995, a survey of data from two major mutual fund information providers in the United States showed that only one-fifth (Morningstar) and one-half (Value Line) of the fund compositions present in the marketed databases had been updated in the previous three months.

[22] For more details on the conditions of use of the two approaches, it would be beneficial to refer to Trzcinka (1997).

portfolio for evaluating the manager is a portfolio made up of the style indices in proportions defined by the portfolio style analysis. This portfolio is the normal portfolio weighted by the style. Formally, it is calculated in the following way:

$$R_{Nt} = w_{1,t-1}S_{1t} + w_{2,t-1}S_{2t} + \cdots + w_{n,t-1}S_{nt} + \varepsilon_{nt}$$

where

R_{Nt}	denotes the return of the style-weighted normal portfolio at date t;
$w_{n,t-1}$	denotes the weight of style index n at the beginning of the time period or the end of the last time period;
S_{nt}	denotes the return of style index n at time t or over the interval from $t-1$ to t;
ε_{nt}	denotes the residual return non-correlated with the n style indices; and
n	denotes the number of style indices in the analysis.

The portfolio with return R_{Nt} is the reference portfolio for evaluating portfolio management and portfolio performance. We note that the manager's alpha is integrated in the error term, whatever the specific portfolio risk. Any return that is not taken into account by the style indices is integrated in the error term. That is the disadvantage of using this method to create normal portfolios compared with the methods based on defining a manager-specific list of securities, which were described in Chapter 2.

When we create a normal portfolio it can track the portfolio of the manager under evaluation with a certain degree of accuracy. The closer the normal portfolio is to the manager's portfolio, the better it will capture his style, but in that case the normal portfolio will only be adapted to a single manager. If, on the other hand, we create a normal portfolio that is a bit more general, it will allow us to evaluate and compare managers with different portfolios but fairly similar styles.

6.4.5.6 Management style characteristics and other methods of classification

Roll (1997) presents an interesting study that allows the relative risk of different management styles to be analysed. The securities were first classified according to the following three style characteristics: size, B/P ratio and E/P ratio. Each security is then given a label, L for low and H for high, for each of the three criteria, depending on whether it is found in the top half or the bottom half of the list. We then construct portfolios containing securities with the same characteristics, i.e. with the same series of labels. This leads to eight portfolios, the first being characterised by three H labels, the last by three L labels, and the intermediate portfolios by different combinations of H and L. This classification is redone each month. The composition of the portfolios is therefore liable to evolve from one month to the next. The portfolio returns are evaluated on a monthly basis.

The goal of the study is to see if the observed differences in returns between the portfolios, which correspond to different styles, are statistically significant. If the response is positive, then we can deduce that the different styles are characterised by different levels of risk. The study was carried out by successively using the CAPM model and a five-factor APT model to explain the returns of the different portfolios. In both cases the results show significant differences in returns between the styles, and hence different levels of risk. In addition, the APT model's risk factors do not allow the performance resulting from the portfolio style to be explained completely. We also observe that the specific returns associated with the style are not stationary over time.

We described the methods that allow the asset styles to be identified with the help of fundamental factors a little earlier. Another useful technique for classifying assets according to their style involves defining style betas (cf. Quinton, 1997) using the same principle as the market betas in Sharpe's CAPM. The return of each asset is described in the following way:

$$R_{\text{stock}} = \alpha + \beta_M R_M + \beta_{G-V} R_{G-V} + \beta_{L-S} R_{L-S}$$

where

α denotes the return not explained by the model;

R_M denotes the monthly market return measured by an index representing the market as a whole;

R_{G-V} denotes the difference between the monthly return of the growth index and the monthly return of the value index;

R_{L-S} denotes the difference between the monthly return of the large-cap index and the monthly return of the small-cap index;

β_M denotes the security's sensitivity to the market index;

β_{G-V} denotes the security's sensitivity to the difference between the growth index and the value index; and

β_{L-S} denotes the security's sensitivity to the difference between the large-cap index and the small-cap index.

The coefficients of this equation are estimated through regression. The stocks for which β_{G-V} is positive are growth stocks and those for which β_{G-V} is negative are value stocks. In the same way, stocks with a positive β_{L-S} are large-cap stocks and those with a negative β_{L-S} are small-cap stocks.

This model defines an APT-type relationship between the returns of the stocks and the returns of the style indices. The betas also provide an accurate measure of the sensitivity of each stock to the different investment styles. Using this analysis we can evaluate the investment style of a portfolio as the weighted mean of the investment styles of the different assets that make up the portfolio.

Brown and Goetzmann (1996) developed an algorithm for classifying funds by category of style which differs from the traditional methods. According to them, the traditional methods do not allow a certain number of problems to be solved satisfactorily, namely explaining future returns of funds, giving indications on the managers' strategies and providing useful benchmarks for evaluating relative performance. The authors indicate that the method that they have developed gives better results for those questions. The algorithm that they developed is consistent with the APT model. The funds are grouped together on the basis of series of past returns and on the responses to specified exogenous factors and endogenous stochastic variables. The results consist of styles that differ from the standard classifications. Their conclusion is that their method would not replace Sharpe's style analysis, but would complement it.

6.4.5.7 Investment style and performance persistence

We saw in Chapter 1 that performance persistence studies do not give very conclusive results as to whether persistence really exists. Over a long period, there is a greater tendency to observe underperformance persistence on the part of poor managers than overperformance persistence from good managers. However, the studies do not take into account the investment style followed by the managers. We do, nevertheless, observe that different investment styles are not all simultaneously favoured by the market. Markets are subject to economic cycles and a style that is favourable for one period, i.e. that offers a performance that is better than that of the market, can be less favourable over another period and lead to underperformance compared with the market. This can be measured by comparing the returns of the different style indices with the returns of a broad market index. The fact that an investment style performs well or badly should not be confused with the manager's skill in picking the right stocks within the style that he has chosen. As we mentioned earlier, a manager's skill in practising a well-defined style should be evaluated in comparison with a benchmark that is adapted to that style.

Few studies have addressed the subject of performance persistence for managers who specialise in a specific style. The results of the studies that have been performed are contradictory and do not allow us to conclude that persistence exists. For example, Coggin *et al.* (1993) carried out a study on American pension funds over the period from 1983 to 1990. Their study relates to identification of both the market timing effect and the selectivity effect. They used two broad indices: the S&P500 index and the Russell 3000 index, and four specialised indices: the Russell 1000 index for large-cap stocks, the Russell 2000 index for small-cap stocks, a Russell index specialised in value stocks and a Russell index specialised in growth stocks. They showed that the timing effect and the selectivity effect were both sensitive to the choice of benchmark and the period of the study. They found a positive selectivity effect compared with the specific indices, while that effect was negative compared with the broad indices. However, they found a negative market timing effect in both cases. The study shows, therefore, that specialisation is a source of value-added. Managers succeed in performing better than their reference style index, even if they do not manage to beat the market as a whole. Over the period studied, the different style indices did not all perform in line with the market. The performance of the value stock index was approximately equal to that of the market, which implies that the study period was favourable for value stocks. The performance of the growth stock index was slightly worse. As far as the small-cap stock index was concerned, its performance was half as good as that of the market index.

However, Kahn and Rudd (1995, 1997) concluded that fund performance was not persistent for a sample of 300 US funds over the period from October 1988 to October 1995.

A final interesting study is that of Chan *et al.* (1999). This study concerns Morningstar funds. The study shows that on the whole there is a certain consistency in the style of the funds. Nevertheless, funds that have performed badly in the past are more liable to modify their style than others. This study shows that it is preferable to avoid managers who change style regularly. They make it more difficult to optimise a portfolio that is shared between several managers and produce worse performances than managers whose style is consistent.

6.5   SUMMARY AND CONCLUSION

Throughout this chapter we have presented the different categories of multi-factor models and their application to portfolio management. The common denominator between all these models is to allow the number of terms employed in calculating the asset variance–covariance matrix to be reduced. By analysing the assets through a reduced number of factors we can express this matrix as a function of the variance–covariance matrix of the factors and the variance–covariance matrix of the asset-specific risks. It therefore becomes easier to analyse large portfolios. In relation to analysing the results of portfolio management, multi-factor models allow us to identify the factors that made the most significant contribution to the performance of a portfolio over a given period.

This chapter also allowed us to appreciate the difficulties linked to the choice and construction of the correct factor model. The results depend above all on the correct fit between the models used and the portfolios studied. Determining the model is therefore a step that should not be neglected. For a long time the models that dominated the market used explicit factors. These models are easier for users to understand because the factors are expressed clearly. But, as we have seen, these models cannot guarantee that the choice of factors is optimal. That is why recent research favours implicit factors, and all the more so since progress in calculating speed and database management allow the factors to be extracted more easily. These models allow the evolution of returns over time to be monitored better, which is why they are very useful for monitoring and managing portfolio risk. If we wish, for example, to use past results to modify the portfolio composition for the following period, or construct a portfolio with levels of risk specified in relation to the different factors with an explicit factor model, we cannot be sure that the model is stable. It is better in that case to be able to turn to an implicit factor model.

However, as far as *ex post* portfolio performance analysis is concerned, we will continue to prefer explicit factor models that allow the sources of portfolio performance to be described by name. They then allow us to produce reports attributing the contribution of each identified risk factor to the total performance of the portfolio.

At the end of this chapter it is interesting to return to the contribution of the APT model and multi-factor models in general, compared with the CAPM. The superiority of these models from a theoretical point of view is unquestionable and unquestioned. However, in practice we observe that the CAPM remains very widely used. Its strength is its great simplicity, even though it has not been the object of rigorous empirical validation. In comparison, the multi-factor models are more cumbersome to implement.

Certain models presented in this section are appropriate for portfolios that are diversified between several asset classes. This is the case for Sharpe's style analysis model and the multi-index model. Others, such as the APT model or the Barra model are more appropriate for analysing a homogeneous class of assets that determines the choice of factors. In Chapter 8, which is devoted to bond investment, we will present versions of these models that are more appropriate for bond portfolios.

APPENDIX 6.1   THE PRINCIPLE OF ARBITRAGE VALUATION

The principle of arbitrage valuation is based on the following reasoning: any portfolio constructed with no capital invested and no risk taken should obtain a null return on average. Such a portfolio is called an arbitrage portfolio.

This portfolio is constructed by considering an investment spread over n assets. It is possible to modify the proportions invested in the different assets without changing the total value of the portfolio, i.e. with no new capital outlay. To do so, we buy and sell in such a way that the total sum of the movements is null. If we take w_i to be the change in the proportion invested in asset i, then the portfolio defined by the weightings, $(w_i)_{1 \leq i \leq n}$, respects the following condition:

$$\sum_{i=1}^{n} w_i = 0 \qquad (A.1)$$

The return obtained by this portfolio is written as follows:

$$R_P = \sum_{i=1}^{n} w_i R_{it}$$

By using the factor relationship assumed by the APT model, or

$$R_{it} = E(R_i) + \sum_{k=1}^{K} b_{ik} F_{kt} + \varepsilon_{it}$$

we obtain the following expression through substitution:

$$R_P = \sum_{i=1}^{n} w_i E(R_i) + \sum_{i=1}^{n} w_i b_{i1} F_1 + \cdots + \sum_{i=1}^{n} w_i b_{iK} F_K + \sum_{i=1}^{n} w_i \varepsilon_{it}$$

Let us now render explicit the conditions that must be respected by the portfolio. The portfolio must be risk-free, which implies that both the systematic and the non-systematic risk are to be eliminated.

The systematic risk in relation to each factor k is given by the vector b_k. To cancel this risk, it is necessary to make the terms containing b_{ik} disappear from the R_P expression. To do that we choose the w_i in such a way that the weighted sum of the components of b_k is null for each factor k, or

$$\sum_{i=1}^{n} w_i b_{ik} = 0 \tag{A.2}$$

for all k.

The non-systematic risk is eliminated by applying the principle of diversification. The number of assets n contained in the portfolio must therefore be large. And the changes in the percentages invested must be small, or

$$w_i \approx 1/n$$

Since the error terms ε_i are independent from each other, the law of large numbers allows us to write that their weighted sum tends towards 0 when n becomes large. Diversification therefore allows us to make the last term of the R_P expression disappear.

Furthermore, since the w_i have been chosen such that

$$\sum_{i=1}^{n} w_i b_{ik} = 0 \quad \text{for all } k$$

all the terms containing the factors have thus been eliminated and the R_P expression becomes simply

$$R_P = \sum_{i=1}^{n} w_i E(R_i)$$

The return on this portfolio is null by definition since it is an arbitrage portfolio. We thus have

$$\sum_{i=1}^{n} w_i E(R_i) = 0 \tag{A.3}$$

We have just established that the vector $(w_i)_{1 \leq i \leq n}$ had to respect the following three conditions:

A.1. $$\sum_{i=1}^{n} w_i = 0$$

A.2. $$\sum_{i=1}^{n} w_i b_{ik} = 0$$

A.3. $$\sum_{i=1}^{n} w_i E(R_i) = 0$$

These three conditions mean that the vector $(w_i)_{1 \leq i \leq n}$ must be orthogonal to the following three vectors: the column vector with all its components equal to 1, the vector of factor loadings, and the vector of expected returns. This last vector must therefore be a linear combination of the other two, or

$$E(R_i) = \lambda_0 + \lambda_1 b_{i1} + \cdots + \lambda_k b_{ik}$$

with

$$\lambda_0 = R_F$$

We thus obtain the so-called arbitrage valuation relationship:

$$E(R_i) - R_F = \lambda_1 b_{i1} + \cdots + \lambda_k b_{ik}$$

BIBLIOGRAPHY

Amenc, N. and Martellini, L., "The Brave New World of Hedge Fund Indices", ACT-Edhec, Working Paper, September 2001.

Barra, "The Barra E2 Multiple-Factor Model", Barra web site, April 1996.

Barra, "US Equity Model Version 3", 1998.

Batteau, P. and Lasgouttes, V., "Modèles multifacteurs des rentabilités boursières", in *Encyclopédie des marchés financiers*, Economica, 1997, pp. 1221–1257.

Bienstock, S. and Sorensen, E., "Segregating Growth from Value: It's not Always Either/Or", Salomon Brothers, Quantitative Equities Strategy, July 1992.

Borger, D.R., "Fundamental Factors in Equity Style Classification", in *The Handbook of Equity Style Management*, T.D. Coggin, F.J. Fabozzi and R.D. Arnott, eds, 2nd edn, Frank J. Fabozzi Associates, 1997.

Brown, S.J. and Goetzmann, W.N., "Mutual Fund Styles", Working Paper, NYU Leonard Stern School of Business, 1996.

Brown, M.R. and Mott, C.E., "Understanding the Differences and Similarities of Equity Style Indexes", in *The Handbook of Equity Style Management*, T.D. Coggin, F.J. Fabozzi and R.D. Arnott, eds, 2nd edn, Frank J. Fabozzi Associates, 1997.

Burmeister, E., Roll, R. and Ross, S., "Using Macroeconomic Factors to Control Portfolio Risk", Working Paper, BIRR Portfolio Analysis, Inc., March 1997. This article is based on the previous version of "A Practitioner's Guide to Arbitrage Pricing Theory", a contribution to *A Practitioner's Guide to Factor Models* for the Research Foundation of the Institute of Chartered Financial Analysts, 1994.

Carhart, M.M., "On Persistence in Mutual Fund Performance", *Journal of Finance*, vol. 52, no. 1, March 1997, pp. 57–82.

Chan, L.K.C., Chen, H.-L. and Lakonishok J., "On Mutual Fund Investment Styles", Working Paper no. 7215, National Bureau of Economic Research, 1999.

Chen, N.-F., Roll, R. and Ross, S., "Economic Forces and the Stock Market", *Journal of Business*, vol. 59, no. 3, 1986.

Coggin, T.D., Fabozzi, F.J. and Arnott, R.D., *The Handbook of Equity Style Management*, 2nd edn, Frank J. Fabozzi Associates, 1997.

Coggin, T.D., Fabozzi, F.J. and Rahman, S., "The Investment Performance of U.S. Equity Pension Fund Managers: An Empirical Investigation", *Journal of Finance*, vol. 48, no. 3, July 1993, pp. 1039–1055.

Connor, G., "The Three Types of Factor Models: A Comparison of their Explanatory Power", *Financial Analysts Journal*, May–June 1995.

Connor, G. and Korajczyk, R.A., "Performance Measurement with the Arbitrage Pricing Theory: A New Framework for Analysis", *Journal of Financial Economics*, March 1986, pp. 373–394.

Copeland, T.E. and Weston, J.F., *Financial Theory and Corporate Policy*, 3rd edn, Addison-Wesley, 1988.

DeRoon, F., Nijman T., and ter Horst, J., "Evaluating Style Analysis", Working Paper, Quantitative Investment Research Europe, 2000.

Eichholtz, P., Op't Veld, H. and Schweitzer, M., "Outperformance: Does Managerial Specialization Pay?", Working Paper, Linburg Institute of Financial Economics, 1997.

Elton, E.J. and Gruber, M.J., *Modern Portfolio Theory and Investment Analysis*, 5th edn, Wiley, 1995.

Elton, E.J., Gruber, M.J., Das, S. and Hlavka, M., "Efficiency with Costly Information: A Reinterpretation of Evidence from Managed Portfolios", *Review of Financial Studies*, vol. 6, no. 1, 1993, pp. 1–22.

Engerman, M., "Using Fundamental and Economic Factors to Explain Stock Returns: A Look at Broad Factors that Affect many Stocks", *Barra Newsletter*, fall 1993.

Fabozzi, F.J., *Investment Management*, Prentice Hall International Editions, 1995.

Fama, E.F. and French, K.R., "The Cross Section of Expected Returns", *Journal of Finance*, vol. 47, June 1992, pp. 427–465.

Fama, E.F. and French, K.R., "Common Risk Factors in the Returns on Stocks and Bonds", *Journal of Financial Economics*, vol. 33, 1993, pp. 3–56.

Fama, E.F. and French, K.R., "Size and Book-to-Market Factors in Earnings and Returns", *Journal of Finance*, vol. 50, no. 1, March 1995, pp. 131–155.

Fama, E.F. and French, K.R., "Multifactor Explanations of Asset Pricing Anomalies", *Journal of Finance*, vol. 51, no. 1, March 1996, pp. 55–84.

Fama, E.F. and MacBeth, J.D., "Risk, Return, and Equilibrium: Empirical Tests", *Journal of Political Economy*, vol. 81, 1973.

Farrell, Jr. J.L., *Portfolio Management, Theory and Application*, McGraw-Hill, 2nd edn, 1997.

Fedrigo, I., Marsh, T.A. and Pfleiderer, P., "Estimating Factor Models of Security Returns: How Much Difference does it Make?", Working Paper, December 1996.

Fontaine, P., *Arbitrage et évaluation internationale des actifs financiers*, Economica, 1987.

Fontaine, P., "Modèles d'arbitrage et multifactoriels internationaux", in *Encyclopédie des marchés financiers*, Economica, 1997, pp. 1164–1185.

Grandin, P., *Mesure de performance des fonds d'investissement, Méthodologie et résultats*, Economica, Gestion poche, 1998.

Grinold, R.C., "The APT, the CAPM, and the Barra Model: How does Barra's Model of Asset Risk Fit the APT and CAPM Models?", *Barra Newsletter*, November–December 1991.

Grinold, R.C. and Kahn, R.N., *Active Portfolio Management*, Irwin, 1995.

Grinold, R.C. and Kahn, R.N., *Active Portfolio Management: A Quantitative Approach for Producing Superior Returns and Controlling Risk*, Irwin, 2nd edn, 2000.

Grinold, R.C., Rudd, A. and Stefek, D., "Global Factors: Fact or Fiction?", *Journal of Portfolio Management*, fall 1989.

Grossman, S.J. and Stiglitz, J., "On the Impossibility of Informationally Efficient Markets", *American Economic Review*, 1980, pp. 393–408.

Hamao, Y., "An Empirical Examination of the Arbitrage Pricing Theory: Using Japanese Data", *Japan and the World Economy*, vol. 1, 1988, pp. 45–61.

Hardy, S., "Return-Based Style Analysis", in *The Handbook of Equity Style Management*, T.D. Coggin, F.J. Fabozzi and R.D. Arnott, eds, 2nd edn, Frank J. Fabozzi Associates, 1997.

Hotelling, H., "Analysis of a Complex of Statistical Variables into Principal Components", *Journal of Educational Psychology*, vol. 24, 1933, pp. 417–441.

Ippolito, R., "Efficiency with Costly Information: a Study of Mutual Fund Performance, 1965–84", *Quarterly Journal of Economics*, vol. 104, 1989, pp. 1–23.

Jegadeesh, N. and Titman, S., "Returns to Buying Winners and Selling Losers: Implications for Stock Market Efficiency", *Journal of Finance*, vol. 48, 1993, pp. 65–91.

Kahn, R.N., "Macroeconomic Risk Perspective", *Barra Newsletter* 161, summer 1993.

Kahn, R.N., "Quantitative Measures of Mutual Fund Risk: An Overview", *Barra Research Publications*, July 1995.

Kahn, R.N. and Rudd, A., "Does Historical Performance Predict Future Performance?", *Financial Analysts Journal*, November–December 1995, pp. 43–52.

Kahn, R.N. and Rudd, A., "The Persistence of Equity Style Performance: Evidence from Mutual Fund Data", in *The Handbook of Equity Style Management*, T.D. Coggin, F.J. Fabozzi and R.D. Arnott, eds, 2nd edn, Frank J. Fabozzi Associates, 1997.

Lawley, D.N. and Maxwell, E., *Factor Analysis as a Statistical Method*, Butterworths, 1963.

Lucas, L. and Riepe, M.W., "The Role of Returns-Based Style Analysis: Understanding, Implementing and Interpreting the Technique", Ibbotson Associates, May 1996.

Marsh, T. and Pfleiderer, P., "The Role of Country and Industry Effects in Explaining Global Stock Returns", Working Paper, September 1997.

Mei, J., "A Semi-Autoregressive Approach to the Arbitrage Pricing Theory", *Journal of Finance*, vol. 48, July 1993, pp. 599–620.

Meier, J., "Performance Attribution and the International Portfolio", *Barra Newsletter*, September–October 1991.

Meier, J., "Global Equity Performance Attribution", *Barra Newsletter*, spring 1994.

Molay, E., "Le modèle de rentabilité à trois facteurs de Fama et French (1993): une application sur le marché français", *Banque et Marchés*, no. 44, January–February 2000.

Mott, C.E. and Coker, D.P., "Understanding the Style Benchmarks", in *Equity Style Management, Evaluating and Selecting Investment Styles*, R.A. Klein and J. Lederman, eds., Irwin, 1995.

Quinton, K., "Style Betas: An Approach to Measuring Style at the Security Level", in *The Handbook of Equity Style Management*, T.D. Coggin, F.J. Fabozzi and R.D. Arnott, eds, 2nd edn, Frank J. Fabozzi Associates, 1997.

Radcliffe, R.C., "Equity Style Information", Working Paper, Department of Finance, Insurance and Real Estate, University of Florida, January 2000.

Roll, R., "Style Return Differentials: Illusions, Risk Premiums, or Investment Opportunities", in *The Handbook of Equity Style Management*, T.D. Coggin, F.J. Fabozzi and R.D. Arnott, eds, 2nd edn, Frank J. Fabozzi Associates, 1997.

Roll, R. and Ross, S., "An Empirical Investigation of the Arbitrage Pricing Theory", *Journal of Finance*, vol. 35, no. 5, December 1980, pp. 1073–1103.

Roll, R. and Ross, S., "The Arbitrage Pricing Theory Approach to Strategic Portfolio Planning", *Financial Analysts Journal*, May–June 1984, pp. 14–26.

Rosenberg, B., "Choosing a Multiple Factor Model", *Investment Management Review*, November–December 1987, pp. 28–35.

Ross, S.A., "The Arbitrage Theory of Capital Asset Pricing", *Journal of Economic Theory*, vol. 13, December 1976, pp. 341–360.

Rudd, A., "On Factor Models", *Barra Newsletter*, September–October 1992.

Salvati, J., "Mesure de performance et gestion de portefeuille", in *Encyclopédie des marchés financiers*, Economica, 1997, pp. 1122–1139.

Sharpe, W.F., "Asset Allocation: Management Style and Performance Measurement", *Journal of Portfolio Management*, vol. 18, winter 1992, pp. 7–19.

Sheikh, A., "Barra's Risk Model", *Barra Research Insights*, 1996.

Simon, Y., *Encyclopédie des marchés financiers*, Economica, 1997.

Trzcinka, C., "Is Equity Style Management Worth the Effort?: Some Critical Issues for Plan Sponsors", in *The Handbook of Equity Style Management*, T.D. Coggin, F.J. Fabozzi and R.D. Arnott, eds, 2nd edn, Frank J. Fabozzi Associates, 1997.

7

Evaluating the Investment Management Process and Decomposing Performance

The theories presented up to now, which are drawn from modern portfolio theory, are based on a bottom-up view of portfolio management, i.e. on an approach that is essentially focused on stock picking. The main aim of the resulting performance models is to evaluate the manager on his capacity to choose securities that are likely to have better than average performance. The earliest approaches to evaluating management strategy examined the timing effect, or, in other words, managing the portfolio according to anticipated movements in the market as a whole. In Chapter 4 we presented methods derived from the Capital Asset Pricing Model (CAPM) that allowed that effect to be measured, but the methods focus more on determining whether the effect exists or not than measuring it quantitatively.

However, the portfolio management profession is increasingly evolving towards a top-down view, which accords more importance to the choice of different markets or asset classes than the individual selection of securities. This is justified in view of studies (cf. Brinson *et al.*, 1986, 1991) that show that these choices determine a large share of the portfolio's risk–return profile. Top-down investment management is broken down into an asset allocation phase, where we determine the allocation of the portfolio between the different asset classes, and a stock picking phase, where we choose the assets within each class. Portfolio performance is then analysed by breaking down the whole result into the different phases of the process, which allows us to highlight the management decisions that made the greatest contribution to performance and use those results to improve the subsequent management of the portfolio.

The investment management phases were briefly presented in Chapter 1 in the section describing the investment process. All these phases can be handled by quantitative methods drawn from modern portfolio theory, even though the methods were originally developed for stock picking purposes. In Section 7.1 we describe those methods and, in particular, the asset allocation methods that have not been discussed until now. The performance decomposition methods will then be presented Section 7.2.

7.1 THE STEPS IN CONSTRUCTING A PORTFOLIO

7.1.1 Asset allocation[1]

Asset allocation consists of choosing the spread of different asset classes within the portfolio. The asset classes can be the major categories of assets (stocks, bonds and money market instruments), industrial sectors for a portfolio of national equities, or countries for a portfolio of international equities. At the outset, investors define the categories of assets that they wish to include in the portfolio, depending on their objectives and constraints. The asset allocation methods may depend on the nature of the assets, but, in all cases, asset allocation is carried out in two stages. We first define the long-term allocation, based on the risk and return estimations

---

[1] Cf. Chapter 28 of Fabozzi (1995) and Chapter 9 of Farrell (1997).

Table 7.1   Results of the Nutall and Nutall (1998) study (Reproduced by permission of Ibbotson Associates)

Nutall & Nutall study (conclusions)		
	Percentage of writers who misinterpret the Brinson survey as a solution to the relationship between asset allocation and the level of returns. For example: "One study suggests that more than 91% of a portfolio's return is attributable to its mix of asset classes. In this study, individual stock selection and market timing together accounted for less than 7% of a diversified portfolio's return." Vanguard Group	75%
	Percentage of writers who misinterpret the Brinson survey as a solution to the impact of choosing one asset allocation policy over another. For example: "A widely quoted study of pension plan managers shows that 91.5% of the difference between one portfolio's performance and another's is explained by asset allocation." Fidelity Investments	10%
	Other erroneous quotations	13%
	Percentage of writers who accurately quoted Brinson (only one correct interpretation)	2%

for each asset class. This is strategic allocation. We can then carry out adjustments based on short-term anticipations. This is tactical allocation.

Today, asset allocation is tending to play a more important role in the investment management process.[2] The interest in asset allocation can be explained by the results established by modern portfolio theory. The latter suggests that financial markets are sufficiently well regulated for the prices of assets to be at equilibrium. The possibility of obtaining substantial gains through stock picking alone is therefore reduced. Besides, Brinson *et al.* (1986)[3] and Brinson *et al.* (1991) showed that a significant share (90%) of portfolio performance could be attributed to the initial allocation decision. The result of this study should however be considered with care, because it has often been incorrectly interpreted.

An analysis carried out in 1998 by Nutall and Nutall (1998) has given us a relative view of the interpretation of the Brinson *et al.* (1991) study, which only gave market timing and stock picking a residual share of the overall performance of funds.

Out of 50 references to the Brinson *et al.* study, Nutall and Nutall showed that only one commentator interpreted the results of their work appropriately (see Table 7.1)

In fact, by comparing the quarterly evolution of the portfolio and the asset classes in which the portfolio is invested, Brinson and his co-authors concluded that more than 90% of the variability in portfolio performance over time is linked to asset allocation.

However, this conclusion, as we have indicated, has been the object of numerous misinterpretations, and criticisms.

Thus, Hansel *et al.* (1991) affirm that the Brinson study is of little interest because it is only stating the obvious: when the representative markets for the asset classes in which the portfolio is invested rise, the value of the portfolio rises (when the water rises, the boats rise!).

---

[2] On this subject, see the beginning of the introduction to Brown and Harlow (1990), who also discuss the role of modern portfolio theory in asset allocation.
[3] A review of this article is given in Jahnke (1997).

Table 7.2 Conclusions of Ibbotson and Kaplan's study (Reproduced by permission of Ibbotson Associates)

Performance Measurement		
	Percentage of the *variability* in returns over time that is due to the asset allocation policy	90%
	Percentage of the variation *between* the funds that is due to different asset allocation policies	40%
	Percentage of the total return that is due to the asset allocation policy	100%

Source: Ibbotson and Kaplan (2000).

Brinson does not ask the right question, which, according to Jahnke (1997), should be "what accounts for the difference in returns between the funds?"

For Surz *et al.* (1999), the right issue, which Brinson did not come up with, is not the measurement of fund return variability over time, but the measurement of the amount or share of the return that is attributable to asset allocation.

In a recent article, Ibbotson and Kaplan (2000) noted that the conclusions and interpretations of the Brinson *et al.* (1991) study were not relevant and, taking a multivarious analysis of a representative sample of US mutual funds and pension funds, concluded that 40% (mutual funds) and 35% (pension funds) of the difference between the fund returns was explained by the asset allocation choice, with the remaining 60% (65) being the result of market timing, stock picking and the funds' fee policies.

In addition, to answer Surz *et al.*'s question, Ibbotson and Kaplan concluded that the average return of the normal portfolios taken as representative benchmarks of the universe of funds explains, over a long period, 100% of the average return of the funds themselves. This conclusion is consistent with the work of Sharpe (1992). It means that, mathematically, the average return of managed funds cannot do better than the average return of the index (in other words, that the whole return is in the market!). This does not exclude large differences in returns between the funds over the short or medium term (see Table 7.2).

To finish up on the subject of questioning the strategic or static allocation dogma, it should be noted that even its most ardent supporters deviate from it. In 1997, Singer, in response to criticism of his 1991 study (Brinson *et al.*, 1991), admitted that when the risk and return values differ significantly from those that justified the initial allocation, the latter should be modified. This pragmatic approach no longer establishes an impassable frontier between strategic (immobile) allocation and tactical (variable) allocation and often uses semantics ("strategic allocation review") to justify its existence.

Finally, we should stress that the impact of asset allocation on the return of a portfolio depends on the investment style. In the case of a passive investment strategy, strategic allocation is indeed the most important decision. However, in the case of active management that practises market timing, the initial allocation has less impact on the returns. We shall give details on the different aspects of asset allocation, and the methods for implementing it, below.

7.1.1.1 Evaluating asset classes

Here we cite, without going into detail, the main methods for evaluating the relative usefulness of the different asset classes compared with one another. We will return to this subject later in the chapter, in the section on tactical allocation. The asset classes with the highest returns are, in principle, the riskiest. The expected return on a class of assets is determined differently depending on its nature.

Bonds are evaluated by taking the rate of return on long-term government loans. Money market positions are represented by the rate of return on short-term T-bills. For equities, several methods are possible. One method is to use historical data on the returns of representative indices. A second method is to use the Dividend Discount Model (DDM), an evaluation model for calculating a rate of return for the stock market, using the rate of return for each stock, and comparing it with the rate of return for the bond market, measured by a long-term interest rate. Finally, there is a third approach, called the scenario method.[4] This method involves defining scenarios that correspond to different configurations for the economy, and their influence on the evolution of different asset classes. A probability of occurrence is then attributed to each of the scenarios. This last method is therefore not very easy to implement.

All of this is valid for a portfolio that is invested in domestic assets only. In the case of an international portfolio,[5] it is necessary to choose the portfolio breakdown by country beforehand. The usefulness of each country is then evaluated using a local index. We also estimate the exchange rates required for expressing all the returns in a reference currency.

The estimation of the returns for the asset classes should be complemented by the estimation of the correlations between the asset classes, which is an essential parameter for choosing the portfolio allocation between the different categories of assets.

7.1.1.2   Strategic allocation

Strategic asset allocation involves choosing an initial portfolio allocation that corresponds to the investor's objectives and constraints. These decisions correspond in reality to the choice of benchmark. This choice is based on the risk and return estimations for the asset classes. It can be carried out quantitatively, with the help of the different methods we describe below.

Applying Markowitz's model to asset allocation[6]
The most widely quoted quantitative model in the strategic allocation literature is Markowitz's optimisation model. This model, which we presented in Chapter 3, was initially developed for stock picking purposes. We saw that the principal difficulty, which was liable to limit its use, was the large number of calculations required to implement it. This model therefore turns out to be particularly appropriate for handling the problem of asset allocation, because the number of asset classes is limited. The number of calculations to be carried out thus becomes reasonable. The input data are the means and the variances, estimated for each asset class, and the correlations between the asset classes. The model provides the optimal percentage to assign to each asset class to obtain the best return for a given level of risk. This optimisation can be produced by defining the constraints linked to the manager's investment style: for example, holding a minimal percentage of stocks in the portfolio. The mathematical models used to solve the Markowitz problem allow these constraints to be taken into account, as we saw in Chapter 3.

---

[4] Cf. Chapter 9 of Farrell (1997). The scenario method is also cited in Bayser (1996).
[5] Cf. Simon and Mannaï (1998), Chapter 11 of Farrell (1997), Chapter 5 of Bito and Fontaine (1989), and Hartpence and Sikorav (1996).
[6] Cf. in particular Chapter 2 of Farrell (1997), Chapter 28 of Fabozzi (1995), Chapter 11 of Broquet and van den Berg (1992), and Chapter 1 of Brown and Harlow (1990).

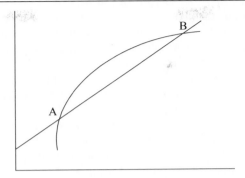

Figure 7.1   Curve of the investor's risk tolerance

In the area of strategic allocation decisions, the Markowitz model can be associated with the notion of shortfall risk.[7] The principle is to integrate a skewed approach to the notion of risk, characterised by a limited shortfall risk, into the model. We thereby define, for a fixed probability, a floor return below which the portfolio should not fall. This condition is translated in the form of a straight line which, placed on the graph of the efficient frontier, marks out the part of the curve that corresponds to the investor's risk tolerance. In Figure 7.1 this part of the curve is marked out by points A and B.

Even though the Markowitz method provides, in theory, a satisfactory response to the problem of determining strategic allocation, it is not in fact very widely used in practice for the following two reasons. First, the optimal proportions are very sensitive to the mean return values; secondly, the mean returns are very difficult to estimate statistically (see, for example, Merton, 1980). As a result, the model often allocates the most significant proportion to the asset class with the largest estimation error!

Taillard (2002) illustrates the limits of Markowitz's model using the following example. The portfolio to be optimised is made up of the stocks in the MSCI World Index. The returns and the variance–covariance matrix are estimated using historical data for the period 1996–2000. The optimal allocation is calculated to achieve a mean expected return of 1% per month. However, if the portfolio had effectively been constructed at the beginning of 2001 with the weights found through optimisation, then its expected mean return would have been −0.47% per month at the end of June 2002. This illustrates the fact that the estimated risk and returns used in Markowitz's model are not reliable. Historical data do not constitute a good representation of the forthcoming period. With this example, Taillard also illustrates the sensitivity of the optimisation method to the data and how it can emphasise data errors and lead to an incoherent allocation. The instability of optimisation can be explained by poor conditioning of the variance–covariance matrix. The matrix conditioning is defined as the parameter that measures the multiplying effect, as a relative value, of an error on the inputs. This parameter is equal to the highest eigenvalue of the matrix, divided by its lowest eigenvalue. Factor analysis shows that the first factor generally explains most of the variance, while the last factors have

[7] Cf. Leibowitz and Langetied (1989) and Leibowitz and Kogelman (1990). These articles are reproduced in *Investing*, the collected works of Martin L. Leibowitz, edited by Frank J. Fabozzi, 1992. The first part of this book discusses asset allocation. This approach is used in Boulier *et al.* (1996), who address the two phases of asset allocation, strategic and tactical, but are more interested in the strategic phase, which is generally less developed than the tactical phase in the literature.

negligible explanatory power. The conditioning parameter may therefore be very high. In the example considered by Taillard, this parameter is equal to 408, so a relative error of 1% on the data may result in an error of 400% on the composition of the portfolio. These considerations mean that we should consider the results of this type of optimisation with reservations. Constrained optimisation does not appear to be a solution to the problem since it tends to reduce portfolio diversification. For example, when short sales are not allowed in the example considered, the optimisation program chooses only four of the 22 markets available.

Another limitation of Markowitz's model is that it uses variance as a risk measure. When a portfolio contains alternative asset classes such as hedge funds, this measure does not provide an accurate representation of the risk of the portfolio. A solution is to add Value-at-Risk constraints to the mean–variance optimisation.

Improving data modelling[8]
Different techniques enable data modelling to be improved. Using only the information available within a sample of data does not allow the effect of parameter uncertainty on optimal portfolio choice to be taken into account. So it is necessary to use additional data, such as information based on the experience or insights of investors or financial analysts. The optimisation is then less dependent on purely statistically estimated data. The optimal combination of sample and non-sample information can be attained with Bayesian statistics. Black and Litterman's (1990) method is one example of the use of Bayesian statistical procedures.

Black and Litterman (1990) proposed an original approach that enabled the problem of applying portfolio optimisation techniques to be partially solved. Their approach involves two steps:

Step 1: obtain the implicit mean returns that allow the market proportions (i.e. proportional to the market capitalisation) to be retrieved as optimal proportions; these mean returns are used as reference values.
Step 2: combine these reference values with "views" or anticipations of the investor's own mean returns.

In this method, managers' anticipations can be provided on only some of the assets, they can be relative between two assets and they can be qualified with a degree of certainty.

Stein estimators are another example of Bayesian techniques. They use the fact that there is probably information in the group of returns of related assets and that the use of this group information can improve parameter estimation for each variable. This results in more intuitive optimised portfolios, and therefore a more coherent asset allocation.

Another possibility for improving the optimisation result is to use resampling techniques. This method allows several estimations to be carried out, producing a set of estimated returns and a variance–covariance matrix for the group of assets each time, instead of just one value for each parameter. An efficient portfolio is then constructed for each estimation. These portfolios are said to be resampled portfolios. The optimal portfolio is then obtained by averaging the results of the different optimisations. More details on the subject can be found in Scherer (2002). This technique reduces the problem of extreme portfolio weights associated with

---

[8] Cf. Michaud (1998), Scherer (2002) and Taillard (2002).

mean–variance efficient portfolios and leads to a portfolio that is less dependent on any particular set of optimisation inputs. Resampled efficient portfolios provide more reliable investments and are more consistent with the results that one would intuitively expect. Still, the difference between Bayesian analysis and resampling is that resampling draws repeatedly from the data without adding any new source of information to the historical data. The true distribution is still unknown and all resampled portfolios inherit the same estimation error relative to the true distribution. So the addition of non-sample information appears to be the best way to achieve more realistic allocations.

We can also cite a recent study by Amenc and Martellini (2002a) who offer a pragmatic response to the problem of optimal strategic allocation in the presence of estimation risk. It involves focusing on the only portfolio on the efficient frontier for which the estimation of mean returns is not necessary, namely the minimal variance portfolio. Using appropriate statistical techniques to improve the estimation of the variance–covariance matrix in a predictive approach, the authors show that the volatility of the minimal variance portfolio is significantly lower than that of a naively diversified portfolio (i.e. an equally weighted portfolio) for a mean return that is not necessarily lower.

In the presence of many assets, a sample variance–covariance matrix of historical returns is likely to generate a high sampling error because there are too many parameters to estimate relative to the available data. The problem is particularly acute in the context of alternative investment strategies, as hedge fund returns are only available on a monthly basis. A possible solution is to impose a structure on the covariance matrix to reduce the number of parameters to be estimated. In their article, Amenc and Martellini consider an implicit linear factor model of low dimension. Imposing a structure enables a low sample error to be obtained and because this structure is endogenous, the specification error is low. Implicit multi-factor forecasts of the asset return covariance matrix can be further improved by noise dressing techniques and optimal selection of the relevant number of factors.

The method used by Amenc and Martellini uses principal component analysis (PCA) to extract a set of implicit factors. From a mathematical point of view, it involves transforming a set of N correlated variables into a set of orthogonal variables, or implicit factors, which reproduces the original information present in the correlation structure. Each implicit factor is defined as a linear combination of original variables.

Define H as the following matrix:

$$H = (h_{it})_{\substack{1 \leq i \leq T \\ 1 \leq i \leq N}}$$

We have N variables h_i, $i = 1, \ldots, N$, i.e. monthly returns for N different funds, and T observations of these variables. PCA enables us to decompose h_{tk} as follows:

$$h_{tk} = \sum_{i=1}^{N} \sqrt{\lambda_i} U_{ik} V_{ti} = \sum_{i=1}^{N} s_{ik} V_{ti}$$

where U is the matrix of the N eigenvectors of $H'H$; and V is the matrix of the N eigenvectors of HH'.

These N eigenvectors are orthonormal. λ_i is the eigenvalue (ordered by degree of magnitude) corresponding to the eigenvector U_i. The N factors V_i are a set of orthogonal variables. The purpose is to describe each variable as a linear function of a reduced number of factors. This is done by selecting a number of factors K such that the first K factors capture a large fraction of asset return variance, while the remaining part can be regarded as statistical noise:

$$h_{tk} = \sum_{i=1}^{N} \sqrt{\lambda_i} U_{ik} V_{ti} + \varepsilon_{tk} = \sum_{i=1}^{N} s_{ik} V_{ti} + \varepsilon_{tk}$$

assuming that the residuals ε_{tk} are uncorrelated between themselves. The percentage of variance explained by the first K factors is given by

$$\sum_{i=1}^{K} \lambda_i \bigg/ \sum_{i=1}^{N} \lambda_i$$

Amenc and Martellini select the relevant number of factors by applying some explicit results from the theory of random matrices (cf. Marchenko and Pastur, 1967). The idea is to compare the properties of an empirical covariance matrix (or equivalently correlation matrix since asset returns have been normalised to have zero mean and unit variance) with a purely random null hypothesis matrix that could be obtained from a finite time series of strictly independent assets. It has been shown (see Johnstone, 2001, for a recent reference and Laloux *et al.*, 1999, for an application to finance) that the asymptotic density of eigenvalues λ of the correlation matrix of strictly independent assets reads

$$f(\lambda) = \frac{T}{2\pi N} \sqrt{\frac{(\lambda - \lambda_{\max})(\lambda - \lambda_{\min})}{\lambda}}$$

$$\lambda_{\max} = 1 + \frac{N}{T} + 2\sqrt{\frac{N}{T}}$$

$$\lambda_{\min} = 1 + \frac{N}{T} - 2\sqrt{\frac{N}{T}}$$

Theoretically this result can be exploited to provide formal testing of the assumption that a given factor represents information and not noise. However, the result is asymptotic and cannot be taken at face value for a finite sample size. One of the most important features here is the fact that the lower bound of the spectrum, $\lambda_{\min}$, is strictly positive (except for $T = N$), and therefore there are no eigenvalues between 0 and $\lambda_{\min}$. A conservative interpretation of this result is used to design a systematic decision rule and to decide to regard as statistical noise all factors associated with an eigenvalue lower than $\lambda_{\max}$. In other words, K is taken such that $\lambda_K > \lambda_{\max}$ and $\lambda_{K+1} < \lambda_{\max}$.

Alternative models to Markowitz's optimisation
Treynor and Black (1973) developed a model in which optimal allocation is achieved by analysing the returns' sources of risk and calculating exposure to each of these sources of risk. A short description of this model can be found in Taillard (2002). Treynor and Black use a single-factor model and integrate portfolio manager forecasts. Each return is separated into a source of systematic risk linked to the factor and a source of specific risk. These two sources of risk are non-correlated. This methodology leads to a more comprehensive portfolio construction process and the resulting allocation can be more easily analysed.

Black and Litterman (1991, 1992) refined Treynor and Black's (1973) idea by introducing uncertainty about the model parameters. Cvitanic *et al.* (2002) propose to improve the

Treynor–Black–Litterman model. They consider the problem of optimal portfolio construction when assets present abnormal returns and when investors are assumed to have views on these abnormal returns and to upgrade those views in a Bayesian way. The model used as a reference is the CAPM, but the approach is more general and can be applied to any multi-factor model. The optimal solution of the problem is derived in a closed form.

Scherer (2002) describes how to use alternative risk measures to derive an optimal portfolio in the framework of scenario optimisation. This is particularly interesting for non-normally distributed returns. The first model uses the mean absolute deviation (MAD), which measures risk as an absolute deviation from the mean. This measure was defined in Section 2.3 of Chapter 2. Optimal portfolios are obtained by minimising the MAD using a linear program. In a second model, allocation choice is obtained by minimising the maximum portfolio loss, also called regret. Here again the solution is obtained by solving a linear program. In the third model, allocation choice is defined by minimising conditional value-at-risk (CVaR), i.e. the expected excess loss over VaR if a loss larger than VaR actually occurs. CVaR offers the advantage of being subadditive. Optimisation is also implemented using linear programming.

Markowitz's approach involves an absolute mean–variance optimisation. Investment management often deals with relative mean–variance optimisation. In that case, the portfolio is optimised relative to its tracking-error. This offers a better control of optimal portfolio weights because the portfolio is kept close to its benchmark. However, the result can be difficult to explain, as can be seen in the example presented in Gaussel (1999), in which tracking-error optimisation underweights the asset with the highest expected return. A solution can be to use equilibrium returns. These returns are defined in relation to the benchmark and enable the deviation of the portfolio allocation from the benchmark to be analysed. If an asset with a high expected return is underweighted, then it simply means that its equilibrium return is higher than the return anticipated by the portfolio manager.

Other approaches to strategic allocation

Asset allocation choices can be made on the basis of forecasts for the economy. Boulier *et al.* (1996) cite this approach without developing it. It involves modelling the consequences over time of a particular choice of allocation in probabilistic form. The allocation is chosen by considering the probability distributions of a certain number of economic elements.

The Sharpe asset allocation model (cf. Sharpe, 1992), presented in Chapter 6, which was devoted to multi-factor models, allows us to identify a portfolio's exposure to the different asset classes on the basis of historical returns, with each asset class represented by a specialised index. It therefore allows us to analyse the asset allocation for a portfolio that has already been constituted, and to define the most appropriate benchmark for monitoring its performance.

Using the VaR, a measure of overall portfolio risk that was presented in Chapter 2, allows us to check whether the asset allocation chosen can be included in the framework fixed by regulatory constraints on the risk exposure of the portfolio under consideration.

As an alternative to asset allocation, Clarke *et al.* (2002) propose solving the optimal portfolio problem by considering risk allocation. Allocation is carried out by choosing the relative contributions of systematic and active risk in the portfolio. Compared with traditional asset allocation, the advantages are better control of the sources of risk in the portfolio and a more efficient trade-off between risk and return. If investors want a portfolio with a low level of total risk, then only a small amount of active management is used. As investors increase their tolerance for risk, more active management can be used in the portfolio. Portfolio optimisation takes place in two steps. First, a long-run benchmark portfolio is chosen based on the risk–return relationships for bearing systematic risk. Then, a decision is made on how to structure the portfolio using a combination of passive and actively managed strategies.

We also find the same idea in the core–satellite portfolio described in Scherer (2002). Core–satellite investing involves separating portfolio management into a passive part, called the core of the portfolio, and an active part, made up of one or more satellites of active managers. The optimal allocation between the core and the satellites will depend on the level of risk tolerance.

The case of international portfolios[9]

In the case of international investment, asset allocation involves, above all, dividing the portfolio between the different countries. This decision, which determines the largest share of portfolio performance, is based on market indices representing each country and the levels of exchange rates between the different countries. Exchange rate forecast models were presented in Chapter 2. Observing the differences compared with the equilibrium values, along with the predicted evolution of macroeconomic variables such as inflation, growth and interest rates, allows us to forecast the evolution of the currency markets and determine, for a given period, the most favourable markets. The methods for allocating the asset classes, presented in the national case, are then applied for each country.

The investment decisions on assets and currencies can be dissociated from each other, which leads, depending on the case, to portfolios that are globally hedged, unhedged, or partially hedged against exchange rate risk.

Some authors have developed specific asset allocation models for international portfolios. In particular, we could cite Emanuelli and Pearson's model (1994), in which the method for evaluating the different markets is based on estimates of company earnings. By relying on analysts' reviews, we can select the countries that will have above average returns.

7.1.1.3 Managing proportions

Several attitudes are possible. An initial solution involves keeping the portfolio structure that was defined at the strategic allocation stage. A second solution is to set up a procedure for readjusting the portfolio proportions automatically, depending on market modifications, so as not to fall below a certain level of return. This method is called portfolio insurance[10] or dynamic allocation. It was briefly presented in Chapter 1 and involves controlling portfolio risk. Here, we come back again to the notion of shortfall risk. The final solution consists of regularly readjusting the proportions of the different asset classes in the portfolio, to take into account short-term forecasts of market movements and the evolution of the economic environment, while respecting the risk constraints defined at the strategic allocation stage. In this case we speak of tactical allocation. The objective is to improve the future return of the portfolio. It is possible to modify the level of risk, as long as we stay within the fixed tracking-error limits. In this section we first give a reminder of the principle of dynamic allocation, and then develop the different methods for implementing tactical allocation. It should be stressed that each time we carry out readjustments, it is necessary to find the right balance between the gain procured and the transaction costs that take away from portfolio performance. The reliability of data forecasts is therefore essential for this stage of the investment management process.

---

[9] Cf. Fontaine (1997), Kahn *et al.* (1996) and Emanuelli and Pearson (1994).
[10] Cf. Black and Jones (1987), Perold and Sharpe (1988) and Chapter 9 of Farrell (1997).

Predictability in asset returns[11]

There is now a consensus in empirical finance that asset class returns are to some extent predictable. Academic studies have found significant evidence of predictability in the systematic component of return, but little evidence of predictability in the (noisier) specific component in the absence of private information. On the subject of predictability in the US markets, pioneering work was carried out by Keim and Stambaugh (1986), Campbell (1987), Campbell and Shiller (1988), Fama and French (1989) and Ferson and Harvey (1991). Investigation on an international basis is more recent. Studies of predictability in various national markets can be found in Bekaert and Hodrick (1992), Ferson and Harvey (1993, 1995), Harvey (1995) and Harasty and Roulet (2000).

This work justifies, on the one hand, the importance of asset allocation compared with stock picking and, on the other, the development of tactical asset allocation strategies and, more recently, of style timing strategies. Tactical asset allocation and style allocation are able to generate superior performance. Kandel and Stambaugh (1996) show that even a low level of statistical predictability can improve portfolio performance: superior returns may be attained even if the market is successfully timed only one out of 100 times.

The ability to predict market returns is part of tactical asset allocation. It has been demonstrated that financial ratio and accounting variables have good predictive power. The subject of our book is not the description of the methods for predicting returns, but how this ability to predict returns can be used in asset allocation, which we will discuss below. We can find numerous studies on the subject of predicting returns. Among the most recent, Lewellen (2002) considers the dividend yield, book-to-market ratio and E/P ratio to forecast market returns, and Berge and Ziemba (2002) look at the association of interest rates and E/P ratios.

Dynamic allocation[12]

Dynamic allocation is a strategy that consists of continuously readjusting the portfolio allocation so as to take into account the evolution of the market. The best known example of dynamic allocation is portfolio insurance. Portfolio insurance brings together strategies that enable the risk of a portfolio losing value to be eliminated, or at least limited. Portfolio insurance can be implemented through techniques that use option replication, by combining an investment in the option's underlying instrument and an investment in cash at the risk-free rate, and continuously adjusting the allocation between the two.

Market timing and tactical allocation[13]

Market timing is a technique that has long been practised. In recent years, and in the area of defining the investment management process as we present it here, it has become more usual to speak of tactical allocation. We observe that most individual securities evolve in the same direction as the market as a whole. Movements in the market therefore determine the core variations in portfolios. The most efficient way of influencing portfolio returns is thus to modify its exposure to the market. Tactical allocation therefore involves adjustments to the proportions

---

[11] Cf. Amenc and Martellini (2002b).

[12] The reader interested in obtaining more details on these methods could refer to Chapter 5 of Amenc and Le Sourd (1998) and the references listed in the Bibliography.

[13] Cf. Chapter 11 of Broquet and van den Berg (1992), Ludwig (1994), Dublanc and Barrioz (1995), Philips *et al.* (1996), Chapter 5 of Bitters (1997), and Grinold and Kahn (1995) who develop the concept of benchmark timing. See also DuBois (1992), Evnine (1992), Clarke and Statman (1992) and Martellini and Sfeir (2002).

in the portfolio, defined at the strategic allocation stage, based on short-term forecasts of the relative values of the various asset classes which are different from the long-term forecasts. The tactical allocation techniques, by affecting the portfolio's exposure to the market, allow us to reduce the risk of the portfolio losing value. Investors should increase their allocation to risky assets in periods of high expected returns (market timing) and decrease their allocation in periods of high volatility (volatility timing).

Tactical asset allocation is a three-step process. The first step involves forecasting asset class returns. The second is to construct portfolios based on the forecasts. Finally, out-of-sample performance tests are performed. A distinction is drawn between discretionary tactical asset allocation, where asset return predictions are based on an expert's forecasting ability, and systematic tactical asset allocation, where predictions are made using a model's forecasting ability. In the latter case, models can be parametric or non-parametric. Parametric models typically are a linear regression where a set of predictor variables is used in a lagged regression analysis (see, for example, Bossaerts and Hillion, 1999). Return forecasting models are selected using statistical criteria. Non-parametric models may, for instance, be neural networks or involve a kernel regression approach, where forecasts are obtained from non-linear filtering of previous returns based on exogenous variables. The performance of a forecast model can then be measured in terms of the *ex post* correlation between the forecast and actual return, and the correlation between the *ex post* class rank and the predicted rank.

Asset allocation therefore relies on the fact that asset returns can be predicted by observing market indicators. If we assume that prices change instantly in response to new information, then the market is efficient and there are no indicators for forecasting asset prices. However, observation of financial markets shows that the efficiency can be defined as semi-strong. We therefore admit that financial markets are not perfectly efficient, or at least that they reveal temporary inefficiencies that are liable to be exploited. We observe, for example, that markets over-react to announcements, and that the stocks then return to equilibrium. Tactical allocation therefore allows us to take advantage of the temporary inefficiencies of the securities in the different asset classes.

In order for tactical allocation to add to the return on the portfolio, the forecasts must be reliable. This method therefore relies on the manager's capacity to anticipate movements in the market. In practice, tactical allocation models tend to recommend contrarian-type trades, i.e. buying risky assets when the markets fall and selling them when the markets rise. This practice is the opposite of that carried out within the framework of portfolio insurance.

The models and processes proposed are based on both the research work carried out in the area of predicting returns, covariances and variances (see for example Campbell *et al.*, 1997, and Lo, 1997), and on the optimal decision rules in the presence of returns with differing degrees of predictability (cf. Barberis, 2000, Brandt, 1999, Campbell and Viceira, 1999, and Brennan *et al.*, 1997).

The success of tactical allocation depends first on the quality of the forecasts on movements in the market. Among the techniques that allow the evolution of the market to be anticipated, we distinguish between fact-based methods and forecast-based methods. The fact-based approach only uses currently available information, while the forecast-based methods are based on a forecast of the future. An example of a fact-based variable is the current level of interest rates, while an example of a forecast-based variable could be the anticipated value of the growth rate. The most widely used strategies favour fact-based approaches. Procedures based on standard observations are easier to implement and more reliable than procedures based on forecasts. These methods are based on the observation of one or more variables, which enable a decision to be taken. In order for the strategy to be liable to improve the portfolio return, there must be a relationship between the indicators that we have chosen to observe and the future performance of the market. The quantitative fact-based methods have the advantage of being compatible with the realisation of historical simulations and the implementation of systematic procedures.

One of the most widely used techniques for carrying out tactical allocation is risk premium valuation. This approach compares the expected returns of the various market sectors considered in order to decide on the portfolio allocation. For example, if the expected return of stocks, compared with that of bonds, is above the mean value for that category of assets, then we will choose to invest a greater share of the portfolio in stocks than in bonds. The most widely used asset classes are stocks, long-term bonds and Treasury bills. We decrease or increase the exposure to the different asset classes, depending on whether the value of their expected return rises or falls. To calculate the expected return of the stock class we can take the average of the returns of the individual securities, weighted by the market capitalisation. The return on individual securities is generally calculated from the Dividend Discount Model. It is therefore dependent on the current price of the securities and on an estimation of future dividends and earnings. It is a bottom-up procedure. We can also use a top-down procedure, consisting for example of calculating the expected market return, by adding an estimation of future earnings, or an estimation of dividend growth, to the current dividend yield for the market as a whole. The disadvantage of the bottom-up approach is that it uses data forecasts, which makes it a forecast-based technique. The top-down approach is more fact-based than forecast-based, which is why we shall prefer it.

To evaluate the bond class we use a bond coupon's rate of return at maturity. The bond's return at maturity can differ significantly from the return actually observed for the bond, even when the bond is held to maturity, because the coupons are reinvested at a rate that is different from the current rates. The return on cash is measured by the return procured by fixed-rate securities with a near-term maturity, which is generally between three and 12 months.

To determine the relative advantages of each of the three asset classes, we estimate the risk premium by calculating the difference between the estimated return of the asset classes taken two by two. The risk premium of stocks compared with Treasury bills is therefore calculated by taking the difference between the expected return for stocks and the expected return for Treasury bills. In the same way, the risk premium for bonds is calculated as the difference between the expected return for bonds and the expected return for Treasury bills. Finally, the risk premium of stocks compared with bonds is obtained by taking the difference between the expected return for stocks and the expected return for bonds.

The risk-premium-based approach has numerous supporters, but it does nevertheless include one disadvantage: it uses long-term expectations for stocks and bonds, while the return used for cash is a short-term value. This final value does not therefore necessarily represent the investor's expected return over the long term. To obtain the true expected returns over the long term for stocks and bonds, we can subtract the inflation rate instead of using an approximation of the risk-free rate.

Frequently investors do not use the valuation methods described above. They evaluate the market for stocks on the basis of ratios such as the value of earnings or dividends compared with the price of the stock, or the *P/E* ratio. These indicators allow the absolute, non-relative advantage of the market for stocks to be determined. The relative advantage of the stock market compared with the bond market is then measured by comparing the return on the stock market with the return on long-term bonds. However, these methods turn out to be less relevant than those described previously.

We also observe that economic cycles influence the price of assets. Variables linked to economic cycles have turned out to be better short-term forecast indicators than the risk premium valuation method in the three cases considered: comparing stocks with T-bills, comparing bonds with T-bills and comparing stocks with bonds.

Let us consider the market for stocks as an example. With the help of the modelling described previously, the return on stocks for the upcoming period is written as a linear function of the following parameters: a term that measures the average return of the market for stocks over the long term and the present value of the indicator chosen to forecast the return on stocks, which is multiplied by the sensitivity of stocks to the indicator, or

$$R_{t+1} = \bar{R} + \beta I_t + e_{t+1}$$

where

R_{t+1} denotes the return on the asset for the upcoming period;
$\bar{R}$ denotes the average return of stocks over the long term;
I_t denotes the value of the indicator at time t;
β denotes the sensitivity of stock returns to a change in the value of the indicator; and
e_{t+1} denotes the residual error term.

The informative content of the indicator is evaluated by calculating the information coefficient associated with the model, i.e. the correlation between the value forecast by the model and the value that was actually produced. The higher the result, the more we can consider that the forecast model is good.

Tactical asset allocation for international portfolios

In the case of an international portfolio, managers can also use a market timing strategy, but in relation to currencies. The strategy involves overweighting the countries that are considered to be attractive and underweighting the other countries. The relative advantage of the countries is evaluated by taking forecasts of the future movements of the currencies in relation to each other. These forecasts are based on exchange rate valuation models and on the differentials compared with the equilibrium values.

The value added by tactical asset allocation and the benefits of international investment in improving portfolio performance have often been considered in separate studies. International portfolio managers have to decide whether to hedge their portfolio or not and how to perform this hedging. Mertens and Zimmermann (2002) describe different ways of integrating currency allocation into the investment process and its effect on portfolio performance. They use a model of time-varying expected returns in dynamic portfolio strategies. Their results suggest that decisions on currency hedging matter more than the implementation of a macroeconomic tactical asset allocation strategy. However, once the hedging decision has been taken, tactical asset allocation can add value. Currency hedging is in fact part of strategic asset allocation. The results are therefore in accordance with those found by Brinson et al. (1986) in a domestic case.

Tactical style allocation[14]

Traditionally, tactical asset allocation has been concerned with allocation between stocks and bonds, but just as we carry out a tactical allocation with regard to asset classes, we can do

---

[14] Cf. Amenc and Martellini (2001, 2002a, 2002b, 2002c) and Martellini and Sfeir (2002).

the same with regard to investment styles. In that case, we speak of tactical style allocation or equity style timing (cf. Fan, 1995). This more recently developed concept, which concerns both traditional investment and alternative investment, can be found in Kao and Shumaker (1999) and Amenc et al. (2002). The different investment styles perform differently depending on the period. Equity style timing therefore involves forecasting the style that will be favoured by the market in the upcoming period in order to orientate the portfolio in that direction and improve its return. In the same way as for market timing with regard to asset classes, this assumes that the markets are not perfectly efficient. There are models that allow us to forecast the best investment style. Here again the result depends on the quality and the reliability of the forecasts.

Tactical style allocation uses predictability in style returns. Evidence of this predictability can be found in Fan (1995), Sorensen and Lazzara (1995) and Avramov (2002). Style timing strategies have been successfully tested and implemented. Ibbotson and Kaplan (2000), in contrast to the Brinson et al. (1986) study, demonstrate that style timing and market timing make a larger contribution to the difference in return between funds than the choice of benchmark.

Amenc et al. (2002) examined whether there is any economic significance in the predictability of hedge fund returns by investigating the implications in terms of a tactical asset allocation model. The performance of the portfolio is measured in terms of the ex post information ratio, and in terms of a portfolio hit ratio, which is the percentage of time that the return on the tactical style allocation portfolio is greater than the return on the benchmark. They find strong evidence of very significant predictability in hedge fund returns. The article shows that a parsimonious set of models captures a very significant amount of predictability for most hedge fund styles. The benefits in terms of tactical style allocation portfolios are potentially very large. Results are also analysed in the case of portfolios that combine hedge funds and traditional investment. Style timing generates comparable levels of average return in the alternative investment universe and the traditional universe.

A tactical style timing strategy is well suited for a portable alpha strategy. It can enhance the performance of an equity portfolio when implemented via a core–satellite approach. The use of futures contracts can allow for more active tactical allocation decisions in the satellite portfolio.

Tactical allocation using risk decomposition
Efficient risk-adjusted portfolios are the result of proper control of their risk, which keeps them exposed to the sources of risk that can generate returns. Emrich and Sharaiha (2002) propose analysing portfolio risk through a decomposition of its tracking risk and derive a portfolio rebalancing algorithm based on risk considerations. The model they present is an improvement on a previous model which was only based on historical tracking risk. They use a predictive risk model to forecast the portfolio tracking risk and analyse the impact of portfolio modification on this tracking risk. Tracking risk is allocated to the top-down and bottom-up decisions of the portfolio manager and each component is decomposed into systematic and idiosyncratic risk in order to identify the profitable sources of risk.

The portfolio rebalancing rule involves reducing the marginal risk induced by the portfolio manager's active decisions. It relies on an analysis of the forecast sensitivity of the tracking risk to these decisions. This can be done at the sector level, as part of a top-down process, but also at the stock level from a bottom-up perspective. Since we are considering an asset allocation problem here, we only describe the case of sector analysis. The algorithm proceeds as follows. It identifies the sector of the portfolio with the largest marginal tracking risk and the sector with the lowest marginal tracking risk. Then it reallocates weights from one sector to another in order to maximise the reduction in overall tracking risk. This procedure can be repeated until the target tracking risk is reached. This type of allocation process, based on risk considerations, is referred to as a re-engineering approach.

Interest-rate-sensitive asset allocation

This method is useful in the case where the strategic allocation is defined by integrating a notion of shortfall risk (cf. Leibowitz *et al.*, 1994). The forecasting of returns is often based on adding a risk premium to an interest rate. If the rates fall, then the probability of falling below the floor threshold that was defined at the strategic allocation stage will increase. It is therefore necessary to adjust the proportions in the portfolio. This method of tactical allocation relies more on the evolution of interest rates than on movements in the market, as was the case for market timing. When rates are high, the proportion of risky assets in the portfolio rises, and when rates fall, the proportion decreases. This technique allows us to keep a constant level of shortfall risk when rates vary.

Furthermore, the tactical allocation approach can be based on maximising a predicted return while staying close to the strategic allocation, i.e. by controlling the tracking-error (cf. Boulier *et al.*, 1996, and Amenc *et al.*, 2001).

7.1.2   Stock picking

This is the last stage in the construction of the portfolio. It takes into account the microeconomic market trends and concerns stocks in particular. Bonds are selected more on the level of duration, the sensitivity and the quality of the issuer, which are parameters that characterise a group of securities, than on the characteristics of the individual securities. In addition to the methods drawn from modern portfolio theory, some methods allow stock picking to be carried out on a quantitative basis. We could cite for example the Graham–Dodd (cf. Cottle *et al.*, 1988) method for valuing assets, and the Dividend Discount Model, outlined in Amenc and Le Sourd (1998).

7.2   PERFORMANCE DECOMPOSITION AND ANALYSIS[15]

Once the portfolio has been constructed, the final stage of the investment management process consists of evaluating its performance. For the sources of portfolio performance to be identified precisely, the performance is broken down into several terms. The first decomposition was proposed by Fama in 1972. The Fama model allows us to go further in our analysis than the simple Treynor, Sharpe and Jensen indicators developed previously. This decomposition consists of isolating the choice of benchmark from the stock picking when calculating portfolio performance.

7.2.1   Fama's decomposition[16]

Fama's decomposition (Fama, 1972) can be applied to a portfolio or a class of assets. It splits portfolio performance into two terms: selectivity and risk. It relies on the CAPM theory since

---

[15] cf. Chapter 30 of Fabozzi (1995).
[16] Cf. Chapter 10 of Broquet and van den Berg (1992), Elton and Gruber (1995), Grandin (1998), Walter (1997) and Chapter 4 of Bitters (1997).

it involves comparing the result of the managed portfolio with that of two theoretical reference portfolios located on the market line.

The procedure is as follows. We take P, the portfolio to be studied. The total risk of this portfolio is denoted by σ_P and its systematic risk by β_P. This portfolio is not, a priori, located on the market line. The principle is to compare its performance with that of two portfolios located on the market line. The first portfolio, P_1, is defined with a beta equal to the beta of portfolio P, or

$$\beta_{P_1} = \beta_P$$

Since this portfolio is located on the market line, its expected return is written as follows:

$$E(R_{P_1}) = E(R_F) + \beta_{P_1}(E(R_M) - E(R_F)) \quad \text{with } \beta_{P_1} = \beta_P$$

The second portfolio, P_2, is defined with a beta equal to the total risk of portfolio P, or

$$\beta_{P_2} = \sigma_P$$

Since this portfolio is also located on the market line, its expected return is given by

$$E(R_{P_2}) = E(R_F) + \beta_{P_2}(E(R_M) - E(R_F)) \quad \text{with } \beta_{P_2} = \sigma_P$$

By using portfolio P_1, the performance of portfolio P is decomposed in the following way:

$$E(R_P) - E(R_F) = (E(R_P) - E(R_{P_1})) + (E(R_{P_1}) - E(R_F))$$

The first term, defined by Fama as the selectivity, measures the performance of the manager's portfolio in comparison with that of a portfolio with the same market risk, but located on the market line, and therefore perfectly diversified. The second term, called risk, corresponds to the choice of a level of beta, and therefore to the choice of benchmark.

Fama proposes taking the analysis further by decomposing each of the two terms again.

7.2.1.1   Decomposing the selectivity

The selectivity, which evaluates the portfolio's additional return compared with the benchmark, is broken down into a net selectivity term and a diversification term. To do this we use portfolio P_2, which was defined previously, and which allows us to write

$$E(R_P) - E(R_{P_1}) = (E(R_P) - E(R_{P_2})) + (E(R_{P_2}) - E(R_{P_1}))$$

By replacing $E(R_{P_1})$ and $E(R_{P_2})$ with their expressions in each of the two terms, in line with the characteristics of portfolio P, we obtain the two decomposition terms for the selectivity:

1. the net selectivity given by

$$E(R_p) - E(R_{P_2}) = E(R_P) - E(R_F) - \sigma_P(E(R_M) - E(R_F))$$

2. the diversification given by

$$E(R_{P_2}) - E(R_{P_1}) = (\sigma_P - \beta_P)(E(R_M) - E(R_F))$$

These two terms are perfectly defined since we know how to calculate the β_P and σ_P parameters for portfolio P. The net selectivity measures the performance differential compared with a portfolio with the same total risk, but located on the market line. The diversification

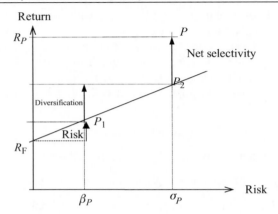

Figure 7.2   Fama's performance decomposition

measures the additional return that comes from taking a greater market risk. The diversification is always positive, but the net selectivity can be negative.

7.2.1.2   Decomposing the risk

The risk term is broken down into manager risk and investor risk. For that reason we define a third portfolio, P_0, with a systematic risk of β_{P_0} corresponding to the investor's desired level of risk. The manager can choose to take a risk β_P different from risk β_{P_0}, based on his forecasts of how the market will evolve. The beta can then be adjusted regularly. This corresponds to a market timing strategy. The decomposition of the risk term is then written as follows:

$$(E(R_{P_1}) - E(R_F)) = (E(R_{P_1}) - E(R_{P_0})) + (E(R_{P_0}) - E(R_F))$$

where the first term corresponds to the manager risk and the second term corresponds to the investor risk.

Figure 7.2 summarises the different decomposition terms.

7.2.1.3   Timing analysis model drawn from the Fama decomposition: the Kon model

The Kon (1983) model seeks to identify the timing effect by using a model that is directly inspired by Fama's performance decomposition. This model assumes that the market return is decomposed into a predictable part and an unanticipated part, π_{Mt}, or

$$R_{Mt} = E(R_{Mt}) + \pi_{Mt}$$

where π_{Mt} denotes the unanticipated market return for period t with $E(\pi_{Mt}) = 0$.

Taking β_T as the fund's risk objective when the manager has the same anticipations as the market and β_t as the risk that was actually taken during period t, then

$$T_t = (\beta_t - \beta_T)\pi_{Mt}$$

allows us to evaluate the share of timing in the fund's performance. This variable is positive if the manager has correctly forecasted market movements and adjusted his risk as a result.

7.2.2 Performance decomposition corresponding to the stages in the investment management process[17]

Fama introduced the principle of performance decomposition, i.e. distinguishing between the choice of benchmark, which characterises the risk taken, and the choice of securities. The models that decompose performance according to the stages in the investment management process still use this principle. Performance decomposition for a national portfolio generally relies on the Brinson *et al.* (1986) study. This was then generalised for the international case by Karnosky and Singer in order to identify the foreign market and currency contribution. This type of model allows us to analyse a portfolio that is made up of several asset classes. The identified effects are then summed for all the asset classes.

The notion of asset class should be seen in the broad sense of the term. We initially distinguish between stocks and bonds. Then, for portfolios invested in assets from a single country, the groupings can be done by industrial sector or by category of bond. For international portfolios, the groupings are done by country, by geographic zone or by quotation currency.

Splitting the overall portfolio performance between the different stages in the investment management process allows us to evaluate the contribution of each management decision. The decomposition is therefore a support tool for rationalising investment management. The performance is divided into asset allocation, stock picking and the currency effect for international portfolios. An additional term that measures the interaction between asset allocation and stock picking is added, but this term is sometimes integrated into either asset allocation or stock picking.

This section presents first the model for portfolios that are only invested in domestic assets, and then its generalisation for international portfolios. Chapter 8 will present a decomposition model that is more specifically adapted to bond portfolios, for which the stock picking term gives little information.

7.2.2.1 The Brinson *et al.* (1986) model[18]

Brinson *et al.* defined the three stages in the investment management process; namely strategic allocation (investment policy), tactical allocation or market timing, and stock picking, and understood the necessity for managers to have a precise evaluation method for the different stages. Their method is comprised of three stages. The first stage considers a benchmark portfolio with weightings that correspond to the long-term allocation. The second stage successively considers a portfolio that combines the strategic allocation with one of the other two components of the return, namely market timing and stock picking. The market timing component is calculated by considering the benchmark return, but by taking the real asset allocation. The stock picking component considers the real returns of the asset classes, but with the benchmark weightings. The final stage calculates the overall portfolio return, obtained from all the return components.

---

[17] Cf. Wainscott (1995) and Chapter 3 of Bitters (1997) who analyses the Brinson *et al.* (1986) study in detail.
[18] Cf. Chapter 3 of Bitters (1997).

For each asset class the components of the benchmark portfolio and the real portfolio can be shown as

Selection Effect

		Real Portfolio	Passive Portfolio
Timing Effect	Real Portfolio	(IV) Real portfolio return	(II) Return on the strategic allocation and the timing
	Passive Portfolio	(III) Return on the strategic allocation and the stock picking	(I) Return on the strategic allocation (benchmark portfolio)

This is written formally as follows:

Selection Effect

		Real Portfolio	Passive Portfolio
Timing Effect	Real Portfolio	(IV) $\sum_i w_{P_i} R_{P_i}$	(II) $\sum_i w_{P_i} R_{B_i}$
	Passive Portfolio	(III) $\sum_i w_{B_i} R_{P_i}$	(I) $\sum_i w_{B_i} R_{B_i}$

where

w_{P_i} denotes the weight of class i in the portfolio;
w_{B_i} denotes the weight of class i in the benchmark;
R_{P_i} denotes the return on class i in the portfolio; and
R_{B_i} denotes the return on class i in the benchmark.

Using this decomposition, we can calculate the manager's active contribution to portfolio performance at each stage of the investment management process. To do so, we calculate the difference between the term that measures the effect in the portfolio and the term that measures the effect in the benchmark, which leads to the following results:

1. The active return due to the timing, or tactical allocation, corresponds to the difference (II) − (I), or

$$\sum_i (w_{P_i} - w_{B_i}) R_{B_i}$$

2. The active return due to stock picking corresponds to the difference (III) − (I), or

$$\sum_i w_{B_i} (R_{P_i} - R_{B_i})$$

3. The interaction term between the allocation and the stock picking corresponds to the expression (IV) − (III) − (II) + (I), or

$$\sum_i (w_{P_i} - w_{B_i})(R_{P_i} - R_{B_i})$$

4. The overall active return corresponds to the difference (IV) − (I), or

$$\sum_i w_{P_i} R_{P_i} - \sum_i w_{B_i} R_{B_i} = \sum_i (w_{P_i} - w_{B_i}) R_{B_i} + \sum_i w_{B_i}(R_{P_i} - R_{B_i})$$
$$+ \sum_i (w_{P_i} - w_{B_i})(R_{P_i} - R_{B_i})$$

The excess portfolio return is therefore divided into a term that comes from an allocation between the asset classes that is different from that of the benchmark, which corresponds to a different level of risk; a term that comes from stock picking, which is different from that of the benchmark within each asset class; and a final term that represents the interaction between the two.

To carry out this study it is necessary to know all the movements that have taken place in the portfolio and break down the overall period into sub-periods during which the portfolio had a fixed composition. The more frequent the fluctuations, the shorter the periods will have to be. It is then necessary to link the results to obtain the result for the whole period. To do this, it may be useful to turn to logarithmic returns. In Appendix 2.1 to Chapter 2 we established the link that exists between the arithmetic expression and the logarithmic expression of returns. The study can also be carried out by using the mean asset weightings for each period. We present a method that allows performance to be broken down into its different effects over several periods a little later on.

The Brinson *et al.* study highlighted the importance of the asset allocation phase in the investment performance result, which led to more attention being paid to this phase and to quantitative asset allocation models being developed. Their result also encouraged the development of index managed funds, because it is possible that the market timing and stock picking phases contribute to a decrease in the portfolio return, while increasing the portfolio risk. It is more and more common for investment firms to use the performance decomposition methods that correspond to the stages in the investment management process. The Frank Russell company is particularly advanced in this area.

7.2.2.2 Some clarifications on the interaction term

We would like to return to the significance of the different effects identified in portfolio performance decomposition in a little more detail. While the asset allocation and stock picking terms are easy to understand, the interaction term can be a little more difficult to explain (see

Laker, 2000). Certain firms choose to add it to one of the other two terms in reports that are presented to clients, so as to avoid having to explain it. More often than not it is added to the stock picking term, but there are no real rules on the subject. If the interaction term has a very low value, then it could be justifiable to proceed in that way. In that case it is appropriate to specify it when the results are presented. But in most cases it seems to be preferable to isolate this term, if only to avoid inconsistency between two managers who do not adopt the same practice. In addition, the interaction term is a term for which the explanatory power can be significant, as we will show in what follows.

The asset allocation term measures the skill in selecting the asset classes or sectors that perform better than the benchmark for the portfolio taken as a whole. The stock picking term measures the skill in choosing the assets that perform best in each of the different sectors. Asset allocation comes from a top-down process, while stock picking results from a bottom-up process. The interaction term measures the effect that results from the conjunction of the two processes.

In order to give this term its full meaning, it must be calculated correctly. In particular, it should not be equated with an error term. Performance attribution should normally be calculated for periods where the composition of the portfolios remains fixed. For capital movements to be taken into account as precisely as possible, the optimal lapse of time is a day. The results should then be compounded to obtain a decomposition for any time interval. This must be done for all the terms, including the interaction term, which should not be calculated as the difference between the overall performance and the sum of the other two terms. Compounding the effects over several periods leads to the appearance of a residual term. The error would then be to integrate this term into the interaction term. It should in fact be spread over the different effects. In the next section we present an attribution method for several periods that spreads the composition residual over the different terms and thereby allows us to obtain a correct interaction term. Turning to an approximation that uses the monthly returns with mean weightings over the period, rather than daily data, is also a source of error for the different terms. Although the approximations could be justified a few years ago, the increase in the storage capacity of computers, along with improved speed of calculation, renders daily attribution easier now.

The contribution of asset allocation to the overall portfolio performance is given by the difference between the weighting of the sector in the portfolio and the weighting of the sector in the benchmark, which is multiplied by the out-performance of the sector compared with the overall portfolio benchmark, or for each sector

$$(w_{P_i} - w_{B_i})(R_{B_i} - R_B)$$

Stock picking for each sector is measured by the difference between the return on the sector in the portfolio and the return on the sector in the benchmark, which is multiplied by the weighting of the sector in the benchmark, or

$$w_{B_i}(R_{P_i} - R_{B_i})$$

The interaction is the product of the difference between the weighting of the sector in the portfolio and the weighting of the sector in the benchmark times the difference between the return on the sector in the portfolio and the return on the sector in the benchmark, or

$$(w_{P_i} - w_{B_i})(R_{P_i} - R_{B_i})$$

The notation used is the same as in the previous section:

w_{P_i} is the weight of class i in the portfolio;

w_{B_i} is the weight of class i in the benchmark;

R_{P_i} is the return on class i in the portfolio;

R_{B_i} is the return on class i in the benchmark; and

$R_B = \sum_i w_i R_{B_i}$ is the portfolio's benchmark.

From the sector allocation point of view, a good decision is to overweight a sector that beats the overall portfolio benchmark. If the manager selects the right assets in the corresponding sector, i.e. if the sector in the portfolio beats the sector index, then the stock picking term is positive for the sector and the corresponding interaction term is also positive. If, on the other hand, the manager has not selected the right assets, then the stock picking term and the interaction term are negative. In this case the interaction term will be even more negative if the differential between the portfolio weightings and the benchmark weightings for that sector is significant. If the sector only had a low weighting in the benchmark, then the stock picking term will only be slightly negative, since it does not use the portfolio weighting. The interaction term will then reflect the bad stock picking results much more significantly.

The interaction therefore measures the combined effect of the management decisions on the portfolio performance and the additional contribution, or on the contrary the decrease in performance, that results. To obtain a positive interaction and thus improve the portfolio performance, it is necessary to know how to identify the best sectors and to choose the best securities within those sectors. A positive interaction is also obtained by underweighting a sector whose performance is worse than that of the overall benchmark, when at the same time the sector in the portfolio does worse than the sector index.

7.2.2.3 Performance attribution over several periods

Earlier, we presented the decomposition of the performance differential between a portfolio and its benchmark over a single time period. We now see how to obtain this decomposition when we consider several periods. The technique presented comes from Menchero (2000). The objective is to obtain an exact additive three-term decomposition, without a residual term: a tactical allocation term, a stock picking term and an interaction term.

The portfolio and benchmark returns over several periods are obtained by calculating the geometric mean of the returns for each period, as described in Chapter 2. If we denote the portfolio return for the whole period as R_P and the benchmark return as R_B, then we have

$$1 + R_P = \prod_{t=1}^{T}(1 + R_{Pt})$$

and

$$1 + R_B = \prod_{t=1}^{T}(1 + R_{Bt})$$

where R_{Pt} and R_{Bt} denote the return of the portfolio and the benchmark for a sub-period, respectively, and T denotes the number of sub-periods.

The performance differential between the portfolio and its benchmark is written as follows:

$$R_P - R_B = \prod_{t=1}^{T}(1 + R_{Pt}) - \prod_{t=1}^{T}(1 + R_{Bt})$$

If the returns are small, then the terms to the power of two or more can be ignored and the performance differential between the portfolio and its benchmark can be approximated by the following expression:

$$R_P - R_B \approx \sum_{t=1}^{T}(R_{Pt} - R_{Bt})$$

However, this approximation is not valid when the returns have high values. A better approach involves multiplying the right-hand side of the equation by a constant, or

$$R_P - R_B \approx A \sum_{t=1}^{T}(R_{Pt} - R_{Bt})$$

We could naively define A as

$$A = \frac{R_P - R_B}{\sum_{t=1}^{T}(R_{Pt} - R_{Bt})}$$

But it is more judicious to replace the R_{Pt} and R_{Bt} returns with their geometric mean, or

$$A = \frac{R_P - R_B}{\sum_{t=1}^{T}\left[\left((1 + R_P)^{1/T} - 1\right) - \left((1 + R_B)^{1/T} - 1\right)\right]}$$

Hence, after simplification:

$$A = \frac{1}{T}\frac{R_P - R_B}{(1 + R_P)^{1/T} - (1 + R_B)^{1/T}}, \quad \text{if } R_P \neq R_B$$

If $R_P = R_B$, then the limiting value of the above expression is

$$A = (1 + R)^{(T-1)/T}$$

The expression for A thus defined does not eliminate the residual term since the equation

$$R_P - R_B \approx A \sum_{t=1}^{T}(R_{Pt} - R_{Bt})$$

is only an approximation. In order to be able to write an exact equation, we introduce a series of corrective terms, α_t, which allow us to spread the residual terms over the different periods. The following exact equation then holds:

$$R_P - R_B = \sum_{t=1}^{T}(A + \alpha_t)(R_{Pt} - R_{Bt})$$

The α_t should be chosen to be as small as possible. The optimal solution is obtained by minimising

$$\sum_{t=1}^{T} \alpha_t^2$$

under the constraint:

$$R_P - R_B = \sum_{t=1}^{T} (A + \alpha_t)(R_{Pt} - R_{Bt})$$

This problem is solved by using the Lagrange multiplier method.[19] The optimal solution is given by

$$\alpha_t = \frac{R_P - R_B - A \sum_{j=1}^{T} (R_{Pj} - R_{Bj})}{\sum_{j=1}^{T} (R_{Pj} - R_{Bj})^2}(R_{Pt} - R_{Bt})$$

In the unlikely event that $R_{Pt} = R_{Bt}$ for all values of t, all the α_t are null.

By setting

$$\beta_t^{\text{opt}} = A + \alpha_t,$$

we can write

$$R_P - R_B = \sum_{t=1}^{T} \beta_t^{\text{opt}}(R_{Pt} - R_{Bt})$$

We established the following relationship for each sub-period in Section 7.2.2.1:

$$\sum_i w_{P_i} R_{P_i} - \sum_i w_{B_i} R_{B_i} = \sum_i (w_{P_i} - w_{B_i})R_{B_i} + \sum_i w_{B_i}(R_{P_i} - R_{B_i})$$
$$+ \sum_i (w_{P_i} - w_{B_i})(R_{P_i} - R_{B_i})$$

or, in a more condensed manner:

$$R_{Pt} - R_{Bt} = \sum_{i=1}^{n} R_{it}^{\text{Allocation}} + \sum_{i=1}^{n} R_{it}^{\text{StockPicking}} + \sum_{i=1}^{n} R_{it}^{\text{Interaction}}$$

We therefore obtain, for the whole period:

$$R_P - R_B = \sum_{t=1}^{T} \beta_t^{\text{opt}} \sum_{i=1}^{n} \left(R_{it}^{\text{Allocation}} + R_{it}^{\text{StockPicking}} + R_{it}^{\text{Interaction}} \right)$$

hence

$$R_P - R_B = \sum_{t=1}^{T} \sum_{i=1}^{n} \beta_t^{\text{opt}} R_{it}^{\text{Allocation}} + \sum_{t=1}^{T} \sum_{i=1}^{n} \beta_t^{\text{opt}} R_{it}^{\text{StockPicking}} + \sum_{t=1}^{T} \sum_{i=1}^{n} \beta_t^{\text{opt}} R_{it}^{\text{Interaction}}$$

---

[19] We described this method in Appendix 3.1 to Chapter 3, on the subject of solving the Markowitz portfolio optimisation problem. The calculations here are much simpler.

We thereby decompose the performance differential between a portfolio and its benchmark into three terms for a complete period, with the help of the effects identified for the sub-periods.

7.2.2.4   The case of an international portfolio[20]

Before discussing the extension of the Brinson *et al.* (1986) decomposition to the international case, we shall initially consider the basic elements that allow the performance of an international portfolio to be analysed. The simplest decomposition involves separating the return into a part that comes from the evolution of the asset prices in their local currency and a part that comes from the evolution of the currencies themselves (cf. Sharpe, 1985). To calculate the first term, we consider that the exchange rate is constant over the period. The second term is then obtained as the difference.

The notation is the same as in Chapter 2:

P_{it}^{Quot} is the price of asset i at time t expressed in the quotation currency;

$d_{it}^{\text{Quot/Ref}}$ is the price of the quotation currency for asset i at time t expressed in the reference currency;

while the price P_{it}^{Ref} of asset i expressed in the reference currency is given by

$$P_{it}^{\text{Ref}} = P_{it}^{\text{Quot}} d_{it}^{\text{Quot/Ref}}$$

and the return on the portfolio of assets is given by

$$(1 + R_{Pt}) = \frac{P_{it}^{\text{Quot}} d_{it}^{\text{Quot/Ref}}}{P_{i,t-1}^{\text{Quot}} d_{i,t-1}^{\text{Quot/Ref}}}$$

The component of return that is exclusively due to variations in the price of the quotation currency is given by

$$\left(1 + R_{Pt}^{\text{Price}}\right) = \frac{P_{it}^{\text{Quot}} d_{i,t-1}^{\text{Quot/Ref}}}{P_{i,t-1}^{\text{Quot}} d_{i,t-1}^{\text{Quot/Ref}}}$$

and the component of return that is exclusively due to variations in the currency is given by

$$\left(1 + R_{Pt}^{\text{Exchange}}\right) = \frac{P_{i,t-1}^{\text{Quot}} d_{i,t}^{\text{Quot/Ref}}}{P_{i,t-1}^{\text{Quot}} d_{i,t-1}^{\text{Quot/Ref}}}$$

and we have

$$(1 + R_{Pt}) = \left(1 + R_{Pt}^{\text{Price}}\right)\left(1 + R_{Pt}^{\text{Exchange}}\right)$$

To analyse further, we can carry out a decomposition by country, or by asset class independently of the country, or more accurately, by asset class for each country using the international version of the model presented in the previous section. The benchmark is then an international market index. The portfolio return is broken down into a term that comes from the benchmark return, a term that comes from the evolution of the markets chosen, a term that comes from the evolution of the currencies and a term that comes from stock picking in each market.

---

[20] Cf. Chapter 6 of Clarke and Kritzman (1996), Ramaswami (1993), Fontaine (1997), Grandin (1998), Clarke and Tullis (1999), AIMR (1998) and the second part of Karnosky and Singer (1994).

A portfolio invested in several countries can be completely hedged against exchange rate risk, partially hedged, or unhedged. The performance attribution methods consider these three situations.

The generalisation of the Brinson *et al.* model to the international case was proposed by Karnosky and Singer. The principle is the same, except that now there is a term measuring the contribution of the currencies. This currency allocation term is constructed on the basis of the same principle as the tactical allocation term. To be even more precise, this currency effect can itself be decomposed. A very thorough presentation of this decomposition is given in Karnosky and Singer (1994). The principle of currency effect decomposition is also well presented, albeit in less detail, in the 1998 AIMR standards update document. Our explanation here draws on that presentation.

The currency effect decomposition takes the spot and forward exchange rates into account. To obtain the decomposition, we divide the return that comes from changes in the spot exchange rates into two separate components:

1. the forward premium, which is known in advance and which is governed by short-term interest rate differentials; and
2. the change in spot rates that is not taken into account by the forward premium and which we call the "currency surprise". This component is calculated as the difference between the variation in the exchange rate and the forward premium.

The first term is based on the exchange rate forecast models. These models were presented briefly in Chapter 2. The second term results from the manager's anticipations.

In practice, the decomposition of an international portfolio containing several asset classes is written as follows:

$$R_P - R_B = \sum_i (w_{P_i} - w_{B_i})(R_{B_i} + f_i) + \sum_i w_{B_i}(R_{P_i} - R_{B_i}) + \sum_j (H_j - H_j^B)(R_{C_j} - f_j) + e$$

$$(1) \qquad\qquad\qquad (2) \qquad\qquad\qquad (3) \qquad\qquad (4)$$

where

w_{P_i} denotes the weight of market i in the portfolio;
w_{B_i} denotes the weight of market i in the benchmark;
R_{P_i} denotes the local return of market i in the portfolio;
R_{B_i} denotes the local return of market i in the benchmark;
R_{C_j} denotes the return on currency j;
f_i denotes the forward premium for market i;
H_j denotes the portfolio's exposure to currency j; and
H_j^B denotes the benchmark's exposure to currency j.

The difference in return between the portfolio and its benchmark is therefore divided up in the following way:

- Term (1) measures the added value that comes from the tactical allocation by using the hedged returns.
- Term (2) measures the added value that comes from the stock picking in each market.
- Term (3) measures the added value that comes from the active management of the currencies. For each market this term is equal to the sum of the currency exposure differences between the portfolio and the benchmark multiplied by the currency surprise term. This term is null

if the exposure to each currency is the same for the portfolio and the benchmark.
• Term (4) is an error term that corresponds to the interaction between the allocation and the stock picking.

The principle behind this decomposition is used by the Frank Russell company. Here again the decomposition is carried out for sub-periods and the results are aggregated for the whole period. The multi-period calculation method presented in Section 7.2.2.3 for a portfolio invested in a single country also applies to international portfolios.

In Chapter 6 of Clarke and Kritzman (1996) we also find a presentation of a performance decomposition model that is more appropriate for portfolios where the proportions between the different asset classes are managed with the help of derivatives.

To conclude the presentation of the decomposition methods, we should mention that a managed portfolio often contains cash, while the benchmark does not. Taking this into account in performance attribution can be delicate. The need to pay attention to this problem is mentioned in the GRAP study (1997).

7.2.3 Technique of replicating portfolios for performance measurement

Engström (2001) proposes to evaluate portfolio performance using replicating portfolios as benchmarks. These portfolios are constructed to replicate the passive strategy of the portfolio to be evaluated, using its holdings. These portfolios are rebalanced whenever necessary in order to follow the evolution of the portfolio they replicate. This work follows that of Grinblatt and Titman (1989), which uses hypothetical portfolios instead of the classic benchmarks. The advantage of using replicating portfolios is that it solves the problem of finding a benchmark that is suitable for all portfolios, since a specific replicating portfolio is constructed for each different portfolio. Moreover, these replicating portfolios allow for a detailed analysis of performance by separating the performance that is due to asset allocation decisions from the performance that is due to tactical asset allocation decisions and evaluating them on a risk-adjusted basis.

Using Jensen's alpha measure, the total alpha is decomposed into a strategic alpha and a tactical alpha.

The performance of strategic decisions is obtained by evaluating the replicating portfolio in relation to a benchmark index:

$$R_{\mathrm{R}it} - R_{ft} = \alpha_{\mathrm{S}i} + \beta_{\mathrm{S}i}(R_{bt} - R_{ft}) + \varepsilon_{\mathrm{S}it}$$

where

$R_{\mathrm{R}it}$ is the return of the replicating portfolio of fund i at time t;
$\alpha_{\mathrm{S}i}$ is the performance of the strategic decisions;
$\beta_{\mathrm{S}i}$ is the risk in the strategic portfolio; and
$R_{bt} - R_{ft}$ is the return on the benchmark in excess of the risk-free asset at time t.

The performance of tactical decisions is obtained by evaluating the fund's return in excess of the replicating portfolio:

$$R_{it} - R_{\mathrm{R}it} = \alpha_{\mathrm{T}i} + \beta_{\mathrm{T}i}(R_{bt} - R_{ft}) + \varepsilon_{\mathrm{T}it}$$

$R_{it} - R_{Rit}$ is the return on fund i in excess of its replicating portfolio or the return on the zero
          investment portfolio;

α_{Ti} is the performance of the tactical decisions;

β_{Ti} is the risk in the tactical portfolio.

Both the fund manager's strategic and tactical decisions can be evaluated in a conditional
setting, following Ferson and Schadt (1996). This allows for time-varying expected returns
and risk.

7.2.4 Comparison between the different performance decomposition methods

We have successively presented performance decomposition methods based on multi-factor
models in Chapter 6, and performance attribution models that follow the stages of the investment management process in this chapter. To conclude this chapter, we compare the different
methods described.

The Fama decomposition and the decomposition in line with the stages in the investment
management process are based on the same principle, namely distinguishing between the
performance that is due to the risk taken and the performance that is due to stock picking. In
the Fama decomposition the investor risk is represented by the choice of level of beta. The
corresponding reference portfolio is the equivalent of the benchmark. The manager risk is
the risk taken by the manager, which is different from the risk desired by the client, in order
to obtain a better performance. This corresponds to the tactical allocation term. The Fama
selectivity term corresponds globally to the Jensen alpha and can be compared to the stock
picking term as defined in the Brinson et al. (1986) decomposition. The latter carry out an
analysis by asset class and then sum the effects of all the classes, while Fama does not make
this distinction. His method is therefore more appropriate to an asset class rather than a whole
portfolio.

Decomposing performance with the help of multi-factor models also uses the principle that
involves isolating the performance that is due to the choice of benchmark from the performance
that is due to stock picking. The benchmark is then constituted from the linear combination
of the returns' explanatory factors, and the residual return term, which is not explained by the
factors, corresponds to the stock picking term. Investment firms generally use performance
decomposition that corresponds to the stages in the investment management process, since it is
easier to understand and explain to clients than the factor model. This is because the model is
additive and follows the manager's approach exactly. The factor models give less information
on the management method, but more information on the characteristics of the securities that
make up the portfolio. They also allow those characteristics to be linked to the performance of
the portfolio in a very precise way.

BIBLIOGRAPHY

AIMR, *Benchmarks and Performance Attribution, Subcommittee Report*, Final Draft, August 1998.
Amenc, N. and Le Sourd, V., *Gestion quantitative des portefeuilles d'actions*, Economica, 1998.
Amenc, N. and Martellini, L., "It's Time for Asset Allocation", *Journal of Financial Transformation*,
    vol. 3, December 2001.
Amenc, N. and Martellini, L., "Portfolio Optimization and Hedge Fund Style Allocation Decisions",
    Journal of Alternative Investments, vol. 5, no. 2, fall 2002a.

Amenc, N. and Martellini, L., "Tactical Style Allocation – A New Form of Active Strategy", Working Paper, September 2002b.

Amenc, N. and Martellini, L., "Asset Allocation", *Encyclopedia of Financial Engineering and Risk Management*, Fitzroy Dearborn Publishers, 2002c.

Amenc, N., el Bied, S. and Martellini, L., "Tactical Style Allocation in the Traditional and Alternative Investment Universes", Working Paper, Edhec Research Program, October 2001.

Amenc, N., el Bied, S. and Martellini, L., "Evidence of Predictability in Hedge Fund Returns and Multi-style Multi-class Tactical Style Allocation Decisions", *Financial Analysts Journal*, 2002.

Avramov, D., "Stock Return Predictability and Model Uncertainty", *Journal of Financial Economics*, vol. 64, no. 3, June 2002.

Barberis, N., "Investing for the Long Run when Returns are Predictable", *Journal of Finance*, vol. 55, no. 1, 2000, pp. 225–264.

Bayser, X., "Allocation stratégique d'actifs : prêt-à-porter ou haute couture?", *Analyse financière*, September 1996.

Bekaert, G. and Hodrick, R., "Characterizing Predictable Components in Excess Returns on Equity and Foreign Exchange Markets", *Journal of Finance*, vol. 47, 1992, pp. 467–509.

Berge, K. and Ziemba, W.T., "The Predictive Ability of the Bond Stock Earnings Yield Differential in World-Wide Equity Markets", Working Paper, 2002.

Bito, C. and Fontaine, P., *Les marchés financiers internationaux*, PUF, "Que sais-je ?", 1989.

Bitters, W.E., *The New Science of Asset Allocation*, Glenlake Publishing Co., 1997.

Black, F. and Jones, R., "Simplifying Portfolio Insurance", *Journal of Portfolio Management*, fall 1987, pp. 48–51.

Black, F. and Litterman, R., "Asset Allocation: Combining Investor Views with Market Equilibrium", Goldman Sachs Fixed Income Research, September 1990.

Black, F. and Litterman, R., "Global Asset Allocation with Equities, Bonds and Currencies", Goldman Sachs Fixed-Income Research, 1991.

Black, F. and Litterman, R., "Global Portfolio Optimization", *Financial Analysts Journal*, September–October, 1992.

Bossaerts, P. and Hillion, P., "Implementing Statistical Criteria to Select Return Forecasting Models: What Do We Learn?", *Review of Financial Studies*, vol. 12, no. 2, 1999, pp. 405–428.

Boulier, J.-F., Bourrette, R. and Danesi, V., "Allocation stratégique et tactique d'actifs : présentation d'une méthode simple", *Banque et Marchés*, November–December 1996.

Brandt, M.W., "Estimating Portfolio and Consumption Choice: A Conditional Euler Equations Approach", *Journal of Finance*, vol. 54, no. 5, 1999, pp. 1177–1189.

Brennan, M.J., Schwartz, E.S. and Lagnado, R., "Strategic Asset Allocation", *Journal of Economic Dynamics and Control*, 1997, pp. 1377–1403.

Brinson, G.P., Hood, L.R. and Beebower, G.L., "Determinants of Portfolio Performance", *Financial Analysts Journal*, July–August 1986.

Brinson, G.P., Singer, B.D. and Beebower, G.L., "Determinants of Portfolio Performance II: An Update", *Financial Analysts Journal*, May–June 1991.

Broquet, C. and van den Berg, A., *Gestion de portefeuille – Actions, Obligations, Options*, 2nd edn, De Boeck Université, 1992.

Brown, K.C. and Harlow, W.V., *The Role of Risk Tolerance in the Asset Allocation Process: A New Perspective*, CFA, 1990.

Cambon, D., "Attribution de performance et création de valeur", *Journées EFE*, May 1997.

Campbell, J. and "Stock Returns and the Term Structure", *Journal of Financial Economics*, vol. 18, 1987, pp. 373–399.

Campbell, J. and Shiller R., "Stock Prices, Earnings and Expected Dividends", *Journal of Finance*, vol. 43, 1988, pp. 661–676.

Campbell, J.Y., Lo, A.W. and MacKinlay, A.C., *The Econometrics of Financial Markets*, Princeton University Press, 1997.

Campbell, J.Y. and Viceira, L.M., "Consumptions and Portfolio Decisions when Expected Returns are Time Varying", *Quarterly Journal of Economics*, 1999.

Clarke, R.G. and Kritzman, M.P., *Currency Management: Concepts and Practices*, The Research Foundation of the Institute of Chartered Financial Analysts, 1996.

Clarke, R.G. and Statman, M., "Does Tactical Asset Allocation Work?", in *Active Asset Allocation, State-of-the-art Portfolio Policies, Strategies and Tactics*, R.D. Arnott and F.J. Fabozzi, eds, Irwin, 1992.

Clarke, R.G. and Tullis, R.M., "How Much International Exposure is Advantageous in a Domestic Portfolio?", *Journal of Portfolio Management*, vol. 25, no. 2, winter 1999, pp. 33–44.

Clarke, R.C., de Silva, H. and Wander, B., "Risk Allocation versus Asset Allocation", *Journal of Portfolio Management*, vol. 29, no. 1, fall 2002.

Conxicoeur, P. and Ryan, T., "Styles de gestion : l'heure des choix", *Revue Banque*, no. 594, July–August 1998.

Cottle, S., Murray, R.F. and Block, F.E., *Graham and Dodd's Security Analysis*, 5th edn, McGraw-Hill, 1988.

Cvitanic, J., Lazrak, A., Martellini, L. and Zapatero, F., "Revisiting Treynor and Black (1973): An Intertemporal Model of Active Portfolio Management", Working Paper, May 2002.

Dublanc, A. and Barrioz, F., *Le guide des indicateurs de marché: Une introduction au market timing*, Valor Editions, 1995.

DuBois, C.H., "Tactical Asset Allocation: A Review of Current Techniques", in *Active Asset Allocation, State-of-the-art Portfolio Policies, Strategies and Tactics*, R.D. Arnott and F.J. Fabozzi, eds, Irwin, 1992.

Elton, E.J. and Gruber, M.J., *Modern Portfolio Theory and Investment Analysis*, 5th edn, Wiley, 1995.

Emanuelli, J.F. and Pearson, R.G., "Using Earnings Estimates for Global Asset Allocation", *Financial Analysts Journal*, March–April 1994.

Emrich, S. and Sharaiha, Y.M., "Portfolio Re-Engineering – A Risk Decomposition Approach", Global Equity and Derivative Markets, Morgan Stanley Quantitative Strategies, September 2002.

Engström, S., "Does Active Trading Create Value? An Evaluation of Fund Managers' Decisions", Working Paper, Stockholm School of Economics, Department of Finance, November 2001.

Evnine, J.J., "Asset Allocation – Reward and Diversification", in *Active Asset Allocation, State-of-the-art Portfolio Policies, Strategies and Tactics*, R.D. Arnott and F.J. Fabozzi, eds, Irwin, 1992.

Fabozzi, F.J., *Investment Management*, Prentice Hall International Editions, 1995.

Fama, E., "Components of Investment Performance", *Journal of Finance*, vol. 17, no. 3, June 1972, pp. 551–567.

Fama, E. and French, K., "Business Conditions and Expected Returns on Stocks and Bonds", *Journal of Financial Economics*, vol. 25, 1989, pp. 23–49.

Fan, S.C., "Equity Style Timing and Allocation", in *Equity Style Management, Evaluating and Selecting Investment Styles*, R.A. Klein and J. Lederman, eds, Irwin, 1995.

Farrell, Jr J.L., *Portfolio Management, Theory and Application*, 2nd edn, McGraw-Hill, 1997.

Ferson, W. and Harvey, C., "Sources of Predictability in Portfolio Returns", *Financial Analysts Journal*, May–June 1991, pp. 49–56.

Ferson, W. and Harvey, C., "The Risk and Predictability of International Equity Returns", *Review of Financial Studies*, vol. 6, 1993, pp. 527–566.

Ferson, W. and Harvey, C., "Predictability and Time-varying Risk in World Equity Markets", *Research in Finance*, vol. 13, 1995, pp. 25–88.

Ferson, W.E. and Schadt, R.W., "Measuring Fund Strategy and Performance in Changing Economic Conditions", *Journal of Finance*, vol. 51, no. 2, June 1996, pp. 425–461.

Fontaine, P., "Modèles d'arbitrage et multifactoriels internationaux", in *Encyclopédie des marchés financiers*, Economica, 1997, pp. 1164–1185.

Gaussel, N., "Portfolio Allocation: Stability of the Results and Consistency of the Expected Returns", AFFI, 16th International Conference in Finance, Aix-en-Provence, France, 1999.

Grandin, P., *Mesure de performance des fonds d'investissement, Méthodologie et résultats*, Economica, Gestion poche, 1998.

GRAP (Groupe de recherche sur l'attribution de performance), *Premier document de synthèse des travaux du groupe*, Paris, March 1997.

Grinblatt, M. and Titman, S., "Mutual Fund Performance: an Analysis of Quarterly Portfolio Holdings", *Journal of Business*, vol. 62, no. 3, 1989, pp. 393–416.

Grinblatt, M. and Titman, S., "Performance Measurement without Benchmarks: an Examination of Mutual Fund Returns", *Journal of Business*, vol. 66, no. 1, 1993, pp. 47–68.

Grinold, R.C. and Kahn, R.N., *Active Portfolio Management*, Irwin, 1995.

Hansel, C.R., Ezra, D.D. and Ilkiw, J.H., "The Importance of the Asset Allocation Decision", *Financial Analysts Journal*, July–August 1991.

Harasty, H. and Roulet, J., "Modeling Stock Market Returns – An Error Correction Model", *Journal of Portfolio Management*, winter 2000, pp. 33–46.

Hartpence, M.-L. and Sikorav, J., "Allocation tactique d'actifs : à la recherche de la valeur", *Quants*, CCF, Mars 1996.

Harvey, C., "Predictable Risk and Returns in Emerging Markets", *Review of Financial Studies*, 1995, pp. 773–816.

Ibbotson, R.G., "The True Impact of Asset Allocation on Returns", Ibbotson Associates, 2000.

Ibbotson, R.G. and Kaplan, P.D., "Does Asset Allocation Policy Explain 49, 90 or 100 Percent of Performance?", *Financial Analysts Journal*, January–February 2000.

Jahnke, W., "The Asset Allocation Hoax", *Journal of Financial Planning*, February 1997.

Johnstone, I., "On the Distribution of the Largest Eigenvalue in Principal Component Analysis", *Annals of Statistics*, 2001.

Kahn, R.N., Roulet, J. and Tajbakhsh, S., "Three Steps to Global Asset Allocation", *Journal of Portfolio Management*, fall 1996.

Kandel, S. and Stambaugh, R., "On the Predictability of Stock Returns: an Asset Allocation Perspective", *Journal of Finance*, vol. 51, 1996, pp. 385–424.

Kao, D.L. and Shumaker, R., "Equity Style Timing", *Financial Analysts Journal*, January–February 1999, pp. 37–48.

Karnosky, D.S. and Singer, B.D., *Global Asset Management and Performance Attribution*, The Research Foundation of the Institute of Chartered Financial Analysts, 1994.

Keim, D. and Stambaugh, R., "Predicting Returns in the Stock and Bond Markets", *Journal of Financial Economics*, vol. 17, 1986, pp.357–390.

Kon, S., "The Market Timing Performance of Mutual Fund Managers", *Journal of Business*, vol. 56, no. 3, 1983.

Laker, D., "What is this Thing Called 'Interaction'?", *Journal of Performance Measurement*, vol. 5, no. 1, fall 2000, pp. 43–57.

Laloux, L., Cizeau, P., Bouchard, J.P. and Potters, M., "Random Matrix Theory", *Risk Magazine*, vol. 12, 1999, p. 69.

Leibowitz, M.L. and Kogelman, S., "Asset Allocation under Shortfall Constraints", *Salomon Brothers Inc.*, June 1990.

Leibowitz, M.L., Kogelman, S., Bader, L.N. and Dravid, A.R., "Interest Rate-sensitive Asset Allocation: A New Approach to Strategic Asset Allocation", *Journal of Portfolio Management*, spring 1994, pp. 8–15.

Leibowitz, M.L. and Langetied, T., "Shortfall Risk and the Asset Allocation Decision: a Simulation Analysis of Stock and Bond Risk Profiles", *Journal of Portfolio Management*, fall 1989.

Lewellen, J., "Predicting Returns with Financial Ratios", Working Paper, no. 4374–02, MIT Sloan School of Management, August 2002.

Lo, A., ed., *Market Efficiency: Stock Market Behaviour in Theory and Practice*, Edward Elgar Publishing, 1997.

Ludwig, J.B., "The Market Timing Approach: A Guide to the Various Strategies", *AAII Journal*, May 1994.

Marchenko, V. and Pastur, L., "Eigenvalue Distribution in some Ensembles of Random Matrices", *Math. USSR Sbornik*, vol. 72, 1967, pp. 536–567.

Martellini, L. and Sfeir, D., "Tactical Asset Allocation", in *Encyclopedia of Financial Engineering and Risk Management*, Fitzroy Dearborn Publishers, 2002.

Menchero, J.G., "An Optimized Approach to Linking Attribution Effects Over Time", *Journal of Performance Measurement*, vol. 25, no. 1, fall 2000, pp. 36–42.

Mertens, E. and Zimmermann, H., "International TAA Strategies and Currencies", Working Paper, University of Basel, February 2002.

Merton, R., "On Estimating the Expected Return on the Market: An Exploratory Investigation", *Journal of Financial Economics*, no. 8, 1980, pp. 323–362.

Michaud, R.O., *Efficient Asset Management – A Practical Guide to Stock Portfolio Optimization and Asset Allocation*, Harvard Business School Press, 1998.

Nuttall, J.A. and Nuttall, J., "Asset Allocation Claims – Truth or Fiction?", Unpublished, 1998.

Perold, A. and Sharpe, W., "Dynamic Strategies for Asset Allocation", *Financial Analysts Journal*, January–February 1988, pp. 16–26.

Philips, T.K., Rogers, G.T. and Capaldi, R.E., "Tactical Asset Allocation 1977–1994: The Long-Term Performance of TAA", *Journal of Portfolio Management*, fall 1996, pp. 57–64.

Ramaswami, M., *Active Currency Management*, The Research Foundation of The Institute of Chartered Financial Analysts, 1993.

Scherer, B., *Portfolio Construction and Risk Budgeting*, Risk Books, 2002.

Sharpe, W.F., *Investments*, 3rd edn, Prentice Hall, 1985.

Sharpe, W.F., "Asset Allocation: Management Style and Performance Measurement", *Journal of Portfolio Management*, vol. 18, winter 1992, pp. 7–19.

Simon, Y. and Mannaï, S., *Techniques financières internationales*, 6th edn, Economica, 1998.

Singer, B., "Asset Allocation, Hoaxes, and the Creation of Straw Men", *Journal of Financial Planning*, October 1997.

Sorensen, E. and Lazzara, C., "Equity Style Management: the Case of Growth and Value", chapter 4 in *Equity Style Management*, Irwin, 1995.

Surz, R., Stevens, D. and Wimer, M., "The Importance of Investment Policy", *Journal of Investing*, vol. 8, no. 4, winter 1999, pp. 80–86.

Taillard, G., "Le point sur . . . L'optimisation de portefeuille", *Banque et Marchés*, no. 60, September–October 2002.

Treynor, J.L. and Black, F., "How to Use Security Analysis to Improve Portfolio Selection", *Journal of Business*, January 1973, pp. 66–88.

Wainscott, C.B., "Attribution Analysis for Equities", *Performance Evaluation, Benchmarks, and Attribution Analysis*, AIMR, 1995.

Walter, C., "Mesure de performance corrigée du risque : une synthèse des méthodes existantes", *Journées EFE*, May 1997.

Walter, C., "Mesure de performance : le retour du gérant", *Revue Banque*, no. 594, July–August 1998.

8

Fixed Income Security Investment

All the developments presented up to this point have been more particularly related to the management of equity portfolios because, historically, modern portfolio theory and the quantitative methods that were drawn from it were developed in order to study equity portfolios. Nevertheless, investors generally hold portfolios that are diversified among several asset classes so as to spread their risk and ensure a certain level of consistency in the performance of their investments. Just as it is useful to practise diversification within each asset class to reduce the portfolio risk, diversification between classes also leads to risk reduction. Moreover, a study by Dietz showed that portfolios containing 35%–60% bonds and 40%–60% stocks are those for which the risk-related expected return is optimal. This is explained by the fact that certain periods are more favourable for stock markets, while others are more favourable for bond markets.

The use of quantitative methods for managing bond portfolios is more recent than for equities, but it is more and more prevalent. In the previous chapter we presented the investment management process as a whole and studied the performance of a diversified portfolio. Here we describe the particular characteristics of bond investment and the specific performance analysis models used for this type of investment. Before defining the risk and return characteristics of bond portfolios, we first present the yield curve modelling methods that are the basis of bond management.

8.1 MODELLING YIELD CURVES: THE TERM STRUCTURE OF INTEREST RATES

The yield curve or term structure of interest rates is the function that associates the level of the interest rate with each maturity. Let $r(t)$ be this function. The term structure of interest rates conditions the prices of bond instruments. Measuring the current rates, forecasting future rates and anticipating shifts in the yield curves allow the future value of rate instruments to be predicted. Modelling the yield curve is therefore essential. The yield curve can be constituted through observation of the prices of financial instruments, by establishing a relationship between the maturities of the securities and the levels of rates. Two alternatives exist: using yield to maturity or using zero-coupon rates.

8.1.1 Yield to maturity and zero-coupon rates[1]

The yield to maturity r of a bond is defined as the rate that makes its quotation price P equal to the discounted sum of its future cash flows $(F_i)_{i=1,\ldots,n}$, or

$$P = \sum_{i=1}^{n} \frac{F_i}{(1 + r)^i}$$

---

[1] Cf. Fitoussi and Sikorav (1991) and Bayser and Pineau (1999).

r constitutes the bond's internal rate of return, but the use of r to define the return that is actually obtained for the bondholder presents a certain number of disadvantages. In order for the rate to correspond to the return obtained at maturity, we must be able to reinvest the coupons at the same rate as r, which is not necessarily the case. In addition, this definition of the rate assumes that the yield curve is flat and that each bond has its own interest rate, while we would wish to have a term structure for the rates with a single rate associated with each maturity. To achieve this, we turn to zero-coupon bonds.

A zero-coupon security is a security that only pays out a single cash flow at its expiry date. Let B_t be the elementary zero-coupon security paying out one euro at date t. The zero-coupon price and its t maturity rate of return respect the following relationship:

$$B_t = \frac{1}{(1 + r_t)^t}$$

assuming that the reference date is 0.

The complete set of rates r_t for the different zero-coupon maturities allows us to define the range of zero-coupon rates. The use of zero-coupon rates allows us to construct a yield curve that associates a single rate with each maturity. The curve that is thereby obtained is then used as a basis for valuing rate instruments and measuring the risks. Any bond that pays out F_i cash flows at dates t_i, $i = 1, \ldots, n$, can be modelled by a portfolio of zero-coupon securities, with each cash flow considered to be a zero coupon.

The number of zero-coupon securities traded on the markets is not sufficient to allow a direct estimate of the yield curve using those securities. Several models have therefore been proposed using government bonds with maturities that allow all yield curves to be covered. These bonds are coupon bonds. In this case, each coupon is equated to a zero-coupon security with a maturity that corresponds to the date on which the coupon falls. We present the models that allow the zero-coupon rates to be constructed theoretically below. We distinguish between static models (Vasicek–Fong), where the rates are constructed using the coupon bond prices or the yield to maturity, and dynamic models (Vasicek, Cox–Ingersoll and Ross) which model the range of rates with the help of state variables such as the short rate, the long rate and the spread between the long rate and the short rate.

8.1.2　Estimating the range of zero-coupon rates from the range of yields to maturity[2]

8.1.2.1　Direct method

We assume that we observe the range of yields to maturity $(a_n)_{n=1,\ldots,N}$. A step-by-step calculation allows us to deduce the range of zero-coupon rates $(r_n)_{n=1,\ldots,N}$.

We recall that a bond's yield to maturity a is defined as the rate that renders its quotation price P equal to the discounted sum of its future cash flows $(F_i)_{i=1,\ldots,n}$, or

$$P = \sum_{i=1}^{n} \frac{F_i}{(1 + a)^i}$$

By using the zero-coupon rates we have

$$P = \sum_{i=1}^{n} \frac{F_i}{(1 + r_i)^i}$$

---

[2] Cf. Poncet *et al.* (1996) and Fabozzi and Fong (1994).

We consider a fixed-rate bond issued at par, i.e. with a market value equal to its face value. We have the following relationship linking the yields to maturity with the zero-coupon rates:

$$1 = \sum_{i=1}^{k} \frac{a_k}{(1 + r_i)^i} + \frac{1}{(1 + r_k)^k}, \quad k = 1, \ldots, n$$

where k represents the maturity. For $k = 1$ we have

$$1 = \frac{a_1}{1 + r_1} + \frac{1}{1 + r_1}$$

and hence

$$r_1 = a_1$$

For $k = 2$ we have

$$1 = \frac{a_2}{1 + r_1} + \frac{1 + a_2}{(1 + r_2)^2}$$

from which

$$(1 + r_2)^2 = \frac{(1 + a_2)(1 + r_1)}{1 + r_1 - a_2}$$

which allows us to calculate r_2.

More generally, we can calculate r_n as a function of a_n and the rates $(r_i)_{i=1,\ldots,n-1}$ by considering a security at par with maturity n whose value is written as follows:

$$1 = \sum_{i=1}^{n-1} \frac{a_n}{(1 + r_i)^i} + \frac{1 + a_n}{(1 + r_n)^n}$$

Hence

$$(1 + r_n)^n = \frac{1 + a_n}{1 - \sum_{i=1}^{n-1} \frac{a_n}{(1 + r_i)^i}}$$

The yield curve for any maturity can then be generated through cubic or linear interpolation methods. These direct methods are theoretically simple and very easy to implement. Unfortunately, significant difficulties prevent us from using them in reality:

- in the markets there are rarely distinct bonds with the same coupon dates, and which also present linearly independent cash flow vectors;
- the method is not robust if the sample of coupon bonds is modified.

8.1.2.2 Indirect methods

These difficulties lead us to consider alternative methods that are often called "indirect methods". The common factor between indirect methods is that they require the market data to be adjusted to a previously specified shape of the yield curve. Although these methods alleviate the practical difficulties mentioned above, they suffer from an eventual specification risk, or model risk. If we choose an inappropriate shape for the yield curve, adjusting the market data to the model will not provide a truly reliable result. A large number of models are used in practice. Here we shall simply present the Vacisek and Fong (1982) model, and, for more details, we encourage the reader to refer to the work of Martellini and Priaulet (2001) in the same collection.

The price of a bond is written as follows:

$$P = \sum_{i=1}^{n} F_i B_{t_i}$$

with

$$B_{t_i} = \frac{1}{(1 + r_{t_i})^{t_i}}$$

where B_t represents the discounting factor at time t which is interpreted as the present value of a cash flow amount of 1 paid out at date t or as the present value of a zero-coupon bond with a face value of 1 paid out at time t; and F_{t_i} denotes the cash flow paid out at time t_i.

The proposal from the model is to write the discounting factor in the following form:

$$B_t = \sum_{i=1}^{m} \beta_i (1 - e^{-\alpha t})^i$$

and to use this expression to calculate the value of the zero-coupon rate. The α and β_i parameters are determined using the prices of bonds quoted on the market. Statistical regression allows a yield curve to be constituted using discrete data. These rates can then be used to discount the cash flow of any bond and therefore to calculate its theoretical price.

8.1.3   Dynamic interest rate models[3]

Empirical studies on the yield curve have highlighted a certain number of characteristics that must be satisfied by any logical model of interest rate dynamics. In particular:

1. The rates cannot become negative.
2. From an historical viewpoint, high rate values tend to be followed, more often than not, by downward movements, which leads us to consider return to the mean effects.
3. Rate volatility tends to be higher for short rates than for long rates; moreover, the level of volatility seems to vary as a function of the absolute level of the rates.

   These studies have made a positive contribution to our understanding of the process followed by the short rate. Here we present some of the models that are most frequently used in practice.

8.1.3.1   The Vasicek model

Vasicek (1977) assumes that only the short rate explains shifts in the zero-coupon yield curve. The short rate follows a diffusion process of the following form:

$$dr_t = \beta(\alpha - r_t)dt + \sigma dW_t$$

where

α denotes the mean interest rate;
β denotes the speed of return to the mean;

---

[3] Cf. Joshi and Swertloff (1999).

σ denotes the volatility of the interest rate; and
W_t denotes a real value Brownian motion representing a shock for short rates.

While the previous model was a static model, this model is a dynamic model. The interest rate is modelled as a random process that oscillates around the level of the long-term interest rate. The short rate converges towards its assumed long-term value of α at a speed of β. The oscillations around the long-term value have an amplitude of σ.

The most widely used method for estimating the model parameters involves extracting them from the price of quoted assets. The model has been presented with constant volatility, but this can be replaced with stochastic volatility. Apart from the difficulty in estimating the parameters, the Vasicek model can produce negative interest rates.

8.1.3.2   The Cox–Ingersoll–Ross (CIR) model

The Cox, Ingersoll and Ross (CIR) (1985) model is again a stochastic interest rate model which models a rate that oscillates around its mean. This model is written as follows:

$$dr_t = \beta(\alpha - r_t)dt + \sigma\sqrt{r_t}W_t$$

where

α denotes the mean interest rate;
β denotes the speed of return to the mean;
σ denotes the volatility of the interest rate; and
W_t is a Brownian motion which characterises a random shock.

The contribution in comparison with the Vasicek model is that the interest rate volatility is heteroskedastic. When the level of rates increases, the volatility also increases, and when the level decreases, the volatility decreases as well. This ensures that the interest rates produced by the model are always non-negative.

8.1.3.3   The Heath–Jarrow–Morton (HJM) model

The approach is analogous to that developed by Black and Scholes (1973) for valuing equity options. By using the spot curve observed on the market, the idea is to equate the underlying with the whole yield curve. This approach is better known as the arbitrage approach. The Heath–Jarrow–Morton (1992) model uses the current forward interest rates to forecast the future short-term interest rates, instead of modelling the rates' dynamics. By considering a model with a dimension of one, i.e. in which a single forward rate explains the whole rate structure, and by denoting the instantaneous forward rate at time t for maturity T as $f(t, T)$, we have the following relationships:

$$df(t, T) = \alpha_1(t, T)dt + \sigma_1(t, T)dW_t$$
$$\frac{dB(t, T)}{B(t, T)} = \alpha_2(t, T)dt - \sigma_2(t, T)dW_t$$

where

α_1 and α_2 denote given functions;
σ_1 denotes the volatility of the forward rate;

σ_2 denotes the volatility of the zero-coupon bond; and
W_t is a Brownian motion with a dimension of one.

The volatilities σ_1 and σ_2 respect the following relationship:

$$\sigma_2(t, T) = \int_t^T \sigma_1(t, u)\mathrm{d}u$$

Implementation of this model is complex.

8.2 MANAGING A BOND PORTFOLIO

The first section of this chapter gave us an overview of the yield curve estimation models, which condition bond prices. We now come to the actual management of bond portfolios. The investment strategy adopted by the manager conditions the performance of the portfolio. It is necessary to dispose of and evaluate the risk factors to which the portfolio is subjected in order to analyse the strategy. Before turning to the definition of the different types of risks for bond portfolios and the analysis of the risks, by studying yield curve shifts, we first describe the quantitative analysis framework for bond portfolios.

8.2.1 Quantitative analysis of bond portfolios[4]

The use of quantitative techniques for managing bond portfolios is becoming more and more widespread. Quantitative techniques are applied to virtually all stages in the portfolio management process. The first stage is to define asset allocation: we choose to divide the portfolio between different asset classes, while taking into account constraints on the duration, the active–passive profile and the diversification and liquidity requirements. The next stage involves choosing the benchmark, or defining a bespoke benchmark. The final stage consists of analysing the performance obtained.

In Chapter 2 we discussed the usefulness of benchmarks and the construction of benchmarks for equity portfolios in particular. Defining a benchmark is also essential for managing a bond portfolio. The benchmark can be a broad bond index or a sector index. This type of index is produced by specialised firms. In the United States, Lehman Brothers produce the Lehman Aggregate index, Salomon Brothers the Salomon Broad Investment Grade (BIG) index and Merrill Lynch the Merrill Lynch Domestic Master index. However, these indices may not correspond to the needs of investors who will prefer, if that is the case, to produce customised benchmarks that accurately reflect the composition of their portfolio. A customised benchmark can be defined using a standard benchmark by only keeping certain sectors, for example. It can also be defined by modifying the percentages of the different categories of bonds compared with an index quoted on the market. Finally, it can be constructed more accurately by using individual investment specifications, in terms of sector allocation, choice of bond categories, the active–passive balance and liquidity, for each investor. Each portfolio has its own objectives and constraints. This can be translated into risk and return terms and conditions the choice of assets that can be included in the portfolio. For the evaluation to be correct, it is therefore important to dispose of a benchmark that is subject to the same constraints as the portfolio to be

---

[4] Cf. Dynkin and Hyman (1998).

evaluated. Once the benchmark has been defined, investors can express their return objectives and risk constraints in terms of deviation from the benchmark.

In Section 8.3 we shall see that performance measurement also relies on the portfolio's benchmark. The evaluation methods for the securities must therefore be consistent, for both the portfolio and its benchmark. This is now ensured by the existence of the AIMR standards.

8.2.2 Defining the risks

A bond is a security with a limited life span. It is a less risky product than a stock. It is however subject to two types of risk that explain the variations in bond returns: the default risk (or spread risk) and the market risk (or risk of interest rate fluctuations). The risk factors for bonds are different from the risk factors for stocks, even though we can draw some comparisons. The duration of a bond, which measures the market risk, can be compared to the beta of a stock, for example.

8.2.2.1 Default risk

The spread risk is connected to the risk of the issuer defaulting. The quality of the issuer is measured through a rating attributed to the bond by the rating agencies. A modification in the rating leads to a variation in the price of the bond and therefore to a modification in its spread. It should be noted that the bonds with the best ratings are those that pay out the lowest coupons, in line with the risk premium principle. In what follows we offer an overview of the methods for approaching the question of default risk. From a schematic point of view, these methods are of two different types: value of the firm-based models (which are also called structural models) and intensity-based models (which are also called reduced-form models).

The value of the firm-based models are characterised by the fact that the default date is determined by the date at which the process describing the value of the firm reaches a frontier. In the seminal works of Black and Scholes (1973) and Merton (1974) it is in fact assumed that the default can only occur on the bond security's maturity date. This framework was generalised by Black and Cox (1976), who consider a default date that is triggered when the value of the firm's assets reaches a given threshold.

The reduced-form models, on the contrary, do not seek to analyse the default process. They prefer to focus on modelling a default that occurs at a random date, which is defined as the first jump date of a Poisson process. This approach has been the subject of a large amount of recent work (Jarrow and Turnbull, 1995; Madan and Unal, 1995; Duffie *et al.*, 1996; Duffie and Singleton, 1997; Duffie and Lando, 1997; and Lando, 1996; for example).

8.2.2.2 Market risk

The risk of a shift in the yield curve is evaluated as a first approximation by the duration. The duration measures the average weighted duration of the time period required for the value of a bond to be paid back by the cash flow that it generates. The duration is the average life span of a bond. In general, it is shorter than the maturity, except in the case of a zero-coupon bond.

For a bond P with a price defined by the yield to maturity r, or

$$P = \sum_{i=1}^{n} \frac{F_i}{(1+r)^i}$$

the duration is written as follows:

$$D = \frac{\displaystyle\sum_{i=1}^{n} \frac{i F_i}{(1+r)^i}}{P}$$

A portfolio's exposure to movements in the yield curve is measured by the modified duration (or sensitivity). The sensitivity is written as follows:

$$S = -\frac{1}{P} \frac{dP}{dr} = \frac{1}{P} \sum_{i=1}^{n} \frac{i F_i}{(1+r)^{i+1}}$$

We can also calculate the convexity, defined by

$$C = \frac{1}{P} \frac{d^2 P}{dr^2} = \frac{1}{P} \sum_{i=1}^{n} \frac{i(i+1)F_i}{(1+r)^{i+2}}$$

The duration assumes that the yield curve is only subject to parallel shifts. However, the yield curve may be subject to three types of shift: a parallel shift, a butterfly shift or a twist. A factor model allows all the possible shifts to be explained completely.

8.2.3   Factor models for explaining yield curve shifts

The factor decomposition methods for the risk rely on statistical analysis of zero-coupon yield curve shifts observed in the past. Several models have been proposed. Since a bond portfolio can be modelled by a set of zero-coupon bonds, which depend on the structure of spot rates, we will show how to describe the spot rates with the help of a factor structure and deduce from this a factorial characterisation of the portfolio's risk and return.

8.2.3.1   Litterman and Scheinkman model[5]

The Litterman and Scheinkman model uses past data to construct a factorial structure for decomposing the shifts in the yield curve. The factors, which cannot be observed, are extracted from the variance–covariance matrix of changes to the spot rates, with the help of a principal component analysis method. We outlined the principles of this method in Chapter 6. Litterman and Scheinkman identify three explanatory factors, with each factor corresponding to a possible shift in the yield curve. The first factor is a level factor which takes into account the parallel shifts in the yield curve. This initial factor is not sufficient to describe the yield curve completely, which is why it is necessary to add other factors. A second factor takes into account a change in the slope of the yield curve. The third factor characterises the curvature. These three factors have decreasing degrees of explanatory power. The first factor explains on average 73% of the variations. Studies have shown that the three factors explained around 95% of the yield curve movements for the United States.

---

[5] Cf. Knez *et al.* (1994).

Some criticisms have been formulated with regard to this method. The first is that since the principal components are linear combinations of movements in the yield curve taken as a whole, they are difficult to forecast. The second criticism is that if the analysis is carried out for a non-American market, then there is no guarantee that the principal components identified will be of the same nature as those proposed in the model. Finally, this approach does not provide a direct measure of a bond or a bond portfolio's sensitivity to changes in the factors. These criticisms are formulated in JP Morgan (1996a), who proposes another method.

8.2.3.2   JP Morgan method

The method proposed by JP Morgan (1996a) should allow us to determine the sensitivity of a bond, or any bond portfolio, to non-parallel shifts in the yield curve, while avoiding the disadvantages of the other methods. The result is a characterisation of the risk of a portfolio in terms of sensitivity to rate movements at different points on the curve.

The spot rate is influenced by a certain number of factors, which are the same for all maturities, but their impact on the portfolio will vary depending on the maturity. The variation in these factors leads to modifications in the value of the rates, depending on the sensitivity of the rates to each of the factors.

The variation in the spot rate with maturity m, in country j and at time t, as a function of the factors is given by

$$\Delta S_t^j(m) = \sum_{k=1}^{K} \beta_k^j(m) \Delta F_{kt}^j$$

where

m denotes the maturity;
$\beta_k(m)$ denotes the sensitivity in relation to factor k; the sensitivities are functions of the
            maturity; and
ΔF_k denotes the change in factor k.

The instantaneous change in the price of a zero coupon resulting from a small change in the spot rate is equal to the change in the spot rate multiplied by the duration of the zero coupon. This duration is equal to its maturity. We therefore have

$$\frac{\Delta Z_t^j(m)}{Z_t^j(m)} = -m \Delta S_t^j(m)$$

where $Z_t^j(m)$ denotes the price of the zero-coupon with maturity m, in country j and at time t.

By replacing the variation in the spot rate as a function of its factorial expression in this expression, we obtain:

$$\frac{\Delta Z_t^j(m)}{Z_t^j(m)} = -m \sum_{k=1}^{K} \beta_k^j(m) \Delta F_{kt}^j$$

We define the duration of the zero-coupon bond with maturity m in relation to the kth factor as

$$D_k^j(m) = m \beta_k^j(m)$$

which allows us to write

$$\frac{\Delta Z_t^j(m)}{Z_t^j(m)} = -\sum_{k=1}^{K} D_k^j(m) \Delta F_{kt}^j$$

Any bond or bond portfolio can be represented by a portfolio of zero-coupon bonds, where each zero-coupon bond corresponds to a cash flow from the bond. The variation in the value of the bond portfolio can therefore be written as a linear combination of the variations in the value of the zero-coupon bonds, or

$$\frac{\Delta B_t^j}{B_t^j} = \sum_{i=1}^{n} x_i \frac{\Delta Z_t^j(m_i)}{Z_t^j(m_i)} = -\sum_{i=1}^{n} x_i \sum_{k=1}^{K} D_k^j(m_i) \Delta F_{kt}^j$$

$$= -\sum_{k=1}^{K} \sum_{i=1}^{n} x_i D_k^j(m_i) \Delta F_{kt}^j$$

where B_t^j denotes the value of the bond portfolio at time t, in country j; and x_i denotes the proportion represented by the current value of the ith cash flow in relation to the total value of the portfolio.

We define the duration of the bond portfolio in relation to the kth factor as

$$D_k^j(B) = \sum_{i=1}^{n} x_i D_k^j(m_i)$$

Hence

$$\frac{\Delta B_t^j}{B_t^j} = -\sum_{k=1}^{K} D_k^j(B) \Delta F_{kt}^j$$

We therefore establish that the return of a bond portfolio depends only on a finite number of factors, rather than a complete spot rate structure. The coefficients of the factorial decomposition are the duration of the portfolio in relation to each of the three shifts in the yield curve.

It is then necessary to construct the explanatory factors. The method used by JP Morgan is based on Ho's (1992) key observable rates approach, but removes the assumption of rate independence and therefore takes into account the correlation between the rates for the different maturities. The factors are obtained by linearly combining the key rates and are orthogonal by construction.

8.2.4 Optimising a bond portfolio[6]

The construction of a bond portfolio relies more on the choice of a category of bonds presenting the same characteristics (duration, maturity, etc.) than on the choice of individual securities.

The factorial structure defined in the previous section allows us to characterise the risk and return of a bond portfolio according to its sensitivity to variations in the factors. The return of a portfolio is written as follows:

$$R_{Pt} - R_{Ft} = \sum_{k=1}^{K} D_k^j(B) \Delta F_{kt}^j$$

where R_{Ft} denotes the risk-free rate.

---

[6] Cf. JP Morgan (1996b).

When we know the current rates and the expected future rates, the optimisation involves determining the portfolio that allows a given level of out-performance to be reached in relation to a benchmark specified in advance with a minimum tracking-error. The performance of the portfolio in excess of that of the benchmark can be characterised in terms of the duration differential between the two portfolios, or

$$R_{Pt} - R_{Bt} = \sum_{k=1}^{K} \left(D_k^j(B) - d_k^j(B) \right) \Delta F_{kt}^j$$

where $d_k^j(B)$ denotes the duration of the benchmark compared with the kth factor.

8.2.5   Bond investment strategies

As a consequence of the particular nature of fixed income securities, the strategies used to manage fixed income portfolios differ from those used to manage equity portfolios. Bonds are characterised by their maturity, the spread, the quality of the security and the coupon rate. A fixed income portfolio could be managed according to a duration strategy, a sector weighting strategy or a maturity distribution strategy. The rate risk indicators such as the duration, the sensitivity and the convexity allow the impact on bonds of variations in interest rates to be measured. The objective is always to obtain the best return for a given level of risk. The portfolio is constructed in accordance with the characteristic bond indicators. The investment strategies used can be passive, such as replicating an index or immunising the portfolio against interest rate risk, or active.

Active investment involves forecasting interest rates to anticipate movements in the bond market as a whole or carrying out an analysis of the market in order to identify the sectors or securities that have been incorrectly valued. In an interest rate strategy the positioning of the portfolio on the maturity spectrum will depend on the anticipated evolution of the yield curve. The security or sector selection requires the preferences to be quantified in accordance with the individual characteristics of the securities. The securities can be classified according to their default risk or according to their spread.

The default risk is the likelihood that the issuer will not respect his contractual obligation, i.e. that he will not be able to redeem the security at its expiry date or that he will no longer be in a position to pay the coupons. A rating is attributed to bonds according to the quality of the issuer. When an issuer's default risk increases, the ranking of the security may be lowered.

Bonds can be grouped together by sector, i.e. by sub-classes that behave in a similar manner. For example, bonds with the same level of ranking will have prices and returns that evolve in the same way. The price differential between bonds in different sectors can undergo modifications in several situations: if the sector's default risk increases, if the market's evaluation of the attributes and characteristics of the securities in the sector is modified or if there are modifications in supply and demand. The difference in return between two sectors, which is usually measured in basis points, is called the spread. Analysing the spread gives a relative evaluation of the interesting sectors. This is useful for investing in the sectors where the securities will have the strongest rate of appreciation.

Individual securities are analysed by evaluating their risk premium, i.e. the difference between the return of the bond and that of the risk-free rate. This risk premium is the investor's compensation for the risk taken.

The manager's investment choices in relation to the maturity of the securities indicate how he has positioned his portfolio on the yield curves and the returns of each maturity class then show the evolution of the rates over the investment period. Choosing securities according to the value of their coupons is also linked to the manager's anticipation of the level of future rates. If he anticipates a rise in rates, then he will choose securities with a high coupon.

8.2.6   International fixed income security investment[7]

In the same way as for equities, international investment widens the field of investment and increases the expected return of the portfolio while limiting the risks. In this case we use an international benchmark. An international fixed income security portfolio's risk is made up of the risk of each local market and a significant share of exchange rate risk. As for equities, the return can be divided into the local return and the currency return. This decomposition has an impact on the variance–covariance matrix, which is broken down into two blocks: one block for the local market and one block for the currency. The two blocks in the matrix are estimated separately.

Although exchange rate risk has little impact on equity investments, it affects fixed income security investments considerably, because the evolution of interest rates and exchange rates is linked. Interest rates influence exchange rates in the short term and exchange rates influence interest rates. To avoid an unfavourable turn in the exchange rates overriding the risk reduction advantage procured through diversification, it is desirable to hedge against exchange rate risk and use a hedged benchmark.

8.3   PERFORMANCE ANALYSIS FOR FIXED INCOME SECURITY PORTFOLIOS

The most thorough studies on performance analysis relate to equity portfolios. The first models were developed from the Capital Asset Pricing Model (CAPM), which only concerns portfolios invested in equities and cash. In addition, portfolio analysis originated in the United States, where portfolios are principally invested in equities. In France, the market for fixed income securities is considerable, but traditional models lead to inappropriate conclusions if the funds contain bonds because the characteristics of bonds are very different from the characteristics of equities. This is why it is necessary to look at specific performance analysis for portfolios, or parts of portfolios, that are invested in bonds.

As for equity portfolios, analysing the performance of bond portfolios initially involves measuring their return and comparing the result with that of the benchmark associated with the portfolio. The performance can then be decomposed and explained. Performance attribution for fixed income securities is still the subject of a large amount of research. The analysis can involve an approach by strategy or a factor approach. The factor approach consists of explaining the return of the portfolio through the return of the identified factors. A multi-factor model allows us to forecast the *ex ante* risk associated with each factor and to measure the return generated by the factors. An approach of this type allows the sources of the portfolio return to be identified in detail, and also allows the statistical significance of the returns to be measured.

It is possible to carry out several types of analysis to study portfolio performance, depending on whether we study the portfolio return in an absolute manner, or in a relative manner compared with a benchmark. In this section we present the different types of portfolio performance analysis and decomposition. We initially describe performance analysis in comparison with

---

[7] Cf. Murphy and Won (1995) and Faillace and Thomas (1997).

a benchmark, and then we give additive decompositions of bond portfolio returns that do not use a multi-factor approach. We then present models that use a multi-factor approach. In Section 8.2 we presented a factorial decomposition of the price of a bond. There are other possible decompositions. The bond performance attribution models are then modelled on these decompositions.

8.3.1 Performance attribution in comparison with a benchmark

Performance attribution in relation to a benchmark involves comparing the portfolio's rate of return with that of its benchmark and evaluating the difference. The benchmark's return is provided by a specialised firm in the case of a standard benchmark. For customised benchmarks, the firms provide returns for each component of the benchmark. The portfolio return is calculated by the manager. Using uniform methods is therefore very important and that is why the AIMR calculation standards are useful.

This analysis takes place within the framework of benchmarked fixed income security investment. The performance differential between the portfolio and its benchmark can then be analysed in order to understand the source of the differential and interpret it in relation to the investment strategy chosen by the manager and his exposure to the different risk factors.

Performance attribution allows us to explain the differences in return between the portfolio and its benchmark, rather than the returns themselves. It does not explain the total return of each security, but rather the relative performance of the portfolio compared with the benchmark in terms of the allocation differences between the two. This allows us, therefore, to analyse the manager's allocation decisions and the benefits procured by the over- or underweighting of the different sectors in the portfolio. For example, if each asset class in the portfolio has had the same return as the asset class in the corresponding benchmark, then the difference in performance between the portfolio and its benchmark will only be due to a different choice of weightings between the portfolio and its benchmark, i.e. the manager's allocation choices.

The analysis can be carried out on several levels. We can, for example, analyse the portfolio by portion of duration, and then analyse the composition by sector within each portion of duration. The excess performance of the portfolio compared with its benchmark can be explained in terms of positioning on the yield curve, sector allocation and security selection. A little later in this chapter we give a detailed presentation of performance decomposition for fixed income security portfolios which corresponds to the stages in the investment management process.

We should mention that there is an additional difficulty for bond portfolios compared with equity portfolios. Since bonds have a limited life span, the composition of the portfolio evolves over time, which gives additional reasons for the portfolio to deviate from its benchmark.

8.3.2 The Lehman Brothers performance attribution model[8]

Lehman Brothers developed a performance attribution model that allows the return of each asset to be decomposed and the different portions of performance to be attributed to the following factors: the passing of time; shifts in the yield curve; changes in volatility and changes in spreads. The results, security by security, of the decomposition are then aggregated at the portfolio level, thereby allowing the portfolio performance to be explained.

---

[8] Cf. Dynkin *et al.* (1998).

The prices of fixed income securities are affected by the passing of time and yield curve movements, with the latter factor accounting for the largest share. The model developed by Lehman Brothers produces an approximation of the real movements in the yield curve by using a combination of the three basic movements: the parallel shift, the twist and the butterfly shift.

For a given month, the model first identifies all the modifications in the market and then divides the return of each security into several components, each being associated with a modification in the market. The model defines the components of the yield curve movements as intuitively as possible and attempts to attribute the realised returns to each component as accurately as possible. The model is based on changes in the official market rates, which can be observed on the market, rather than rates obtained through calculation. For each month, the real changes in the yield curve are described with the help of the three basic movements. Each of these components is a linear function by portions using two-, five-, 10- and 30-year variations in rates.

The return that comes from a parallel shift in the yield curve (the shift return) is expressed as the average change in the official two-, five-, 10- and 30-year market rates, or

$$s = 1/4(\Delta y_2 + \Delta y_5 + \Delta y_{10} + \Delta y_{30})$$

The slope of the yield curve can undergo modifications, such as a flattening or, on the contrary, an increase in the slope around the five-year rate. The resulting return (the twist return) is quantified through the change in the spread between the official two- and 30-year market rates, or

$$t = \Delta y_{30} - \Delta y_2$$

The slope of the yield curve may also be subject to a butterfly shift when the middle of the curve moves in the opposite direction to its extremities. The resulting return (the butterfly return) is determined through the differential between the average of the two- and 30-year rates and the five-year rate, or

$$b = 1/2(\Delta y_2 + \Delta y_{30}) - \Delta y_5$$

The residual return, or shape return, is the yield curve return that is not explained by the three types of yield curve shift.

The Lehman Brothers model constructs a sequence of progressive changes to move from the environment at the start of the month to the environment at the end of the month. The bonds are valued at each of these stages. Each component of return is given by the difference in price between two successive valuations.

The Lehman Brothers method presents an advantage over methods that use the sensitivities at the start of the month. The methods that use the start of the month parameters do not integrate the fact that changes in the yield curve modify the risk characteristics of all securities with cash flow that depends on the interest rates, which can lead to significant errors when calculating the components of the return.

The yield curve shift decomposition in the Lehman Brothers model was developed on the basis of statistical studies on the historical behaviour of government loans. Tests were carried out to validate the model. The tests showed that the model gave more accurate explanations of shifts in the yield curve than other models such as principal component analysis.

This decomposition applied to the return of a portfolio and that of its benchmark allows the performance of the portfolio to be analysed within the framework of both passive investment and active investment. In active investment, the manager seeks to obtain a higher return for his portfolio by choosing a strategy based on his anticipations for the market in terms of yield curve evolution. To do this, the portfolio will voluntarily deviate from the benchmark on one or more aspects. Separating the portfolio return into several components allows us to analyse the effect of the different investment strategies on the overall performance of the portfolio. In the case of passive investment, where the objective is to track the performance of the benchmark, the return differentials between the portfolio and the benchmark must be monitored closely. It is therefore useful to have a precise understanding of the origins of the return differences between the portfolio and the benchmark, in the case of underperformance, so as to carry out the necessary modifications to the portfolio.

8.3.3   Additive decomposition of a fixed income portfolio's performance[9]

We have seen that the study of performance attribution for fixed income portfolios must be based on indicators that are characteristic of this class of assets, such as the duration, the maturity and the spread. These indicators can be tricky to estimate. Fong *et al.* (1983) proposed a solution for decomposing the return of a fixed income portfolio.

The principle consists of separating the portfolio return into two components: a component that comes from the financial environment, over which the manager has no control, and a component that corresponds to the manager's value-added, or

$$R = I + C$$

where I denotes the effect of the interest rates' financial environment; and C denotes the manager's contribution.

Each of these two terms can be decomposed again. I corresponds to the return of the bond market considered globally. It can be decomposed into two terms: a predictable component and an unanticipated component, which comes from changes in the interest rates, or

$$I = E + U$$

where E denotes the share of return obtained in the absence of modifications to the rate structure; and U denotes the share of return that comes from a modification in the rate structure.

The value of I is observed on the market: it is given by the value of a fixed income security index. The value of E must be estimated and the value of U is then obtained by calculating the difference between I and E.

The manager's value-added is obtained globally as the difference between the portfolio return and the return I of the fixed income security index. This component can then be divided into three terms: a term linked to the choice of maturity, a term linked to the choice of sector and finally a security selection term, or

$$C = M + S + B$$

where

M denotes the share of return that comes from managing the maturity (or managing the duration);

S denotes the share of return that comes from managing the spreads; and

B denotes the share of return that comes from the choices of individual securities.

---

[9] Cf. Fabozzi and Fong (1994), la Bruslerie (1990), Elton and Gruber (1995), Fabozzi (1995) and Grandin (1998).

The management of the maturity has the greatest impact on portfolio performance. The success of the manager's decisions depends on his capacity to anticipate evolutions in interest rates. To estimate this component, we simulate the portfolio result by eliminating the effects of the other two components.

Managing the sector and the quality relates to how the portfolio is divided between the different compartments of the fixed income security market. It involves measuring the manager's capacity to identify the right sector at the right time. This component is estimated by carrying out a simulation in which the other two effects are neutralised.

The individual selection of securities consists of choosing, within each bond category, the securities for which we anticipate the best performance. This effect is measured as the difference between the overall portfolio return and all the other effects identified.

This performance decomposition method is suitable for a portfolio that is solely invested in domestic assets. Solnik proposed a decomposition model in the international framework, which we present in the following section.

8.3.4   International Performance Analysis (IPA)[10]

This model was developed by Solnik. It focuses on the effect on performance of the choices between the different international markets, without entering into performance decomposition within each market. The return of each portfolio currency compartment is initially evaluated independently. If we take V_j^t as the value of the assets held in currency j at time t, then the return on the portfolio compartment in currency j is given by

$$R_j = \frac{V_j^t}{V_j^{t-1}} - 1$$

Part of the value of V_j is made up of income such as the coupons cashed in during the period. The overall return can therefore be decomposed into two terms:

$$R_j = P_j + C_j - 1$$

where P_j denotes the gain or loss of capital, as a relative value; and C_j denotes the current return, which comes from the income.

The return can be converted into the reference currency by using the exchange rate S_j for currency j, or

$$R_j^{\text{Ref}} = \frac{S_j^t V_j^t}{S_j^{t-1} V_j^{t-1}} - 1$$

We define the percentage currency gain, or loss, over the period as s, which gives us

$$1 + s_j = \frac{S_j^t}{S_j^{t-1}}$$

Hence

$$R_j^{\text{Ref}} = (1 + s_j)(1 + R_j) - 1$$

---

[10] This model is described in la Bruslerie (1990) and in Solnik (1999).

and by replacing R_j with its decomposition:

$$R_j^{\text{Ref}} = P_j + C_j + s_j(P_j + C_j) - 1$$

This expression reveals a term that measures the impact of exchange rate fluctuations on the return expressed in the reference currency. We shall call this term e_j. We have

$$e_j = s_j(P_j + C_j)$$

and hence

$$R_j^{\text{Ref}} = P_j + C_j + e_j - 1$$

Let us now consider the return of our entire portfolio. It is equal to the weighted sum of the investment returns in each currency. Taking x_j as the weighting of each compartment in the portfolio, the overall portfolio return is given by

$$R_P = \sum_j x_j P_j + \sum_j x_j C_j + \sum_j x_j e_j - 1$$

The portfolio performance realised on a market j can be compared with the performance I_j of an index on that market. The overall portfolio performance can then be rewritten in the following manner:

$$R_P = \sum_j x_j I_j + \sum_j x_j(P_j + C_j - I_j) + \sum_j x_j e_j - 1$$

The first term represents the weighted mean of the local market indices. It gives the return of a well-diversified international portfolio. The second term measures the manager's selection capacity in each market. The third term corresponds to the contribution of the exchange rate gains or losses to the overall portfolio performance.

This analysis considers that the portfolio weightings remain constant, but in practice the manager regularly adjusts his portfolio between the different markets, which contributes to the performance result. By introducing the weighting differentials between the managed portfolio and an international reference index, we can identify three terms in the performance evaluation: strategic allocation, tactical allocation or timing, and stock picking. This was presented in detail in Chapter 7. We discuss an adaptation of the model presented in Chapter 7 to the specific case of bonds below.

8.3.5 Performance decomposition in line with the stages in the investment management process

Decomposing performance in accordance with the stages in the investment management process, as it was presented in Chapter 7, is valid for all asset classes, but the particular nature of bonds has led to the development of more appropriate decompositions. In the case of bonds, the asset allocation term remains useful because it measures the contribution to the excess return that comes from the portfolio's exposure to a given risk. But the stock picking term provides little information. It is more useful to replace it with a decomposition term according to the sensitivities to the risk factors. The share of return that is not explained by the risk factors constitutes a residual stock picking term.

The complete decomposition identifies the following terms (see Kuberek, 1995):

1. A return term that comes from the currency effect, which is written as follows:

$$\sum_h (w_{ph} - w_{bh})\tilde{x}_h$$

where

w_{ph} denotes the weight of currency h in the portfolio;
w_{bh} denotes the weight of currency h in the benchmark; and
$\tilde{x}_h$ denotes the hedged return of currency h.

2. A return term that comes from asset allocation, which is written as follows:

$$\sum_i (w_{pi} - w_{bi})\tilde{H}_i$$

where

w_{pi} denotes the weight of class i in the portfolio;
w_{bi} denotes the weight of class i in the benchmark; and
$\tilde{H}_i$ denotes the excess return of class i.

The asset classes are represented by specific indices.

3. A term that comes from the decomposition of the return according to the risk factors within each asset class, which is written as follows:

$$\sum_i w_{pi} \sum_j (b_{pij} - b_{bij})\tilde{Q}_{ij}$$

where

w_{pi} denotes the weight of class i in the portfolio;
b_{pij} denotes the portfolio's exposure to risk factor j for class i;
b_{bij} denotes the benchmark's exposure to risk factor j for class i; and
$\tilde{Q}_{ij}$ denotes the excess return compared to risk factor j.

The risk factors used are characteristic of fixed income securities and can be the duration, the maturity or the sector. This term allows the performance to be explained precisely by groups of bonds with the same characteristics.

4. Finally, an ultimate residual term that comes from security selection, once all the other effects have been eliminated, which is written:

$$\tilde{R}_P - \sum_h w_{ph}\tilde{x}_h - \sum_i w_{pi}\tilde{H}_i - \sum_i w_{pi} \sum_j (b_{pij} - b_{bij})\tilde{Q}_j$$

where $\tilde{R}_P$ denotes the total portfolio return.

As in all the decompositions presented, the size of the study periods chosen is important. Originally monthly or quarterly, performance attribution is evolving in the direction of daily analysis, which ensures that the portfolio composition is fixed over the calculation period.

8.3.6   Performance decomposition for multiple currency portfolios

To complement the performance decomposition model proposed by Kuberek, we present the model developed by McLaren (2002), which gives details on performance attribution for a multiple-currency portfolio. This model provides a precise explanation for the relationship between portfolio performance and the manager's investment decisions and explicitly accounts for the duration decisions. The model is initially described from a single-currency perspective and then a currency return analysis is performed.

The portfolio analysis is carried out sector by sector, where a sector represents any grouping of assets (for example, type of issuer, credit quality or industrial sector). The total performance is then obtained by adding together the performance of each sector. Comparing the performance of the portfolio with that of the benchmark allows us to identify four effects: the duration contribution, the spread contribution, the selection effect and the interaction effect.

We define the following variables:

L_{a_i} is the local return of the fund for sector i;
L_{p_i} is the local return of the benchmark for sector i;
L_{y_i} is the local return of the yield curve for sector i;
W_{a_i} is the weight of the fund for sector i; and
W_{p_i} is the weight of the benchmark for sector i.

Using this notation, the return of sector i is given by $W_{a_i} L_{a_i}$ for the portfolio and by $W_{p_i} L_{p_i}$ for the benchmark. The analysis involves decomposing the difference between these two terms into several components. Initially, we will only consider single-currency analysis.

The duration contribution is defined as that part of the total contribution that would have been achieved if the fund were invested in bonds that have no risk premium or credit component. The duration contribution is then the result of under- or overweighting segments of the yield curve relative to the normal weights identified by the benchmark or policy:

$$(W_{a_i} - W_{p_i})L_{y_i}$$

The spread contribution is that part of the total contribution that is not explained by the duration contribution. Its value is obtained by under- or overweighting the various spreads relative to the normal weights identified by the benchmark or policy:

$$(W_{a_i} - W_{p_i})(L_{p_i} - L_{y_i})$$

The selection term measures the active investment decisions concerning the bonds within each sector:

$$S_{r_i} = W_{p_i}(L_{a_i} - L_{p_i})$$

The interaction term is due to the interaction between the allocation and bond selection contributions:

$$I_i = (L_{a_i} - L_{p_i})(W_{a_i} - W_{p_i})$$

Using these four terms, we can write the following decomposition:

$$W_{a_i} L_{a_i} - W_{p_i} L_{p_i} = (W_{a_i} - W_{p_i})L_{y_i} + (W_{a_i} - W_{p_i})(L_{p_i} - L_{y_i})$$
$$+ W_{p_i}(L_{a_i} - L_{p_i}) + (L_{a_i} - L_{p_i})(W_{a_i} - W_{p_i})$$

This model can be extended to analyse multiple-currency portfolios by adding a currency component. McLaren describes two different ways of analysing this component: comparing the fund currency returns with the benchmark currency returns, and comparing the fund currency returns with forward currency returns. We have chosen to limit the presentation to the benchmark analysis. The reader interested in further analysis should refer to McLaren's article.

We define the following variables: CR_{a_i} is the currency return of the fund for sector i; and CR_{p_i} is the currency return of the benchmark for sector i.

Using this notation, the currency contribution of the fund sector is given by $C_{a_i} = W_{a_i} CR_{a_i}$ and the currency contribution of the benchmark is given by $C_{p_i} = W_{p_i} CR_{p_i}$. The outperformance of the portfolio as a result of currency decisions is the difference between these two terms.

We identify the following two components:

1. The currency allocation, defined as that part of the outperformance resulting from allocation decisions:

$$(W_{a_i} - W_{p_i})CR_{p_i}$$

2. The currency timing, measuring the difference between the fund and benchmark currency returns encountered when trading occurred during the period. Here the interaction between allocation and timing has been added to the pure currency timing term:

$$CT_{r_i} = W_{a_i}(CR_{a_i} - CR_{p_i})$$

We can then write the following decomposition for the currency term:

$$C_{r_i} = W_{a_i} CR_{a_i} - W_{p_i} CR_{p_i} = (W_{a_i} - W_{p_i})CR_{p_i} + W_{a_i}(CR_{a_i} - CR_{p_i})$$

8.3.7   The APT model applied to fixed income security portfolios

This model, which was developed by Elton *et al.* (1995), uses both indices and macroeconomic variables to explain the returns and expected returns of bonds. The authors underline the fact that, in spite of the importance of the fixed income security markets, little attention has been given to applying models based on Ross's APT to the valuation of bonds. Nevertheless, the APT model, which was presented in detail in Chapter 6, can also be used for fixed income security portfolios.

The factors used are indices traded on the markets and factors measuring the unanticipated variations in economic variables. The return of a security is given by

$$R_{it} = \mathrm{E}(R_i) + \sum_{j=1}^{J} \beta_{ij}(R_{jt} - \mathrm{E}(R_j)) + \sum_{k=1}^{K} \gamma_{ik} g_{kt} + \eta_{it} \qquad (8.1)$$

where

R_{it} denotes the return on asset i at time t;
R_{jt} denotes the return on a tradable portfolio j at time t;

g_{kt} denotes the unexpected change in the kth economic variable at time t with $E(g_k) = 0$;
β_{ij} denotes the sensitivity of asset i to the innovation of the jth portfolio;
γ_{ik} denotes the sensitivity of asset i to the innovation of the kth economic factor; and
η_{it} denotes the return on asset i at time t, not explained by the factors and the indices, with
$\quad E(\eta_i) = 0$.

Arbitrage reasoning allows us to write the following:

$$E(R_i) = R_{Ft} + \sum_{j=1}^{J} \beta_{ij}\lambda_j + \sum_{k=1}^{K} \gamma_{ik}\lambda_k$$

where

R_{Ft} denotes the return of the risk-free asset;
λ_j denotes the risk premium of index j; and
λ_k denotes the risk premium of the kth economic variable.

When the variables are indices traded on the markets, the risk premium is written as follows:

$$\lambda_j = E(R_j) - R_F$$

Through substitution, we obtain the following:

$$E(R_i) = R_{Ft} + \sum_{j=1}^{J} \beta_{ij}(E(R_j) - R_F) + \sum_{k=1}^{K} \gamma_{ik}\lambda_k$$

By bringing this expression into equation (8.1) we obtain:

$$R_{it} = R_{Ft} + \sum_{j=1}^{J} \beta_{ij}(R_{jt} - R_{Ft}) + \sum_{k=1}^{K} \gamma_{ik}(\lambda_k + g_{kt}) + \eta_{it}$$

which can also be written

$$R_{it} - R_{Ft} = \alpha_i + \sum_{j=1}^{J} \beta_{ij}(R_{jt} - R_{Ft}) + \sum_{k=1}^{K} \gamma_{ik}g_{kt} + \eta_{it}$$

where

$$\alpha_i = \sum_{k=1}^{K} \gamma_{ik}\lambda_k$$

This model is a multi-factor model in which α_i must respect a particular relationship. The model was tested with several series of factors. Once the model has been developed and the parameters set, it can be used to evaluate the performance of fixed income security portfolios.

8.3.8   The Khoury, Veilleux and Viau model

This model is a performance attribution model for fixed income security portfolios. The form of the model is multiplicative, so as to be able to handle investments over several periods. The model identifies 11 factors that are liable to influence the value of bonds. For the moment, the model has been studied more often than it has been applied.

Traditionally, multi-factor models are formulated in the following way:

$$R_{Pt} = \sum_{k=1}^{K} \beta_{Pk} F_{kt} + u_{Pt}$$

where

R_{Pt} denotes the return of portfolio P for period t;
β_{Pk} denotes the sensitivity of the portfolio to factor k;
F_{kt} denotes the return of factor k over period t; and
u_{Pt} denotes the specific return of the portfolio over period t.

In order to be able to combine the returns over time, the model can be written in multiplicative form, or

$$(1 + R_{Pt}) = \prod_{k=1}^{K} (1 + \beta_{Pk} F_{kt})(1 + u_{Pt})$$

The factors proposed are divided between factors linked to the spread risk and factors linked to the risk of yield curve shift. The latter factors take into account the different types of possible shift: parallel shifts, changes in curvature and butterfly risk.

With this formula, the portfolio and benchmark performance results are compared by calculating their return ratio, or

$$\frac{(1 + R_{Pt})}{(1 + R_{Bt})} = \frac{\prod_{k=1}^{K}(1 + \beta_{Pk} F_{kt})(1 + u_{Pt})}{\prod_{k=1}^{K}(1 + \beta_{Bk} F_{kt})(1 + u_{Bt})}$$

where the benchmark is decomposed in the same way as the portfolio.

The Khoury et al. (1997) article presents the construction of the explanatory factors in detail.

8.3.9   The Barra model for fixed income security portfolios[11]

Kahn (1991) describes the performance attribution model for bond portfolios used by Barra. It is a multi-factor model. The factors used to explain the return of the portfolio for each period are the usual specific factors for bonds, linked to the maturity, the spread, the quality of the issuer and the risk of yield curve shift. Applied to a single period, this model allows us to identify the sources of portfolio performance period by period. The results for each period can then be combined to evaluate the manager and separate the share of performance due to luck from the share of performance due to skill. This multi-period analysis involves studying the series of returns attributed to each factor. The study allows us to check whether the return attributed to a factor for a period remains significant over time. To do so, we evaluate the t-statistic of the series, a notion that we defined in Chapter 4.

---

[11] Cf. Algert and Leverone (1992), Davis (1991) and Kahn (1991).

8.3.10 Decomposition with hedging of the exchange rate risk

The excess return, compared with a benchmark portfolio, of an international fixed income portfolio that is hedged against exchange rate risk can be decomposed into three terms. The first term measures the return linked to the allocation by country. It measures the impact of a different benchmark allocation in terms of countries by assuming that the durations in each country are equal to their optimal levels. The second term measures the return that comes from a different allocation within each country and gives the excess return of a portfolio invested, like the benchmark, in terms of allocation by country, but with different durations within each country. The final term measures the return compared with the different exchange rate hedging parameters. The precise formula is described in the appendix to JP Morgan (1996b). We discussed this point in the previous chapter, when analysing the investment management process for an international portfolio.

BIBLIOGRAPHY

Algert, S. and Leverone, M., "Fixed Income Performance Analysis Over Time", *Barra Newsletter*, January–February 1992.

Banque Stratégie, "Les marchés obligataires", January 1999.

Bayser, X. (de) and Pineau, F., "La gestion obligataire quantitative modélisée", *Banque Stratégie* no. 156, January 1999, pp. 19–22.

Black, F. and Cox, J.C., "Valuing Corporate Securities: Some Effects of Bond Indenture Provisions", *Journal of Finance*, vol. 31, May 1976, pp. 351–367.

Black, F. and Scholes, M., "The Pricing of Options and Corporate Liabilities", *Journal of Political Economy*, vol. 81, 1973, pp. 637–659

la Bruslerie, H. (de), *Gestion obligataire internationale, tome 2 : Gestion de portefeuille et contrôle*, Economica, 1990.

Cox, J.C., Ingersoll, J.E. and Ross, S.A., "A Theory of the Term Structure of Interest Rates", *Econometrica*, vol. 53, no. 2, 1985, pp. 385–407.

Davis, M., "Fixed Income Performance Attribution", *Barra Newsletter*, July–August 1991.

Duffie, D. and Lando, D., "Term Structures of Credit Spreads with Incomplete Accounting Information", Working Paper, Stanford University, 1997.

Duffie, D. and Singleton, K., "Modeling Term Structures of Defaultable Bonds", Working Paper, Stanford University, 1997.

Duffie, D., Schroder, M. and Skiadas, C., "Recursive Valuation of Defaultable Securities and the Timing of Resolution of Uncertainty", *Annals of Applied Probability*, vol. 6, 1996, pp. 1075–1090.

Dynkin, L. and Hyman, J., "Quantitative Analysis of Fixed Income Portfolios Relative to Indices", in *Handbook of Portfolio Management*, F.J. Fabozzi, ed., Frank J. Fabozzi Associates, 1998.

Dynkin, L., Hyman, J. and Konstantinovsky, V., "A Return Attribution Model for Fixed Income Securities", in *Handbook of Portfolio Management*, F.J. Fabozzi, ed., Frank J. Fabozzi Associates, 1998.

Elton, E.J. and Gruber, M.J., *Modern Portfolio Theory and Investment Analysis*, 5th edn, Wiley, 1995.

Elton, E.J., Gruber, M.J. and Blake, C.R., "Fundamental Economic Variables, Expected Returns, and Bond Fund Performance", *Journal of Finance*, vol. 50, no. 4, September 1995, pp. 1229–1256.

Fabozzi, F.J., *Investment Management*, Prentice Hall International Editions, 1995.

Fabozzi, F.J., *Handbook of Portfolio Management*, Frank J. Fabozzi Associates, 1998.

Fabozzi, F.J. and Fong, G., *Advanced Fixed Income Portfolio Management, The State of the Art*, Irwin, 1994.

Faillace, A.L. and Thomas, L.R., "International Fixed Income Investment: Philosophy and Process", in *Managing Fixed Income Portfolios*, F.J. Fabozzi, ed., Frank J. Fabozzi Associates, 1997.

Fitoussi, B. and Sikorav, J., "Courbe de taux et zéro-coupons : quel prix pour l'argent ?", *Quants*, CCF, 1991.

Fong, G., Pearson, C. and Vasicek, O., "Bond Performance Analyzing Sources of Return", *Journal of Portfolio Management*, spring 1983, pp. 46–50.

Grandin, P., *Mesure de performance des fonds d'investissement, Méthodologie et résultats*, Economica, Gestion poche, 1998.

Heath, D., Jarrow, R. and Morton, A., "Bond Pricing and the Term Structure of Interest Rates: A New Methodology for Contingent Claims Valuation", *Econometrica*, vol. 60, 1992, pp. 77–105.

Ho, T.S.Y., "Key Rates Durations: Measures of Interest Rate Risks", *Journal of Fixed Income*, 1992.

Jarrow, R. and Turnbull, S., "Pricing Derivatives on Financial Securities Subject to Credit Risk", *Journal of Finance*, vol. 50, March 1995, pp. 53–85.

Joshi, J.P. and Swertloff, L., "A User's Guide to Interest Rate Models: Applications for Structured Finance", *Journal of Risk Finance*, fall 1999, pp. 106–114.

Kahn, R.N., "Bond Performance Analysis: A Multifactor Approach", *Barra Newsletter*, July–August 1991 and *Journal of Portfolio Management*, fall 1991.

Kahn, R.N., "Fixed Income Risk Modeling", in *The Handbook of Fixed Income Securities*, F.J. Fabozzi, ed., 5th edn, Frank J. Fabozzi Associates, 1997.

Khoury, N., Veilleux, M. and Viau, R., "A Performance Attribution Model for Fixed-Income Portfolios", Working Paper, 1997.

Knez, P.J., Litterman, R. and Scheinkman, J., "Explorations into Factors Explaining Money Market Returns", *Journal of Finance*, vol. 49, no. 5, December 1994, pp. 1861–1882.

Kuberek, R.C., "Attribution Analysis for Fixed Income", *Performance Evaluation, Benchmarks, and Attribution Analysis*, AIMR, 1995.

Lando, D., "Modeling Bonds and Derivatives with Default Risk", Working Paper, University of Copenhagen, 1996.

McLaren, A., "A Framework for Multiple Currency Fixed Income Attribution", *Journal of Performance Measurement*, vol. 6, no. 4, summer 2002.

Madan, D. and Unal, H., "Pricing the Risks of Default", Working Paper, College of Business and Management, University of Maryland, 1995.

Martellini, L. and Priaulet, P., Fixed-Income Securities: Dynamic Methods for Interest Rate Risk Pricing and Hedging, Wiley, 2001.

JP Morgan, "Multi-Factor Duration", Internal documents, Capital Market Research, London, 1996a.

JP Morgan, "Fixed Income Optimization", Internal documents, Capital Market Research, London, 1996b.

Merton, R.C., "On the Pricing of Corporate Debt: the Risk-Structure of Interest Rates", *Journal of Finance*, vol. 29, 1974, pp. 449–470.

Munro, J., "Performance Attribution for Global Fixed Income Portfolios", *Global Investor*, November 1996.

Murphy, B.P. and Won, D., "Valuation and Risk Analysis of International Bonds", in *The Handbook of Fixed Income Securities*, F.J. Fabozzi, ed., 4th edn, Frank J. Fabozzi Associates, 1995.

Poncet, P., Portait, R. and Hayat, S., *Mathématiques financières : Evaluation des actifs et analyse du risque*, 2nd edn, Dalloz, 1996.

Solnik, B., *International Investments*, 4th edn, Addison-Wesley, 1999.

Vasicek, O.A., "An Equilibrium Characterisation of the Term Structure", *Journal of Financial Economics*, vol. 5, 1977, pp. 177–188.

Vasicek, O.A. and Fong, H.G., "Term Structure Modeling using Exponential Splines", *Journal of Finance*, vol. 37, no. 2, May 1982, pp. 339–348.

Conclusion

Although the source of modern portfolio theory was a conceptual progression in terms of asset allocation, through the idea of diversification, researchers and practitioners have, in recent years, devoted most of their efforts to stock or fund picking.

The increasing number of studies on the persistence of alphas and the less than encouraging conclusions of most of these have not altered this state of affairs, with style specialisation probably having given a new lease of life to fund or manager selection.

Today, however, under the twin influence of researchers who are questioning the dogma of the lack of usefulness of active portfolio allocation, and multi-management professionals who wish to justify their value added as "allocators", research into the share of performance that is due to active allocation, whether involving market or style timing, or into diversifications, is taking up considerable space in the literature devoted to performance analysis.

The development of decorrelation techniques or frameworks, such as alternative investments, is a consecration of this interest in portfolio "betas". While some may doubt that persistence exists for hedge fund alphas, nobody questions their usefulness for diversification.

We hope that the balance that we have attempted to maintain between the analysis of stock picking models and techniques and portfolio allocation concepts and tools will allow the reader to approach the next few years, which are predicted to be the years of active investment and "decorrelation", with serenity and a sense of perspective.

Index

Index compiled by Terry Halliday

Printed and bound by CPI Group (UK) Ltd, Croydon, CR0 4YY

24/04/2025

14661402-0001